Philosophical Perspectives on Punishment

Second Edition

Philosophical Perspectives on Punishment

Second Edition

Edited by

Gertrude Ezorsky

Published by State University of New York Press, Albany

© 2015 State University of New York

Printed in the United States of America

For information, contact State University of New York Press, Albany, NY
www.sunypress.edu

Production, Ryan Morris
Marketing, Anne M. Valentine

Library of Congress Cataloging-in-Publication Data

Ezorsky, Gertrude, 1926– compiler.
   Philosophical perspectives on punishment / edited by Gertrude Ezorsky.
– Second edition.
        pages cm
   Includes bibliographical references.
   ISBN 978-1-4384-5855-7 (hc : alk. paper)—978-1-4384-5856-4 (pb : alk. paper)
   ISBN 978-1-4384-5857-1 (e-book)
   1. Punishment. I. Title.

HV8675.E9 2015
303.3'6–dc23   2014047344

10 9 8 7 6 5 4 3 2 1

For Michael Jacobson
whose work made this book possible.

Chapter Six: Solitary Confinement

Chapter Seven: Possible Alternatives to Punishment

Gertrude Ezorsky

The Ethics of Punishment

"Punishment," writes McTaggart, "is pain and to inflict pain on any person obviously needs justification." But if the need to justify punishment is obvious, the manner of so doing is not. Philosophers have advanced an array of diverse and conflicting arguments to justify punitive institutions. I shall sort their claims into three varieties: teleological, retributivist, and teleological retributivist.

What are the distinctive claims of our three kinds of philosophers?

Teleologists believe that punishment should yield, in fact, some further effect, which is desirable. Thus Bentham, a utilitarian, held that while the suffering of punishment is itself evil, nevertheless the threat of punishment, strengthened by enforcement, may serve a good purpose, e.g., deterrence of aspiring criminals and a consequent reduction in the misery wrought by crime. Notice that this sort of view may be empirically confirmed, or refuted, by a factual investigation, for punishment is conceived as a causal means which, given our laws of nature, will yield the effect of crime prevention.

Retributivists, however, take a different view of the matter. They claim that necessarily the distribution of deserved suffering for wrongdoing is either just or intrinsically valuable, irrespective of any further good consequence, e.g., crime prevention. Some philosophers might put the matter in this fashion: punishment for immorality would exemplify justice or have worth not merely in our familiar world, but in any possible world.

Teleological retributivists pay their respects to a plurality of principles. Thus, they share with utilitarians the notion that penal laws should yield some demonstrable beneficial consequences. Justice is not served by the infliction of deserved suffering for its own sake. But they derive the following view from retributivism: justice is served if teleological aims are held in check by principles of justice, e.g., that the suffering of punishment should not exceed the offender's desert.

Let us consider the merits—and the demerits—of these three perspectives on punishment.

Teleology

Teleologists view punishment as desirable either primarily for the guilty man, i.e., making him a better person, or primarily for the world, e.g., by isolating and reforming criminals or deterring potential offenders, punishment makes the world a better place.

Early better man thinkers, like Plato and Aristotle, conceived crime as a spiritual disease, curable by the bitter medicine of punishment. For Hegel, (as interpreted by McTaggart) the pain of punishment yields repentance, whereby the criminal recognizes his sin. He does not merely change his ways. Fear of future punishment might yield this superficial reform. He really becomes a better man; thus, Hegel declares, he realizes his true nature.

It is tempting to challenge curative theories by pointing to the sparsity of supporting evidence. (Do hardened criminals really mend their ways, either superficially or in depth, when punished?) But there are more fundamental objections at hand. Let us assume that in some cases punishment really does produce the effects claimed by these philosophers. It would not follow then that punishment is justified. Suppose the social costs of producing the punitive cure required were very burdensome? Or suppose that symptoms of a propensity to commit crime appeared before crimes were committed? Should preventive punishment—if effective—be imposed as we might impose preventive medicine against communicable disease? Imagine that a very severe punishment cured someone guilty of a petty offense. Would not such a punishment be undeserved, hence unjust?

The same sort of problems arise for those who see treatment, e.g., psychoanalytic therapy or drugs, as an alternative to punishment. Should preventive treatment be imposed on persons who will most likely commit crimes? Should the bill for slightly successful, but very costly, treatment be imposed on society? Remember, too, that cures can be more painful than punishments. According to a 1966 experiment performed in a Canadian mental hospital, treatment can, to some extent, reduce the amount of liquor ingested by alcoholics.

The treatment? Intravenous injection of 20 mgs. of succinylcholine chloride which induces paralysis and suppression of respiration, that is, a *drowning to death* experience. Surely no reasonable person would suggest treating alcoholic petty offenders in this fashion. The treatment would, of course, not be imposed as a punishment. Yet who would hesitate to call it undeserved? The moral problems raised by curative theories of punishment (or treatment) require, not merely an account of beneficial effects on the criminal, but a comprehensive moral perspective. Utilitarians claim to have it.

Utilitarians are better world teleologists. They evaluate punishment as follows. A moral agent ought to choose that act which of all feasible alternatives, has maximum utility. (The utility of an act is measured by its efficacy in producing happiness or reducing suffering, for everyone.) How does the suffering of punishment fit into this scheme? Bentham puts the matter in this fashion:

> The general object which all laws have, or ought to have in common, is to augment the total happiness of the community: and therefore, in the first place, to exclude, as far as may be, every thing that tends to subtract from that happiness; in other words, to exclude mischief . . . But all punishment is mischief; all punishment is in itself evil. Upon the principle of utility, if it ought at all to be admitted, it ought only to be admitted in as far as it promises to exclude some greater evil. (*Principles of Morals and Legislation*, Ch. XII).

Punishment serves to "exclude some greater evil" when by the workings of isolation, reform, and deterrence, the misery and insecurity created by crime is reduced.

It may be objected that the reform and deterrence effects of punishment have been exaggerated. Nevertheless, it is reasonable to suppose that some criminals, when punished, do not repeat an offense and that the threat of punishment stays the hands of some persons tempted to crime. In such cases, if punishment, as compared to other alternatives, e.g., psychiatric treatment, has maximum utility, the utilitarian is obligated by his views to endorse punishment.

Critics of utilitarianism claim that punishment which passes utilitarian standards may be undeserved, hence unjust. Indeed, as they see the matter, utilitarians are committed to undeserved punishment of two sorts, legal and illegal.

Let us consider the legal variety first. A legal punishment is undeserved when the offender is not morally responsible for the offense or if his prescribed punishment is excessive. An offender is not morally responsible when the following conditions obtain: he is punished either retroactively (by ex post facto law), or vicariously (for the act of another), or he has a valid excuse for committing the offense, i.e., insanity, ignorance or mistake of fact, necessity, incompetence, or automatism. When such excuses are not accepted, the offender is being held *strictly liable*.

How could retroactive sanctions, vicarious punishment, or strict liability serve utilitarian purposes?

Consider the following sort of situation. Suppose death and injury due to shooting were very much on the upgrade because too many people had guns. In that case there may be a utilitarian rationale for the following laws prescribing undeserved punishment.

Retail gun sellers are held strictly liable if any of their guns are found on a person without a permit. Sellers of guns would become extra careful in scrutinizing permits and protecting their stocks from theft. The iron clad rule, "No excuses," toughens the deterrent threat of punishment.

Vicarious punishment is prescribed by law for parents if any of their children under twenty-one is discovered in possession of a gun. Parents, consequently, would make a greater effort to ensure that their children have no guns.

An ex post facto law prohibits the use of guns by individuals against unarmed persons trespassing on their property. As a consequence of this law, shootings by persons not covered by the law, e.g., armed guards, decline because they fear future ex post facto laws under which they would be retroactively punished.

It is perfectly possible that laws prescribing these three sorts of undeserved punishment would maximize utility by reducing deaths and injuries due to shootings. But consider the injustices that might be perpetrated under such laws.

Suppose gun sellers were held strictly liable if one of their guns were found in the possession of an individual without a permit. F, a scrupulously honest retailer, sells a gun to G, who has a permit. G plants the gun on H, who has no permit. Discovery of the gun on H sends faultless F to prison.

Imagine that parents are vicariously liable if a gun is discovered on the person of any of their children. An eight-year-old girl on a treasure hurt with her classmates finds a package which she brings back to school as her "treasure." The child's parents, ardent pacifists, are convicted and serve a prison sentence.

Suppose an ex post facto law makes it a criminal offense to shoot unarmed trespassers on one's property for any reason whatsoever. Before enactment of this law, the following incident occurred. Gangsters threatened to kidnap Jones's children. Jones saw three of them on his property making off with his child. He fired at one who is unarmed. Note that at the time Jones's act was not only morally defensible, it was perfectly legal. But when the ex post facto law is enacted, Jones is convicted and punished, retroactively.

Laws prescribing excessive punishment, i.e., undeserved in light of the offense, may also satisfy utilitarian standards. Imagine a community where loitering is so widespread as to be a public nuisance. A law is enacted prescribing one year in prison for loitering. It might very well be the case that only one person would be punished under this law. The threat of such severe punishment, reinforced by infliction on one offender, is sufficient to deter all other potential offenders. The good utilitarian effects of the law may very well outweigh the bad ones. But a one-year jail sentence for loitering is certainly undeserved, hence unjust.

Finally, we may note that the guilt of an offender is usually held to decrease with extenuating circumstances, e.g., that the crime was committed in a state of passion. But, as Bentham noted, where the temptation to commit an offense is greater, the threat of more severe punishment is required to overcome the temptation. Thus, to secure effective deterrence, crimes committed in extenuating circumstances should be punished more severely. However, these are precisely the circumstances where the offender, being less responsible, deserves a lighter penalty.

In all cases just described, punishment while either wholly or partially undeserved would, by hypothesis, be perfectly legal. But utilitarians, it may be argued, are also committed to undeserved punishment which is illegal.

Let us suppose there has been a wave of vicious crimes, and the police are unable to find the culprit. Since no one is punished for these offenses, the deterrent threat of punishment becomes increasingly ineffective, and more persons are tempted into committing the crime. To frame and punish an innocent for these offenses may reinforce the deterrent threat of punishment. A few such scapegoat punishments might avert great harm and be worthwhile utility-wise.

It may be objected that those who hold a revised form of utilitarianism, namely, rule utilitarianism, are not committed to such illegal punishment of the innocent. A rule utilitarian believes that our conduct should be guided by estimating the utility not of any single, particular action, but of the general practice of that kind of act. Rule utilitarians may argue that they are not committed to what Professor Rawls calls "telishment," the illegal punishment of innocent scapegoats. Such punishment might, in a particular case, maximize utility, but it is doubtful that the general practice of "telishment" would meet utilitarian standards. Consider that the deterrence effect of the general practice of "telishment" depends on the success of systematic deception. Unless the general public believes the innocent scapegoat is guilty, the desired deterrence effect would not be achieved. But it is extremely difficult to imagine that such systematic deception could be maintained successfully. Hence the practice of "telishment" cannot be justified on rule utilitarian grounds.

Notice, however, that the rule utilitarian argument against illegal punishment has no application to legal undeserved sanctions. Excessive penalties, strict liability, retroactive and vicarious punishment are perfectly compatible with rule utilitarian principles. No deception is required to sustain the practice of these undeserved punishments. Provision for such punishments can and has been incorporated into public law.

Moreover, it seems false that the rule utilitarian is never committed to "telishment."

Suppose that D, the sovereign of a powerful nation, has a grievance against Smith, a citizen of a small nation. D demands that E, the sovereign of Smith's country, ensure that Smith be convicted and imprisoned for some particularly disgraceful offense of which Smith is innocent, e.g., sexual assault on a child. Unless innocent Smith is convicted and punished, D will launch an attack on E's country and massacre the whole population. E can with the aid of a few trusted security police manufacture evidence which would convict Smith in a court of law. The massacre of a whole nation would surely have more disutility than the harmful effect of Smith's illegal punishment. Thus, it seems that for rule utilitarianism, in this rare kind of case where averting a catastrophe depends on an innocent's being "telished," the rule should be, "telish" him.[1]

It may be objected that in this kind of case the rule utilitarian's violation of justice is warranted. We might reluctantly agree to the punishment of one innocent in order to prevent the massacre of a whole nation. But as Hart notes "we should do so with the sense of sacrificing an important principle." However, the rule utilitarian is not sacrificing any of his principles. On the contrary, punishing innocent Smith satisfies his principles.

Retributivism

Pure retributivists claim that deserved punishment is necessarily either just or of some moral worth. Undeserved punishment is always either unjust or of negative moral worth. As Kant sees the matter, to perpetrate undeserved punishment for any purpose whatsoever is to use a person as a means only, rather than as an end in himself.

For some retributivists punishment for wrongdoing is just because it restores the moral balance disturbed by crime. What is a state of moral balance? One version derives from Kant. A moral balance is exemplified by "a proportion between welfare and well-doing." The good are happy and the wicked suffer for their misdeeds. Thus an imbalance obtains when a criminal fails to suffer for his crime. Punishing him sets matters right, with respect to the criminal. Full moral balance is achieved, however, when the criminal is punished and the victim is compensated. Then a proper proportion between welfare and well-doing is achieved.

---

1. This sort of case is suggested by Alan Donagan. See "Is There a Credible Form of Utilitarianism?" in *Contemporary Utilitarianism*, ed. M. Bayles, Anchor Books, 1968.

The trouble with this moral balance view is that if it justifies punishment it can also justify crime. Suppose a moral disproportion obtains in M's case. He has been made to suffer excessively for his crimes. However, a moral disproportion also obtains in N's case. Given N's conduct his happiness is excessive. (N is good, but not that good.) Suppose M commits a crime against N. It is possible that M's crime against N may achieve a state of moral balance for both M and N. Thus, if obtaining a moral balance justifies punishment, it can do the same service for crime.

For all retributivists punishment has moral worth independently of any further desirable effects. *Ceteris paribus*, the world is better, morally speaking, when the vicious suffer. Thus it is not surprising that retributivism is sometimes characterized as the vindictive theory of punishment.

We may test this position by imagining a world in which punishing criminals has no further effects worth achieving. Thus the criminal, punished, is perfectly ready to go out and commit his crime all over again. Ordinary men are not deterred in the slightest from crime by the threat of punishment. Victims of crime have no desire for retaliation, and the pleasure of vengeance is unknown. According to retributivists, individuals in this world are still obliged to bear the burden of maintaining institutions of punishment. Indeed, they have an obligation to sacrifice so that punishment is kept going. But what sort of sacrifice is anyone obligated to make for the sake of utterly useless punishment? I suggest that in this case there is no obligation whatsoever to punish wrongdoing.

Retributivists believe, presumably, that their views should find expression in actual systems of law. Is this possible? Remember, these philosophers emphasize that only the guilty may be punished. But no infallible method for determining guilt has ever been devised. Indeed, it is a virtual certainty that honest, reasonable jurors have convicted defendants who appeared guilty but were, in fact, innocent. Thus, as it turns out, the price of a system which punishes the guilty is sacrifice of some innocents. Unless retributivists avoid punishing the guilty, they will be unable to avoid punishing the innocent.

Moreover, it is possible that more innocents would be punished in a society governed by retributivist, rather than utilitarian, principles. Here is why: for utilitarians, punishment is justified only if, by comparison with other alternatives, e.g., treatment, punishment would maximize utility. Suppose a painless but expensive pill were devised which cured any propensity to crime. The pill's utility surpassed that of other alternatives to punishment and slightly exceeded that of punishment itself. In that case utilitarians should endorse adoption of the crime cure pill and abolition of punishment. But retributivists believe that punishment of the guilty is either necessarily just or has some intrinsic value. In that case retributivists might refuse to substitute the crime cure pill for punishment. But juries would most likely remain fallible. Thus some innocents would be punished along with the guilty. Hence, if retributivist principles held sway, some innocents would, as a consequence, be punished. While if utilitarians had their way, not a single innocent would suffer punishment.

Teleological Retributivism

Teleological retributivists, whom I shall call TR philosophers, are pluralists. They mediate between a teleological principle, i.e., utilitarianism, and principles of justice held by retributivists. Let us contrast utilitarianism and retributivism with one plausible version of TR pluralism. I shall refer to a philosopher who holds this version as TR, to the retributivist as R, and to the utilitarian as U.

Consider (A1).

(A1) *If X deserves to suffer, then the amount of suffering in the world ought to be increased by X's suffering, as much as he deserves.*

(A1), a claim about the *amount* of suffering in the world, is an aggregative desert principle. R believes (A1). However, both TR and U deny that (A1) is true. TR and U believe a different aggregative principle, (A2).

(A2) *The total amount of suffering in the world ought not be increased by anyone's suffering.*

Consider now (D).

(D)   *If either X or Y is to suffer, and X but not Y deserves to suffer, then X not Y ought to suffer (but not more than he deserves).*

(D) is a distributive principle, since (D) is a claim about how suffering ought to be distributed. Both TR and R believe (D). However, U denies that (D) is true. Only the amount of suffering matters to the utilitarian. Who does the suffering is morally indifferent. Thus TR shares a distributive desert principle, (D), with R and an aggregative utilitarian principle, (A2), with U.

The different views of TR, R, and U may be illustrated in the following cases.

Suppose three men know they will die within 24 hours. The first, a philosopher, is not in pain, but the other two—a sadistic ex-SS criminal and his former victim—are suffering and to an equal degree. The philosopher has two pain-killing capsules, each totally effective for 24 hours. If the philosopher were TR or U, he would, following (A2), give each sufferer a tablet. However, if he were R, he would, following (A1), refuse to give the Nazi criminal a tablet.

Imagine now that the philosopher had only one such indivisible pill. If he were R or TR, then he would, in accord with (D), give the pill to the innocent man, not the criminal. However, if the philosopher were U, he would have no reason to alleviate the innocent's pain rather than the criminal's. After all (A2) would be satisfied by either choice.

How would our TR philosopher justify punishment?

Consider the case of C who has committed a crime. If he were punished, as he deserves, then, and only then, would he be deterred from committing a further crime against some innocent person. Hence, punishing C, a criminal, would prevent the suffering of an innocent. Our TR philosopher, following (D), would claim that C ought to be punished.

Notice, however, that (D) is an affirmative principle indicating when the guilty should be punished. But TR philosophers, like retributivists, also hold some negative principle of justice, e.g., Kant's principle of humanity, which implies that undeserved punishment is wrong.

Kant, we recall, urged that a person ought not be treated as a means only, but always as an end-in-himself. Suppose that an undeserved punishment would serve utility. Then, as Raphael, a TR philosopher, puts the matter:

> The claim of social utility is opposed by the claims of the individual to be treated as an "end-in-himself" and not merely as a means to the ends of society.

(HP) is an application of Kant's principle of punishment.

> (HP) Never treat a person as a means by punishing him undeservedly in order to benefit others.

Both TR and R would endorse (HP). Thus TR is committed to three principles: (HP), (D), and (A2). [R adheres to (HP), (D), and (A1), while U is committed to (A2)].

Are TR's three principles really compatible? Remember innocent Smith. Unless Smith's sovereign punishes him for a disgraceful offense of which Smith is innocent, the head of a powerful nation will have the entire population of Smith's country massacred. Suppose Smith's sovereign were TR. He could not adhere to both (HP) and (A2). By punishing Smith he violates (HP). But by not punishing Smith he violates (A2). [If Smith's sovereign were R or U, he would have no problem. R is committed to (HP) but not to (A2). Hence R would refuse to punish Smith and allow the nation to be massacred. U is committed to (A2) but not to (HP). Hence U would punish Smith to prevent the massacre.]

Some TR philosophers, e.g., Ross, hold that an innocent should be punished "that the whole nation perish not."

If our TR sovereign took this view he would sacrifice a principle of justice, (HP), in favor of a utilitarian principle, (A2). But TR's view of undeserved punishment would still be quite different from the utilitarian's. Remember U is not committed to (HP). Hence U would endorse undeserved punishment to achieve a slight gain in utility. But TR would abandon (HP) and opt for undeserved punishment only to avert a catastrophe. In that case TR would avowedly be sacrificing one of his principles, (HP), in favor of another, (A2). But in punishing innocent Smith, U sacrifices no principle whatsoever. TR's position is, I believe, closer to our common morality.

A complete TR view of punishment would incorporate two types of principles. The first may be dubbed a *recognized first order* principle, e.g., (A2), (D), or (HP). However, such principles may, as we have seen, conflict. Hence, some *absolute, second order* principle is required to referee the outcome. Thus our TR sovereign would, by punishing Smith, be following some absolute, second order principle which implies that in catastrophe cases, (A2) takes priority over (HP).

Criminal Desert

R believes that deserved punishment, *in toto*, should be inflicted on the criminal. While for TR the deserved penalty merely sets the upper limit of permissible punishment. But the notion of a deserved penalty is not easy to explicate.

Note first that the deserved penalty may differ from the penalty a state is legally entitled to impose. A government is legally entitled to inflict any punishment whatsoever—no matter how undeserved—if law permits. Thus, should cutting off an offender's hand be the legal penalty for petty thievery, then a judge is legally entitled to impose such sentence. But plainly the penalty is undeserved. Legal entitlement is not a moral concept. We ascertain legal entitlement by consulting a legal code. But a legal code cannot suffice to determine what a criminal deserves to suffer as a penalty. The misery he deserves depends on the moral wrong he has committed. Thus desert is a moral, not a legal notion. Suppose that torture of children were perfectly legal and shoplifting were illegal. It would be true, nevertheless, that those who torture children deserve to suffer more than shoplifters.

To determine the deserved penalty, one must decide how much misery an offender deserves for his wrongdoing. In such assessment, two kinds of questions may arise, one of degree and one of scope.

Let us look at the degree problem first. Consider the following kinds of offenses.

> A: *blackmail, kidnapping, rape, murder*
> B: *loitering, shoplifting, tax evasion, petty theft.*

Type A offenses are usually more grave, morally speaking, than type B. Hence it is usually reasonable to claim that a type B offender deserves a lesser degree of suffering as punishment. But such a comparative claim is crucially incomplete. We should like to know just how much misery a blackmailer or petty thief deserves.

Suppose we ranked offenses in an ascending order of moral gravity and penalties in a parallel order of severity. Could we then match offense to deserved punishment? What would constitute deserved punishment for the most serious moral wrongs?

Hobbes describes the punishment for high treason in seventeenth-century England as follows:

> To be drawn upon a Hurdle from the Prison to the Gallows, and there be hanged by the Neck, and laid upon the ground alive, and have his Bowels taken out, and burnt, whilst he is yet living; to have his Head cut off, his Body to be divided into four parts, and his Head, and Quarters to be placed as the King shall assign.

By comparison a one-year prison sentence seems mild indeed. But would we not consider a one-year sentence too severe for a mild offense (e.g., loitering)?

Note again that plausible comparative rankings of offenses by their degree of moral seriousness and penalties by their degree of severity seem possible. But such rankings cannot determine the non-comparative degree of suffering deserved for a specific offense.

The difficulty may arise in part because desert is a moral, not a legal, notion. Yet our intuitions of criminal desert are moored to our legal code, i.e., what seems mild or severe by that code.

Some philosophers suggest that a punishment is deserved if it fits the crime. But a criterion of fittingness is notoriously difficult to explicate. Consider one plausible formulation of such a criterion:

> A punishment is fitting if and only if the degree of suffering inflicted on the criminal equals the degree of suffering imposed by the criminal on his victim.

Is it? Compare a criminal who assaults a helpless invalid with one who assaults a healthy adult. Suppose both victims endured an equal degree of suffering. The first criminal would still deserve a more severe penalty. His offense is, after all, much worse morally speaking.

A fitting penalty should match the moral evil of the offense. But how does one know when the match is made? For example, how many years in prison does the first criminal deserve for his crime?

I turn now to the problem of scope.

Suppose one could match deserved misery to moral evil. Let us assume then that (α) is true.

(α) *A penalty of Z' and no more than Z' is deserved for the offense of Z, of Y' and no more than Y' for the offense of Y, of X' and no more than X' for the offense of X.*

Consider Jones, who committed the offense of X, a performance which ended at time t_1. Since (α) is true, so is (I).

(I) Jones deserves to suffer X' and no more than X' for committing X.

But can we assume that (II) is also true?

(II) Jones deserves to suffer X' and no more than X' at t_1.

If Jones had committed other offenses before t_1, (II) might be false. Let us assume however that, in fact, X is the only offense Jones committed in his whole life. Can we now assume that (II) is true?

Suppose that before committing X at t_1, Jones had suffered X' at time t_0 in a natural disaster, e.g., a flood. Then, one might claim—and not incredibly—that Jones had paid his desert debt in advance. His preoffense ordeal of X' at t_0, nullifies his post-X desert debt of X' at t_1. Hence, while he deserves to suffer X' for committing X, he does not deserve to suffer X' at t_1. Although (I) is true, (II) is false.

Let us call this perspective on criminal desert, the whole life view. It may be objected that this view seems plainly misguided. Jones's flood ordeal was both prior to his crime, and nonpenal, i.e., came about through natural causes. Hence that ordeal has no bearing on the penalty Jones deserves at t_1, after he committed his crime. If this objection is sound, then criminal desert at a given time should be unaffected by two items:

(1) suffering prior to an offense
(2) nonpenal suffering

Let us consider the first item. Suppose that an immoral government penalized Jones by X' at t_0 for an offense he did not commit.

Jones served an undeserved prison sentence of one year. A new and idealistic regime is installed and Jones proceeds to commit X at t_1. Jones might inform these idealists that he deserves compensation for the undeserved penalty he suffered. But the standard to which compensation should, where possible, conform is *restitution*, i.e., restoring the equivalent of what was taken. At t_0 Jones was undeservedly deprived of his freedom from incarceration for one year. Deserved restitution at t_1 can only be made by giving Jones one year of freedom from incarceration, i.e., suspending his deserved one-year prison sentence for committing X. Hence, what Jones deserves at t_1 is that he not endure his deserved X' penalty for committing X. Thus, he does not deserve X' at t_1.

To so compensate Jones would of course be moral madness. As a consequence any person punished undeservedly would earn the right to commit a crime. But remember that *what* reason forbids is treating Jones *as he deserves* at t_1.

I conclude that criminal desert, at a given time, may be altered by item (1), i.e., suffering prior to the offense. But can such desert be affected by item (2), nonpenal suffering, e.g., an ordeal caused by some natural disaster.

Imagine a world, W, quite different from our own. Only one sort of evil obtains in W. A class of persons, dubbed Fists, occasionally feels sadistic impulses which they vent on others. How? Fists have very powerful right fists which they use when so inclined to pummel others. Moreover, Fists are so strong and so swift that they can neither be controlled nor deterred in the slightest. A potential victim can only try to stay away from these Fists. But once assaulted the victim feels no desire for vengeance. Indeed, Fists aside, inhabitants of W are (by our standards) remarkably pacific and reasonable. They know that even if punishment of Fists were possible, no good would come of it. A Fist would not be affected in the slightest by punishment.

However when a Fist attacks, then as a causal consequence, he feels severe pain—just the degree he deserves—in his right hand. Thus in W, there are only two sorts of misery, undeserved pain inflicted by Fists and deserved pain which these Fists endure as a consequence. Since Fists receive their full measure of deserved pain through natural causes they deserve to suffer no more. Hence, both R and TR would agree that there are no occasions in W for penal intervention. (A1) as well as (D) are superfluous principles in W.

Reflection on W should serve to remind us that, from the perspective of criminal desert, punishment intervenes to accomplish what, in fact, could come about through perfectly natural causes. Hence, it is false that such nonpenal suffering cannot affect criminal desert.

If the whole life view of criminal desert is correct, then R and TR are in serious difficulty. Assessment of a criminal's desert after an offense would require that one balance all of his moral wrongs against the suffering of his entire life. But such reckoning is usually beyond ordinary mortals. An omniscient deity could of course know all the wrongs a person has committed as well as the tribulations he has endured. However those who determine legal penalties are not omniscient. To rely on them for such life-spanning estimates of desert is plainly out of the question. In that case how can we be certain that when an offender is penalized, he does in fact deserve to be so treated?

Moreover, we may, I believe, safely assume the following: first, a large number of legal offenders have led miserable, deprived lives. Second, at least some, and possibly, a great many, such offenders, do not, when punished, deserve their ordeal. If we persist in legal punishment, for society's benefit, we violate (HP), a principle of justice to which both R and TR are committed.

Let us now make a rash assumption. Only a penal system can prevent crime. No alternative can do the job. Should we then secure protection against crime by legal punishment, at the expense of (HP)?

How would our three principled philosophers view the matter?

Only U could accept the situation with equanimity. He, after all, had no commitment to (HP) in the first place.

R's dilemma, however, would be most extreme. R, we recall, feels a double obligation: to punish deservedly (A1) and not to punish undeservedly (HP). But now it seems that both sorts of punishment arrive in one package, tagged, a human penal system. Moreover R did not expect his principles to conflict. He, unlike TR, is not the man for compromise.

I imagine that R would give up and wash his hands entirely of our penal system, i.e., one not directed by an omniscient deity. Perhaps he will spend his time dreaming of a possible world where an all-knowing and righteous god rains deserved suffering—just the right amount—on those who fall from virtue.

And TR? He of course is not averse to compromise. For TR, the sacrifice of (HP), to avoid a massacre, was not out of the question. But would TR endorse a penal system where injustice may be an everyday matter? Or would he, like R, turn away from a reality so resistant to his moral principles.

I say TR would face up to moral fact and strain his principles to the utmost. Perhaps he would pose the issue in the following fashion. Many offenders, punished, would not deserve to be so treated. But many who would suffer at the hands of criminals, undeterred, would not deserve to be so victimized. In that case, TR may opt for legal punishment. But he can take little pleasure in his choice.

TR aspired to that best of all plausible moral worlds, one where both justice and utility receive their due. Only in some exceptional circumstance would justice be denied. But now TR knows that in a human penal system justice may be set aside, not on some rare and grim occasion, but with dreadful regularity. In that case he could only regard the practice of legal punishment as a most unhappy compromise.

Chapter One

Concepts of Punishment

Thomas Hobbes

Of Punishments and Rewards*

> A Punishment, is an Evill inflicted by publique Authority, on him that hath done, or omitted that which is Judged by the same Authority to be a Transgression of the Law; to the end that the will of men may thereby the better be disposed to obedience.

Before I inferre any thing from this definition, there is a question to be answered, of much importance; which is, by what door the Right, or Authority of Punishing in any case, came in. For by that which has been said before, no man is supposed bound by Covenant, not to resist violence; and consequently it cannot be intended, that he gave any right to another to lay violent hands upon his person. In the making of a Common-wealth, every man giveth away the right of defending another; but not of defending himselfe. Also he obligeth himselfe, to assist him that hath the Soveraignty, in the Punishing of another; but of himselfe not. But to covenant to assist the Soveraign, in doing hurt to another, unlesse he that so covenanteth have a right to doe it himselfe, is not to give him a Right to Punish. It is manifest therefore that the Right which the Common-wealth (that is, he, or they that represent it) hath to Punish, is not grounded on any concession, or gift of the Subjects. But I have also shewed formerly, that before the Institution of Common-wealth, every man had a right to every thing, and to do whatsoever he thought necessary to his own preservation; subduing, hurting, or killing any man in order thereunto. And this is the foundation of that right of Punishing, which is exercised in every Common-wealth. For the Subjects did not give the Soveraign that right; but onely in laying down theirs, strengthned him to use his

---

*Thomas Hobbes, *Leviathan* (New York: E. P. Dutton & Co., 1950), 266–69.

own, as he should think fit, for the preservation of them all: so that it was not given, but left to him, and to him onely; and (excepting the limits set him by naturall Law) as entire, as in the condition of meer Nature, and of warre of every one against his neighbour.

From the definition of Punishment, I inferre, First, that neither private revenges, nor injuries of private men, can properly be stiled Punishment; because they proceed not from publique Authority.

Secondly, that to be neglected, and unpreferred by the publique favour, is not a Punishment; because no new evill is thereby on any man Inflicted; he is onely left in the estate he was in before.

Thirdly, that the evill inflicted by publique Authority, without precedent publique condemnation, is not to be stiled by the name of Punishment; but of an hostile act; because the fact for which a man is Punished, ought first to be Judged by publique Authority, to be a transgression of the Law.

Fourthly, that the evill inflicted by usurped power, and Judges without Authority from the Soveraign, is not Punishment; but an act of hostility; because the acts of power usurped, have not for Author, the person condemned; and therefore are not acts of publique Authority.

Fifthly, that all evill which is inflicted without intention, or possibility of disposing the Delinquent, or (by his example) other men, to obey the Lawes, is not Punishment; but an act of hostility; because without such an end, no hurt done is contained under that name.

Sixthly, whereas to certain actions, there be annexed by Nature, divers hurtfull consequences; as when a man in assaulting another, is himselfe slain, or wounded; or when he falleth into sicknesse by the doing of some unlawfull act; such hurt, though in respect of God, who is the author of Nature, it may be said to be inflicted, and therefore a Punishment divine; yet it is not contaned in the name of Punishment in respect of men, because it is not inflicted by the Authority of man.

Seventhly, If the harm inflicted be lesse than the benefit, or contentment that naturally followeth the crime committed, that harm is not within the definition; and is rather the Price, or Redemption, than the Punishment of a Crime: Because it is of the nature of Punishment, to have for end, the disposing of men to obey the Law; which end (if it be lesse that the benefit of the transgression) it attaineth not, but worketh a contrary effect.

Eighthly, If a Punishment be determined and prescribed in the Law it selfe, and after the crime committed, there be a greater Punishment inflicted, the excesse is not Punishment, but an act of hostility. For seeing the aym of Punishment is not a revenge, but terrour; and the terrour of a great Punishment unknown, is taken away by the declaration of a lesse, the unexpected addition is no part of the Punishment. But where there is no Punishment at all determined by the Law, there whatsoever is inflicted, hath the nature of Punishment. For he that goes about the violation of a Law, wherein no penalty is determined, expecteth an indeterminate, that is to say, an arbitrary Punishment.

Ninthly, Harme inflicted for a Fact done before there was a Law that forbad it, is not Punishment, but an act of Hostility: For before the Law, there is no transgression of the Law: But Punishment supposeth a fact judged, to have been a transgression of the Law; Therefore Harme inflicted before the Law made, is not Punishment, but an act of Hostility.

Tenthly, Hurt inflicted on the Representative of the Common-wealth, is not Punishment, but an act of Hostility: Because it is of the nature of Punishment, to be inflicted by publique Authority, which is the Authority only of the Representative it self.

Lastly, Harme inflicted upon one that is a declared enemy, fals not under the name of Punishment: Because seeing they were either never subject to the Law, and therefore cannot transgresse it; or having been subject to it, and professing to be no longer so, by consequence deny they can transgresse it, all the Harmes that can be done them, must be taken as acts of Hostility. But in declared Hostility, all infliction of evill is lawfull. From whence it followeth, that if a subject shall by fact, or word, wittingly, and deliberatly deny the authority of the Representative of the Common-wealth, (whatsoever penalty hath been formerly ordained for Treason,) he may lawfully be made to suffer whatsoever the Representative will: For in denying subjection, he denyes such Punishment as by the Law hath been ordained; and therefore suffers as an enemy of the Common-wealth; that is, according to the will of the Representative. For the Punishments set down in the Law, are to Subjects, not to Enemies; such as are they, that having been by their own act Subjects, deliberately revolting, deny the Soveraign Power.

A. M. Quinton

On Punishment*

I. Introductory

There is a prevailing antinomy about the philosophical justification
of punishment. The two great theories—retributive and utilitarian—
seem, and at least are understood by their defenders, to stand in
open and flagrant contradiction. Both sides have arguments at their
disposal to demonstrate the atrocious consequences of the rival theory. Retributivists, who seem to hold that there are circumstances in
which the infliction of suffering is a good thing in itself, are charged
by their opponents with vindictive barbarousness. Utilitarians, who
seem to hold that punishment is always and only justified by the
good consequences it produces, are accused of vicious opportunism.
Where the former insists on suffering for suffering's sake, the latter
permits the punishment of the innocent. Yet, if the hope of justifying
punishment is not to be abandoned altogether, one of these apparently unsavory alternatives must be embraced. For they exhaust the
possibilities. Either punishment must be self-justifying, as the retributivists claim, or it must depend for its justification on something other
than itself, the general formula of "utilitarianism" in the wide sense
appropriate here.

In this paper I shall argue that the antinomy can be resolved,
since retributivism, properly understood, is not a moral but a logical doctrine, and that it does not provide a moral justification of
the infliction of punishment but an elucidation of the use of the
word. Utilitarianism, on the other hand, embraces a number of possible moral attitudes toward punishment, none of which necessarily involves the objectionable consequences commonly adduced by

*A. M. Quinton, "On Punishment," *Analysis*, 14 (1954): 512–17. Reprinted by
permission of the author and the publisher.

retributivists, provided that the word "punishment" is understood in the way that the essential retributivist thesis lays down. The antinomy arises from a confusion of modalities, of logical and moral necessity and possibility, of "must" and "can" with "ought" and "may." In brief, the two theories answer different questions: retributivism the question "when (logically) can we punish?," utilitarianism the question "when (morally) may we or *ought* we to punish?" I shall also describe circumstances in which there is an answer to the question "when (logically) *must* we punish?" Finally, I shall attempt to account for this difference in terms of a distinction between the establishment of rules whose infringement involves punishment from the application of these rules to particular cases.

II. The Retributive Theory

The essential contention of retributivism is that punishment is only justified by guilt. There is a certain compellingness about the repudiation of utilitarianism that this involves. We feel that whatever other considerations may be taken into account, the primary and indispensable matter is to establish the guilt of the person to be punished. I shall try to show that the peculiar outrageousness of the rejection of this principle is a consequence, not of the brutality that such rejection might seem to permit, but of the fact that it involves a kind of lying. At any rate the first principle of retributivism is that it is necessary that a man be guilty if he is to be punished.

But this doctrine is normally held in conjunction with some or all of three others which are logically, if not altogether psychologically, independent of it. These are that the function of punishment is the negation or annulment of evil or wrongdoing, that the punishment must fit the crime (the *lex talionis*) and that offenders have a right to punishment, as moral agents they ought to be treated as ends not means.

The doctrine of "annulment," however carefully wrapped up in obscure phraseology, is clearly utilitarian in principle. For it holds that the function of punishment is to bring about a state of affairs in which it is as if the wrongful act had never happened. This is to justify punishment by its effects, by the desirable future consequences which it brings about. It certainly goes beyond the demand that only the guilty he punished. For, unlike this demand, it seeks to prescribe exactly what the punishment should be. Holding that whenever wrong has been done it must be annulled, it makes guilt—the state of one who has done wrong—the sufficient as well as the necessary condition of punishment. While the original thesis is essentially negative, ruling out the punishment of the innocent, the annulment doctrine is positive, insisting on the punishment and determining the degree of punishment of the guilty. But the doctrine is only applicable to a restricted class of cases, the order of nature is inhospitable to attempts to put the clock back. Theft and fraud can be compensated, but not murder, wounding, alienation of affection, or the destruction of property or reputation.

Realizing that things cannot always be made what they were, retributivists have extended the notion of annulment to cover the infliction on the offender of an injury equal to that which he has caused. This is sometimes argued for by reference to Moore's theory of organic wholes, the view that sometimes two blacks make a white. That this, the *lex talionis*, revered by Kant, does not follow from the original thesis is proved by the fact that we can always refrain from punishing the innocent hut that we cannot always find a punishment to fit the crime. Some indeed would argue that we can never fit punishment to wrongdoing, for how are either, especially wrongdoing, to be measured? (Though, as Ross has pointed out, we can make ordinal judgments of more or less about both punishment and wrongdoing.)

Both of these views depend on a mysterious extension of the original thesis to mean that punishment and wrongdoing must necessarily be somehow equal and opposite. But this is to go even further than to regard guilt and punishment as necessitating one another. For this maintains that only the guilty are to be punished and that the guilty are always to be punished. The equal and opposite view maintains further that they are to be punished to just the extent that they have done wrong.

Finally retributivism has been associated with the view that if we are to treat offenders as moral agents, as ends and not as means, we must recognize their right to punishment. It is an odd sort of right whose holders would strenuously resist its recognition. Strictly interpreted, this view would entail that the sole relevant consideration in determining whether and how a man should be punished is his own moral regeneration. This is utilitarian and it is also immoral, since it neglects the rights of an offender's victims to compensation and of society in general to protection. A less extreme interpretation would be that we should never treat offenders merely as means in inflicting punishment but should take into account their right to treatment as moral agents. This is reasonable enough; most people would prefer a penal system which did not ignore the reformation of offenders. But it is not the most obvious correlate of the possible view that if a man is guilty he ought to be punished. We should more naturally allot the correlative right to have him punished to his victims or society in general and not to him himself.

III. The Retributivist Thesis

So far I have attempted to extricate the essentials of retributivism by excluding some traditional but logically irrelevant associates. A more direct approach consists in seeing what is the essential principle which retributivists hold utilitarians to deny. Their crucial charge is that utilitarians permit the punishment of the innocent. So their fundamental thesis must be that only the guilty are to be punished, that guilt is a necessary condition of punishment. This hardly lies open to the utilitarian countercharge of pointless and vindictive barbarity, which could only find a foothold in the doctrine of annulment and in the *lex talionis*. (For that matter, it is by no means obvious that the charge can be sustained even against them, except in so far as the problems of estimating the measure of guilt lead to the adoption of a purely formal and external criterion which would not distinguish between the doing of deliberate and accidental injuries.)

Essentially, then, retributivism is the view that only the guilty are to be punished. Excluding the punishment of the innocent, it permits the other three possibilities: the punishment of the guilty, the non-punishment of the guilty, and the nonpunishment of the innocent. To add that guilt is also the sufficient condition of punishment, and thus to exclude the nonpunishment of the guilty, is another matter altogether. It is not entailed by the retributivist attack on utilitarianism and has none of the immediate compulsiveness of the doctrine that guilt is the necessary condition of punishment.

There is a very good reason for this difference in force. For the necessity of not punishing the innocent is not moral but logical. It is not, as some retributivists think, that we may not punish the innocent and *ought* only to punish the guilty, but that we cannot punish the innocent and must only punish the guilty. Of course, the suffering or harm in which punishment consists can be and is inflicted on innocent people, but this is not punishment, it is judicial error or terrorism or, in Bradley's characteristically repellent phrase, "social surgery." The infliction of suffering on a person is only properly described as punishment if that person is guilty. The retributivist thesis, therefore, is not a moral doctrine, but an account of the meaning of the word "punishment." Typhoid carriers and criminal lunatics are treated physically in much the same way as ordinary criminals; they are shut up in institutions. The essential difference is that no blame is implied by their imprisonment, for there is no guilt to which the blame can attach. "Punishment" resembles the word "murder"; it is infliction of suffering on the guilty and not simply infliction of suffering, just as murder is wrongful killing and not simply killing. Typhoid carriers are no more (usually) criminals than surgeons are (usually) murderers. This accounts for the flavor of moral outrage attending the notion of punishment of the innocent. In a sense a contradiction in terms, it applies to the common enough practice of inflicting the suffering involved in punishment on innocent people and of sentencing them to punishment with a lying imputation of their responsibility and guilt. Punishment cannot be inflicted on the innocent; the suffering associated with punishment may not be inflicted on them, firstly, as brutal and secondly, if it is represented as punishment, as involving a lie.

This can be shown by the fact that punishment is always *for* something. If a man says to another "I am going to punish you" and is asked "what for?" he cannot reply "nothing at all" or "something you have not done." At best, he is using "punish" here as a more or less elegant synonym for "cause to suffer." Either that or he does not understand the meaning of "punish." "I am going to punish you for something you have not done" is as absurd a statement as "I blame you for this event for which you were not responsible." "Punishment implies guilt" is the same sort of assertion as "ought implies can." It is not *pointless* to punish or blame the innocent, as some have argued, for it is often very useful. Rather the very conditions of punishment and blame do not obtain in these circumstances.

IV. An Objection

But how can it be useful to do what is impossible? The innocent can be punished and scapegoats are not logical impossibilities. We do say "they punished him for something he did not do." For A to be said to have punished B it is surely enough that A thought or said he was punishing B and ensured that suffering was inflicted on B. However innocent B may be of the offense adduced by A, there is no question that, in these circumstances, he has been punished by A. So guilt cannot be more than a *moral* precondition of punishment.

The answer to this objection is that "punish" is a member of that now familiar class of verbs whose first-person-present use is significantly different from the rest. The absurdity of "I am punishing you for something you have not done" is analogous to that of "I promise to do something which is not in my power." Unless you are guilty I am no more in a position to punish you than I am in a position to promise what is not in my power. So it is improper to say "I am going to punish you" unless you are guilty, just as it is improper to say "I promise to do this" unless it is in my power to do it. But it is only *morally* improper if I do not *think* that you are guilty or that I can do the promised act. Yet, just as it is perfectly proper to say of another "he promised to do this," whether he thought he could do it or not, provided that he *said* "I promise to do this," so it is perfectly proper to say "they punished him," whether they thought him guilty or not, provided that they *said* "we are going to punish you" and inflicted suffering on him. By the first-person-present use of these verbs we prescribe punishment and *make* promises; these activities involve the satisfaction of conditions over and above what is required for *reports* or *descriptions* of what their prescribers or makers represent as punishments and promises.

Understandably "reward" and "forgive" closely resemble "punish." Guilt is a precondition of forgiveness, desert—its contrary—of reward.

One cannot properly say "I am going to reward you" or "I forgive you" to a man who has done nothing. Reward and forgiveness are always for something. But, again, one can say "they rewarded (or forgave) him for something he had not done." There is an interesting difference here between "forgive" and "punish" or "reward." In this last kind of assertion "forgive" seems more peculiar, more inviting to inverted commas, than the other two. The three undertakings denoted by these verbs can be divided into the utterance of a more or less ritual formula and the consequences authorized by this utterance. With punishment and reward the consequences are more noticeable than the formula, so they come to be sufficient occasion for the use of the word even if the formula is inapplicable and so improperly used. But, since the consequences of forgiveness are negative, the absence of punishment, no such shift occurs. To reward involves giving a reward, to punish inflicting a punishment, but to forgive involves no palpable consequence, e.g., handing over a written certificate of pardon.

Within these limitations, then, guilt is a *logically* necessary condition of punishment and, with some exceptions, it might be held, a morally necessary condition of the infliction of suffering. Is it in either way a sufficient condition? As will be shown in the last section there are circumstances, though they do not obtain in our legal system, nor generally in extralegal penal systems (e.g., parental), in which guilt is a logically sufficient condition of at least a sentence of punishment. The parallel moral doctrine would be that if anyone is guilty of wrong-doing he ought morally to be punished. This rather futile rigorism is not embodied in our legal system with its relaxations of penalties for first offenders. Since it entails that offenders should never be forgiven it is hardly likely to commend itself in the extralegal sphere.

V. The Utilitarian Theory

Utilitarianism holds that punishment must always be justified by the value of the consequences. I shall refer to this as "utility" for convenience without any implication that utility must consist in pleasure. The view that punishment is justified by the value of its consequences is compatible with any ethical theory which allows meaning to be attached to moral judgments. It holds merely that the infliction of suffering is of no value or of negative value and that it must therefore be justified by further considerations. These will be such things as prevention of and deterrence from wrongdoing, compensation of victims, reformation of offenders, and satisfaction of vindictive impulses. It is indifferent for our purposes whether these are valued as intuitively good, as productive of general happiness, as conducive to the survival of the human race or are just normatively laid down as valuable or derived from such a norm.

Clearly there is no *logical* relation between punishment and its actual or expected utility. Punishment *can* be inflicted when it is neither expected, nor turns out, to be of value and, on the other hand, it can be foregone when it is either expected, or would turn out, to be of value.

But that utility is the morally necessary or sufficient condition, or both, of punishment are perfectly reputable moral attitudes. The first would hold that no one should be punished unless the punishment would have valuable consequences; the second that if valuable consequences would result punishment ought to be inflicted (without excluding the moral permissibility of utility-less punishment). Most people would no doubt accept the first, apart from the rigorists who regard guilt as a morally sufficient condition of punishment. Few would maintain the second except in conjunction with the first. The first says when you may not but not when you ought to punish, the second when you ought to but not when you may not.

Neither permits or encourages the punishment of the innocent, for this is only logically possible if the word "punishment" is used in an unnatural way, for example as meaning any kind of deliberate infliction of suffering. But in that case they cease to be moral doctrine about punishment as we understand the word and become moral doctrines (respectively, platitudinous and inhuman) about something else.

So the retributivist case against the utilitarians falls to the ground as soon as what is true and essential in retributivism is extracted from the rest. This may be unwelcome to retributivists since it leaves the moral field in the possession of the utilitarians. But there is a compensation in the fact that what is essential in retributivism can at least be definitely established.

VI. Rules and Cases

So far what has been established is that guilt and the value or utility of consequences are relevant to punishment in different ways. A further understanding of this difference can he gained by making use of a distinction made by Sir David Ross in the appendix on punishment in *The Right and the Good*. This will also help to elucidate the notion of guilt which has hitherto been applied uncritically.

The distinction is between laying down a rule which attaches punishment to actions of a certain kind and the application of that rule to particular cases. It might be maintained that the utilitarian theory was an answer to the question "What *kinds* of action should be punished?" and the retributive theory an answer to the question "On what particular occasions should we punish?" On this view both punishment and guilt are defined by reference to these rules. Punishment is the infliction of suffering attached by these rules to certain kinds of action, guilt the condition of a person to whom such a rule applies. This accounts for the logically necessary relation holding between guilt and punishment. Only the guilty can be punished because unless a person is guilty, unless a rule applies to him, no infliction of suffering on him is properly called punishment, since punishment is infliction of suffering as laid down by such a rule. Considerations of utility, then, are alone relevant to the determination of what in general, what *kinds* of action, to punish. The outcome of this is a set of rules. Given these rules, the question of whom in particular to punish has a definite and necessary answer. Not only will guilt be the logically necessary but also the logically sufficient condition of punishment or, more exactly, of a sentence of punishment. For declaration of guilt will be a declaration that a rule applies and, if the rule applies, what the rule enjoins—a sentence of punishment applies also.

The distinction between setting up and applying penal rules helps to explain the different parts played by utility and guilt in the justification of punishment, in particular the fact that where utility is a moral, guilt is a logical, justification. Guilt is irrelevant to the setting up of rules, for until they have been set up the notion of guilt is undefined and without application. Utility is irrelevant to the application of rules, for once the rules have been set up, punishment is determined by guilt; once they are seen to apply, the rule makes a sentence of punishment necessarily follow.

But this account is not an accurate description of the very complex penal systems actually employed by states, institutions, and parents. It is, rather, a schema, a possible limiting case. For it ignores an almost universal feature of penal systems (and of games, for that matter, where penalties attend infractions of the rules)—discretion. For few offenses against the law is one and only one fixed and definite punishment laid down. Normally only an upper limit is set. If guilt, the applicability of the rule, is established no fixed punishment is entailed but rather, for example, one not exceeding a fine of forty shillings or fourteen days' imprisonment. This is even more evident in the administration of such institutions as clubs or libraries and yet more again in the matter of parental discipline. The establishment of guilt does not close the matter; at best it entails some punishment or other. Precisely how much is appropriate must be determined by reference to considerations of utility. The variety of things is too great for any manageably concise penal code to dispense altogether with discretionary judgment in particular cases.

But this fact only shows that guilt is not a logically *sufficient* condition of punishment; it does not affect the thesis that punishment entails guilt. A man cannot be guilty unless his action falls under a penal rule and he can only be properly said to be punished if the rule in question prescribes or permits some punishment or other. So all applications of the notion of guilt necessarily contain or include all applications of the notion of punishment.

Kurt Baier

Is Punishment Retributive?[*]

It would seem that punishment must of its nature be retributive, and also that it cannot be. It must be, for the infliction of hardship on someone is not punishment, unless it is as retribution *for* something he has done. It cannot be, for it makes sense to say that someone was punished for something he did not do. This seemingly simple, but actually quite intricate problem, was recently discussed by Professor A. G. N. Flew in an article entitled "The Justification of Punishment"[1] and by Mr. A. M. Quinton in a paper entitled "On Punishment."[2] Both appear to me to misrepresent the nature of punishment. I shall begin by stating briefly what I hold to be the correct solution, and then point out where exactly they went wrong.

1. To say that someone has punished someone else is to say that someone entitled to administer the penalty for a certain offense has administered this penalty to the person who has been found guilty of this offence by someone with the authority to do so. The question whether or not someone has punished someone else could not even arise unless he belonged to a group which had the practice of punishing people. We could not say of a group that it had the practice of punishing people unless all the following conditions were satisfied. There must be someone, such as a father or legislator, whose job it is to prescribe or prohibit the doing of certain things or types of thing by certain people, in the form of commands or regulations, someone whose task it is to decree how a person disobeying these commands or regulations shall be treated, someone, such as a father or policeman,

---

[*]Kurt Baier, "Is Punishment Retributive?" *Analysis*, 16 (1955): 25–32. Reprinted by permission of the author and the publisher.

1. *Philosophy*, October, 1954.

2. *Analysis*, June, 1954.

entrusted with the task of detecting cases of disobedience, someone, such as a father or judge, charged with meting out the penalty for such disobedience, and someone, such as a father or executioner, charged with administering it. Of course, all these different tasks may be entrusted to one and the same person, as in the case of punishment by a father or teacher.

It should be noticed that "punishing" is the name of only a part-activity belonging to a complex procedure involving several stages. Giving orders or laying down laws, affixing penalties to them, ascertaining whether anyone has disobeyed the commands or laws, sentencing persons found guilty, are not themselves punishing or part of the activity of punishing. Yet these activities must be performed and must precede the infliction of hardship if we are to speak of punishment at all. Of course, these activities may take only rudimentary forms. A father does not legislate, but gives orders; he does not necessarily affix penalties to breaches of these orders before the breaches occur, but determines the penalty after a breach or disobedience has occurred; he often does not take much trouble in finding out whether his child really is guilty, nor does he formally "find him guilty" or pronounce sentence. All this is merely tacitly implied, but it is quite definitely implied. It would be just as odd for a father to send his son to bed without supper for being late, if he had found the son not guilty of this—either because the son was not told to be home by a certain time or because he was home by the time mentioned—as it would be for a judge to pronounce sentence on the accused when he has just been acquitted by the jury.

It follows from the nature of this whole "game," consisting of rule-making, penalization, finding guilty of a breach of a rule, pronouncing sentence, and finally administering punishment, that the last act cannot be performed unless things have gone according to the rules until then. It is one of the constitutive rules of this whole "game" that the activity called punishing, or administering punishment, cannot be performed if, at a previous stage of the "game," the person in question has been found "not guilty." The "game" has to proceed differently after the verdict "not guilty," from the way it must proceed after the verdict "guilty." It is only if the verdict is "guilty" that there is any question of a sentence and its being carried out. And if, after the jury has found the accused "not guilty," the judge continues as if the jury had found him guilty, then his "I sentence you to three years' hard labor" is not the pronouncement of the sentence, but mere words. If, for some reason, the administration acts on these words, then what they do to the accused is not the infliction of punishment, but something for which (since it never happens) we do not even have a word.

A method of inflicting hardship on someone cannot he called "punishment" unless at least the following condition is satisfied. It must be the case that when someone is found "not guilty" it is not permissible to go on to pronounce sentence on him and carry it out. For "punishment" is the name of a method, or system, of inflicting hardship, *the aim of which* is to hurt all and only those who are guilty of an offence. For this reason, a system of punishment requires a more or less elaborate apparatus for detecting those who are guilty and for allotting to them the hardship prescribed by the system. To say that it is of the very nature of punishment to be retributive, is to say that a system of inflicting hardship on someone could not be properly called "punishment," unless it is the aim of this system to hurt all and only those guilty of an offence. Hence inflicting hardship on a person who has been found "not guilty" (logically) cannot be punishing. This is a conceptual point about punishment.

The correct answer to our problem is that punishment is indeed of its very nature retributive, since the very aim of inflicting hardship *as punishment* would be destroyed, if it were inflicted on someone who had been found "not guilty." But at the same time, someone may be punished, i.e., have hardship inflicted on him as *punishment*, although he was guilty of no offence, since he may have been *found* guilty without *being* guilty. For all judges and jurymen are fallible and some are corrupt.

2. Flew holds a different view. He says[3] that punishment is of its very nature retributive, but thinks that this applies only to the system of punishment as a whole, not to individual instances of punishing, because "The term is sufficiently vague to permit us to speak *in single cases and provided these do not become too numerous* (if they

---

3. *Loc. cit.*, p. 298.

do become too numerous, then *ispo facto* the use, the meaning, of 'punishment' has changed) of punishing a man who has broken no law (or even done no wrong)."[4]

My first point is that Flew has got the analysis wrong. Punishment, whether a system or a single case, is of its nature retributive. Flew says it "would he pedantic to insist in *single cases* that people (logically) cannot be punished for what they have not done,"[5] but that "a system of inflicting unpleasantness on scapegoats . . . could scarcely be called a system of punishment at all." These contrasts are misleading. It is not pedantic, but plain wrong, to insist in single cases that people (logically) cannot be punished for what they have not done. But this is not a statistical matter at all. True, a system of inflicting unpleasantness on scapegoats as such is not a system of punishment, but then a single case of inflicting unpleasantness on a scapegoat as such is not a case of punishment either. In Ruritania, everyone who has been punished during the last year or the last ten years may have been innocent, for in Ruritania the judges and jurymen and the police and prison authorities are very inefficient and very corrupt. A system of punishing people does not turn into a system of inflicting unpleasantness on scapegoats, simply in virtue of the fact that in this system innocent people happen frequently to get punished.

It is surely not true that, if under a certain system of punishment it happens that very many innocent people get punished, the meaning and use of "punishment" has ipso facto changed. Let us envisage such a deterioration in our own legal system. It is not logically necessary that we should come to know about it. Even now many people claim to have been unjustly condemned. Every now and then we hear of a ghastly judicial error, and there may be many more than we hear of. Think of the many cases in which people accuse the police of having used third degree methods for getting "confessions." For all I know, a very large percentage of people who are found guilty, and are later punished, are really innocent. At least, this is conceivable. Yet, if it were true, the meaning and use of "punishment" could not change *eo ipso*.

---

4. Ibid., p. 299/300.

5. Ibid., p. 293.

Or suppose we knew about it. What would we say? Simply that judges, police, and so on, were inefficient and/or corrupt, and that very many people got punished wrongly, i.e., unjustly, or by mistake.

Flew may have confused the unsound point he is making with another point which is sound. Suppose a group had what is properly called a system of punishment. It may then happen once in a while that a judge goes on to "pronounce sentence" even after the jury has found the accused "not guilty." Or, to take a more probable case, that a teacher goes on to hit a pupil even after he has realised, perhaps even admitted, that the pupil is innocent. Now, it is true that we would still say that the group had a system of punishment even if such cases occurred, provided they were exceptional. We would not, however, say that they had a system of punishment, if these were not exceptions, but if the group had a system of doing just this sort of thing.

This is true, but again it is not a matter of statistics, not a matter of happening frequently or infrequently. It is a matter of being an exception rather than the rule, in the sense that it is understood to be *a breach of the rule*, rather than merely out of the ordinary. Not merely that judges usually, but not always, discharge the accused when he has been found "not guilty," but that it is their *job* or duty to do so. If, after the jury has found the accused "not guilty," the judge says "I sentence you to three years' hard labour," this is not just an unusual case of punishing the man who is innocent, but not a case of punishment at all. And here it would not only not be pedantic, let alone wrong, but perfectly right to say that this case was not a case of punishment.

Flew, I suspect, may have been taken in by the word "system." He is, of course, right in saying that a system of inflicting unpleasantness on scapegoats, or a system of "punishing" people who had broken no laws cannot be called a system of punishment. This obvious truth, together with the obvious truth that men who have not broken any laws can be and sometimes are correctly said to have been punished, leads him to the view that the solution to the puzzle how one can say the one, but not the other, must be found in the difference between systems and single cases, which he takes to be the difference between the great majority of cases, and single cases.[6]

---

6. *Loc. cit.*, pp. 302/3

But it is more complicated than that. The expression "a system *of* 'punishing' people who had broken no laws" means "system whose declared and recognised nature it is to 'punish' those who had broken no laws." Hence the importance of "exception." If it is still the declared and recognised nature of the group's infliction of hardship on people that it is to be directed to all and only those who are found guilty of an offence, then the cases of inefficient and corrupt judges, and judges guilty of flagrant breaches of the law, are clearly exceptions. And while these single cases are exceptions, the whole system can still be called a system of punishment, otherwise it is a system of something else.

3. Mr. Quinton, on the other hand, does not think the solution of our problem lies in the distinction between systems and single cases of punishment, but he thinks it lies in the recognition "that 'punish' is a member of that now familiar class of verbs whose first-person-present use is significantly different from the rest."[7] As soon as we recognise that while "I am punishing you for something you have not done" is as absurd as "I promise to do something which is not in my power," we see that "he punished him for something he had not done" is no more absurd than is "he promised to do something that was not in his power."

My first point is that it is simply not true that "I am punishing you for something you have not done" is as absurd as "I promise you to do something which is not in my power." It need not be absurd at all. The executioner may whisper it to the man who has been sentenced to death. "I am punishing you for something you have not done" would be analogous to "I promise you to do this which is not in my power" only if to say "I am punishing you . . ." were to punish you, just as "I promise you . . ." is to promise you. In other words, the verb "to promise" is a performatory word, "to punish" is not. And if it were used performatorily in "I hereby punish you . . ." (not, by the way, as Quinton has it, "I am punishing you . . ."), then it would mean the same as "I hereby sentence you . . ." and saying it would still not be punishing anyone, but merely sentencing him. Thus, Quinton's account is not true of punishing but at best of sentencing.

---

7. *Loc. cit.*, p. 138

A similar mistake was made some time ago by Professor H. L. A. Hart in his important paper "The Ascription of Responsibility and Rights."[8] For the view he there expresses[9] is that judicial decisions are ascriptions of responsibility or rights and that these are "performatory utterances," "nondescriptive statements," statements not capable of being true or false. But while this is so of some judicial decisions such as pronouncing a sentence, it is not true of others such as verdicts. When the jury says "Guilty," the accused is "guilty in law" and may have no further recourse against such a judicial decision, but that does not mean that he really is guilty. The verdict "guilty" could be a performatory utterance only if uttering these words were making the accused guilty, as uttering the words "I promise" is making a promise. It might be said that the jury uses the word in a technical legal sense, different from the ordinary. When the jury says "Jury-Guilty," the accused is not indeed made guilty, but he is made jury-guilty. But this won't do, for what does jury-guilty come to? It simply means "to be held guilty," "to be regarded or treated as guilty." But this is not what the jury is asked to decide or what it says. The jury is asked to give its opinion on whether the accused *is* guilty, not on whether he is to be *treated* as guilty, for different considerations might enter into the second question. For the purpose of the legal consequences, the jury's opinion about his guilt is authoritative. Thus, it is not true that the jury says "Jury-Guilty," and thereby makes the accused jury-guilty. What is true is that the jury says "guilty" and thereby makes the accused jury-guilty that is to be held guilty. Hence the performatory model is out of place here, for when I say "I promise," I am making a promise, not an "uttered promise."

It might be thought that Quinton had seen this point, for he says[10] "There is an interesting difference here between 'forgive' and 'punish' or 'reward' . . . The three undertakings denoted by these verbs can be divided into the utterance of a more or less ritual formula and the consequences authorized by this utterance. With punishment and reward the consequences are more noticeable than the formula,

---

8. *Proc. Arist. Soc.* 1948–9. Reprinted in Flew, *Logic and Language*, Vol. I.

9. *Logic and Language*, pp. 155, 157, 159. 161.

10. Ibid., p. 139.

so they come to be sufficient occasion for the use of the word *even if the formula is inapplicable and so improperly used.* But, since the consequences of forgiveness are negative, the absence of punishment, no such shift occurs." At first sight, this distinction between the ritual formula and the consequences authorized by it might be taken to be the same distinction as the one I have drawn between sentencing and punishing. But on closer inspection, this turns out not to be so.

For while to say "I forgive you" is indeed to use a formula, the use of this formula or ritual is not performatory in the way in which the use of "I promise" or "I hereby sentence you to . . ." is. For if I say the latter in the appropriate circumstances, then I have promised or pronounced sentence. But when I say "I forgive you" I may merely say so. It is moreover wrong to think that "I forgive you" authorizes the nonimposition of punishment. The assaulted girl, with her last words, may forgive her assailant, but this does not authorize "the absence of punishment." Nor is the infliction of punishment authorized by the formula "I don't forgive you." The former indicates the injured party's intention not to seek revenge, to resume friendly relations, and so on, the latter the opposite. On the other hand, the infliction of punishment is authorized by the formula "guilty" or equivalent formulae, the noninfliction by the formula "not guilty" and perhaps the Home Secretary's pardon. Thus, the difference Quinton has in mind is not the difference I have drawn between pronouncing sentence and punishing.

Lastly, it should be emphasised that it is not true to say that punishing is the utterance of a ritual formula involving certain palpable consequences whereas forgiving is merely the utterance of a ritual formula involving no palpable consequences, and that, therefore, "punishing" sometimes refers merely to the palpable consequences even when the ritual formula is inappropriate, whereas this never happens in the case of forgiving. On the contrary, punishing and forgiving alike are certain kinds of doings, but they are doings which presuppose the correct completion of a certain more or less formal procedure culminating in the finding someone guilty of an offence. If and only if this procedure has been followed correctly to its very conclusion, can there be any question of someone's being or not being punished or forgiven or pardoned. One of the important differences between forgiving and punishing is that they presuppose different sorts of formalities. Forgiving is involved only where a man has been found guilty of an injury. Punishment is involved only where he has been found guilty of an offence. Many systems of crime and punishment make injuries offences, but not all offences are necessarily injuries. Vindictiveness and forgiveness, revenge and turning the other cheek are individual, punishment and reward are social ways of dealing with objectionable behaviour.

Although the infliction of hardship on an individual cannot be called punishment unless it is preceded by his having been found "guilty" of an offence, the procedure leading up to this finding need only be formally and not materially correct. That is to say, as long as he was found "guilty" in the proper way, even though he is not in fact guilty, the infliction of hardship which then follows will be punishment, provided no further slip occurs.

Joel Feinberg

The Expressive Function of Punishment*

It might well appear to a moral philosopher absorbed in the classical literature of his discipline, or to a moralist sensitive to injustice
and suffering, that recent philosophical discussions of the problem of
punishment have somehow missed the point of his interest. Recent
influential articles[1] have quite sensibly distinguished between questions of definition and justification, between justifying general rules
and particular decisions, between moral and legal guilt. So much is
all to the good. When these articles go on to *define* "punishment,"
however, it seems to many that they leave out of their ken altogether
the very element that makes punishment theoretically puzzling and
morally disquieting. Punishment is defined, in effect, as the infliction
of hard treatment by an authority on a person for his prior failing in
some respect (usually an infraction of a rule or command).[2] There
may be a very general sense of the word "punishment" which is well

---

*Joel Feinberg, "The Expressive Function of Punishment," *The Monist*, 49:3,
(La Salle, IL, 1965): 397–408. Reprinted by permission of the author and the
publisher.

1. See especially the following: A. Flew, "The Justification of Punishment,'
Philosophy, 29 (1954): 291–307; S. I. Benn, "An Approach to the Problems of
Punishment," *Philosophy*, 33 (1958): 325–341; and H. L. A. Mart, "Prolegomenon
to the Principles of Punishment," *Proceedings of the Aristotelian Society*, 60
(1959–60): 1–26.

2. Hart and Benn both borrow Flew's definition. In Hart's paraphrase, punishment
"(i) . . . must involve pain or other consequences normally considered
unpleasant. (ii) It must be for an offense against legal rules. (iii) It must be
of an actual or supposed offender for his offense. (iv) It must be intentionally
administered by human beings rather than the offender. (v) It must be imposed
and administered by an authority constituted by a legal system against which the
offense is committed" (*op. cit.*, p. 4.).

expressed by this definition; but even if that is so, we can distinguish a narrower, more emphatic sense that slips through its meshes. Imprisonment at hard labor for committing a felony is a clear case of punishment in the emphatic sense; but I think we would be less willing to apply that term to parking tickets, offside penalties, sackings, flunkings, and disqualifications. Examples of the latter sort I propose to call penalties (merely), so that I may inquire further what distinguishes punishment, in the strict and narrow sense that interests the moralist, from other kinds of penalties.[3]

One method of answering this question is to focus one's attention on the class of nonpunitive penalties in an effort to discover some clearly identifiable characteristic common to them all, and absent from all punishments, on which the distinction between the two might be grounded. The hypotheses yielded by this approach, however, are not likely to survive close scrutiny. One might conclude, for example, that mere penalties are less severe than punishments, but although this is generally true, it is not necessarily and universally so. Again we might be tempted to interpret penalties as mere "price tags" attached to certain types of behavior that are generally undesirable, so that only those with especially strong motivation will be willing to

---

3. The distinction between punishments and penalties was first called to my attention by Dr. Anita Fritz of the University of Connecticut. Similar distinctions in different terminologies have been made by many. Pollock and Maitland speak of "true afflictive punishments" as opposed to outlawry, private vengeance, fine, and emendation (*History of English Law*, 2d ed., II, pp. 451 ff). The phrase "afflictive punishment" was invented by Bentham (*Rationale of Punishment*, London, 1830): "These [corporal] punishments are almost always attended with a portion of ignominy, and this does not always increase with the organic pain, but principally depends upon the condition [social class] of the offender" (p. 83). James Stephen says of legal punishment that it "should always connote . . . moral infamy" (*History of the Criminal Law*, II, p. 171). Lasswell and Donnelly distinguish "condemnation sanctions" and "other deprivations" ("The Continuing Debate over Responsibility: An Introduction to Isolating the Condemnation Sanction," *Yale Law Journal*, 68, 1959). The traditional common law distinction is between "infamous" and "noninfamous" crimes and punishments. Conviction of an "infamous crime" rendered a person liable to such post-punitive civil disabilities as incompetence to be a witness.

pay the price.[4] So, for example, deliberate efforts on the part of some western states to keep roads from urban centers to wilderness areas few in number and poor in quality are essentially no different from various parking fines and football penalties. In each case a certain kind of conduct is discouraged without being absolutely prohibited: Anyone who desires strongly enough to get to the wilderness (or park overtime, or interfere with a pass) may do so provided he is willing to pay the penalty (price). On this view penalties are, in effect, licensing fees, different from other purchased permits in that the price is often paid afterward rather than in advance. Since a similar interpretation of punishments seems implausible, it might be alleged that this is the basis of the distinction between penalties and punishments. However, while a great number of penalties can, no doubt, plausibly be treated as retroactive license fees, this is hardly true of all of them. It is certainly not true, for example, of most demotions, firings, and flunkings, that they are "prices" paid for some already consumed benefit; and even parking fines are sanctions for rules "meant to be taken seriously as . . . standard [s] of behavior,"[5] and thus are more than mere public parking fees.

Rather than look for a characteristic common and peculiar to the penalties on which to ground the distinction between penalties and punishments, we would be better advised, I think, to cast our attention to the examples of punishments. Both penalties and punishments are authoritative deprivations for failures; but apart from these common features, penalties have a miscellaneous character, whereas punishments have an important additional characteristic in common. That characteristic or specific difference, I shall argue, is

---

4. That even punishments proper are to be interpreted as taxes on certain kinds of conduct is a view often associated with O. W. Holmes, Jr. For an excellent discussion of Holmes's fluctuations of this question see Mark DeWolfe Howe, *Justice Oliver Wendell Holmes: Volume II: The Proving Years, 1870–1882* (Cambridge, MA: Harvard University Press, 1963), 74–80. See also Lon L. Fuller, *The Morality of Law* (New Haven, CT: Yale University Press, 1964). Chap. II, part. 7, and H. L. A. Hart, *The Concept of Law* (Oxford, 1961), 39, for illuminating comparisons and contrasts of punishment and taxation.

5. H. L. A. Hart, *loc. cit.*

a certain expressive function. Punishment is a conventional device for the expression of attitudes of resentment and indignation, and of judgments of disapproval and reprobation, either on the part of the punishing authority himself or of those "in whose name" the punishment is inflicted. Punishment, in short, has a *symbolic significance* largely missing from other kinds of penalties.

The reprobative symbolism of punishment and its character as "hard treatment," while never separate in reality, must be carefully distinguished for purposes of analysis. Reprobation is itself painful, whether or not it is accompanied by further "hard treatment"; and hard treatment, such as fine or imprisonment, because of its conventional symbolism, can itself be reprobatory; but still we can conceive of ritualistic condemnation unaccompanied by any *further* hard treatment, and of inflictions and deprivations which, because of different symbolic conventions, have no reprobative force. It will be my thesis in this essay that (1) both the hard treatment aspect of punishment and its reprobative function must be part of the *definition* of legal punishment; and (2) each of these aspects raises its own kind of question about the justification of legal punishment as a general practice. I shall argue that some of the jobs punishment does, and some of the conceptual problems it raises, cannot be intelligibly described unless (1) is true; and that the incoherence of a familiar form of the retributive theory results from failure to appreciate the force of (2).

I. Punishment as Condemnation

That the expression of the community's condemnation is an essential ingredient in legal punishment is widely acknowledged by legal writers. Henry M. Hart, for example, gives eloquent emphasis to the point:

> What distinguishes a criminal from a civil sanction and all that distinguishes it, it is ventured, is the judgment of community condemnation which accompanies . . . its imposition. As Professor Gardner wrote not long ago, in a distinct but cognate connection:

'The essence of punishment for moral delinquency lies in the criminal conviction itself. One may lose more money on the stock market than in a court-room; a prisoner of war camp may well provide a harsher environment than a state prison; death on the field of battle has the same physical characteristics as death by sentence of law. It is the expression of the community's hatred, fear, or contempt for the convict which alone characterizes physical hardship as punishment.'

If this is what a 'criminal' penalty is, then we can say readily enough what a 'crime' is. . . . It is conduct which, if duly shown to have taken place, will incur a formal and solemn pronouncement of the moral condemnation of the community. . . . Indeed the condemnation plus the added [unpleasant physical] consequences may well be considered, compendiously, as constituting the punishment.[6]

Professor Hart's compendious definition needs qualification in one respect. The moral condemnation and the "unpleasant consequences" that he rightly identifies as essential elements of punishment are not as distinct and separate as he suggests. It is not always the case that the convicted prisoner is first solemnly condemned and then subjected to unpleasant physical treatment. It would be more accurate in many cases to say that the unpleasant treatment itself expresses the condemnation, and that this expressive aspect of his incarceration is precisely the element by reason of which it is properly characterized as punishment and not mere penalty. The administrator who regretfully suspends the license of a conscientious but accident-prone driver can inflict a deprivation without any scolding, express or implied; but the reckless motorist who is sent to prison for six months is thereby inevitably subject to shame and ignominy—the very walls of his cell condemn him and his record becomes a stigma.

To say that the very physical treatment itself expresses condemnation is to say simply that certain forms of hard treatment have

---

6. Henry M. Hart, "The Aims of the Criminal Law," *Law and Contemporary Problems*, 23 (1958), 11, A, 4.

become the conventional symbols of public reprobation. This is neither more nor less paradoxical than to say that certain words have
become conventional vehicles in our language for the expression of
certain attitudes, or that champagne is the alcoholic beverage traditionally used in celebration of great events, or that black is the color
of mourning. Moreover, particular kinds of punishment are often used
to express quite specific attitudes (loosely speaking, this is part of their
"meaning"); note the differences, for example, between beheading a
nobleman and hanging a yeoman, burning a heretic and hanging a
traitor, hanging an enemy soldier and executing him by firing squad.

It is much easier to show that punishment has a symbolic significance than to say exactly what it is that punishment expresses.
At its best, in civilized and democratic countries, punishment surely
expresses the community's strong disapproval of what the criminal did.
Indeed it can be said that punishment expresses the judgment (as
distinct from any emotion) of the community that what the criminal
did was wrong. I think it is fair to say of our community, however,
that punishment generally expresses more than judgments of disapproval; it is also a symbolic way of getting back at the criminal, of
expressing a kind of vindictive resentment. To any reader who has in
fact spent time in a prison, I venture to say, even Professor Gardner's
strong terms—"hatred, fear, or contempt for the convict"—will not
seem too strong an account of what imprisonment is universally taken
to express. Not only does the criminal feel the naked hostility of
his guards and the outside world—that would he fierce enough—
but that hostility is self-righteous as well. His punishment bears the
aspect of legitimized vengefulness; hence there is much truth in J.
F. Stephen's celebrated remark that "The criminal law stands to the
passion of revenge in much the same relation as marriage to the
sexual appetite."[7]

If we reserve the less dramatic term "resentment" for the various
vengeful attitudes, and the term "reprobation" for the stern judgment of disapproval, then perhaps we can characterize condemnation
(or denunciation) as a kind of fusing of resentment and reprobation.
That these two elements are generally to be found in legal punish-

---

7. *General View of the Criminal Law of England*, 1st ed. (London, 1863), p. 99.

ment was well understood by the authors of the Report of the Royal Commission on Capital Punishment:

> Discussion of the principle of *retribution* is apt to be confused because the word is not always used in the same sense. Sometimes it is intended to mean vengeance, sometimes reprobation. In the first sense the idea is that of satisfaction by the State of a wronged individual's desire to be avenged; in the second it is that of the State's *marking its disapproval* of the breaking of its laws by a punishment proportionate to the gravity of the offense. [Feinberg's emphasis][8]

II. Some Derivative Symbolic Functions of Punishment

The relation of the expressive function of punishment to its various central purposes is not always easy to trace. Symbolic public condemnation added to deprivation may help or hinder deterrence, reform, and rehabilitation—the evidence is not clear. On the other hand, there are other functions of punishment, often lost sight of in the preoccupation with deterrence and reform that presuppose the expressive function and would be impossible without it.

1. *Authoritative Disavowal.* Consider the standard international practice of demanding that a nation whose agent has unlawfully violated the complaining nation's rights should punish the offending agent. For example, suppose that an airplane of nation A fires on an airplane of nation B while the latter is flying over international waters. Very likely high authorities in nation B will send a note of protest to their counterparts in nation A demanding, among other things, that the transgressive pilot he punished. Punishing the pilot is an emphatic, dramatic, and well understood way of *condemning* and thereby *disavowing* his act. It tells the world that the pilot had no

---

8. *Report of the Royal Commission on Capital Punishment* (London: H.M.S.O., 1953), pp. 17–18, cited in Joel Feinberg, "The Expressive Function of Punishment," in his *Doing and Deserving: Essays in the Theory of Responsibility* (Princeton, NJ: Princeton University Press, 1970), p. 101.

right to do what he did, that he was on his own in doing it, that his government does not condone that sort of thing. It testifies thereby to government A's recognition of the violated rights of government B in the affected area, and therefore to the wrongfulness of the pilot's act. Failure to punish the pilot tells the world that government A does not consider him to have been personally at fault. That in turn is to claim responsibility for the act, which in effect labels that act as an "instrument of deliberate national policy," and therefore an act of war. In that case either formal hostilities or humiliating loss of face by one side or the other almost certainly follows. None of this makes any sense without the well understood reprobative symbolism of punishment. In quite parallel ways punishment enables employers to disavow the acts of their employees (though not civil liability for those acts), and fathers the destructive acts of their sons.

2. *Symbolic Non-Acquiescence: "Speaking in the Name of the People."* The symbolic function of punishment also explains why even those sophisticated persons who abjure resentment of criminals and look with small favor generally on the penal law are likely to demand that certain kinds of conduct be punished when or if the law lets them go by. In the state of Texas, so-called "paramour killings" are regarded by the law as not merely mitigated, but completely justifiable.[9] Many humanitarians, I believe, will feel quite spontaneously that a great injustice is done when such killings are left unpunished. The sense of violated justice, moreover, might be distinct and unaccompanied by any frustrated *schaden-freude* toward the killer, lust for blood or vengeance, or metaphysical concern lest the universe stay "out of joint." The demand for punishment in cases of this sort may instead represent the feeling that paramour killings deserve to be condemned, that the law in condoning, even feeling that paramour killings deserve to be *con-*

---

9. The Texas Penal Code (Art. 1220) states: "Homicide is justifiable when committed by the husband upon one taken in the act of adultery with the wife, provided the killing takes place before the parties to the act have separated. Such circumstances cannot justify a homicide when it appears that there has been on the part of the husband, any connivance in or assent to the adulterous connection." New Mexico and Utah have similar statutes. For some striking descriptions of perfectly legal paramour killings in Texas, see John Bainbridge, *The Super-Americans* (Garden City, NY, 1961), pp. 238 ff.

demned, that the law in condoning, even approving of them, speaks for all citizens in expressing a wholly inappropriate attitude toward them. For, in effect, the law expresses the judgment of the "people of Texas." in whose name it speaks, that the vindictive satisfaction in the mind of a cuckolded husband is a thing of greater value than the very life of his wife's lover. The demand that paramour killings be punished may simply be the demand that this lopsided value judgment be withdrawn and that the state go on record against paramour killings, and the law *testify to the recognition* that such killings are wrongful. Punishment no doubt would also help deter killers. This too is a desideratum and a closely related one, but it is not to be identified with reprobation; for deterrence might be achieved by a dozen other techniques, from simple penalties and forfeitures to exhortation and propaganda; but effective public denunciation and, through it, symbolic non-acquiescence in the crime, seem virtually to require punishment.

This symbolic function of punishment was given great emphasis by Kant, who, characteristically, proceeded to exaggerate its importance. Even if a desert island community were to disband, Kant argued, its members should first execute the last murderer left in its jails, "for otherwise they might all be regarded as participators in the [unpunished] murder. . . ."[10] This Kantian idea that in failing to punish wicked acts society endorses them and thus becomes *particeps criminis* does seem to reflect, however dimly, something embedded in common sense. A similar notion underlies whatever is intelligible in the widespread notion that all citizens share the responsibility for political atrocities. Insofar as there is a coherent argument behind the extravagant distributions of guilt made by existentialists and other literary figures, it can be reconstructed in some such way as this: To whatever extent a political act is done "in one's name," to that extent one is responsible for it. A citizen can avoid responsibility in advance by explicitly disowning the government as his spokesman, or after the fact through open protest, resistance, and so on. Otherwise, by "acquiescing" in what is done in one's name, one incurs the responsibility for it. The root notion here is a kind of "power of attorney" a government has for its citizens.

---

10. *The Philosophy of Law*, trans. W. Hastie (Edinburgh, 1887), p. 198.

3. *Vindication of the Law.* Sometimes the state goes on record through its statutes, in a way that might well please a conscientious citizen in whose name it speaks, but then through official evasion and unreliable enforcement, gives rise to doubts that the law really means what it says. It is murder in Mississippi, as elsewhere, for a white man intentionally to kill a Negro; but if grand juries refuse to issue indictments or if trial juries refuse to convict, and this is well understood by most citizens, then it is in a purely formal and empty sense indeed that killings of Negroes by whites are illegal in Mississippi.

Yet the law stays on the books, to give ever-less-convincing lip service to a noble moral judgment. A statute honored mainly in the breach begins to lose its character as law, unless, as we say, it is vindicated (emphatically reaffirmed); and clearly the way to do this (indeed the only way) is to punish those who violate it.

Similarly, *punitive damages,* so-called, are sometimes awarded the plaintiff in a civil action, as a supplement to compensation for his injuries. What more dramatic way of vindicating his violated right can be imagined than to have a court thus forcibly condemn its violation through the symbolic machinery of punishment?

4. *Absolution of Others.* When something scandalous has occurred and it is clear that the wrongdoer must be one of a small number of suspects, then the state, by punishing one of these parties, thereby relieves the others of suspicion, and informally absolves them of blame. Moreover, quite often the absolution of an accuser hangs as much in the balance at a criminal trial as the inculpation of the accused. A good example of this can be found in James Gould Cozzens's novel, *By Love Possessed.* A young girl, after an evening of illicit sexual activity with her boyfriend, is found out by her bullying mother, who then insists that she clear her name by bringing criminal charges against the boy. He used physical force, the girl charges; she freely consented, he replies. If the jury finds him guilty of rape, it will by the same token absolve her from (moral) guilt and her reputation as well as his rides on the outcome. Could not the state do this job without punishment? Perhaps, but when it speaks by punishing, its message is loud and sure of getting across. . . .

Chapter Two

The Justification of Punishment

1. Teleological Theories

Plato	Punishment as Cure
J. E. McTaggart	Hegel's Theory of Punishment
Jeremy Bentham	Utility and Punishment
H. Rashdall	Punishment and the Individual
T. L. S. Sprigge	A Utilitarian Reply to Dr. McCloskey
John Austin	Rule Utilitarianism (I)
John Rawls	Rule Utilitarianism (II)
Richard Brandt	Rule Utilitarianism (III)

2. Retributivism

Immanuel Kant	Justice and Punishment
G. W. F. Hegel	Punishment as a Right

1. Teleological Theories

Plato

Punishment as Cure*

SOCRATES: . . . of two who suffer evil either in body or in soul, which is the more wretched, the man who submits to treatment and gets rid of the evil, or he who is not treated but still retains it?

POLUS: Evidently the man who is not treated.

SOCRATES: And was not punishment admitted to be a release from the greatest of evils, namely wickedness?

POLUS: It was.

SOCRATES: Yes, because a just penalty disciplines us and makes us more just and cures us of evil.

POLUS: I agree.

SOCRATES: Then the happiest of men is he who has no evil in his soul, since this was shown to be the greatest of evils?

POLUS: That is plain.

SOCRATES: And second in order surely is he who is delivered from it.

POLUS: Apparently.

SOCRATES: And we found this was the man who is admonished and rebuked and punished.

POLUS: Yes.

SOCRATES: Then his life is most unhappy who is afflicted with evil and does not get rid of it.

POLUS: Evidently.

SOCRATES: And is not this just the man who does the greatest wrong and indulges in the greatest injustice and yet contrives to escape admonition, correction, or punishment—the very condition you describe as achieved by Archelaus and other tyrants, orators, and potentates?

POLUS: It seems so.

---

*Plato, *Gorgias*, in *The Collected Dialogues of Plato*, ed. with an intro. E. Hamilton and H. Cairns. (Princeton, NJ: Princeton University Press, 1961), 262–63.

SOCRATES: For what these have contrived, my good friend, is pretty much as if a man afflicted with the most grievous ailments should contrive not to pay to the doctors the penalty of his sins against his body by submitting to treatment, because he is afraid, like a child, of the pain of cautery or surgery. Do you agree?

POLUS: I do.

SOCRATES: He is evidently ignorant of the meaning of health and physical fitness. For apparently, as our recent admissions prove, those who escape punishment also act much in the same way, Polus. They see its painfulness but are blind to its benefit and know not how much more miserable than a union with an unhealthy body is a union with a soul that is not healthy but corrupt and impious and evil, and so they leave nothing undone to avoid being punished and liberated from the greatest of ills, providing themselves with money and friends and the highest attainable powers of persuasive rhetoric. But if we have been right in our admissions, Polus, do you see the results of our argument, or shall we sum them up together?

POLUS: Yes, if you wish.

SOCRATES: Is not our conclusion then that injustice and the doing of wrong is the greatest of evils?

POLUS: Evidently.

SOCRATES: And it was shown that punishment rids us of this evil?

POLUS: Apparently.

SOCRATES: And when punishment is evaded, the evil abides?

POLUS: Yes.

SOCRATES: Then wrongdoing itself holds the second place among evils, but first and greatest of all evils is to do wrong and escape punishment.

POLUS: So it seems.

SOCRATES: Now did we not differ, my friend, about this very point, when you maintained that Archelaus was happy because he remained unpunished despite the enormity of his crimes, whereas I was of the contrary opinion—that Archelaus or any other man who escapes punishment for his misdeeds must be miserable far beyond all other men, and that invariably the doer of wrong is more wretched than his victim, and he who escapes punishment than he who is punished? Was not that what I was saying?

POLUS: Yes.

SOCRATES: And has it not been proved that it is true?

POLUS: Clearly.

J. E. McTaggart

Hegel's Theory of Punishment[*]

. . . Hegel does not deny that punishment may deter, prevent, or improve, and he does not deny that this will be an additional advantage. But he says that none of these are the chief object of punishment, and none of them express its real nature. It would seem, therefore, that he must intend to advocate vindictive punishment. And this is confirmed by the fact that he expressly says the object of punishment is not to do "this or that" good.

Nevertheless, I believe that Hegel had not the slightest intention of advocating what we have called vindictive punishment. For he says, beyond the possibility of a doubt, that in punishment the criminal is to be treated as a moral being—that is, one who is potentially moral, however immoral he may be in fact, and one in whom this potential morality must be called into actual existence. He complains that in the deterrent theory we treat a man like a dog to whom his master shows a whip, and not as a free being. He says that the criminal has a right to be punished, which indicates that the punishment is in a sense for his sake. And, still more emphatically, "in punishment the offender is honored as a rational being, since the punishment is looked on as his right."[1]

Now this is incompatible with the view that Hegel is here approving of vindictive punishment. For he says that a man is only to be punished because he is a moral being, and that it would be an injury to him not to punish him. The vindictive theory knows nothing of all this. It inflicts pain on a man, not for his ultimate good, but because, as it says, he has deserved to suffer pain. And, on Hegel's theory,

---

[*]J. E. McTaggart, "Hegel's Theory of Punishment," *International Journal of Ethics* 6 (1896), pp. 482–99.

1. "Philosophy of Law." Sections 99 and 100.

punishment depends on the recognition of the criminal's rational and moral nature, so that, in his phrase, it is an honor as well as a disgrace. Nothing of the sort exists for vindictive punishment. It does not care whether the sinner can or will do good in the future. It punishes him because he has done wrong in the past. If we look at the doctrine of hell—which is a pure case of vindictive punishment—we see that it is possible to conceive punishment of this sort when the element of a potential moral character has entirely disappeared, for I conceive that the supporters of this doctrine would deny the possibility of repentance, since they deny the possibility of pardon.

What, then, is Hegel's theory? It is, I think, briefly this. In sin, man rejects and defies the moral law. Punishment is pain inflicted on him because he has done this, and in order that he may, by the fact of his punishment, be forced into recognizing as valid the law which he rejected in sinning, and so repent of his sin—really repent, and not merely be frightened out of doing it again.

Thus the object of punishment is that the criminal should repent of his crime, and by so doing realize the moral character, which has been temporarily obscured by his wrong action, but which is, as Hegel asserts, really his truest and deepest nature. At first sight this looks very much like the reformatory theory of punishment, which Hegel has rejected. But there is a great deal of difference between them. The reformatory theory says that we ought to reform our criminals while we are punishing them. Hegel says that punishment itself tends to reform them. The reformatory theory wishes to pain criminals as little as possible, and improve them as much as possible. Hegel's theory says that it is the pain which will improve them, and therefore, although it looks on pain in itself as an evil, is by no means particularly anxious to spare it, since it holds that through the pain the criminals will be raised, and that we have therefore no right to deny it to them.

When Hegel says, therefore, as we saw above, that the object of punishment is not to effect "this or that good," we must not, I think, take him to mean that we do not look for a good result from punishment. We must rather interpret him to mean that it is not in consequence of some *accidental* good result that punishment is to be defended, but that, for the criminal, punishment is inherently good. This use of "this or that" to express an accidental or contingent good seems in accordance with Hegel's usual style. And we must also remember that Hegel, who hated many things, hated nothing more bitterly than sentimental humanitarianism, and that he was in consequence more inclined to emphasize his divergence from a reformatory theory of punishment than his agreement with it.

We have thus reached a theory quite different from any of the four which we started this paper by considering. It is not impossible that we may find out that the world has been acting on the Hegelian view for many ages, but as an explicit theory it has found little support. We all recognize that a man can be frightened into or out of a course of action by punishment. We all recognize that a man can sometimes be reformed by influences applied while he is being punished. But can he ever be reformed simply by punishment? Reform and repentance involve that he should either see that something was wrong which before he thought was right, or else that the intensity of his moral feelings should be so strengthened that he is enabled to resist a temptation, to which before he yielded. And why should punishment help him to do either of these things?

There is a certain class of people in the present day who look on all punishment as essentially degrading. They do not, in their saner moods, deny that there may be people for whom it is necessary. But they think that, if anyone requires punishment, he proves himself to be uninfluenced by moral motives, and only to be governed by fear, which they declare to be degrading. (It is curious, by the way, that this school is rather fond of the idea that people should be governed by rewards rather than punishments. It does not seem easy to understand why it is less degrading to be bribed into virtue than to be frightened away from vice.) They look on all punishment as implying deep degradation in someone—if it is justified, the sufferer must be little better than a brute; if it is not justified, the brutality is in the person who inflicts it.

This argument appears to travel in a circle. Punishment, they say, is degrading, therefore it can work no moral improvement. But this begs the question. For if punishment could work a moral improvement, it would not degrade but elevate. The humanitarian argument alternately proves that punishment can only intimidate because it is brutalizing, and that it is brutalizing because it can only intimidate. The real reason, apparently, of the foregone conviction which tries to justify itself by this confusion, is an unreasoning horror of the infliction of pain which has seized on many very excellent and disinterested people. That pain is an evil cannot be denied. It may, perhaps, be reasonably asserted that it is the ultimate evil. But to assert that it is always wrong to inflict it is equivalent to a declaration that there is no moral difference between a dentist and a wife-beater. No one can deny that the infliction of pain may in the long run increase happiness—as in the extraction of an aching tooth. If pain, in spite of its being evil *per se*, can thus be desirable as a means, the general objection to pain as a moral agent would seem to disappear also.

Of course, there is nothing in simple pain, as such, which can lead to repentance. If I get into a particular train, and break my leg in a collision, that cannot make me repent my action in going by the train, though it will very possibly make me regret it. For the pain in this case was not a punishment. It came, indeed, because I got into the train, but not because I had done wrong in getting into the train.

Hegel's theory is that punishment, that is, pain inflicted because the sufferer had previously done wrong, may lead to repentance for the crime which caused the punishment. We have now to consider whether this is true. Our thesis is not that it always produces repentance—which, of course, is not the case—but that there is something in its nature as punishment which tends to produce repentance. And this, as we have seen, is not a common theory of punishment. "Men do not," says George Eliot in "Felix Holt," (Chap. 41,)—"men do not become penitent and learn to abhor themselves by having their backs cut open with the lash; rather, they learn to abhor the lash." That the principle expressed here is one which often operates, cannot be denied. Can we so far limit its application that Hegel's theory shall also be valid?

We have so far defined punishment as pain inflicted because the sufferer has done wrong. But, looking at it more closely, we should have to alter this definition, which is too narrow, and does not include cases of unjust or mistaken punishment. To bring these in we must say that it is pain inflicted because the person who inflicts it thinks that the person who suffers it has done wrong. Repentance, again, is the realization by the criminal, with sufficient vividness to govern future action, that he has done wrong. Now, is there anything in the nature of punishment to cause the conviction in the mind of the judge to be reproduced in the mind of the culprit? If so, punishment will tend to produce repentance.

I submit that this is the case under certain conditions. When the culprit recognizes the punishing authority as one which embodies the moral law, and which has a right to enforce it, then punishment may lead to repentance, but not otherwise.

Let us examine this a little more closely. A person who suffers punishment may conceive the authority which inflicts it as distinctly immoral in its tendencies. In this case, of course, he will not be moved to repent of his action. The punishment will appear to him unjust, the incurring of the punishment will present itself in the light of a duty, and he will consider himself not as a criminal, but as a martyr. On the other hand, if the punishment causes him to change his line of action, this, his convictions being as we have supposed, will not be repentance, but cowardice.

Or again, he may not regard it as distinctly immoral—as punishing him for what it is his duty to do, but he may regard it as non-moral—as punishing him for what he had a right, though not a duty, to do. In this case, too, punishment will not lead to repentance. He will not regard himself as a martyr, but he will be justified in regarding himself as a very badly treated individual. If the punishment does cause him to abstain from such action in future, it will not be the result of repentance, but of prudence. He will not have come to think it wrong, but he may think it not worth the pain it will bring on him.

If, however, he regards the authority which punishes him as one which expresses, and which has a right to express, the moral law, his attitude will be very different. He will no longer regard his punishment either as a martyrdom or as an injury. On the contrary, he will feel that it is the proper consequence of his fault. And to feel this, and to be able to accept it as such, is surely repentance.

But it may be objected that this will lead to a dilemma. The punishment cannot have this moral effect on us unless it comes from an authority which we recognize as expressing the moral law, and therefore valid for us. But if we recognize this, how did we ever come to commit the sin, which consists in a defiance of the moral law? Does not the existence of the sin itself prove that we are not in that submissive position to the moral law, and to the power which is enforcing it, which alone can make the punishment a purification?

I do not think this is the case. It is, in the first place, quite possible for a recognition of the moral law to exist which is not sufficiently strong to prevent our violating it at the suggestion of our passions or our impulses, but which is yet strong enough, when the punishment follows, to make us recognize the justice of the sentence. After all, most cases of wrongdoing, which can be treated as criminal, are cases of this description, in which a man defies a moral law which he knows to be binding, because the temptations to violate it are at that moment too strong for his desire to do what he knows to be right. In these cases the moral law is, indeed, recognized—for the offender knows he is doing wrong—but not recognized with sufficient strength; for, if it was, he would abstain from doing wrong. And, therefore, the moral consciousness is strong enough to accept the punishment as justly incurred, though it was not strong enough to prevent the offender from incurring it. In this case, the significance of the punishment is that it tends to produce that vividness in the recognition of the moral law, which the occurrence of the offence shows to have been previously wanting. The pain and coercion involved in punishment present the law with much greater impressiveness than can, for the mass of people, be gained from a mere admission that the law is binding. On the other hand, the fact that the pain coincides with that intellectual recognition, on the part of the offender, that the law is binding, prevents the punishment having a merely intimidating effect, and makes it a possible stage in a moral advance.

Besides these cases of conscious violation of a moral law, there are others where men sincerely believe in a certain principle, and yet systematically fail to see that it applies in certain cases, not because they really think these cases are exceptions, but because indolence or prejudice has prevented them from ever applying their general principle to those particular instances. Thus, there have been nations who conscientiously believed murder to be sinful, and yet fought duels with a good conscience. If pressed, they would have admitted duels to be attempts to murder. But no one ever did press them, and they never pressed themselves. As soon as a set of reformers arose, who did press the question, duels were found to be indefensible and disappeared. So for many years the United States solemnly affirmed the right of all men to liberty, while slavery was legally recognized. Yet they would not have denied that slaves were men.

When such cases occur with a single individual, punishment might here, also, lead to repentance. For it was only possible to accept the general law, and reject the particular application, by ignoring the unanswerable question, Why do not you in this case practise what you preach? Now, you can ignore a question, but you cannot ignore a punishment, if it is severe enough. You cannot put it on one side; you must either assert that it is unjust, or admit that it is just. And in the class of cases we have now been considering, we have seen that when the question is once asked, it must condemn the previous line of action. Here, therefore, punishment may lead to repentance.

A third case is that in which the authority is recognized, but in which it is not known beforehand that it disapproved of the act for which the punishment is awarded. Here, therefore, there is no difficulty in seeing that recognition of the authority is compatible with transgression of the law, because the law is not known till after it has been transgressed. It may, perhaps, be doubted whether it is strictly correct to say in this case that punishment may lead to repentance, since there is no willful fault to repent, as the law was, by the hypothesis, not known at the time it was broken. The question is, however, merely verbal. There is no doubt that in such cases the punishment coming from an authority accepted as moral, may lead a man to see that he has done wrong, though not intentionally, may lead him to regret it and to avoid it in future. Thus, at any rate, a moral advance comes from the punishment, and it is of no great importance whether we grant or deny it the name of repentance.

It may be objected, however, that punishment in the two last cases we have mentioned would be totally unjust. We ought to punish, it may be said, only those acts which were known by their perpetrators at the time when they did them to be wrong. And therefore we have no right to punish a man for any offence, which he did not know to be an offence, whether because he did not know of the existence of the law, or because he did not apply it to the particular case.

I do not think, however, that on examination we can limit the proper application of punishment to cases of conscious wrongdoing, plausible as such a restriction may appear at first sight. We must remember, in the first place, that not to know a moral law may be a sign of greater moral degradation than would be implied in its conscious violation. If a man really believed that he was morally justified in treating the lower animals without any consideration, he would not be consciously doing wrong by torturing them. But we should, I think, regard him as in a lower moral state than a man who was conscious of his duty to animals, though he occasionally disregarded it in moments of passion. Yet the latter in these moments would be consciously doing wrong. A man who could see nothing wrong in cowardice would be surely more degraded than a man who recognized the duty of courage, though he sometimes failed to carry it out. Thus, I submit, even if punishment were limited to cases of desert, there would be no reason to limit it to cases of conscious wrongdoing, since the absence of the consciousness of wrongdoing may itself be a mark of moral defect.

But we may, I think, go further. There seems no reason why we should inquire about any punishment, whether the criminal deserved it or not. For such a question really brings us, if we press it far enough, back to the old theory of vindictive punishment, which few of us, I suppose, would be prepared to advocate. On any other theory a man is to be punished, not to avenge the past evil, but to secure some future good. Of course, a punishment is only to be inflicted for a fault, for the effect of all punishment is to discourage the repetition of the action punished, and that would not be desirable unless the action was wrong. But to inquire into how far the criminal is to be blamed for his action seems irrelevant. If he has done wrong, and if the punishment will cure him, he has, as Hegel expresses it, a right to his punishment. If a dentist is asked to take out an aching tooth, he does not refuse to do so, on the ground that the patient did not deliberately cause the toothache, and that therefore it would be unjust to subject him to the pain of the extraction. And to refuse a man the chance of a moral advance—when the punishment appears to afford one—seems equally unreasonable.

Indeed, any attempt to measure punishment by desert gets us into hopeless difficulties. If we suppose that every man is equally responsible for every action which is not done under physical compulsion, we ignore the effect of inherited character, of difference of education, of difference of temptation, and, in fact, most of the important circumstances. Punishments measured out on such a system may, perhaps, be defended on the ground of utility, but certainly not on the ground of desert. On the other hand, if we endeavored to allow for different circumstances in fixing punishments, we should have no punishments at all. That a man commits an offence in given circumstances is due to his character, and, even if we allowed a certain amount of indeterminate free-will, we could never know that a change in the circumstances would not have saved him from the crime, so that we could never say that it was his own fault.

The only alternative seems to be to admit that we punish, not to avenge evil, but to restore or produce good, whether for society or the criminal. And on this principle we very often explicitly act. For example, we do not punish high treason because we condemn the traitors, who are often moved by sincere, though perhaps mistaken, patriotism. We punish it because we believe that they would, in fact, though with the best intentions, do harm to the state. Nor do parents, I suppose, punish young children for disobedience, on the ground that it is their own fault that they were not born with the habit of obedience developed. They do it, I should imagine, because punishment is the most effective way of teaching them obedience, and because it is desirable, for their own sakes, that they should learn it.

We must now return to the cases in which punishment can possibly produce repentance, from which we have been diverted by the question as to whether the punishment inflicted in the second and third cases could be considered just. There is a fourth and last case. In this the authority which inflicts the punishment was, before its infliction, recognized, indeed theoretically and vaguely, as embodying the moral law, and therefore as being a valid authority. But the recognition was so languid and vague that it was not sufficient to prevent disobedience to the authority's commands. This, it will be seen, is rather analogous to the second case. There the law was held so vaguely that the logical applications of it were never made. Here the authority is recognized, but not actively enough to influence conduct. It is scarcely so much that the criminal recognizes it, as that he is not prepared to deny it.

Here the effect of punishment may again be repentance. For punishment renders it impossible any longer to ignore the authority, and it is, by the hypothesis, only by ignoring it that it can be disobeyed. The punishment clearly proves that the authority is in possession of the power. If it is pressed far enough, there are only two alternatives—to definitely rebel, and declare the punishment to be unjust, or to definitely submit and to acknowledge it to be righteous. The first is here impossible, for the criminal, by the hypothesis, is not prepared definitely to reject the authority. There remains therefore only the second.

Perhaps the best example of this state of things may be found in the attitude of the lower boys of a public school towards the authority of the masters. Their conviction that this is a lawful and valid authority does not influence them to so great an extent as to produce spontaneous and invariable obedience. But it is, I think, sufficient to prevent them from considering the enforcement of obedience by punishment unjust, except in the cases where their own code of morality comes explicitly in conflict with the official code—cases which are not very frequent. In fact, almost all English school systems would break down completely if they trusted to their punishments being severe enough to produce obedience by fear. That they do not break down would seem important evidence that punishment can produce other effects than intimidation, unless, indeed, any ingenious person should suggest that they could get on without punishment altogether.

We have now seen that when punishment is able to fulfil the office which Hegel declares to be its highest function—that of producing repentance—it does so by emphasizing some moral tie which the offender was all along prepared to admit, although it was too faint or incomplete to prevent the fault. Thus it essentially works on him as, at any rate potentially, a moral agent, and thus, as Hegel expresses it, does him honor. It is no contradiction of this, though it may appear so at first sight, to say that a punishment has such an effect only by the element of disgrace which all deserved punishment contains. Here it differs from deterrent punishment. A punishment deters from the repetition of the offence, not because it is a punishment, but because it is painful. An unpleasant consequence which followed the act, not as the result of moral condemnation, but as a merely natural effect, would have the same deterrent result. A man is equally frightened by pain, whether he recognizes it as just or not. And so a punishment may deter from crime quite as effectually when it is not recognized as just, and consequently produces no feeling of disgrace. But a punishment cannot lead to repentance unless it is recognized as the fitting consequence of a moral fault, and it is this recognition which makes a punishment appear disgraceful.

It seems to be a fashionable theory at present that it is both cruel and degrading to attempt to emphasize the element of disgrace in punishment, especially in the education of children. We are recommended to trust principally to rewards, and, if we should be unhappily forced to inflict pain, we must represent it rather as an inconvenience which it would be well to avoid for the future, than as a punishment for an offence which deserved it. And for this reason all punishments, which proclaim themselves to be such, are to be avoided.

I must confess that it is the modern theory which seems to me the degrading one. To attempt to influence by the pleasures of rewards and, by the pain element in punishment, implies that the person to be influenced is governed by pleasure and pain. On the other hand, to trust to the fact that his punishment will appear to him a disgrace implies that he is to some degree influenced by a desire to do right; for, if not, he would feel no disgrace in a punishment for doing wrong. And on the whole it would seem that the latter view of a child's nature is the more hopeful and the less degrading of the two.

There seems to be in this argument a confusion between degradation and disgrace. A man is degraded by anything which lowers his moral nature. A punishment which did this would of course stand condemned. But he is disgraced by being made conscious of a moral defect. And to become conscious of a defect is not to incur a new one. It is rather the most hopeful chance of escaping from the old one. It can scarcely be seriously maintained that, if a fault has been committed, the offender is further degraded by being ashamed of it.

This confusion seems to be at the root of the discussion as to whether the corporal punishment of children is degrading. There is no doubt that it expresses, more unmistakably and emphatically than any substitute that has been proposed for it, the fact that it is a punishment. It follows that, unless the offender is entirely regardless of the opinions of the authority above him, that it is more calculated than other punishments to cause a feeling of disgrace. But, supposing it to be inflicted on the right occasions, this is surely the end of punishment. That it produces any degradation is entirely a separate assertion, which demands a separate proof—a demand which it would be difficult to gratify.

But although a punishment must, to fulfil its highest end, be disgraceful, it does not follow that we can safely trust to the disgrace involved in the offence itself as a punishment—a course which is sometimes recommended. The aim of punishment is rather to produce repentance, and, as a means to it, disgrace. If we contented ourselves with using as a punishment whatever feeling of disgrace arose independently in the culprit's mind, the result would be that we should only affect those who were already conscious of their fault, and so required punishment least, while those who were impenitent, and so required it most, would escape altogether. We require, therefore, a punishment which will produce disgrace where it is not, not merely utilize it where it is. Otherwise we should not only distribute our punishments precisely in the wrong fashion, but we should also offer a premium on callousness and impenitence. As a matter of prudence, it is as well to make sure that the offender, even if he refuses to allow his punishment to be profitable to him, shall, at any rate, find it painful.

And in this connection we must also remember that the feeling of disgrace which ensues on punishment need be nothing more introspective or morbid than a simple recognition that the punishment was deserved. On the other hand, an attempt to influence any one—especially children—by causing them to reflect on the disgrace involved in the fault itself, must lead to a habitual self-contemplation, the results of which are not unlikely to be both unwholesome to the penitent and offensive to his friends.

I have thus endeavored to show that there are certain conditions under which punishment can perform the work which Hegel assigns to it. The question then arises: When are these conditions realized? We find the question of punishment prominent in jurisprudence and in education. It is found also in theology, in so far as the course of the world is so ordered as to punish sin. Now it seems to me that Hegel's view of punishment cannot properly be applied in jurisprudence, and that his chief mistake regarding it lay in supposing that it could.

In the first place, the paramount object of punishment from the point of view of the state ought, I conceive, to be the prevention of crime and not the reformation of the criminal. The interests of the innocent are to be preferred to those of the guilty—for there are more of them, and they have on the whole a better claim to be considered. And the deterrent effect of punishment is far more certain than its purifying effect. (I use the word purifying to describe the effect of which Hegel treats. It is, I fear, rather stilted, but the word reformatory, which would be more suitable, has by common consent been appropriated to a different theory.) We cannot, indeed, eradicate crime, but experience has shown that by severe and judicious punishment we can diminish it to an enormous extent. On the other hand, punishment can only purify by appealing to the moral nature of the criminal. This may be always latent, but is sometimes far too latent for us to succeed in arousing it. Moreover, the deterrent effect of a punishment acts not only on the criminal who suffers it, but on all who realize that they will suffer it if they commit a similar offence. The purifying influence can act only on those who suffer the punishment. For these reasons it would appear that if the state allows its attention to be distracted from the humble task of frightening criminals from crime, by the higher ambition of converting them to virtue, it is likely to fail in both, and so in its fundamental object of diminishing crime.

And in addition there seems grave reason to doubt whether, in a modern state, the crimes dealt with and the attitude of the criminal to the state are such that punishment can be expected to lead to repentance. The crimes which a state has to deal with may be divided into two classes. The first and smaller class is that in which the state, for its own welfare, endeavors to suppress by punishment conduct which is actuated by conscientious convictions of duty. Examples may be found in high treason and breaches of the law relating to vaccination. Now in these cases the criminal has deliberately adopted a different view of his duty to that entertained by the state. He is not likely, therefore, to be induced to repent of his act by a punishment which can teach him nothing except that he and the state disagree in their views of his duty—which he knew before. His punishment may appear to him to be unjust persecution, or may be accepted as the inevitable result of difference of opinion, but can never be admitted by him as justly deserved by his action, and cannot therefore change the way in which he regards that action.

In the second, and much larger, class of criminal offences, the same result happens, though from very different reasons. The average criminal, convicted of theft or violence, is, no doubt, like all of us, in his essential nature, a distinctly moral being. And, even in action, the vast majority of such criminals are far from being totally depraved.

But, by the time a man has become subject to the criminal law for any offence, he has generally become so far callous, with regard to that particular crime, that his punishment will not bring about his repentance. The average burglar may clearly learn from his sentence that the state objects to burglary. He might even, if pressed, admit that the state was from an objective point of view more likely to be right than he was. But, although he may have a sincere abhorrence of murder, he is probably in a condition when the disapproval of the state of his offences with regard to property will rouse no moral remorse in him. In such a case repentance is not possible. Punishment can, under the circumstances I have mentioned above, convince us that we have done wrong. But it cannot inspire us with the desire to do right. The existence of this is assumed when we punish with a view to the purification of an offender, and it is for this reason that the punishment, as Hegel says, honors him. Where the desire to do right is, at any rate as regards one field of action, hopelessly dormant, punishment must fall back on its lower office of intimidation. And this would happen with a large proportion of those offences which are dealt with by the criminal law.

Many offences, no doubt—especially those committed in a moment of passion, or by persons till then innocent—are not of this sort, but do coexist with a general desire to do right, which has been overpowered by a particular temptation. Yet I doubt if, at the present day, repentance in such cases would be often the result of punishment by the state. If the criminal's independent moral will was sufficiently strong, he would, when the particular temptation was removed, repent without the aid of punishment. If it was not sufficiently strong, I doubt if the punishment would much aid it. The function of punishment, as we have seen, in this respect, was to enforce on the offender the disapproval with which his action was considered by an authority, whom he regarded as expressing the moral law. But why should the modern citizen regard the state as expressing the moral law? He does not regard it as something above and superior to himself, as the ancient citizen regarded his city, as the child regards his parents, or the religious man his God. The development of individual conscience and responsibility has been too great for such an attitude. The state is now for him an aggregate of men like himself. He regards obedience to it, within certain limits, as a duty. But this is because matters which concern the whole community are matters on which the whole community is entitled to speak. It does not rest on any belief that the state can become for the individual the interpreter of the moral law, so that his moral duty lies in conforming his views to its precepts. Not only does he not feel bound, but he does not feel entitled, to surrender in this way his moral independence. He must determine for himself what he is himself to hold as right and wrong. The result of this is that if he sees for himself that his action was wrong, he will repent without waiting for the state to tell him so, and, if he does not see it for himself, the opinion of the state will not convince him. I do not assert that there are no cases in which a man finds himself in the same childlike relation to the state as was possible in classical times, but they are too few to be of material importance. And except in such cases we cannot expect the punishment of jurisprudence to have a purifying effect.

Hegel's mistake, in applying his conception of punishment to criminal law, resulted from his high opinion of the state as against the individual citizen. The most significant feature of all his writings on the metaphysics of society is the low place that he gives to the conscience and opinions of the individual. He was irritated—not without cause, though with far less cause than we have today—at the follies of the writers who see nothing in morality but conscientious convictions, or "the good will." It would almost seem, according to some exponents of these views, that it is entirely unimportant, from a moral point of view, what you do, if only you can manage to persuade yourself that you are doing right. But he did not lay enough emphasis on the fact that, though the approval of conscience does not carry you very far, by itself, towards a satisfactory system of morality, yet that without the approval of the individual conscience no modern system of morality can be satisfactory. As between adult human beings, it has become in modern times impossible for one man to yield up his conscience into the hands of any other man or body of men. A child, while it is young enough to be treated entirely as a child, can and ought to find its morality in the commands of others. And those who believe in a divine revelation, will naturally endeavor to place themselves in an attitude of entire submission to what appears to them to be the divine will, whether manifested through books or through some specially flavored organization of men. But a man is not a child, and the state is not God, and the surrender of our consciences to the control of others has become impossible. A man may indeed accept the direction of a teacher whom he has chosen—even accept it implicitly. But then this is by virtue of his own act of choice. We cannot now accept any purely outward authority as having, of its own right, the power of deciding for us on matters of right and wrong.

Jeremy Bentham

Utility and Punishment*

Chapter XIII

GENERAL VIEW OF CASES UNMEET FOR PUNISHMENT

I. *The end of law is, to augment happiness.* The general object which all laws have, or ought to have, in common, is to augment the total happiness of the community; and therefore, in the first place, to exclude, as far as may be, every thing that tends to subtract from that happiness: in other words, to exclude mischief.

II. *But punishment is an evil.* But all punishment is mischief: all punishment in itself is evil. Upon the principle of utility, if it ought at all to be admitted, it ought only to be admitted in as far as it promises to exclude some greater evil.

III. *Therefore ought not to be admitted;* It is plain, therefore, that in the following cases punishment ought not to be inflicted.

1. *Where groundless.* Where it is *groundless:* where there is no mischief for it to prevent; the act not being mischievous upon the whole.

2. *Inefficacious.* Where it must be *inefficacious:* where it cannot act so as to prevent the mischief.

3. *Unprofitable.* Where it is *unprofitable,* or too *expensive:* where the mischief it would produce would be greater than what it prevented.

4. *Or needless.* Where it is *needless:* where the mischief may be prevented, or cease of itself, without it: that is, at a cheaper rate.

---

*Jeremy Bentham, *An Introduction to the Principles of Morals and Legislation* (New York: Hafner, 1948), ch. 13, sec. 1; ch. 14, sec. 1–26.

Chapter XIV

I. *Recapitulation.* We have seen that the general object of all laws is to prevent mischief; that is to say, when it is worth while; but that, where there are no other means of doing this than punishment, there are four cases in which it is *not* worth while.

II. *Four objects of punishment.* When it *is* worth while, there are four subordinate designs or objects, which, in the course of his endeavours to compass, as far as may be, that one general object, a legislator, whose views are governed by the principle of utility, comes naturally to propose to himself.

III. 1. *1ˢᵗ Object—to prevent all offences.* His first, most extensive, and most eligible object, is to prevent, in as far as it is possible, and worth while, all sorts of offenses whatsoever: in other words, so to manage, that no offense whatsoever may be committed.

IV. 2. *2d Object—to prevent the worst.* But if a man must needs commit an offense of some kind or other, the next object is to induce him to commit an offense *less* mischievous, *rather* than one *more* mischievous: in other words, to choose always the *least* mischievous, of two offenses that will either of them suit his purpose.

V. 3. *3d Object—to keep down the mischief.* When a man has resolved upon a particular offense, the next object is to dispose him to do *no more* mischief than is *necessary* to his purpose: in other words, to do as little mischief as is consistent with the benefit he has in view.

VI. 4. *4ᵗʰ Object—to act at the least expense.* The last object is, whatever the mischief be, which it is proposed to prevent, to prevent it at as *cheap* a rate as possible.

VII. *Rules of proportion between punishments and offences.* Subservient to these four objects, or purposes, must be the rules or canons by which the proportion of punishments to offenses is to be governed.

VIII. Rule 1. *Outweigh the profit of the offence.* The first object, it has been seen, is to prevent, in as far as it is worth while, all sorts of offenses; therefore,

The value of the punishment must not less in any case than what is sufficient to outweigh that of the profit of the offense.

If it be, the offence (unless some other considerations, independent of the punishment should intervene and operate efficaciously in the character of tutelary motives) will be sure to be to committed notwithstanding: the whole lot of punishment will be thrown away: it will be altogether *inefficacious*.

IX. *The propriety of taking the strength of the temptation for a ground of abatement, no objection to this rule.* The above rule has been often objected to, on account of its seeming harshness: but this can only have happened for want of its being properly understood. The strength of the temptation, *cæteris paribus*, is as the profit of the offense: the quantum of the punishment must rise with the profit of the offense: *cæteris paribus*, it must therefore rise with the strength of the temptation. This there is no disputing. True it is, that the stronger the temptation, the less conclusive is the indication which the act of delinquency affords of the depravity of the offender's disposition. So far then as the absence of any aggravation, arising from extraordinary depravity of disposition, may operate, or at the utmost, so far as the presence of a ground of extenuation, resulting from the innocence or beneficence of the offender's disposition, can operate, the strength of the temptation may operate in abatement of the demand for punishment. But it can never operate so far as to indicate the propriety of making the punishment ineffectual, which it is sure to be when brought below the level of the apparent profit of the offense.

The partial benevolence which should prevail for the reduction of it below this level, would counteract as well those purposes which such a motive would actually have in view, as those more extensive purposes which benevolence ought to have in view: it would be cruelty not only to the public, but to the very persons in whose behalf it pleads: in its effects, I mean, however opposite in its intention. Cruelty to the public, that is cruelty to the innocent, by suffering them, for want of an adequate protection, to lie exposed to the mischief of the offense: cruelty even to the offender himself, by punishing him to no purpose, and without the chance of compassing that beneficial end, by which alone the introduction of the evil of punishment is to be justified.

X. Rule 2. *Venture more against a great offence than a small one.* But whether a given offence shall be prevented in a given degree by a given quantity of punishment, is never any thing better than a chance; for the purchasing of which, whatever punishment is employed, is so much expended into advance. However, for the sake of giving it the better chance of outweighing the profit of the offence,

The greater the mischief of the offense, the greater is the expense which it may be worth while to be at, in the way of punishment.

XI. Rule 3. *Cause the least of two offences to be preferred.* The next object is, to induce a man to choose always the least mischievous of two offenses; therefore,

Where two offences come in competition, the punishment for the greater offence must be sufficient to induce a man to prefer the less.

XII. Rule 4. *Punish for each particle of the mischief.* When a man has resolved upon a particular offense, the next object is, to induce him to do no more mischief than what is necessary for his purpose: therefore

The punishment should be adjusted in such manner to each particular offence, that for every part of the mischief there may be a motive to restrain the offender from giving birth to it.

XIII. Rule 5. *Punish in no degree without special reason.* The last object is, whatever mischief is guarded against, to guard against it at as cheap a rate as possible: therefore

The punishment ought in no case to be more than what is necessary to bring it into conformity with the rules here given.

XIV. Rule 6. *Attend to circumstances influencing sensibility.* It is further to be observed, that owing to the different manners and degrees in which persons under different circumstances are affected by the same exciting cause, a punishment which is the same in name will not always either really produce, or even so much as appear to others to produce, in two different persons the same degree of pain: therefore

That the quantity actually indicted on each individual offender may correspond to the quantity intended for similar offenders in general, the several circumstances influencing sensibility ought always to be taken into account.

XV. *Comparative view of the above rules.* Of the above rules of proportion, the first four, we may perceive, serve to mark out limits on the side of diminution; the limits *below* which a punishment ought not to be *diminished*: the fifth the limits on the side of increase; the limits *above* which it ought not to be *increased*. The five first are calculated to serve as guides to the legislator: the sixth is calculated in some measure, indeed, to the same purpose; but principally for guiding the judge in his endeavors to conform, on both sides, to the intentions of the legislator.

XVI. *Into the account of the value of a punishment must be taken its deficiency in point of certainty and proximity.* Let us look back a little. The first rule, in order to render it more conveniently applicable to practice, may need perhaps to be a little more particularly unfolded. It is to be observed, then, that for the sake of accuracy, it was necessary, instead of the word *quantity* to make use of the less perspicuous term *value.* For the word *quantity* will not properly include the circumstances either of certainty or proximity: circumstances which, in estimating the value of a lot of pain or pleasure, must always be taken into the account. Now, on the one hand, a lot of punishment is a lot of pain; on the other hand, the profit of an offense is a lot of pleasure, or what is equivalent to it. But the profit of the offense *is* commonly more *certain* than the punishment, or, what comes to the same thing, *appears* so at least to the offender. It is at any rate commonly more *immediate.* It follows, therefore, that, in order to maintain its superiority over the profit of the offense, the punishment must have its value made up in some other way, in proportion to that whereby it falls short in the two points of *certainty* and *proximity.* Now there is no other way in which it can receive any addition to its *value,* but by receiving an addition in point of *magnitude.* Wherever then the value of the punishment falls short, either in point of *certainty,* or of *proximity,* of that of the profit of the offence, it must receive a proportionable addition in point of *magnitude.*

XVII. Also, *into the account of the mischief, and profit of the offence, the mischief and profit of other offences of the same habit.* Yet farther. To make sure of giving the value of the punishment the superiority over that of the offence, it may be necessary, in some cases, to take into account the profit not only of the *individual* offence to which the punishment is to be annexed, but also of such *other* offences of the *same sort* as the offender is likely to have already committed without detection. This random mode of calculation, severe as it is, it will be impossible to avoid having recourse to, in certain cases: in such, to wit, in which the profit is pecuniary, the chance of detection very small, and the obnoxious act of such a nature as indicates a habit: for example, in the case of frauds against the coin. If it be *not* recurred to, the practice of committing the offence will be sure to be, upon the balance of the account, a gainful practice. That being the case, the legislator will be absolutely sure of *not* being able to suppress it, and the whole punishment that is bestowed upon it will be thrown away. In a word (to keep to the same expressions we set out with) that whole quantity of punishment will be *inefficacious*.

XVIII. Rule 7. *Want of certainty must be made up in magnitude.* These things being considered, the three following rules may be laid down by way of supplement and explanation to Rule 1.

To enable the value of the punishment to outweigh that of the profit of the offense, it must be increased, in point of magnitude, in proportion as it falls short in point of certainty.

XIX. Rule 8. *(So also want of proximity.) Punishment must be further increased in point of magnitude, in proportion as it falls short in point of proximity.*

XX. Rule 9. *(For acts indicative of a habit punish as for the habit.) Where the act is conclusively indicative of a habit, such an increase must be given to the punishment as may enable it to outweigh the profit not only of the individual offence, but of such other like offenses as are likely to have been committed with impunity by the same offender.*

XXI. *The remaining rules are of less importance.* There may be a few other circumstances or considerations which may influence, in some small degree, the demand for punishment: but as the propriety of these is either not so demonstrable, or not so constant, or the application of them not so determinate, as that of the foregoing, it may be doubted whether they be worth putting on a level with the others.

XXII. Rule 10. *(For the sake of quality, increase quantity.) When a punishment, which in point of quality is particularly well calculated to answer its intention, cannot exist in less than a certain quantity, it may sometimes be of use, for the sake of employing it, to stretch a little beyond that quantity which, on other accounts, would be strictly necessary.*

XXIII. Rule 11. *(Particularly for a moral lesson.) In particular, this may sometimes be the case, where the punishment proposed is of such a nature as to be particularly well calculated to answer the purpose of a moral lesson.*

XXIV. Rule 12. *Attend to circumstances which may render punishment unprofitable.* The tendency of the above considerations is to dictate an augmentation in the punishment: the following rule operates in the way of diminution. There are certain cases (it has been seen) in which, by the influence of accidental circumstances, punishment may be rendered unprofitable in the whole: in the same cases it may chance to be rendered unprofitable as to a part only. Accordingly,

In adjusting the quantum of punishment, the circumstances, by which all punishment may be rendered unprofitable, ought to be attended to.

XXV. Rule 13. *For simplicity's sake, small disproportions may be neglected.* It is to be observed, that the more various and minute any set of provisions are, the greater the chance is that any given article in them will not be borne in mind: without which, no benefit can ensue from it. Distinctions, which are more complex than what the conceptions of those whose conduct it is designed to influence can take in, will even be worse than useless. The whole system will present a confused appearance: and thus the effect, not only of the proportions established by the articles in question, but of whatever is connected with them, will be destroyed. To draw a precise line of direction in such case seems impossible. However, by way of memento, it may be of some use to subjoin the following rule.

Among provisions designed to perfect the proportion between punishments and offences, if any occur, which, by their own particular good effects, would not make up for the harm they would do by adding to the intricacy of the Code, they should be omitted.

XXVI. *Auxiliary force of the physical, moral, and religious sanction, not here allowed for—why.* It may be remembered, that the political sanction, being that to which the sort of punishment belongs, which in this chapter is all along in view, is but one of four sanctions, which may all of them contribute their share towards producing the same effects. It may be expected, therefore, that in adjusting the quantity of political punishment, allowance should be made for the assistance it may meet with from those other controlling powers. True it is, that from each of these several sources a very powerful assistance may sometimes be derived. But the case is, that (setting aside the moral sanction, in the case where the force of it is expressly adopted into and modified by the political) the force of those other powers is never determinate enough to be depended upon. It can never be reduced, like political punishment, into exact lots, nor meted out in number, quantity, and value. The legislator is therefore obliged to provide the full complement of punishment, as if he were sure of not receiving any assistance whatever from any of those quarters. If he does, so much the better: but lest he should not, it is necessary he should, at all events, make that provision which depends upon himself.

H. Rashdall

Punishment and the Individual*

It is sometimes supposed that the utilitarian view of punishment is inconsistent with a proper respect for human personality: it involves, we are told, the treatment of humanity as a means and not as an end. If by the "utilitarian" theory is meant a view resting upon a hedonistic theory of Ethics, I have nothing to say in its favour; if by "utilitarian" is meant simply a view which treats punishment as a means to some good, spiritual or otherwise, of some conscious being, I should entirely deny the justice of the criticism. In the first place I should contend humanity as a means. When a servant is called upon to black the boots of his master, or a soldier to face death or disease in the service of his country, society is certainly treating humanity as a means: the men do these things not for their own sakes, but for the sake of other people. Kant himself never uttered anything so foolish as the maxim which indiscreet admirers are constantly putting into his mouth, that we should never treat humanity as a means: what he did say was that we should never treat humanity *only* as a means, but always *also* as an end. When a man is punished in the interest of society, he is thereby violated, if his good is treated as of equal importance with the end of other human beings. Social life would not be possible without constant subordination of the claims of individuals to the like claims of a greater number of individuals; and there may be occasions when in punishing a criminal we have to think more of the good of society generally than of the individual who is punished. No doubt it is a duty to think also of the individual so far as that can be done consistently with justice to other individuals: it is obviously the duty of State to endeavour to make its punishments as far as possible reformatory as well as deterrent and educational to others. And how

---

*Hastings Rashdall, *Theory of Good and Evil*, 2d ed. (Oxford: Clarendon Press, 1924), 303–04. By permission of Oxford University Press.

the reformatory view of punishment can be accused of disrespect for human personality, because forsooth it uses a man's animal organism or his lower psychical nature as a means to the good of his higher self, I cannot profess to understand. The retributive view of punishment justifies the infliction of evil upon a living soul, even though it will do neither him nor anyone else any good whatsoever. If it is to do anybody any good, punishment is not inflicted for the sake of retribution. It is the retributive theory which shows a disrespect for human personality by proposing to sacrifice human life and human Well-being to a lifeless fetish styled the Moral Law, which apparently, though unconscious, has a sense of dignity and demands the immolation of victims to avenge its injured *amour propre*. . . .

T. L. S. Sprigge

A Utilitarian Reply to Dr. McCloskey*

. . . McCloskey's main argument against a utilitarian theory of punishment lies in examples which he presents of moral judgments which
he supposes would follow from utilitarian theory, and which clash
with our common moral consciousness, even presumably when this
has been altered to meet the demands of critical reflection. Such
examples may be of two types. They may be moral judgments regarding situations of a kind which actually occur or they may regard
situations of a kind which do not occur. Or, to put it another way,
these moral judgments may be deducible from the utility principle
and certain contingent truths (or from fictions akin to such truths)
or they may be deducible from the utility principle in conjunction
with contingent factual premises which include falsehoods. Although
McCloskey recognizes this distinction, he evidently does not think it
of much importance. For he says: "Against the utilitarian who seeks
to argue that utilitarianism docs not involve unjust punishment, there
is a very simple argument, namely, that whether or not unjust punishments are in fact useful, it is logically possible that they will at
some time become useful, in which case utilitarians are committed
to them."

Actually, I have a certain hesitation regarding the sense of this
passage. Is there an especial significance in the future tense? Presumably if it is logically possible that they will become useful, it
is logically possible that they are useful now. After all it is logically
possible that Britain and the United States are now at war, Use of
the future tense suggests that perhaps by its being logically possible

*T. L. S. Sprigge, "A Utilitarian Reply to Dr. McCloskey," *Inquiry* 8
(Universitetsforlaget, Olso, 1965), 272–84. Reprinted by permission of the author
and the publisher. Dr. McCloskey's paper is reprinted in this volume, p. 125.

that they will become useful, McCloskey really means the quite different thing that *for all we know* they may become useful one day. It is an important question which is meant. For it is very easy indeed to establish the logical possibility that something like punishment of the innocent will be (is, or was) useful. One can for instance imagine the most basic facts of human nature altered for this purpose. But it is a more empirical task to establish that *for all we know* they will become useful one day. Since the "we" presumably does not refer just to one perhaps ignorant person, one must show that there are not (say) well confirmed principles of psychology which give us firm reasons for saying that things will not develop that way.

Situations instanced in which utilitarian judgments are alleged to be offensive to our common moral consciousness (understand henceforth: even when purified by critical attention) may be of three kinds. First, they may be actual or relevantly akin to actual situations. Second, they may be situations not establishable as actual or akin to such, but not establishable either as such as will never have occurred. Thirdly, they may be logically possible situations, but ones which there is good reason to suppose will never have occurred. Of course, this rough classification is capable of refinement.

McCloskey presumably would think a situation on which a utilitarian judgment shocks our moral consciousness counts equally against utilitarianism to whichever type it belongs. For this he could argue as follows. The principle of utility is a theory about what would be right and wrong under any conceivable (i.e., logically possible) circumstances. Our common moral consciousness also provides us with principles about what would be right or wrong under any conceivable circumstances. If therefore they clash in their judgment on a conceivable situation, however out of the question such a situation is, they do indeed clash, and one must be discarded.

I accept this description of the principle of utility, but not of our common moral consciousness. I do not think the latter is thus thought of by most people we might consider typical vehicles of it. Plain men will probably admit that if the empirical nature of the world had been very different then different moral sentiments would often have been appropriate. For instance, Christians who urge more or less strongly the principle of turning the other cheek, are wont to support it with references to the contrary effects of love and hate. However basic such facts about love and hate are, they are in the last resort contingent. Similarly with the kind of support most people would give for our sentiments in favour of just rather than unjust punishment. Utilitarianism then is not eccentric in basing the rightness of some very fundamental moral sentiments on ultimately contingent facts.

Now if one considers some fantastic situations of the third type one does of course consider them as a person with certain moral sentiments, the strength of which in society as it is, is an important utilitarian good. These sentiments are offended. A utilitarian will see no point in trying to imagine oneself looking with approval on the imaginary situation, since this is likely to weaken the feelings while not serving as a preparation for any actual situation. If in fact punishing the innocent (say) always is and always will be harmful, it is likewise harmful to dwell on fanciful situations in which it would be beneficial, thus weakening one's aversion to such courses. Thus the utilitarian shares (quite consistently so) in the unease produced by these examples. Although he may admit that in such a situation punishment of the innocent would be right, he still regards favourably the distaste which is aroused at the idea of its being called right.

Certainly, if one imagines the world as other than it is, one may find oneself imagining a world in which utilitarianism implies moral judgments which shock our moral sentiments. But if these moral sentiments are quite appropriate to the only world there is, the real world, the utilitarian is glad that moral judgements in opposition to them seen repugnant. He sees no need for moral acrobatics relevant only to situations which in fact are quite out of the question.

We must be very careful therefore in using the fact that strong and, we feel, right-minded antipathies are aroused at the thought of certain utilitarian type judgments on type three examples, as an argument against utilitarianism. For the utilitarian himself will commend this distaste as something to be kept alive in himself and others, and is perhaps claiming for the offended moral sentiments as much as, on reflection, most people would be prepared to do.

There is another reason for caution in discussing type three situations. Suppose one describes a case where punishment of an innocent man would yield a balance of good, and insures that this is so simply by stipulating certain striking benefits which will derive from it, and explicitly eliminating all the harms one can think of. If one finds oneself still half-inclined to call such punishment wrong, it may well be because one does not really succeed in envisaging the situation just as described, but surrounds it with those circumstances of real life which would in fact create a greater probability of unhappiness in its consequences than happiness.

We may conclude that it would be more convincing if examples of conflict between the common moral consciousness and utilitarianism were looked for in type one situations rather than in type three, while situations of type two (clearly) have a degree of relevance here lying between the other two.

McCloskey's Examples

Let us now consider McCloskey's individual examples. I shall not dwell much on his first example, as he himself lays more weight on his second, which is a modified version of it. But I should like to comment on one oddity in his discussion of the first.

The sheriff is supposed to have framed an innocent Negro to prevent a series of lynchings which he knows will occur if no one is "punished" for the offence. It is urged that this is obviously the right course from a utilitarian point of view.

One line of objection to this conclusion appeals to the likelihood that the facts will become known. I may urge parenthetically that in the real world such a likelihood is likely (surely) to be pretty strong. The utilitarian may then insist on a variety of evils which would result from its becoming known, such as a loss of confidence in the impartiality and fairness of the legal system, of a belief that lawful behaviour pays, etc. Now McCloskey says that "even if everyone came to know, surely, if utilitarianism is thought to be the true moral theory, the general body of citizens ought to be happier believing that their sheriff is promoting what is right rather than promoting non-utilitarian standards of justice." This strikes me as absurd. Let us consider first the white citizenry. It is quite obvious that they are not utilitarians, or that even if by chance some are in theory, their feelings are not in fact governed by utilitarian theory. For if they were utilitarians they would not be charging around the country lynching people. For who could seriously believe that this was the best way of creating the greatest happiness of the greatest number? If they were utilitarians (in practice) the sheriff would not be in the situation he is in. As it is, he has to think about them as they are. How they *would* react to the fact that the sheriff framed the Negro is a different matter, but for a utilitarian to expect their satisfaction because he has done the right thing from a utilitarian point of view would be absurd. You might as well suggest that a utilitarian penologist should urge that all prisons should be without bars, on the grounds that once it is explained to the offenders how useful it is for society that they should be punished they will see the wrongness of escaping. Let us now consider the Negroes. There is not the same evidence within the very hypothesis that their actions and feelings are opposed to utilitarian precepts. But one may take it that whatever their ethical views, they are filled with bitterness at white behaviour. They are hardly going to be overjoyed at learning that a Negro up for trial is likely to be framed in order to sate the fury of brutish whites. Will not their incentives to law-abidingness be decreased when they learn that someone else's crime may just as well get them punished as one of their own? Is racial harmony really going to be advanced by such an event?

But I shall now turn to the second supposedly more forceful example. Here a utilitarian visitor from outside the area bears incriminating false witness against a Negro so that his being "punished" for a rape will put an end to a series of riots and lynchings. One main point of thus changing the example presumably is to eliminate such harms as might be supposed to ensue from a local figure, especially a legal authority, practising the deception.

Before commenting on this example in further detail I should like to ask the reader (or McCloskey himself) to stand back for a moment and consider the prima facie implausibility of what McCloskey tries to show. Forget for a moment all question of the rightness or wrongness of utilitarian theory, forget morality, and imagine simply that you are a reasonable being with one overriding aim, to create as much happiness as possible at the cost of as little unhappiness as possible. Does it really seem on the cards that in a situation where race riots are going on as a result of a rape, you will find no more effective way of forwarding your aim in this area than to bear false witness against some unfortunate Negro, thus ensuring that at least one human being is thoroughly miserable? Does not a vague unanalysed sense of how the world really works inform one that this is not a type of action which increases human happiness? People who lack this commonsense grasp of how the world runs are dangerous whatever moral backing they may claim for their actions.

Let us now turn to details. Our utilitarian is said to *know* "that a quick arrest will stop the riots and lynchings." How does he know this? How does he know that they aren't going to die down soon anyway? Even if he has good reason to think that they will go on unless such an arrest is made, does he know how intense they will be, how many people are actually going to get lynched? One thing he does know is that if he bears false witness (successfully) an innocent man is going to get punished. We are not told what the punishment will be, but it is likely either to be death or a long term of imprisonment, which will mean the ruin of the man's life. Suppose he does not bear the false witness, that the riots go on as he expected, but that no deaths or permanent injuries take place. Isn't it likely that the suffering in this case is less than that of a man sentenced to execution (together with the sufferings of his family) or languishing for long years in prison?

Utilitarian judgment that the false witness would be right must be based on its foreseeable consequences. Now an event can be foreseen as a probable (or certain) consequence of a given action on two roughly distinguishable grounds. It may be a well confirmed generalization that actions of that broad type in that broad type of situation very often (or always) have such a consequence. But an action may (also) be characterized by features too unusual to figure in such generalizations. If these are to provide a basis for prediction it must be because of some hunch about the situation which will be no more rational than an indefinite number of other hunches. Reliance on such hunches is something which often leads people wildly wrong. (This is well confirmed, I suggest.) This suggests that a product (such as happiness) will be increased in the long run more by those who base their expectations on well confirmed generalizations than on hunches, and that therefore the utilitarian should stick to the former, especially where the amounts of happiness or unhappiness are large. The situation is quite different from that of scientific research. Here the hunches are needed for major advances, and can be put to the test and abandoned if necessary, with no harm done. And indeed in ethical decisions which do not have consequences of too great import, action on such hunches may be useful as a mode of experiment.

Now I suggest that the prediction of misery for the innocent man if he is successfully framed rests on well confirmed generalizations, but that the prediction that this will stop lynchings, etc., which would otherwise have occurred, will be based on a hunch about the character of the riots. In that case the sensible utilitarian will attach a predominating weight to the former prediction, and refrain from framing the man.

McCloskey may, however, insist that the utilitarian has the very firmest grounds for his beliefs about the duration and degree of the rioting if no punishment takes place, and concerning the preventability of all this by the means in question. I'm inclined to suggest then that a man with such a rich knowledge of the nature of these riots should devote himself fully to a documented study of them with a view to putting his knowledge before such organizations as can arrange by propaganda and other means to alleviate their causes. If he has something to hide concerning his own illicit means of checking them, he will not be at ease in drawing up a report on the situation and will therefore not do his work properly, work which will stop more riot-caused suffering in the end than this isolated act.

If these last remarks seen somewhat fanciful I should urge that the situation in which a man knows that the riots will go on unless he tells this lie is also fanciful, and is an example of type two perilously close to type three. In an actual situation this would probably only be a hunch, of little weight besides the well-supported belief that a successful frame-up will produce massive suffering for the innocent man and his family, There is also good reason for believing that facing a man and telling lies which will ruin his life will blunt one's sensibilities in a way which may well lead one to use such methods again with still less justification. I should suspect, moreover, that a utilitarian who persuaded himself that such an act was useful would be finding an outlet for harmful impulses which it would behoove him not to indulge; for instance an urge to exert power in a secret God-like manner, and without scruple. It is dangerously easy for someone who wants to do something for motives of which he is ashamed to persuade himself that the general good would be served by it. This gives another reason for suspicion of "hunches."

None of this has appealed to any such principle as that the suffering of an innocent man is a worse thing in itself than that of a guilty one. What of this principle? The utilitarian cannot consistently say that one is worse in itself if the degree of suffering is the same. But if there is reason to believe that more suffering is involved in a given punishment for an innocent man than for a guilty man this is something of which the utilitarian should take account.

There does seem some reason to believe this. An innocent man is liable to suffer more shock at being thus punished. He will suffer from an indignant fury as the guilty man will not. Whatever the utilitarian thinks of the appropriateness of such indignation (a matter too complicated for comment here) he must take it into account as a fact. But apart from the indignation, the punishment will come on him as much more of a surprise, and thus be something he is less able to cope with psychologically (accept) or even practically. The distress caused to his relatives will also probably be greater, since it is likely to come as more of a shock to them also. His wife may be ill prepared in every way for life alone, and she will also be more likely to be dismayed if she now believes her husband guilty. Moreover punishment of the innocent (especially in a case like that described) is very likely to arouse emotions leading to antisocial action on the part of someone previously law-abiding.

Of course McCloskey can deal with each specific point by imagining a situation in which it would not arise. Let the innocent man be without family and a natural pessimist always prepared for the worst. But what sort of investigation prior to his false witness is our wily utilitarian to make into these matters? It is hard to believe that a man of such tenacity will not find less costly ways of advancing racial harmony.

It seems to me, then, highly unlikely that in a situation at all like the one described by McCloskey a man guided by a cool assessment of probabilities rather than by wild surmises will see such bearing of false witness as the most felicific act. This applies even if we ignore the effects on the utilitarian's own character, still more if we take these into account.

Still, I should not say it was absolutely *out of the question* that situations may arise where a sensible utilitarian would think it right to implicate an innocent man. As I have explained at length, he could still think the resultant punishment *unjust*, although his production of it was right or justified. In such a situation the good to be achieved by the punishment would presumably be predictable as near certain on well confirmed principles, and be great enough to outweigh harms of the sort we have described, and such other evils (especially evils of injustice) as might arise. It would also have to be unobtainable at less cost. I suspect that with such goods to be gained our utilitarian's action would be such as many plain men (not just official utilitarians) would condone or approve.

What plain men would feel, however, is an uneasiness at the situation, and a deep regret about it. Now sometimes one gets a picture of the utilitarian who can feel no regret at any overriding of conventional moral principles provided his sums come out all right. This is a travesty of the utilitarian outlook.

There is indeed a certain problematicness about regret on any ethical theory. Everyone must admit that on occasion the action which on balance one ought to do, has characteristics or consequences which considered in themselves suggest the wrongness of the act. A general fighting for a good cause may well regard the dead and injured on the field of battle with a terrible regret that he should have brought this about, and yet think he acted rightly—although he always knew there would be a sacrifice like this. Moreover his regret may in a sense be a moral regret, different in character from the regret one feels at the sacrifice of one's own interests for the sake of duty. An unimaginative moral philosopher might say that such regret was inapposite, if he had really done the right thing. Most of us do not feel this way and utilitarianism offers at least two justifications for our attitude. First, a man who was not sad at producing suffering would lack the basic sentiment which inspires the utility principle, namely a revulsion at the suffering and a delight in the happiness of any sentient being. Second, sentiments such as the love of justice, respect for human life and so on, are sentiments which utilitarian considerations bid us cherish in ourselves and others. When the promptings of these sentiments have to be set aside in the interests of a greater good, the man who feels no regret can have them little developed, and the man who checks all regret will blunt them. Regret in such situations is therefore a desirable state of mind according to utilitarianism.

Feeling regret must not be confused with a judgement that it would be a good thing to feel regret. There is no such confusion here. Whether I feel regret is a psychological fact not normally in my control. All I have argued is that the utilitarian who feels regret need not think that his theory demands an attempt to set it aside as a weakness. Rather he should be troubled by his character if he does not feel it.

So even if on some rare occasion a greater good demands some such injustice as the punishment of an innocent man, the utilitarian will certainly accept this as an appropriate matter for regret.

Further Examples

Among further examples which McCloskey gives of unjust but useful laws are scapegoat punishment and collective punishment. He does not make it very clear, however, what his own moral attitude to such punishments is, or what he takes to be that of the common moral consciousness. Certainly he thinks they are unjust even when useful—and that is something with which the utilitarian can agree—but does he think that they are sometimes justified nonetheless? He seems at least to leave it open that they may be, and in one case, collective punishment in schools, he goes further. Now to say that they are unjust but all the same morally right or justified is a position which the utilitarian who really believed they produced more good than evil would probably adopt.

Consider the type of scapegoat punishment he mentions. It is within the bounds of possibility that a commander whose chances of victory demanded some sort of cooperation from the local people, and who had good reason to believe that without this victory the common good of humanity would suffer, finding this method of securing the population's cooperation the only workable one, would rightly consider that it was justified. I say that it is within the bounds of possibility, but it is also perhaps more probable that such a method is not even the most efficient for his end, or at least not more efficient than other means less damaging to the goods of justice. But if the circumstances really were as described, most people who condone war at all would probably think the act was right.

In saying that such an undesirable means to a desirable end might possibly on rare occasions be justified, one is not giving one's general approval to such methods of gaining one's ends. There is, however, always the danger that when once one has allowed the justifiability of such means on one occasion, one will be ready to use them again on other occasions where although immediately convenient the same justifying conditions do not hold. The fact that an act may be a bad example to oneself and others (even if supposing this fact left out of account it would be justified) may often finally tip the balance against the rightness of doing it. As an example, I should like to take the bombing of centers of civilian population in wartime. For many such raids the British may well have had acceptable justification. This was certainly the belief of quite decent people in Britain. The victory of the allies really was an overwhelming good for humanity and this may have been an unavoidable means to it. But once moral scruples against such bombings were set aside in the interests of a greater good the capacity for moral reflection on the matter seems to have become blunted, and we have the bombing of Dresden which it is widely agreed served no essential purpose. In the same kind of way injustices in the treatment of an occupied country are likely to escalate, and this consideration should probably tip the balance in any cases (if there are such) where it might otherwise have been justified from a utilitarian point of view.

Just about the same can be said regarding collective punishments as scapegoat punishments.

In both cases one doubts whether these acts really ever are justified from a utilitarian point of view. Anyone concerned to gain the cooperation of an occupied territory without making it a slave population will presumably be concerned to gain its good will, to which end these methods are hardly conducive. The purposes for which the occupation is undertaken are obviously relevant here. On the whole, the more immoral the purposes the more such methods will seem required.

Although I am not attempting in this reply any account of what constitutes the goods (and evils) of justice (and injustice), I should perhaps mention a good of this type which would be prevented by scapegoat and collective punishment. One of the great goods furthered by various legal and quasilegal institutions when properly conducted is the increased chance they give to everyone to control their own futures (so far as these depend on human agency) within limits imposed by the common good. This can perhaps be called one of the goods of justice, when it is the result of such institutions. (A similar good arising from a different cause might not be so called.) But the good of justice with which I am concerned is rather the *maintenance* of institutions serving this purpose. This can be called a major good of justice. Among such institutions we may include various habits of people wielding authority even where they are not directed to act thus by some positive law. It should not be very controversial to urge that the maintenance of institutions which (or of those aspects of them which) increase a person's opportunities to plan his future is a great utilitarian good.

An institution which serves the purposes in question will ensure that such evils as may arise for a man through human agency and frustrate his plans, when they are also such that their attempted elimination (by—or in the case of punishment from—the institutions in question) would be predominantly harmful, are at least so far as possible predictable by him, and preferably dependent for their occurrence on circumstances within his control. Thus, although customs which ensured that a man could never lose his job would doubtless be harmful on the whole, habits of employment according to which a man knows under what circumstances he will lose his job, especially if these circumstances are within his control, serve the purpose we have described and action which weakens such habits is so far unjust. Now we may accept that punishment (like the sack) is necessary evil, but granted that, we should try to preserve institutions according to which a man can predict and control the circumstances in which he will suffer it. Acts which weaken such institutions will be so far unjust, and be so even on those rare occasions where they may effect a predominating good and so be right.

It is not difficult to see that the infliction of scapegoat or collective punishment will be unjust from this point of view. There are various rules adherence to which is generally regarded as a criterion of just punishment. A main one is the rule that a man should only be punished for an action if he knew before doing it that he was likely to be punished for it, and could have refrained from the act if he had chosen. Various departures from this rule are in fact countenanced without people feeling that there is an injustice. For instance, it is accepted that a man may be punished if in some sense he should have known that punishment might be inflicted for something he has done, even if in fact he did not know this. That is a rather minor departure. But there are also cases such as some punishments of war criminals where the rule is departed from more strikingly, and yet not everyone regards such punishment as unjust. I think we may say, however, that a departure from this rule always gives some reason for talk of injustice.

Adherence to this rule is an institution such as I have been describing. So long as a person is only punished in conformity to it the evil he suffers is such as he could have anticipated and avoided. If we weaken this institution we are acting against the major good of justice I have mentioned, and forwarding the opposing evil.

Now infliction of a scapegoat or collective punishment represents a breaking of the rule in question. A collective punishment can hardly be a secret affair, and it is not very clear that a scapegoat punishment can be. (For we do not call such frame-ups as were discussed in the last section scapegoat punishments.) In acting against the rule we create a general sense that this institution (adherence to the rule) is breaking down, and this acts in various ways to bring about that result. Even if in some examples the result is supposed avoided, it is unrealistic to imagine it possible thus to act without weakening one's own tendency to abide by the rule. One's adherence to the rule represents a personal habit and sentiment, which when once broken for what seem good reasons is much more likely than before to be broken for bad reasons. It seems then that collective and scapegoat punishment will always weaken the institution in question, and will be so far *unjust*, using this word according to the utilitarian account I have adumbrated.

It is of course theoretically possible that a punishment of this sort will bring about more good than evil, even when the weakening of the institution and the intrinsic evil of the punishment itself are both taken into account, and I would not care to insist that it was not sometimes a practical possibility. But there are two different possibilities here which must be distinguished. One is that the goods which outweigh these evils are other goods of justice. The other is that these goods are of a different type. In the former case we may wish to describe the punishment as on the whole just, in spite of seeming unjust when one aspect of the situation only is considered. Such might be the case with the punishment of war criminals. In the latter case, however, we will allow that the punishment was unjust, but urge that nonetheless it was justified by the special good it did. It seems likely that whatever other goods can be described as goods of justice besides that major one which we have considered, they will never be forwarded by scapegoat and collective punishment. So that the utilitarian can accept that such punishments are always unjust.

The possibility remains that these unjust punishments may on occasion be right and proper, because useful in some other way. This possibility seems, however, to be allowed by McCloskey. It is not at all clear in my judgment that occasions of this kind actually occur. At any rate the utilitarian has every reason for urging the serious damage done to the goods of justice on any likely occasion of scapegoat or collective punishment, and for insisting therefore on the extreme gravity of any decision to use them.

John Austin

Rule Utilitarianism (I)*

The *tendency* of a human action (as its tendency is this understood) is the whole of its tendency: the sum of its probable consequences, in so far as they are important or material: the sum of its remote and collateral, as well as of its direct consequences, in so far as any of its consequences may influence the general happiness.

Trying to collect its tendency (as its tendency is thus understood), we must not consider the action as if it were *single* and *insulated*, but must look at the *class* of actions to which it belongs. The probable specific consequences of doing that single act, of forbearing from that single act, or of omitting that single act, are not the objects of the inquiry. The question to be solved is this: — If acts of the *class* were *generally* done, or *generally* forborne or omitted, what would be the probable effect on the general happiness or good?

Considered by itself, a mischievous act may seem to be useful or harmless. Considered by itself, a useful act may seem to be pernicious.

For example, If a poor man steal a handful from the heap of his rich neighbour, the act, considered by itself, is harmless or positively good. One man's poverty is assuaged with the superfluous wealth of another.

But suppose that thefts were general (or that the useful right of property were open to frequent invasions), and mark the result.

Without security for property, there were no inducement to save. Without habitual saving on the part of proprietors, there were no accumulation of capital. Without accumulation of capital, there were no fund for the payment of wages, no division of labour, no elaborate and costly machines: there were none of those helps to labour which

---

*John Austin, *The Province of Jurisprudence Determined and the Uses of the Study of Jurisprudence*, intro. H. L. A. Hart (New York: The Noonday Press, (1954), 38–40.

augment its productive power, and, therefore, multiply the enjoyments of every individual in the community. Frequent invasions of property would bring the rich to poverty; and, what were a greater evil, would aggravate the poverty of the poor.

If a single and insulated theft seem to be harmless or good, the fallacious appearance merely arises from this: that the vast majority of those who are tempted to steal abstain from invasions of property; and the detriment to security, which is the end produced by general security.

Again: If I evade the payment of a tax imposed by a good government, the *specific* effects of the mischievous forbearance are indisputably useful. For the money which I unduly withhold is convenient to myself; and, compared with the bulk of the public revenue, is a quantity too small to be missed. But the regular payment of taxes is necessary to the existence of the government. And I, and the rest of the community, enjoy the security which it gives, because the payment of taxes is rarely evaded.

In the cases now supposed, the act or omission is good, considered as single or insulated; but, considered with the rest of its class, is evil. In other cases, an act or omission is evil, considered as single or insulated; but, considered with the rest of its class, is good.

For example, A punishment, as a solitary fact, is an evil: the pain inflicted on the criminal being added to the mischief of the crime. But, considered as part of a system, a punishment is useful or beneficent. By a dozen or score of punishments, thousands of crimes are prevented. With the sufferings of the guilty few, the security of the many is purchased. By the lopping of a peccant member, the body is saved from decay.

It, therefore, is true generally (for the proposition admits of exceptions), that, to determine the true tendency of an act, forbearance, or omission, we must resolve the following question:—What would be the probable effect on the general happiness or good, if *similar* acts, forbearances, or omissions were general or frequent?

Such is the *test* to which we must usually resort, if we would try the true *tendency* of an act, forbearance, or omission: Meaning, by the true *tendency* of an act, forbearance, or omission, the sum of its probable effects on the general happiness or good, or its agreement or disagreement with the principle of general utility.

John Rawls

Rule Utilitarianism (II)*

In this paper I want to show the importance of the distinction between justifying a practice[1] and justifying a particular action falling under it, and I want to explain the logical basis of this distinction and how it is possible to miss its significance. While the distinction has frequently been made,[2] and is now becoming commonplace, there remains the

---

*John Rawls, "Two Concepts of Rules," *The Philosophical Review* 44 (1955), intro., sec. 1., pp. 3–13. Reprinted by permission of the author and *The Philosophical Review*. http://www.ditext.com/rawls/rules.html

1. I use the word "practice" throughout as a sort of technical term meaning any form of activity specified by a system of rules which defines offices, roles, moves, penalties, defenses, and so on, and which gives the activity its structure. As examples one may think of games and rituals, trials and parliaments.

2. The distinction is central to Hume's discussion of justice in *A Treatise of Human Nature*, bk. III, pt. ii, esp. secs. 2–4. It is clearly stated by John Austin in the second lecture of *Lectures on Jurisprudence* (4th ed.; London, 1873), I, 116ff. (1st ed., 1832). Also it may be argued that J. S. Mill took it for granted in *Utilitarianism*; on this point cf. J. o. Urmson, "The Interpretation of the Moral Philosophy of J. S. Mill," *Philosophical Quarterly*, vol. III (1953). In addition to the arguments given by Urmson there are several clear statements of the distinction in *A System of Logic* (8th ed.; London, 1872), bk. VI, ch. xii pars. 2, 3, 7. The distinction is fundamental to J. D. Mabbott's important paper, "Punishment," *Mind*, n.s., vol. XLVIII (April, 1939). More recently the distinction has been stated with particular emphasis by S. E. Toulmin in *The Place of Reason in Ethics* (Cambridge, 1950), see esp. ch. xi, where it plays a major part in his account of moral reasoning. Toulmin doesn't explain the basis of the distinction, nor how one might overlook its importance, as I try to in this paper, and in my review of this book (*Philosophical Review*, vol. LX [October, 1951]), as some of my criticisms show, I failed to understand the force of it. See also H. D. Aiken, "The Levels of Moral Discourse," *Ethics*, vol. LXII (1952), A. M. Quinton, "Punishment," *Analysis*, vol. XIV (June, 1954), and P. H. Nowell-Smith, *Ethics* (London, 1954): 236–39, 271–73.

task of explaining the tendency either to overlook it altogether, or to fail to appreciate its importance.

To show the importance of the distinction I am going to defend utilitarianism against those objections which have traditionally been made against it in connection with punishment and the obligation to keep promises. I hope to show that if one uses the distinction in question then one can state utilitarianism in a way which makes it a much better explication of our considered moral judgments than these traditional objections would seem to admit.[3] Thus the importance of the distinction is shown by the way it strengthens the utilitarian view regardless of whether that view is completely defensible or not.

To explain how the significance of the distinction may be overlooked, I am going to discuss two conceptions of rules. One of these conceptions conceals the importance of distinguishing between the justification of a rule or practice and the justification of a particular action falling under it. The other conception makes it clear why this distinction must be made and what is its logical basis.

I

The subject of punishment, in the sense of attaching legal penalties to the violation of legal rules, has always been a troubling moral question.[4] The trouble about it has not been that people disagree as to whether or not punishment is justifiable. Most people have held that, freed from certain abuses, it is an acceptable institution. Only a few have rejected punishment entirely, which is rather surprising when one considers all that can be said against it. The difficulty is with the justification of punishment: various arguments for it have

---

3. On the concept of explication see the author's paper *Philosophical Review*, vol. LX (April, 1951).

4. While this paper was being revised, Quinton's appeared; footnote 2 supra. There are several respects in which my remarks are similar to his. Yet as I consider some further questions and rely on somewhat different arguments, I have retained the discussion of punishment and promises together as two test cases for utilitarianism.

been given by moral philosophers, but so far none of them has won any sort of general acceptance; no justification is without those who detest it. I hope to show that the use of the aforementioned distinction enables one to state the utilitarian view in a way which allows for the sound points of its critics.

For our purposes we may say that there are two justifications of punishment. What we may call the retributive view is that punishment is justified on the grounds that wrongdoing merits punishment. It is morally fitting that a person who does wrong should suffer in proportion to his wrongdoing. That a criminal should be punished follows from his guilt, and the severity of the appropriate punishment depends on the depravity of his act. The state of affairs where a wrongdoer suffers punishment is morally better than the state of affairs where he does not, and it is better irrespective of any of the consequences of punishing him.

What we may call the utilitarian view holds that on the principle that bygones are bygones and that only future consequences are material to present decisions, punishment is justifiable only by reference to the probable consequences of maintaining it as one of the devices of the social order. Wrongs committed in the past are, as such, not relevant considerations for deciding what to do. If punishment can be shown to promote effectively the interest of society it is justifiable, otherwise it is not.

I have stated these two competing views very roughly to make one feel the conflict between them: one feels the force of *both* arguments and one wonders how they can be reconciled. From my introductory remarks it is obvious that the resolution which I am going to propose is that in this case one must distinguish between justifying a practice as a system of rules to be applied and enforced, and justifying a particular action which falls under these rules; utilitarian arguments are appropriate with regard to questions about practices, while retributive arguments fit the application of particular rules to particular cases.

We might try to get clear about this distinction by imagining how a father might answer the question of his son. Suppose the son asks, "Why was *J* put in jail yesterday?" The father answers, "Because he robbed the bank at B. He was duly tried and found guilty. That's why he was put in jail yesterday." But suppose the son had asked a different question, namely, "Why do people put other people in jail?" Then the father might answer, "To protect good people from bad people" or "To stop people from doing things that would make it uneasy for all of us; for otherwise we wouldn't be able to go to bed at night and sleep in peace." There are two very different questions here. One question emphasizes the proper name: It asks why *J* was punished rather than someone else, or it asks what he was punished for. The other question asks why we have the institution of punishment: Why do people punish one another rather than, say, always forgiving one another?

Thus the father says in effect that a particular man is punished, rather than some other man, because he is guilty, and he is guilty because he broke the law (past tense). In his case the law looks back, the judge looks back, the jury looks back, and a penalty is visited upon him for something he did. That a man is to be punished, and what his punishment is to be, is settled by its being shown that he broke the law and that the law assigns that penalty for the violation of it.

On the other hand we have the institution of punishment itself, and recommend and accept various changes in it, because it is thought by the (ideal) legislator and by those to whom the law applies that, as a part of a system of law impartially applied from case to case arising under it, it will have the consequence, in the long run, of furthering the interests of society.

One can say, then, that the judge and the legislator stand in different positions and look in different directions: one to the past, the other to the future. The justification of what the judge does, *qua* judge, sounds like the retributive view; the justification of what the (ideal) legislator does, *qua* legislator, sounds like the utilitarian view. Thus, both views have a point (this is as it should be since intelligent and sensitive persons have been on both sides of the argument); and one's initial confusion disappears once one sees that these views apply to persons holding different offices with different duties, and situated differently with respect to the system of rules that make up the criminal law.[5]

---

5. Note the fact that different sorts of arguments are suited to different offices. One way of taking the differences between ethical theories is to regard them as accounts of the reasons expected in different offices.

One might say, however, that the utilitarian view is more fundamental since it applies to a more fundamental office, for the judge
carries out the legislator's will so far as he can determine it. Once
the legislator decides to have laws and to assign penalties for their
violation (as things are there must be both the law and the penalty)
an institution is set up which involves a retributive conception of
particular cases. It is part of the concept of the criminal law as a
system of rules that the application and enforcement of these rules
in particular cases should be justifiable by arguments of a retributive
character. The decision whether or not to use law rather than some
other mechanism of social control, and the decision as to what laws
to have and what penalties to assign, may be settled by utilitarian
arguments; but if one decides to have laws then one has decided on
something whose working in particular cases is retributive in form.[6]

The answer, then, to the confusion engendered by the two views
of punishment is quite simple: One distinguishes two offices, that of
the judge and that of the legislator, and one distinguishes their different stations with respect to the system of rules which make up the
law; and then one notes that the different sorts of considerations which
would usually be offered as reasons for what is done under the cover
of these offices can be paired off with the competing justifications
of punishment. One reconciles the two views by the time-honored
device of making them apply to different situations.

But can it really be this simple? Well, this answer allows for
the apparent intent of each side. Does a person who advocates the
retributive view necessarily advocate, as an *institution*, legal machinery whose essential purpose is to set up and preserve a correspondence
between moral turpitude and suffering? Surely not.[7] What retributionists have rightly insisted upon is that no man can be punished unless
he is guilty, that is, unless he has broken the law. Their fundamental
criticism of the utilitarian account is that, as they interpret it, it sanctions an innocent person's being punished (if one may call it that)
for the benefit of society.

---

6. In this connection see Mabbott, *op. cit.*, pp. 163–64.

7. On this point see Sir David Ross, *The Right and the Good* (Oxford, 1930),
57–60.

On the other hand, utilitarians agree that punishment is to be inflicted only for the violation of law. They regard this much as understood from the concept of punishment itself.[8] The point of the utilitarian account concerns the institution as a system of rules: utilitarianism seeks to limit its use by declaring it justifiable only if it can be shown to foster effectively the good of society. Historically it is a protest against the indiscriminate and ineffective use of the criminal law.[9] It seeks to dissuade us from assigning to penal institutions the improper, if not sacrilegious, task of matching suffering with moral turpitude. Like others, utilitarians want penal institutions designed so that, as far as humanly possible, only those who break the law run afoul of it. They hold that no official should have discretionary power to inflict penalties whenever he thinks it for the benefit of society; for on utilitarian grounds an institution granting such power could not be justified.[10]

---

8. See Hobbes's definition of punishment in *Leviathan*, ch. xxviii; and Bentham's definition in *The Principle of Morals and Legislation*, ch. xii, par. 36, ch. xv, par. 28, and in *The Rationale of Punishment*, (London, 1830), bk. I, ch. i. They could agree with Bradley that: "Punishment is punishment only when it is deserved. We pay the penalty, because we owe it, and for no other reason; and if punishment is inflicted for any other reason whatever than because it is merited by wrong, it is a gross immorality, a crying injustice, an abominable crime, and not what it pretends to be." *Ethical Studies* (2nd ed.; Oxford, 1927), 26–27. Certainly by definition it isn't what it pretends to be. The innocent can only be punished by mistake; deliberate "punishment" of the innocent necessarily involves fraud.

9. Cf. Leon Radzinowicz, *A History of English Criminal Law: The Movement for Reform 1750–1833* (London, 1948), esp. ch. xi on Bentham.

10. Bentham discusses how corresponding to a punitory provision of a criminal law there is another provision which stands to it as an antagonist and which needs a name as much as the punitory. He calls it, as one might expect, the *anaetiosostic*, and of it he says: "The punishment of guilt is the object of the former one: the preservation of innocence that of the latter." In the same connection he asserts that it is never thought fit to give the judge the option of deciding whether a thief (that is, a person whom he believes to be a thief, for the judge's belief is what the question must always turn upon) should hang or not, and so the law writes the provision: "The judge shall not cause a thief to be hanged unless he have been duly convicted and sentenced in course of law." (*The Limits of Jurisprudence Defined*, ed. C. W. Everett [New York, 1945], pp. 238–39).

The suggested way of reconciling the retributive and the utilitarian justifications of punishment seems to account for what both sides have wanted to say. There are, however, two further questions which arise, and I shall devote the remainder of this section to them.

First, will not a difference of opinion as to the proper criterion of just law make the proposed reconciliation unacceptable to retributionists? Will they not question whether, if the utilitarian principle is used as the criterion, it follows that those who have broken the law are guilty in a way which satisfies their demand that those punished deserve to be punished? To answer this difficulty, suppose that the rules of the criminal law are justified on utilitarian grounds (it is only for laws that meet his criterion that the utilitarian can be held responsible). Then it follows that the actions which the criminal law specifies as offenses are such that, if they were tolerated, terror and alarm would spread in society. Consequently, retributionists can only deny that those who are punished deserve to be punished if they deny that such actions are wrong. This they will not want to do.

The second question is whether utilitarianism doesn't justify too much. One pictures it as an engine of justification which, if consistently adopted, could be used to justify cruel and arbitrary institutions. Retributionists may be supposed to concede that utilitarians *intend* to reform the law and to make it more humane; that utilitarians do not *wish* to justify any such thing as punishment of the innocent; and that utilitarians may appeal to the fact that punishment presupposes guilt in the sense that by punishment one understands an institution attaching penalties to the infraction of legal rules, and therefore that it is logically absurd to suppose that utilitarians in justifying *punishment* might also have justified punishment (if we may call it that) of the innocent. The real question, however, is whether the utilitarian, in justifying punishment, hasn't used arguments which commit him to accepting the infliction of suffering on innocent persons if it is for the good of society (whether or not one calls this punishment). More generally, isn't the utilitarian committed in principle to accepting many practices which he, as a morally sensitive person, wouldn't want to accept? Retributionists are inclined to hold that there is no way to stop the utilitarian principle from justifying too much except by adding to it a principle which distributes certain rights to individuals.

Then the amended criterion is not the greatest benefit of society *simpliciter*, but the greatest benefit of society subject to the constraint that no one's rights may be violated. Now while I think that the classical utilitarians proposed a criterion of this more complicated sort, I do not want to argue that point here.[11] What I want to show is that there is *another* way of preventing the utilitarian principle from justifying too much, or at least of making it much less likely to do so: namely, by stating utilitarianism in a way which accounts for the distinction between the justification of an institution and the justification of a particular action failing under it.

I begin by defining the institution of punishment as follows: a person is said to suffer punishment whenever he is legally deprived of some of the normal rights of a citizen on the ground that he has violated a rule of law, the violation having been established by trial according to the due process of law, provided that the deprivation is carried out by the recognized legal authorities of the state, that the rule of law clearly specifies both the offense and the attached penalty, that the courts construe statutes strictly, and that the statute was on the books prior to the time of the offense.[12] This definition specifies what I shall understand by punishment. The question is whether utilitarian arguments may be found to justify institutions widely different from this and such as one would find cruel and arbitrary.

This question is best answered, I think, by taking up a particular accusation. Consider the following from Carritt:

> . . . the utilitarian must hold that we are justified in inflicting pain always and only to prevent worse pain or bring about greater happiness. This, then, is all we need to consider in so-called punishment, which must be purely preventive. But if some kind of very cruel crime becomes common, and none

---

11. By the classical utilitarians I understand Hobbes, Hume, Bentham, J. S. Mill, and Sidgwick.

12. All these features of punishment are mentioned by Hobbes; cf. *Leviathan*, ch. xxviii.

of the criminals can be caught, it might be highly expedient, as an example, to hang an innocent man, if a charge against him could be so framed that he were universally thought guilty; indeed this would only fail to be an ideal instance of utilitarian 'punishment' because the victim himself would not have been so likely as a real felon to commit such a crime in the future; in all other respects it would be perfectly deterrent and therefore felicific.[13]

Carritt is trying to show that there are occasions when a utilitarian argument would justify taking an action which would be generally condemned; and thus that utilitarianism justifies too much. But the failure of Carritt's argument lies in the fact that he makes no distinction between the justification of the general system of rules which constitutes penal institutions and the justification of particular applications of these rules to particular cases by the various officials whose job it is to administer them. This becomes perfectly clear when one asks who the "we" are of whom Carritt speaks. Who is this who has a sort of absolute authority on particular occasions to decide that an innocent man shall be "punished" if everyone can be convinced that he is guilty? Is this person the legislator, or the judge, or the body of private citizens, or what? It is utterly crucial to know who is to decide such matters, and by what authority, for all of this must be written into the rules of the institution. Until one knows these things one doesn't know what the institution is whose justification is being challenged; and as the utilitarian principle applies to the institution one doesn't know whether it is justifiable on utilitarian grounds or not.

Once this is understood it is clear what the countermove to Carritt's argument is. One must describe more carefully what the *institution* is which his example suggests, and then ask oneself whether or not it is likely that having this institution would be for the benefit of society in the long run. One must not content oneself with the vague thought that, when it's a question of *this* case, it would be a

---

13. *Ethical and Political Thinking* (Oxford, 1947), p. 65.

good thing if *somebody* did something even if an innocent person were to suffer.

Try to imagine, then, an institution (which we may call "telishment") which is such that the officials set up by it have authority to arrange a trial for the condemnation of an innocent man whenever they are of the opinion that doing so would be in the best interests of society. The discretion of officials is limited, however, by the rule that they may not condemn an innocent man to undergo such an ordeal unless there is, at the time, a wave of offenses similar to that with which they charge him and telish him for. We may imagine that the officials having the discretionary authority are the judges of the higher courts in consultation with the chief of police, the minister of justice, and a committee of the legislature.

Once one realizes that one is involved in setting up an *institution*, one sees that the hazards are very great. For example, what check is there on the officials? How is one to tell whether or not their actions are authorized? How is one to limit the risks involved in allowing such systematic deception? How is one to avoid giving anything short of complete discretion to the authorities to telish anyone they like? In addition to these considerations, it is obvious that people will come to have a very different attitude towards their penal system when telishment is adjoined to it. They will be uncertain as to whether a convicted man has been punished or telished. They will wonder whether or not they should feel sorry for him. They will wonder whether the same fate won't at any time fall on them. If one pictures how such an institution would actually work, and the enormous risks involved in it, it seems clear that it would serve no useful purpose. A utilitarian justification for this institution is most unlikely.

It happens in general that as one drops off the defining features of punishment one ends up with an institution whose utilitarian justification is highly doubtful. One reason for this is that punishment works like a kind of price system: by altering the prices one has to pay for the performance of actions, it supplies a motive for avoiding some actions and doing others. The defining features are essential if punishment is to work in this way; so that an institution which lacks these features, for example, an institution which is set up to "punish" the innocent, is likely to have about as much point as a price system (if one may call it that) where the prices of things change at random from day to day and one learns the price of something after one has agreed to buy it.[14]

If one is careful to apply the utilitarian principle to the institution which is to authorize particular actions, then there is *less* danger of its justifying too much. Carritt's example gains plausibility by its indefiniteness and by its concentration on the particular case. His argument will only hold if it can be shown that there are utilitarian arguments which justify an institution whose publicly ascertainable offices and powers are such as to permit officials to exercise that kind of discretion in particular cases. But the requirement of having to build the arbitrary features of the particular decision into the institutional practice makes the justification much less likely to go through.

---

14. The analogy with the price system suggests an answer to the question how utilitarian considerations insure that punishment is proportional to the offense. It is interesting to note that Sir David Ross, after making the distinction between justifying a penal law and justifying a particular application of it, and after stating that utilitarian considerations have a large place in determining the former, still holds back from accepting the utilitarian justification of punishment on the grounds that justice requires that punishment be proportional to the offense, and that utilitarianism is unable to account for this. Cf. *The Right and the Good*, pp. 61–62. I do not claim that utilitarianism can account for this requirement as Sir David might wish, but it happens, nevertheless, that if utilitarian considerations are followed penalties will be proportional to offenses in this sense: the order of offenses according to seriousness can be paired off with the order of penalties according to severity. Also the absolute level of penalties will be as low as possible. This follows from the assumption that people are rational (i.e., that they are able to take into account the "prices" the state puts on actions), the utilitarian rule that a penal system should provide a motive for preferring the less serious offense, and the principle that punishment as such is an evil. All this was carefully worked out by Bentham in *The Principles of Morals and Legislation*, chs. xiii–xv.

Richard Brandt

Rule Utilitarianism (III)*

The essence of the rule-utilitarian theory, we recall, is that our actions, whether legislative or otherwise, should be guided by a set of prescriptions, the conscientious following of which by all would have maximum net expectable utility. As a result, the utilitarian is not, just as such, committed to any particular view about how antisocial behavior should be treated by society—or even to the view that society should do anything at all about immoral conduct. It is only the utilitarian principle *combined* with statements about the kind of laws and practices which will maximize expectable utility that has such consequences. Therefore, utilitarians are free to differ from one another about the character of an ideal system of criminal justice; some utilitarians think that the system prevalent in Great Britain and the United States essentially corresponds to the ideal, but others think that the only system that can be justified is markedly different from the actual systems in Western countries. We shall concentrate our discussion, however, on the traditional line of utilitarian thought which holds that roughly the actual system of criminal law, say in the United States, is morally justifiable, and we shall follow roughly the classic exposition of the reasoning given by Jeremy Bentham—but modifying this freely when we feel amendment is called for. At the end of the chapter we shall look briefly at a different view.

Traditional utilitarian thinking about criminal justice has found the rationale of the practice, in the United States, for example, in three main facts. (Those who disagree think the first two of these "facts" happen not to be the case.) (1) People who are tempted to misbehave, to trample on the rights of others, to sacrifice public welfare for personal gain, can usually be deterred from misconduct by fear

---

*Richard B. Brandt, *Ethical Theory: The Problems of Normative and Critical Ethics* (Englewood Cliffs, NJ: Prentice-Hall, Inc., 1959), 490–95.

of punishment, such as death, imprisonment, or find. (2) Imprisonment or fine will teach malefactors a lesson; their characters may be improved, and at any rate a personal experience of punishment will make them less likely to misbehave again. (3) Imprisonment will certainly have the result of physically preventing past malefactors from misbehaving, during the period of their incarceration.

In view of these suppositions, traditional utilitarian thinking has concluded that having laws forbidding certain kinds of behavior on pain of punishment, and having machinery for the fair enforcement of these laws, is justified by the fact that it maximizes expectable utility. Misconduct is not to be punished just for its own sake; malefactors must be punished for their past acts, according to the law, as a way of maximizing expectable utility.

The utilitarian principle, of course, has implications for decisions about the severity of punishment to be administered. Punishment is itself an evil, and hence should be avoided where this is consistent with the public good. Punishment should have precisely such a greater degree of severity (not more or less) that the probable disutility of greater severity just balances the probable gain in utility (less crime because of the more serious threat). The cost, in other words, should be counted along with the value of what is bought; and we should buy protection up to the point where the cost is greater than the protection is worth. How severe will such punishment be? Jeremy Bentham had many sensible things to say about this. Punishment, he said, must be severe enough so that it is to no one's advantage to commit an offense even if he receives the punishment; a find of $10 for bank robbery would give no security at all. Further, since many criminals will be undetected, we must make the penalty heavy enough in comparison with the prospective gain from crime, that a prospective criminal will consider the risk hardly worth it, even considering that it is not certain he will be punished at all. Again, the more serious offenses should carry the heavier penalties, not only because the greater disutility justifies the use of heavier penalties in order to prevent them, but also because criminals should be motivated to commit a less serious rather than a more serious offense. Bentham thought the prescribed penalties should allow for some variation at the discretion of the judge, so that the actual suffering caused should roughly be the same in all cases; thus, a heavier fine will be imposed on a rich man than on a poor man.

Bentham also argued that the goal of maximum utility requires that certain facts should excuse from culpability, for the reason that punishment in such cases "must be inefficacious." He listed as such (1) the fact that the relevant law was passed only after the act of the accused, (2) that the law had not been made public, (3) that the criminal was an infant, insane or was intoxicated, (4) that the crime was done under physical compulsion, (5) that the agent was ignorant of the probable consequences of his act or was acting on the basis of an innocent misapprehension of the facts, such that the act the agent thought he was performing was a lawful one, and (6) that the motivation to commit the offense was so strong that no threat of law could prevent the crime. Bentham also thought that punishment should be remitted if the crime was a collective one and the number of the guilty so large that great suffering would be cause by its imposition, or if the offender held an important post and his services were important for the public, or if the public or foreign powers would be offended by the punishment; but we shall ignore this part of his view.

Bentham's account of the logic of legal "defenses" needs amendment. What he should have argued is that *not* punishing in certain types of cases (cases where such defenses as those just indicated can be offered) reduces the amount of suffering imposed by law and the insecurity of everybody, and that failure to impose punishment in these types of case will cause only a negligible increase in the incidence of crime.

How satisfactory is this theory of criminal justice? Does it have any implications that are far from being acceptable when compared with concrete justified convictions about what practices are morally right?[1]

---

1. Act-utilitarians face some special problems. For instance, if I am an act-utiltiaran and serve on a jury, I shall work to get a verdict that will do the most good, irrespective of the charges of the judge, and of any oath I may have taken to give a reasonable answer to certain questions on the basis of the evidence presented—unless I think my doing so will have indirect effects on the institution of the jury, public confidence in it, and so on. This is certainly not what we think a juror should do. Of course, neither a juror nor a judge can escape his prima facie obligation to do what good he can; this obligation is present in some form in every theory. The act-utilitarian, however, makes this the whole of one's responsibility.

Many criminologists, as we shall see at the end of this chapter, would argue that Bentham was mistaken in his facts: the deterrence value of threat of punishment, they say, is much less than he imagined, and criminals are seldom reformed by spending time in prison. If these contentions are correct, then the ideal rules for society's treatment of malefactors are very different from what Bentham thought, and from what actual practice is today in the United States. To say all this, however, is not to show that the utilitarian *principle* is incorrect, for in view of these facts presumably the attitudes of a "qualified" person would not be favorable to criminal justice as practiced today. Utilitarian theory might still be correct, but its implications would be different from what Bentham thought—and they might coincide with justified ethical judgments. We shall return to this.

The whole utilitarian approach, however, has been criticized on the ground that it ought not in consistency to approve of *any* excuses from criminal liability.[2] Or at least, it should do so only after careful empirical inquiries. It is not obvious, it is argued, that we increase net expectable utility by permitting such defenses. At the least, the utilitarian is committed to defend the concept of "strict liability." Why? Because we could get a more strongly deterrent effect if everyone knew that *all behavior* of a certain sort would be punished, irrespective of mistaken supposals of fact, compulsion, and so on. The critics admit that knowledge that all behavior of a certain sort will be punished will hardly deter from crime the insane, persons acting under compulsion, persons acting under erroneous beliefs about facts, and others, but, as Professor Hart points out, it does not follow from this that general knowledge that certain acts will always be punished will not be salutary.

The utilitarian, however, has a solid defense against charges of this sort. We must bear in mind (as the critics do not) that the utilitarian principle, *taken by itself, implies nothing whatever* about whether a system of law should excuse persons on the basis of certain defenses.

---

2. See H. L. A. Hart, "Legal Responsibility and Excuses," in Sidney Hook (ed.), *Determinism and Freedom* (New York: New York University Press, 1958), pp. 81–104; and David Braybrooke, "Professor Stevenson, Voltaire, and the Case of Admiral Byng," *Journal of Philosophy*, LIII (1956), 787–96.

What the utilitarian does say is that when we *combine* the principle of utiltarianism with *true* propositions about a certain thing or situation, then we shall come out with true statements about obligations. The utilitarian is certainly not committed to saying that one will derive true propositions about obligations if one starts with *false* propositions about fact or about what will maximize welfare, or with no such propositions at all. Therefore the criticism sometimes made (for example, by Hart), that utilitarian theory does not render it "obviously" or "necessarily" the case that recognized excuses from criminal liability should be accepted as excusing from punishment, is beside the point. Moreover, in fact the utilitarian can properly claim that we do have excellent reason for believing that the general public would be no better motivated to avoid criminal offenses than it now is, if the insane and others were also punished along with intentional wrongdoers. Indeed, he may reasonably claim that the example of punishment of these individuals could only have a hardening effect—like public executions. Furthermore, the utilitarian can point out that abolition of the standard exculpating excuses would lead to serious insecurity. Imagine the pleasure of driving an automobile if one knew one could be executed for running down a child whom it was absolutely impossible to avoid striking! One certainly does not maximize expectable utility by eliminating the traditional excuses. In general, then, the utilitarian theory is not threatened by implications about exculpating excuses.

It might also be objected against utilitarianism that it cannot recognize the validity of *mitigating* excuses (which presumably have the support of "qualified" attitudes). Would not consequences be better if the distinction between premeditated and impulsive acts were abolished? The utilitarian can reply that people who commit impulsive crimes, in the heat of anger, do not give a thought to legal penalties; they would not be deterred by a stricter law. Moreover, such a person is unlikely to repeat his crime, so that a mild sentence saves an essentially good man for society.[3] Something can

---

3. The utilitarian must admit that the same thing is true for many deliberate murders, and probably he should also admit that some people who commit a crime in the heat of anger would have found time to think had they known a grave penalty awaited them.

also be said in support of the practice of judges in giving a milder sentence when a person's temptation is severe: at least the *extended* rule-utilitarian can say, in defense of the practice of punishing less severely the crime of a man who has had few opportunities in life that a judge ought to do what he can to repair inequalities in life, and that a mild sentence to a man who has had few opportunities is one way of doing this. There are, then, utilitarian supports for recognizing the mitigating excuses.

Sometimes it is objected to utilitarianism that it must view imprisonment for crime as morally no different from quarantine. This, it is said, shows that the utilitarian theory must be mistaken, since actually there is a vast moral difference between being quarantined and being imprisoned for crime. *Why* is it supposed utilitarian theory must view imprisonment as a kind of quarantine? The answer is that utilitarianism looks to the future; the treatment is prescribes for individuals is treatment with an eye to maximizing net expectable utility. The leper is quarantined because otherwise he will expose others to disease. The criminal is imprisoned because otherwise he (or she), or others who are not deterred by the threat of punishment, will expose the public to crime. Both the convicted criminal and the leper are making contributions to the public good. So, quarantine an imprisonment are essentially personal sacrifices for the public welfare, if we think of punishment as the utilitarian does. But in fact, the argument goes on, we feel there is a vast difference. The public is obligated to do what is possible to make the leper comfortable, to make his necessary sacrifice as easy for him and his family as possible. But we feel no obligation to make imprisonment as comfortable as possible.

Again the utilitarian has a reply. He can say that people cannot help contracting leprosy, but they can avoid committing crimes—and the very discomforts and harshness of prison life are deterring factors. If prison life were made attractive, there might be more criminals— not to mention the indolent who would commit a crime in order to enjoy the benefits of public support. Furthermore, the utilitarian can say, why should we feel that we "ought to make it up to" a quarantined leper? At least partly because it is useful to encourage willingness to make such sacrifices. But we do not at all wish to encourage the criminal to make his "sacrifice" rather, we wish him not to commit his crimes. There is all the difference between the kind of treatment justified on utilitarian grounds for a person who may have to make a sacrifice for the public welfare through no fault of his own, and for a person who is required to make a sacrifice because he has selfishly and deliberately trampled on the rights of others, in clear view of the fact that if he is apprehended society must make an example of him. There are all sorts of utilitarian reasons for being kindly to persons of the former type, and stern with people of the latter type.

Another popular objection to the utilitarian theory is that the utilitarian must approve of prosecutors or judges occasionally withholding evidence known to them, for the sake of convicting an innocent man, if the public welfare really is served by so doing. Critics of the theory would not deny that there *can* be circumstances where the dangers are so severe that such action is called for they only say that utilitarianism calls for it all too frequently. Is this criticism justified? Clearly, the utilitarian is not committed to advocating that a provision should be written into the *law* so as to permit punishment of persons for crimes they did not commit if to do so would serve the public good. Any such provision would be a shattering blow to public confidence and security. The question is only whether there should be an informal moral rule to the same effect, for the guidance of judges and prosecutors. Will the rule-utilitarian necessarily be committed to far too sweeping a moral rule on this point? We must recall that he is not in the position of the act-utilitarian, who must say that an innocent man must be punished if in *his particular case* the public welfare would be served by his punishment. The rule-utilitarian rather asserts only that an innocent man should be punished if he falls within a class of cases such that net expectable utility is maximized if *all* members of the class are punished, taking into account the possible disastrous effects on public confidence if it is generally known that judges and prosecutors are guided by such a rule. Moreover, the "extended" rule-utilitarian has a further reason for not punishing an innocent man unless he has had more than his equal share of the good things of life already; namely, that there is an obligation to promote equality of welfare, whereas severe punishment is heaping "illfare" on one individual person. When we take these considerations into account, it is *not* obvious that the rule-utilitarian (or the "extended" rule-utilitarian) is committed to action that we are justifiably convinced is immoral.[4]

In recent years, some philosophers have sought to rescue the utilitarian from his supposed difficulty of being committed to advocate the punishment of innocent men, by a verbal point. Their argument is that it is *logically* guaranteed that only a guilty man be *punished*. "Punishment," it is said, like "reward" and "forgive," has a backward reference; we properly speak of "punishing for . . . ," and if we inflict suffering on someone for the sake of utility and irrespective of guilt for some offense, it is a misuse of the word "punishment" to speak of such a person as being punished.[5] It is not clear, however, that anything is accomplished by this verbal move. If these writers are correct, then it is self-contradictory to say "innocent men may be punished for the sake of the public good," and no one can say that utilitarian theory commits one to uttering such self-contradiction. But it may still be that utilitarian theory commits one to advocating that prosecutors suppress evidence on certain occasions, that judges aid in conducting unfair trials and pronounce sentences out of line with custom for a particular type of case in times of public danger and, in short that innocent men be locked up or executed—only not "punished"—for the sake for the public welfare. So, if there is a difficulty here at all for the utilitarian theory, the verbal maneuver of these philosophers seems to remove it.

Everything considered, the utilitarian theory seems to be in much less dire distress in respect of its implications for criminal justice, than has sometimes been supposed. It does not seem possible to show that in any important way its implications are clearly in conflict with our

---

4. In any case, a tenable theory of punishment must approve of punishing persons who are *morally* blameless. Suppose someone commits treason for moral reasons. We may have to say that this deed is not reprehensible at all and night even (considering the risk it took for his principles) be morally admirable. Yet we think such persons must be punished no matter what their motives; people cannot be permitted to take the law into their own hands.

5. For some discussion of the grammar of "punish," see A. M. Quinton, "On Punishment," *Analysis* XIV (1954), 133–42; and K. Baier, "Is Punishment Retributive?" *Analysis* XVI (1955) 25–32.

valid convictions about what is right. The worst that can be said is that utilitarian theory does not in a clear-cut way definitely require us to espouse some practices we are inclined to espouse. But to this the utilitarian may make tow replies. First, that there is reason to think our ordinary convictions about punishment for crime ought to be thoroughly reexamined in important respects. We shall briefly examine later some proposals currently receiving the strong support of criminologists. Second, the utilitarian may reply that if we consider our convictions about the punishments we should administer *as a parent*—and this is the point where our moral opinions are least likely to be affected by the sheer weight of tradition—we shall find that we regard their punishment of their children as justified only in view of the future good of the child, and in order to make life in the home tolerable and in order to distribute jobs and sacrifices equally.

II. Retributivism

Immanuel Kant

Justice and Punishment[*]

What we call good must be, in the judgment of every reasonable man, an object of the faculty of desire, and the evil must be, in everyone's eyes, an object of aversion. Thus, in addition to sense, this judgment requires reason. So it is with truthfulness as opposed to a lie, with L. W. Beck (New York: Liberal Arts Press, 1956), part 1, bk. 1, from ch. 2, "justice in contrast to violence," etc. But we can call something an ill, however, which everyone at the same time must acknowledge as good, either directly or indirectly.

Whoever submits to a surgical operation feels it without doubt as an ill, but by reason he and everyone else will describe it as good. When, however, someone who delights in annoying and vexing peace-loving folk receives at last a right good beating, it is certainly an ill, but everyone approves of it and considers it as a good in itself even if nothing further results from it; nay, even he who gets the beating must acknowledge, in his reason, that justice has been done to him, because he sees the proportion between welfare and well-doing, which reason inevitable holds before him, here put into practice.

---

[*]Immanuel Kant, *Critique of Practical Reason*, trans. and ed. with an intro.

Immanuel Kant

Justice and Punishment** (continued)

E. The Right of Punishing and of Pardoning

I: THE RIGHT OF PUNISHING

The right of administering punishment, is the right of the sovereign as the supreme power to inflict pain upon a subject on account of a crime committed by him. The head of the state cannot therefore be punished; but his supremacy may be withdrawn from him. Any transgression of the public law which makes him who commits it incapable of being a citizen, constitutes a crime, either simply as a private crime (*crimen*), or also as a public crime (*crimen publicum*). Private crimes are dealt with by a civil court; public crimes by a criminal court. —Embezzlement or peculation of money or goods entrusted in trade, fraud in purchase or sale, if done before the eyes of the party who suffers, are private crimes. On the other hand, coining false money or forging bills in exchange of theft, robbery, etc., are public crimes, because the commonwealth, and not merely some particular individual, is endangered thereby. Such crimes may be divided into those of *base* character (*indolis abjectae*) and those of violent character (*indolies violentiae*).

Judicial or juridical punishment (*poena forensis*) is to be distinguished from natural punishment (*poena naturalis*), in which crime as vice punishes itself, and does not as such come within the cognizance of the legislator. Juridical punishment can never be administered merely as a means for promoting another good, either with

---

**Immanuel Kant, *The Philosophy of Law*, Part II, translated by W. Hastie, (Edinburgh: T. T. Clark, 1887), 194–98.

regard to the criminal himself or to civil society, but must in all cases be imposed only because the individual on whom it is inflicted has committed a crime. For one man ought never to be dealt with merely as a means subservient to the purpose of another, nor be mixed up with the subjects of real right. Against such treatment his inborn personality has a right to protect him, even although he may be condemned to lose his civil personality. He must first be found guilty and punishable, before there can be any thought of drawing from his punishment any benefit for himself or his fellow-citizens. The penal law is a categorical imperative; and woe to him who creeps through the serpent-windings of utilitarianism to discover some advantage that may discharge him from the justice of punishment, or even from the due measure of it, according to the pharisaic maxim: "It is better that one man should die than that the whole people should perish." For if justice and righteousness perish, human life would no longer have any value in the world. — What, then, is to be said of such a proposal as to keep a criminal alive who has been condemned to death, on his being given to understand that if he agreed to certain dangerous experiments being performed upon him, he would be allowed to survive if he came happily through them? It is argued that physicians might thus obtain new information that would be of value to the commonweal. But a court of justice would repudiate with scorn any proposal of this kind if made to it by the medical faculty; for justice would cease to be justice, if it were bartered away for any consideration whatever.

But what is the mode and measure of punishment which public justice takes as its principle and standard? It is just the principle of equality, by which the pointer of the scale of justice is made to incline no more to the one side than the other. It may be rendered by saying that the undeserved evil which any one commits on another, is to be regarded as perpetrated on himself. Hence it may be said: "If you slander another, you slander yourself; if you steal from another, you steal from yourself; if you strike another, you strike yourself; if you kill another, you kill yourself." This is the right of retaliation (*Jus talionis*); and properly understood, it is the only principle which in regulating a public court, as distinguished from mere private judgment, can definitely assign both the quality and the quantity of a just penalty. All other standards are wavering and uncertain; and on account of other considerations involved in them, they contain no principle conformable to the sentence of pure and strict justice. It may appear, however, that difference of social status would not admit the application of the principle of retaliation, which is that of "like with like." But although the application may not in all cases be possible according to the letter, yet as regards the effect it may always be attained in practice, by due regard being given to the disposition and sentiment of the parties in the higher social sphere. Thus a pecuniary penalty on account of a verbal injury, may have no direct proportion to the injustice of slander; for one who is wealthy may be able to indulge himself in this offence for his own gratification. Yet the attack committed on the honour of the party aggrieved may have its equivalent in the pain inflicted upon the pride of the aggressor, especially if he is condemned by the judgment of the court, not only to retract and apologize, but to submit to some meaner ordeal, as kissing the hand of the injured person. In like manner, if a man of the highest rank has violently assaulted an innocent citizen of the lower orders, he may be condemned not only to apologize but to undergo a solitary and painful imprisonment, whereby, in addition to the discomfort endured, the vanity of the offender would be painfully affected, and the very shame of his position would constitute an adequate retaliation after the principle of like with like. But how then would we render the statement: "If you steal from another, you steal from yourself"? In this way, that whoever steals anything makes the property of all insecure; he therefore robs himself of all security in property, according to the right of retaliation. Such a one has nothing, and can acquire nothing, but he has the will to live; and this is only possible by others supporting him. But as the state should not do this gratuitously, he must for this purpose yield his powers to the state to be used in penal labour; and thus he falls for a time, or it may be for life, into a condition of slavery. — But whoever has committed murder, must die. There is, in this case, no juridical substitute or surrogate that can be given or taken for the satisfaction of justice. There is no likeness or proportion between life, however painful, and death; and therefore there is no equality between the crime of murder and the retaliation of it but what is judicially accomplished by the execution of the criminal. His death, however, must be kept free from all maltreatment that would make the humanity suffering in his person loathsome or abominable. Even if a civil society resolved to dissolve itself with the consent of all its members—as might be supposed in the case of a people inhabiting an island resolving to separate and scatter themselves throughout the whole world—the last murderer lying in the prison ought to be executed before the resolution was carried out. This ought to be done in order that every one may realize the desert of his deeds, and that blood guiltiness may not remain upon the people; for otherwise they might all be regarded as participators in the murder as a public violation of justice.

The equalization of punishment with crime, is therefore only possible by the cognition of the judge extending even to the penalty of death, according to the right of retaliation . . .

G. W. F. Hegel

Punishment as a Right*

The injury [the penalty] which falls on the criminal is not merely *implicitly* just—as just, it is *eo ipso* his implicit will, an embodiment of his freedom, his right; on the contrary, it is also a right *established* within the criminal himself, i.e., in his objectively embodied will, in his action. The reason for this is that his action is the action of a rational being and implies that it is something universal and that by doing it the criminal has laid down a law which he has explicitly recognized in his action and under which in consequence he should be brought as under his right.

As is well known, Beccaria denied to the state the right of inflicting capital punishment. His reason was that it could not be presumed that the readiness of individuals to allow themselves to be executed was included in the social contract, and that in fact the contrary would have to be assumed. But the state is not a contract at all nor is its fundamental essence the unconditional protection and guarantee of the life and property of members of the public as individuals. On the contrary, it is that higher entity which even lays claim to this very life and property and demands its sacrifice. Further, what is involved in the action of the criminal is not only the concept of crime, the rational aspect which the state has to vindicate, but also the abstract rationality of the individual's *volition*. Since that is so, punishment is regarded as containing the criminal's right and hence by being punished he is honoured as a rational being. He does not receive this due of honour unless the concept and measure of his punishment are derived from his own act. Still less does he receive it if he is treated either as a harmful animal who has to be made harmless, or with a view to deterring and reforming him.

---

*G. W. F. Hegel, *The Philosophy of Right*, trans. T. M. Knox (London: Oxford University Press, 1969), sec. 100.

Moreover, apart from these considerations, the form in which the righting of wrong exists in the state, namely punishment, is not only form, nor is the state a precondition of the principle of righting wrong. [A.]

F. H. Bradley

The Vulgar Notion of Responsibility*

If there is any opinion to which the man of uncultivated morals is attached, it is the belief in the necessary connexion of punishment and guilt. Punishment is punishment, only where it is deserved. We pay the penalty, because we owe it, and for no other reason; and if punishment is inflicted for any other reason whatever than because it is merited by wrong, it is a gross immorality, a crying injustice, an abominable crime, and not what it pretends to be. We may have regard for whatever considerations we please—our own convenience, the good of society, the benefit of the offender; we are fools, and worse, if we fail to do so. Having once the right to punish, we may modify the punishment according to the useful and the pleasant; but these are external to the matter, they cannot give us a right to punish, and nothing can do that but criminal desert. This is not a subject to waste words over: if the fact of the vulgar view is not palpable to the reader, we have no hope, and no wish, to make it so.

I am not to be punished, on the ordinary view, unless I deserve it. Why then (let us repeat) on this view do I merit punishment? It is because I have been guilty. I have done "wrong." I have taken into my will, made a part of myself, have realized my being in something which is the negation of "right," the assertion of not-right. Wrong can be imputed to me. I *am* the realization and the standing assertion of wrong. Now the plain man may not know what he means by "wrong," but he is sure that, whatever it is, it "ought" not to exist, that it calls and cries for obliteration; that, if he can remove it, it is his business to do so; that, if he does not remove it, it rests also upon him, and that the destruction of guilt, whatever be the consequences, and even if there be no consequences at all, is still a good in itself; and this, not

---

*F. H. Bradley, *Ethical Studies*, 2nd ed. (London: Oxford University Press, 1927), 26–29.

because a mere negation is a good, but because the denial of wrong is the assertion of right (whatever "right" means); and the assertion of right is an end in itself.

Punishment is the denial of wrong by the assertion of right, and the wrong exists in the self, or will, of the criminal; his self is a wrongful self, and is realized in his person and possessions; he has asserted them in his wrongful will, the incarnate denial of right; and in denying that assertion, and annihilating, whether wholly or partially, that incarnation by fine, or imprisonment, or even by death, we annihilate the wrong and manifest the right; and since this, as we saw, was an end in itself, so punishment is also an end in itself.

Yes, in despite of sophistry, and in the face of sentimentalism, with well-nigh the whole body of our self-styled enlightenment against them, our people believe to this day that *punishment is inflicted for the sake of punishment*; though they know no more than our philosophers themselves do, that there stand on the side of the unthinking people the two best-known names of modern philosophy.

But, even were we able, it is not our task here to expound to the reader, what this, or again what the other metaphysician understands by punishment. The above is no more than the theoretical expression of the popular view, viz. that punishment is justice; that justice implies the giving what is due; that suppression of its existence, in one form or other, is due to guilt, and so to the guilty person; and that against his will, to give or take from a man what is not due, is, on the other hand, injustice.

G. E. Moore

An Organic Unity*

There remains one point which must not be omitted in a complete description of the kind of questions which Ethics has to answer. The main division of these questions is, as I have said, into two; the question what things are good in themselves, and the question to what other things these are related as effects. The first of these, which is the primary ethical question and is presupposed by the other, includes a correct comparison of the various things which have intrinsic value (if there are many such) in respect of the degree of value which they have; and such comparison involves a difficulty of principle which has greatly aided the confusion of intrinsic value with mere "goodness as a means." It has been pointed out that one difference between a judgment which asserts that a thing is good in itself, and a judgment which asserts that it is a means to good, consists in the fact that the first, if true of one instance of the thing in question, is necessarily true of all; whereas a thing which has good effects under some circumstances may have bad ones under others. Now it is certainly true that all judgments of intrinsic value are in this sense universal; but the principle which I have now to enunciate may easily make it appear as if they were not so but resembled the judgment of means in being merely general. There is, as will presently be maintained, a vast number of different things, each of which has intrinsic value; there are also very many which are positively bad; and there is a still larger class of things, which appear to be indifferent. But a thing belonging to any of these three classes may occur as part of a whole, which includes among its other parts other things belonging both to the same and to the other two classes; and these wholes, as such, may also have intrinsic value. The paradox, to which it is necessary

---

*G. E. Moore, *Principia Ethica* (Cambridge: Cambridge University Press, 1903), ch. 1, sec. 18, 19; ch. 6, sec 128, 130.

to call attention, is that *the value of such a whole bears no regular proportion to the sum of the values of its parts.* It is certain that a good thing may exist in such a relation to another good thing that the value of the whole thus formed is immensely greater than the sum of the values of the two good things. It is certain that a whole formed of a good thing and an indifferent thing may have immensely greater value than that good thing itself possesses. It is certain that two bad things or a bad thing and an indifferent thing may form a whole much worse than the sum of badness of its parts. And it seems as if indifferent things may also be the sole constituents of a whole which has great value, either positive or negative. Whether the addition of a bad thing to a good whole may increase the positive value of the whole, or the addition of a bad thing to a bad may produce a whole having a positive value, may seem more doubtful; but it is, at least, possible, and this possibility must be taken into account in our ethical investigations. However we may decide particular questions, the principle is clear. *The value of a whole must not be assumed to be the same as the sum of the values of its parts.*

A single instance will suffice to illustrate the kind of relation in question. It seems to be true that to be conscious of a beautiful object is of great intrinsic value; whereas the same object, if no one be conscious of it, has certainly comparatively little value, and it is commonly held to have none at all. But the consciousness of a beautiful object is certainly a whole of some sort in which we can distinguish as parts the object on the one hand and the being conscious on the other. Now this latter factor occurs as part of a different whole, whenever we are conscious of anything; and it would seem that some of these wholes have at all events very little value, and may even be indifferent or positively bad. Yet we cannot always attribute the slightness of their value to any positive demerit in the object which differentiates them from the consciousness of beauty; the object itself may approach as near as possible to absolute neutrality. Since, therefore, mere consciousness does not always confer great value upon the whole of which it forms a part, we cannot attribute the great superiority of the consciousness of a beautiful thing over the beautiful thing itself to the mere addition of the value of consciousness to that of the beautiful thing. Whatever the intrinsic value of consciousness may be, it does not give to the whole of which it forms a part a value proportional to the sum of its value and that of its object. If this be so, we have here an instance of a whole possessing a different intrinsic value from the sum of that of its parts; and whether it be so or not, what is meant by such a difference is illustrated by this case.

There are, then, wholes which possess the property that their value is different from the sum of the values of their parts, and the relations which subsist between such parts and the whole of which they form a part have not hitherto been distinctly recognised or received a separate name. Two points are especially worthy of notice. (1) It is plain that the existence of any such part is a necessary condition for the existence of that good which is constituted by the whole. And exactly the same language will also express the relation between a means and the good thing which is its effect. But yet there is a most important difference between the two cases, constituted by the fact that the part is, whereas the means is not, a part of the good thing for the existence of which its existence is a necessary condition. The necessity by which, if the good in question is to exist, the means to it must exist is merely a natural or causal necessity. If the laws of nature were different, exactly the same good might exist, although what is now a necessary condition of its existence did not exist. The existence of the means has no intrinsic value; and its utter annihilation would leave the value of that which it is now necessary to secure entirely unchanged. But in the case of a part of such a whole as we are now considering, it is otherwise. In this case the good in question cannot conceivably exist, unless the part exist also. The necessity which connects the two is quite independent of natural law. What is asserted to have intrinsic value is the existence of the whole; and the existence of the whole includes the existence of its part. Suppose the part removed, and what remains is *not* what was asserted to have intrinsic value; but if we suppose a means removed, what remains is just what *was* asserted to have intrinsic value. And yet (2) the existence of the part may *itself* have no more intrinsic value than that of the means. It is this fact which constitutes the paradox of the relation which we are discussing. It has just been said that what has intrinsic value is the existence of the whole, and that this includes the existence of the part; and from this it would seem a natural inference that the existence of the part has intrinsic value. But the inference would be as false as if we were to conclude that, because the number of two stones was two, each of the stones was also two. The part of a valuable whole retains exactly the same value when it is, as when it is not, a part of that whole. If it had value under other circumstances, its value is not any greater, when it is part of a far more valuable whole; and if it had no value by itself, it has none still, however great be that of the whole of which it now forms a part. We are not then justified in asserting that one and the same thing is under some circumstances intrinsically good, and under others not so; as we are justified in asserting of a means that it sometimes does and sometimes does not produce good results. And yet we are justified in asserting that it is far more desirable that a certain thing should exist under some circumstances than under others; namely when other things will exist in such relations to it as to form a more valuable whole. *It* will not have more intrinsic value under those circumstances than under others; it will not necessarily even be a means to the existence of things having more intrinsic value; but it will, like a means, be a necessary condition for the existence of that which *has* greater intrinsic value, although, unlike a means, it will itself form a part of the more valuable existent. . . .

But, finally, it must be insisted that pleasure and pain are completely analogous in this: that we cannot assume either that the presence of pleasure always makes a state of things better *on the whole,* or that the presence of pain always makes it worse. This is the truth which is most liable to be overlooked with regard to them; and it is because this is true, that the common theory, that pleasure is the only good and pain the only evil, has its grossest consequences in misjudgments of value. Not only is the pleasantness of a state *not* in proportion to its intrinsic worth; it may even add positively to its vileness. We do not think the successful hatred of a villain the less vile and odious, because he takes the keenest delight in it; nor is there the least need, in logic, why we should think so, apart from an unintelligent prejudice in favour of pleasure. In fact it seems to be the case that wherever pleasure is added to an evil state of either of our first two classes, the whole thus formed is *always* worse than if no pleasure had been there. And similarly with regard to pain. If pain be added to an evil state of either of our first two classes, the whole thus formed is *always* better, *as a whole*, than if no pain had been there;

though here, if the pain be too intense, since that is a great evil, the state may not be better *on the whole*. It is in this way that the theory of vindictive punishment may be vindicated. The infliction of pain on a person whose state of mind is bad may, if the pain be not too intense, create a state of things that is better *on the whole* than if the evil state of mind had existed unpunished. Whether such a state of things can ever constitute a *positive* good, is another question. . . .

But what we have now to consider are cases of wholes, in which one or more parts have a great *negative* value—are great positive evils. And first of all, we may take the *strongest* cases, like that of retributive punishment, in which we have a whole, exclusively composed of two great positive evils—wickedness and pain. Can such a whole ever be positively good *on the whole*?

(1) I can see no reason to think that such wholes ever are positively good *on the whole*. But from the fact that they may, nevertheless, be less evils, than either of their parts taken singly, it follows that they have a characteristic which is most important for the correct decision of practical questions. It follows that, quite apart from *consequences* or any value which an evil may have as a mere means, it may, *supposing* one evil already exists, be worthwhile to create another, since, by the mere creation of this second, there may be constituted a whole less bad than if the original evil had been left to exist by itself. And similarly, with regard to all the wholes which I am about to consider, it must be remembered, that, even if they are not goods *on the whole*, yet, where an evil already exists, as in this world evils do exist, the existence of the other part of these wholes will constitute a thing desirable *for its own sake*—that is to say, not merely a means to future goods, but one of the *ends* which must be taken into account in estimating what that best possible state of things is, to which every right action must be a means.

Herbert Morris

Persons and Punishment*

. . . Let us first turn attention to the institutions in which punishment is involved. The institutions I describe will resemble those we ordinarily think of as institutions of punishment; they will have, however, additional features we associate with a system of just punishment.

Let us suppose that men are constituted roughly as they now are, with a rough equivalence in strength and abilities, a capacity to be injured by each other and to make judgments that such injury is undesirable, a limited strength of will, and a capacity to reason and to confirm conduct to rules. Applying to the conduct of these men are a group of rules, ones I shall label "primary," which closely resemble the core rules of our criminal law, rules that prohibit violence and deception and compliance with which provides benefits for all persons. These benefits consist in noninterference by others with what each person values, such matters as continuance of life and bodily security. The rules define a sphere for each person, then, which is immune from interference by others. Making possible this mutual benefit is the assumption by individuals of a burden. The burden consists in the exercise of selforestraint by individuals over inclinations that would, if satisfied, directly interfere or create a substantial risk of interference with other sin proscribed ways. If a person fails to exercise self-restraint even though he might have and gives in to such inclinations, he renounces a burden which others have voluntarily assumed and thus gains an advantage which others who have restrained themselves, do not possess. This system, then, is one in which the rules establish a mutuality of benefit and burden and in which the benefits of noninterference are conditional upon the assumption of burdens.

---

*Herbert Morris, "Persons and Punishment," *The Monist* 52:4 (La Salle, IL, 1968), 476–79. Reprinted by permission of the publisher and the author.

Connecting punishment with the violation of these primary rules, and making public the provision for punishment, is both reasonable and just. First, it is only reasonable that those who voluntarily comply with the rules be provided some assurance that they will not be assuming burdens which others are unprepared to assume. Their disposition to comply voluntarily will diminish as they learn that others are with impunity renouncing burdens they are assuming. Second, fairness dictates that a system in which benefits and burdens are equally distributed have a mechanism designed to prevent a maldistribution in the benefits and burdens. Thus, sanctions are attached to noncompliance with the primary rules so as to induce compliance with the primary rules among those who may be disinclined to obey. In this way the likelihood of an unfair distribution is diminished.

Third, it is just to punish those who have violated the rules and cause the unfair distribution of benefits and burdens. A person who violates the rules has something others have—the benefits of the system—but by renouncing what others have assumed, the burdens of self-restraint, he has acquired an unfair advantage. Matters are not even until this advantage is in some way erased. Another way of putting it is that he owes something to others, for he has something that does not rightfully belong to him. Justice—that is punishing such individuals—restores the equilibrium of benefits and burdens by taking from the individual what he owes, that is, exacting the debt. It is important to see that the equilibrium may be restored in another way. Forgiveness—with its legal analogue of a pardon—while not the righting of an unfair distribution by making one pay his debt is, nevertheless, a restoring of the equilibrium by forgiving the debt. Forgiveness may be viewed, at least in some types of cases, as a gift after the fact, erasing a debt, which had the gift been given before the fact, would not have created a debt. But the practice of pardoning has to proceed sensitively, for it may endanger in a way the practice of justice does not, the maintenance of an equilibrium of benefits and burdens. If all are indiscriminately pardoned less incentive is provided individuals to restrain their inclinations, thus increasing the incidence of persons taking what they do not deserve.

There are also in this system we are considering a variety of operative principles compliance with which provides some guarantee that the system of punishment does not itself promote an unfair distribution of benefits and burdens. For one thing, provision is made for a variety of defenses, each one of which can be said to have as its object diminishing the chances of forcibly depriving a person of benefits others have if that person has not derived an unfair advantage. A person has not derived an unfair advantage if he could not have restrained himself or if it is unreasonable to expect him to behave otherwise than he did. Sometimes they provide a defense if on a particular occasion a person lacked the capacity to conform his conduct to the rules. Thus, someone who in an epileptic seizure strikes another is excused. Punishment in these cases would be punishment of the innocent, punishment of those who do not voluntarily renounce a burden others have assumed. Punishment in such cases, then, would not equalize but rather cause an unfair distribution in benefits and burdens.

Along with principles providing defenses there are requirements that the rules be prospective and relatively clear so that persons have a fair opportunity to comply with the rules. There are, also, rules governing, among other matters, the burden of proof, who shall bear it and what it shall be, the prohibition on double jeopardy, and the privilege against self-incrimination. Justice requires conviction of the guilty, and requires their punishment, but in setting out to fulfill the demands of justice we may, of course, because we are not omniscient, cause injustice by convicting and punishing the innocent. The resolution arrived at in the system I ham describing consists in weighing as the greater evil the punishment of the innocent. The primary function of the system of rules was to provide individuals with a sphere of interest immune from interference. Given this goal, it is determined to be a greater evil for society to interfere unjustifiably with an individual by depriving him of good than for the society to fail to punish those that have unjustifiably interfered.

Finally, because the primary rules are designed to benefit all and because the punishments prescribed for their violation are publicized and the defenses respected, there is some plausibility in the exaggerated claim that in choosing to do an act violative of the rules an individual has chosen to be punished. This way of putting matters brings to our attention the extent to which, when the system is as I have described it, the criminal "has brought the punishment upon himself" in contrast to those cases where it would be misleading to say "he has brought it upon himself," cases, for example, where one does not know the rules or is punished in absence of fault. . . .

H. J. McCloskey

A Non-Utilitarian Approach to Punishment*

Although the view that punishment is to be justified on utilitarian grounds has obvious appeal, an examination of utilitarianism reveals that, consistently and accurately interpreted, it dictates unjust punishments which are unacceptable to the common moral consciousness. In this rule-utilitarianism is no more satisfactory than in act-utiliarianism. Although the production of the greatest good, or the greatest happiness, of the greatest number is obviously a relevant consideration when determining which punishments may properly be inflicted, the question as to which punishment is just is a distinct and more basic question and one which must be answered before we can determine which punishments are morally permissible. That a retributivist theory, which is a particular application of a general principle of justice, can account more satisfactorily for our notion of justice in punishment is a positive reason in its support.

I. Introduction

At first glance there are many obvious considerations which seem to suggest a utilitarian approach to punishment. Crime is an evil and what we want to do is not so much to cancel it out after it occurs as to prevent it. To punish crime when it occurs is, at best, an imperfect state of affairs. Further, punishment, invoking as it does evils such as floggings, imprisonment, and death, is something which does not commend itself to us without argument. An obvious way of attempting to justify such deliberately created evils would be in terms of their utility.

*H. J. McCloskey, "A Non-Utilitarian Approach to Punishment," *Inquiry* 8 (1965), pp. 239–55. Reprinted by permission of the author and the publisher. A reply to Dr. McCloskey is reprinted in this volume p. 68.

This is how crime and punishment impress on first sight. A society in which there was no crime and no punishment would be a much better society than one with crime and resulting punishments. And punishment, involving evils such as deliberately inflicted suffering and even death, and consequential evils such as the driving of some of its victims into despair and even insanity, etc., harming and even wrecking their subsequent lives, and often also the lives of their relatives and dependents, obviously needs justification. To argue that it is useful, that good results come from such punishment, is to offer a more plausible justification than many so-called retributive justifications. It is obviously more plausible to argue that punishment is justified if and because it is useful than to argue that punishment is justified because society has a right to express its indignation at the actions of the offender, or because punishment annuls and cancels out the crime, or because the criminal, being a human being, merits respect and hence has a right to his punishment, Such retributive type justifications have some point, but they are nonetheless implausible in a way that the utilitarian justification is not. Yet I shall be concerned to argue that the key to the morality of punishment is to be found in terms of a retributive theory, namely, the theory that evils should be distributed according to desert and that the vicious deserve to suffer. In so arguing, I shall be bringing together and adding to a number of arguments I have set out elsewhere.[1]

II. How Our Common Moral Consciousness Views Punishment

Is the punishment which commends itself to the moral consciousness always useful punishment? And is all punishment that is useful such that we should consider it to be morally just and permissible? Punishment which we commonly consider to be just is punishment which is deserved. To be deserved, punishment must be of an offender who is guilty of an offence in the morally relevant sense of "offence." For

---

1. "An Examination of Restricted Utilitarianism," *Philosophical Review*, Vol. LXVI, 4 (Oct., 1957); "The Complexity of the Concepts of Punishment," *Philosophy*, Vol. XXXVII, pp. 307–25 (Oct., 1962).

instance, the punishing of a man known to be innocent of any crime shocks our moral consciousness and is seen as a grave injustice. Similarly, punishment of a person not responsible for his behaviour, e.g., a lunatic, is evidently unjust and shocking. Punishment for what is not an offence in the morally significant sense of "offence" is equally unjust. To punish a man who has tried his hardest to secure a job during a period of acute and extensive unemployment for "having insufficient means of support," or to punish a person under a retroactive law is similarly unjust. So too, if the offence for which the person punished is one against a secret law which it was impossible for him to know of, the punishment is gravely unjust. Similarly, punishment of other innocent people—e.g., as scapegoats—to deter others, is unjust and morally wrong. So too is collective punishment—killing all the members of a village or family for the offences of one member. Whether such punishments successfully deter seems irrelavant [sic] to the question of their justice. Similarly, certain punishments of persons who are offenders in the morally relevant sense of "offenders" also impress us as gravely unjust. We now consider to have been gravely unjust the very severe punishments meted out to those punished by hanging or transportation and penal servitude for petty thefts in the 18th century. Comparable punishments, e.g., hanging for shoplifting from a food market, would be condemned today as equally unjust. It is conceivable that such unjust punishments may, in extreme circumstances, become permissible, but this would only be so if a grave evil has to be perpetrated to achieve a very considerable good.

In brief, our moral consciousness suggests that punishment, to be just, must be merited by the committing of an offence. It follows from this that punishment, to be justly administered, must involve care in determining whether the offending person is really a responsible agent. And it implies that the punishment must not be excessive. It must not exceed what is appropriate to the crime. We must always be able to say of the person punished that he deserved to be punished as he was punished. It is not enough to say that good results were achieved by punishing him. It is logically possible to say that the punishment was useful but undeserved, and deserved but not useful. It is not possible to say that the punishment was just although undeserved.

These features of ordinary moral thinking about just punishment appear to be features of which any defensible theory of punishment needs to take note. Punishment of innocent people—through collective punishments, scapegoat punishment, as a result of inefficient trial procedures, corrupt police methods, mistaken tests of responsibility, etc., or by using criteria of what constitute offences which allow to be offences, offences under secret and retroactive laws—is unjust punishment, as is punishment which is disproportionate with the crime. Thus the punishment which we consider, after critical reflection, to be just punishment, is punishment which fits a retributive theory. It is to be noted that it is just punishment, not morally permissible punishment, of which this is being claimed. Sometimes it is morally permissible and obligatory to override the dictates of justice. The retributive theory is a theory about justice in punishment and tells only part of the whole story about the morality of punishment. It points to a very important consideration in determining the morality of punishment—namely, its justice—and explains what punishments are just and why they are just.

Before proceeding further, some comment should be made concerning these allusions to "what our common moral consciousness regards as just or unjust." Utilitarians frequently wish to dismiss such appeals to our moral consciousness as amounting to an uncritical acceptance of our emotional responses. Obviously they are not that. Our uncritical moral consciousness gives answers which we do not accept as defensible after critical reflection, and it is the judgements which we accept after critical reflection which are being appealed to here. In any case, before the utilitarian starts questioning this approach, he would do well to make sure that he himself is secure from similar criticism. It might well be argued that his appeal to the principle of utility itself rests upon an uncritical emotional acceptance of what prima facie appears to be a high-minded moral principle but which, on critical examination, seems to involve grave moral evils. Thus the problem of method, and of justifying the use of this method, is one which the utilitarian shares with the nonutilitarian. It is not possible here to argue for the soundness of this mode of argument beyond noting that whether an intuitionist or non-cognitivist meta-ethic be true, this sort of appeal is what such meta-ethical theories suggest to be appropriate.

III. What Utilitarianism Appears to Entail in Respect of Punishment

Is all useful punishment just punishment, and is all just punishment useful? Here it is necessary first to dispose of what might not unfairly be described as "red herring." A lot of recent utilitarian writing is to the effect that punishment of the innocent is logically impossible, and hence that utilitarianism cannot be committed to punishment of the innocent. Their point is that the concept of punishment entails that the person being punished be an actual or supposed offender, for otherwise we do not call it punishment but injury, harm-infliction, social quarantining, etc. There are two good reasons for rejecting this argument as nothing but a red herring. Not all unjust punishment is punishment of the innocent. Much is punishment which is excessive. Thus even if punishment of the innocent were not logically possible, the problem of justice in punishment would remain in the form of showing that only punishments commensurate with the offence were useful. Secondly, the verbal point leaves the issue of substance untouched. The real quarrel between the retributionist and the utilitarian is whether a system of inflictions of suffering on people without reference to the gravity of their offences or ever to whether they have committed offences, is just and morally permissible. It is immaterial whether we call such deliberate inflictions of sufferings punishment, social surgery, social quarantining, etc. In any case, as I have elsewhere tried to show, the claim is evidently false. We the observers and the innocent victims of such punishment call it punishment, unjust punishment. In so referring to it there is no straining of language.

To consider now whether all useful punishment is just punishment. When the problem of utilitarianism in punishment is put in this way, the appeal of the utilitarian approach somewhat diminishes. It appears to be useful to do lots of things which are unjust and undesirable. Whilst it is no doubt true that harsh punishment isn't necessarily the most useful punishment, and that punishment of the guilty person is usually the most useful punishment, it is nonetheless easy to call to mind cases of punishment of innocent people, of mentally deranged people, of excessive punishment, etc., inflicted because it was believed to be useful. Furthermore, the person imposing such punishment seems not always to be mistaken. Similarly, punishment which is just may be less useful than rewards. With some criminals, it may be more useful to reward them. As Ross observes:

> A utilitarian theory, whether of the hedonistic or of the 'ideal' kind, if it justifies punishment at all, is bound to justify it solely on the ground of the effects it produces. . . . In principle, then, the punishment of a guilty person is treated by utilitarians as not different in kind from the imposition of inconvenience, say by quarantine regulations, on innocent individuals for the good at the community.[2]

What is shocking about this, and what most utilitarians now seek to avoid admitting to be an implication of utilitarianism, is the implication that grave injustices in the form of punishment of the innocent, of those not responsible for their acts, or harsh punishments of those guilty of trivial offences, are dictated by their theory. We may sometimes best deter others by punishing, by framing, an innocent man who is generally believed to be guilty, or by adopting rough and ready trial procedures, as is done by army courts martial in the heat of battle in respect of deserters, etc.; or we may severely punish a person not responsible for his actions, as so often happens with military punishments for cowardice, and in civil cases involving sex crimes where the legal definition of insanity may fail to cover the relevant cases of insanity. Sometimes we may deter others by imposing ruthless sentences for crimes which are widespread, as with car stealing and shoplifting in food markets. We may make people very thoughtful about their political commitments by having retroactive laws about their political affiliations, and we may, by secret laws, such as make to be major crimes what are believed simply to be antisocial practices and not crimes at all, usefully encourage a watchful, public-spirited behaviour. If the greatest good or the greatest happiness of the greatest number is the foundation of the morality and justice of punishment, there can be no guarantee that some such injustices

---

2. W. D. Ross, *The Right and the Good*, Oxford University Press, Oxford 1930, p. 56.

may not be dictated by it. Indeed, one would expect that it would depend on the details of the situation and on the general features of the society, which punishments and institutions of punishment were most useful. In most practical affairs affecting human welfare, e.g., forms of government, laws, social institutions, etc., what is useful is relative to the society and situation. It would therefore be surprising if this were not also the case with punishment. We should reasonably expect to find that different punishments and systems of punishment were useful for different occasions, times, communities, peoples, and be such that some useful punishments involved grave and shocking injustices. Whether this is in fact the case is an empirical matter which is best settled by social and historical research, for there is evidence available which bears on which of the various types of punishments and institutions work best in the sense of promoting the greatest good. Although this is not a question for which the philosopher qua philosopher is well equipped to deal, I shall nonetheless later briefly look at a number of considerations which are relevant to it, but only because the utilitarian usually bases his defence of utilitarianism on his alleged knowledge of empirical matters of fact, upon his claim to know that the particular punishments and that system of punishment which we regard as most just, are most conducive to the general good. J. Bentham, and in our own day, J. J. C. Smart, are among the relatively few utilitarians who are prepared—in the case of Smart, albeit reluctantly—to accept that utilitarian punishment may be unjust by conventional standards, but morally right nonetheless.

Against the utilitarian who seeks to argue that utilitarianism does not involve unjust punishment, there is a very simple argument, namely, that whether or not unjust punishments are in fact useful, it is logically possible that they will at some time become useful, in which case utilitarians are committed to them. Utilitarianism involves the conclusion that if it is useful to punish lunatics, mentally deranged people, innocent people framed as being guilty, etc., it is obligatory to do so. It would be merely a contingent fact, if it were a fact at all, that the punishment which works is that which we consider to be morally just. In principle, the utilitarian is committed to saying that we should ask "Is the punishment deserved?" The notion of desert does not arise for him. The only relevant issue is whether the punishment produces greater good.

IV. What Utilitarianism in Fact Entails in the Light of Empirical Considerations

What is the truth about the utility of the various types of punishments? As I have already suggested, it would be astonishing if, in the sphere of punishment, only those punishments and that institution of punishment we consider to be just, worked best. To look at particular examples.

In an article cited above, I argued that a utilitarian would be committed to unjust punishment, and used the example of a sheriff framing an innocent Negro in order to stop a series of lynchings which he knew would occur if the guilty person were not immediately found, or believed to have been found.[3] I suggested that if the sheriff were a utilitarian he would frame an innocent man to save the lives of others. Against this example, it is suggested that we cannot know with certainty what the consequences of framing the Negro would be, and that there may be other important consequences besides the prevention of lynchings. Utilitarians point to the importance of people having confidence in the impartiality and fairness of the legal system, a belief that lawful behavior pays, etc. However, as the example is set up, only the sheriff, the innocent victim and the guilty man and not the general public, would know there had been a frame-up. Further, even if a few others knew, this would not mean that everyone knew; and even if everyone came to know, surely, if utilitarianism is thought to be the true moral theory, the general body of citizens ought to be happier believing that their sheriff is promoting what is right rather than promoting nonutilitarian standards of justice. Since complex factors are involved, this example is not as decisive as is desirable. It can readily be modified so as to avoid many of these complications and hence become more decisive. Suppose a utilitarian were visiting an area in which there was racial strife, and that, during his visit, a Negro rapes a white woman, and that race riots occur as a result of the crime, white mobs, with the connivance of the police, bashing and killing Negroes, etc. Suppose too that our utilitarian is in the area of the crime when it is committed such that his testimony would

---

3. "An Examination of Restricted Utilitarianism," *op. cit.*, pp. 468–469 [reprinted above, pp. 120–21].

bring about the conviction of a particular Negro. If he knows that a quick arrest will stop the riots and lynchings, surely, as a utilitarian, he must conclude that he has a duty to bear false witness in order to bring about the punishment of an innocent person. In such a situation, he has, on utilitarian theory, an evident duty to bring about the punishment of an innocent man. What unpredictable consequences, etc., are present here other than of a kind that are present in every moral situation? Clearly, the utilitarian will not be corrupted by bearing false witness, for he will be doing what he believes to be his duty. It is relevant that it is rare for any of us to be in a situation in which we can usefully and tellingly bear false witness against others.

We may similarly give possible examples of useful punishments of other unjust kinds. Scapegoat punishment need not be and typically is not of a framed person. It may be useful. An occupying power which is experiencing trouble with the local population may find it useful to punish, by killing, some of the best loved citizen leaders, each time an act of rebellion occurs; but such punishments do not commend themselves to us as just and right. Similarly, collective punishment is often useful—consider its use in schools. There we consider it unjust but morally permissible because of its great utility. Collective punishments of the kind employed by the Nazis in Czechoslovakia—destroying a village and punishing its inhabitants for the acts of a few—are notorious as war crimes. Yet they appear to have been useful in the sense of achieving Nazi objectives. It may be objected that the Nazi sense of values was mistaken, that such punishment would not contribute towards realizing higher values and goods. But it is partly an accident of history that it was the Nazis who, in recent times, resorted to this method. If we had had to occupy a Nazi territory with inadequate troops, this might have been the only effective way of maintaining order. As with human affairs generally, it would depend on many factors, including the strength of our troops, the degree of hostility of the occupied people, their temper and likely reaction to this sort of collective punishment, etc. Punishment of relatives could also be useful. It would be an interesting social experiment in those modern democracies which are plagued by juvenile delinquency, for parents as well as the teenage delinquents to be punished. Such punishment would be unjust but it might well be useful. It would need a number of social experiments to see whether it is or is not useful.

It is not a matter we can settle by intuitive insight. If it did prove useful, it is probable people would come to think of such punishment of parents as punishment for the offence of being a parent of a delinquent! This would obscure the awareness of the injustice of such punishment, but it would nonetheless be unjust punishment.

Similarly with punishment for offences under secret and retroactive laws. Such laws, it is true, would be useful only if used sparingly and for very good reasons but it is not hard to imagine cases where the use of a retroactive law might be useful in the long as well as in the short run. That a plausible case could have been made out for introducing retroactive laws in postwar Germany on utilitarian grounds as well as on the other sorts of grounds indicated by legal theorists, suggests that such cases do occur. They may be the most useful means, they may, in the German case, even have been morally permissible means and the means of achieving greater total justice; but they are nonetheless means which in themselves are unjust. Retroactive laws are really a kind of secret law. Their injustice consists in this; and secret laws, like them, seem useful if used sparingly and with discretion. The Nazis certainly believed them to be very useful but again it will no doubt be said that this was because their system of values was mistaken. However, unless the system of values includes respect for considerations of justice, such secret laws are possibly useful instruments for promoting good.

In our own community we define "offence" in such a way, with various laws, that we condone unjust punishment because of its utility. The vagrancy law is a very useful law but what it declares to be an offence is hardly an offence in the morally relevant sense. And it is not difficult to imagine countries in which it would be useful to have a law making it an offence to arouse the suspicions of the government. Suppose there were a democratic revolution in Spain, or in Russia, which led to the perilous existence of a democratic government. Such a government might find that the only way in which it could safely continue in existence was by having such a law and similar laws involving unjust punishments. It would then have to consider which was morally more important—to avoid the unjust punishments which such a law involves, or to secure and make permanent a democratic form of government which achieved greater over-all injustice. That is, it would face conflicting claims of justice.

In an ignorant community it might well be useful to punish as responsible moral agents "criminals" who in fact were not responsible for their actions but who were generally believed to be responsible agents. The experts suggest that many sex offenders and others who commit the more shocking crimes, are of this type, but even in reasonably enlightened communities the general body of citizens do not always accept the judgments of the experts. Thus, in communities in which enlightened opinion generally prevails (and these are few) punishment of mentally deranged "criminals" would have little if any deterrent value, whereas in most communities some mentally deranged people may usefully be punished, and in ignorant, backward communities very useful results may come from punishing those not responsible for their actions. Similarly, very undesirable results may come from not punishing individuals generally believed to be fully responsible moral agents. Yet, clearly, the morality of punishing such people does not depend on the degree of the enlightenment of the community. Utilitarian theory suggests that it does, that such punishment is right and just in ignorant, prejudiced communities, unjust in enlightened communities. The utility of such punishment varies in this way, but not its justice. The tests of responsible action are very difficult to determine, although this need not worry the utilitarian who should use the test of utility in this area as elsewhere. However, to make my point, we need not consider borderline cases. The more atrocious and abominable the crime, the more pointless its brutality is, the more likely it is that the criminal was not responsible and the more likely that the general public will believe him to be fully responsible and deserving of the severest punishment.

Utilitarians often admit that particular punishments may be useful but unjust and argue that utilitarianism becomes more plausible and indeed, acceptable, if it is advanced as a theory about the test of rules and institutions. These utilitarians argue that we should not test particular punishments by reference to their consequences; rather, we should test the whole institution of punishment in this way, by reference to the consequences of the whole institution.

This seems an incredible concession; yet rule-utilitarianism enjoys widespread support and is perhaps the dominant version of utilitarianism. It is argued that particular utilitarian punishments may be unjust but that useful systems of punishment are those which are just systems in the judgment of our reflective moral consciousness. This modification of utilitarianism involves a strange concession. After all, if the test of right and wrong rules and institutions lies in their utility, it is surely fantastic to suggest that this test should be confined to rules and institutions, unless it is useful so to confine its application. Clearly, when we judge the utility of particular actions, we should take note of the effects on the institution or rule, but surely, it is individual acts and their consequences which ultimately matter for the utilitarian. There are therefore good reasons for believing that the half-hearted utilitarianism of rule-utilitarianism involves an indefensible compromise between act-utilitarianism and Ross's theory of a plurality of irreducible prima facie duties.

To consider now the implications of rule-utilitarianism. As with act-utilitarianism, it would be surprising if what was useful was also at all times just, and that what was the most useful institution of punishment was the same under all conditions and for all times. For example, what we in Australia regard as useful and just, fair trial procedures—and these are an important part of justice in punishment—for example, rules about the burden of proof, strict limitation of newspaper comment before and during the trial, selection of the jury, provision of legal aid for the needy, etc., differ from those found useful in dictatorships. Also, obviously a country emerging from the instability of a great revolution cannot afford to take risks with criminals and counterrevolutionaries which a stable, secure, well established community can afford to take. In Australia we can take the risk of allowing a few traitors to escape deserved punishment as a result of our careful procedures directed at ensuring that the innocent be not punished in error. During a war we may take fewer risks but at the expense of injustices. In an unstable community, immediately after a revolution, a more cavalier approach to justice is usually found to be the most useful approach. And there are differences within anyone community. What is useful for civil courts is not necessarily what is most useful for military courts, and the most useful "institution" for the whole community may be a mixture of different systems of justice and punishment. Thus not only particular punishments but also whole institutions of punishment may be useful but of a kind we consider to be gravely unjust. It is these difficulties of utilitarianism—of act- and rule-utilitarianism—and the facts which give rise to these difficulties which give to the retributive theory, that the vicious deserve to suffer, its initial plausibility.

V. Positive Considerations for a Retributive Theory of Punishment

There are many positive considerations in support of the retributive theory of punishment, if it is constructed as the theory that the vicious deserve to suffer. Firstly, it is a particular application of a general principle of justice, namely, that equals should be treated equally and unequals unequally. This is a principle which has won very general acceptance as a self-evident principle of justice. It is the principle from which the more celebrated, yet opposed accounts of justice, are derived. It is a principle which has wide application and which underlies our judgments of justice in the various areas. We think of it as applying—other things being equal—to fair prices, wages, and treatment generally. It is in terms of such a principle that we think that political discrimination against women and peoples of special races is unjust, and that against children, just. Justice in these areas involves treating equals equally, unequals unequally—where the equals are equal in the relevant respect, and the unequals unequal in the relevant respect. Hence it is that we think it just to deny women some jobs because of their weaker physique, but unjust to exclude a woman from a post such as librarian or violinist if she is more proficient as such than other candidates for the post. So too with justice and punishment. The criminal is one who has made himself unequal in the relevant sense. Hence he merits unequal treatment. In this case, unequal treatment amounts to deliberate infliction of evils—suffering or death.

We need now to consider whether our retributive theory implies that there is a duty to punish with full, deserved punishment. Look at the other areas of justice, for example, wage justice. If it is just, say, to pay a labourer £20 a week, there is no breach of justice if the employer shows benevolence and pays £25, whereas there is a grave breach if he pays only £15. Similarly with retributive justice, but in a reverse way. We do not act unjustly if, moved by benevolence, we impose less than is demanded by justice, but there is a grave injustice if the deserved punishment is exceeded. If the deserved punishment is inflicted, all we need to do to justify it is to point out that the crime committed deserved and merited such punishment. Suppose that the just punishment for murder is imprisonment for 15 years. Suppose also that the judge knows that the murderer he is about to sentence will never be tempted to commit another murder, that he is deeply and genuinely remorseful, and that others will not be encouraged to commit murders if he is treated leniently. If the judge imposed a mild penalty we should probably applaud his humanity, but if he imposed the maximum penalty we should not be entitled to condemn him as unjust. What we say in cases like this is that the judge is a hard, even harsh, man, not that he is an unjust man.

Is only deserved punishment morally permissible? Obviously not. Here we might take an analogy with other parts of morality. It is wrong to lie, to break promises, or to steal. This is not to say that we are never obliged to lie, break promises, steal, etc. What it means is that we need to have another, conflicting, more stringent duty which overrides the duty to tell the truth, keep our promise, or not steal, if we are to be justified in lying, breaking our promise, or stealing. Similarly with justice in punishment. The fact that a punishment is just entitles the appropriate authority to inflict it, but that is not to say that it must be inflicted nor that more cannot properly be inflicted. Many considerations may weigh with the relevant authority and make it morally right to inflict more or less than is strictly just; and not all such considerations will be utilitarian considerations—some may be other considerations of justice. We determine what punishment ought to be inflicted by taking into account firstly what punishment is deserved, and then other considerations. Relevant here are considerations such as that the criminal's wife and children may be the real victims of the punishment, that the criminal would be unable to make restitution to the person whose property he has stolen; of benevolence, e.g., in not imposing the punishment because the criminal has already suffered greatly in blinding himself in attempting to blow a safe; of the general good, as in making an example of the criminal and inflicting more than the deserved punishment because of the grave consequences that will come about if this type of crime is not immediately checked, etc. Production of the greatest good is obviously a relevant consideration when determining which punishment may properly be inflicted, but the question as to which punishment is just is a much more basic and important consideration. When considering that question we need to determine whether the person to be punished committed an offence in the morally relevant sense of "offence" and what punishment is commensurate with the offence.

It is important here to note and dismiss a commonly made criticism of this retributive theory, namely, that there is no objective test of the gravity of a crime except in terms of the penalty attached to the crime. If the penalty is hanging, then, it is argued, the crime is a serious one; if the penalty is a £2 fine, it is a trivial offence. This criticism is often reinforced by the contention that if all the people in any given group were to make out lists of crimes in order of their gravity, they would give significantly different lists such that what appear as grave crimes on one list are minor crimes on other lists. Obviously, if this criticism were sound, it would mean that one very important element of the retributive theory would be nullified, for punishment could not be other than commensurate with the offence. However, this criticism is unsound and rests on a number of confusions.

It is true that we speak of a crime as serious if the penalty is hanging, but this is not to say that it is therefore a grave crime in the morally significant sense of "grave crime." The fact that hanging was the penalty for stealing a loaf of bread made that a serious offence in one sense but not in another, for we speak of the punishment as gravely disproportionate and as treating the offence as much more serious than it really is. It is on this basis that we can and do speak of penalties as being too light or too heavy, even where similar offences have similar penalties. It is unjust that the theft of a loaf of bread should meet with the same punishment as murder. Further, the fact that we reach different conclusions about the relative gravity of different crimes constitutes no difficulty for the retributive theory. Most of us would agree that murder is a very serious crime and that shoplifting a cake of soap is a considerably lesser offence. We should perhaps differ about such questions as to whether kidnapping is more or less serious than blackmail, whether embezzlement should be treated as a lesser crime than housebreaking, whether stealing a car worth £2,000 is less serious than stealing £2,000 worth of jewelry. We do disagree, and most of us would have doubts about the right order of the gravity of crimes. This shows very little. We have the same doubts—and disagreements—in other areas of morality where we are uncertain about which duties are more stringent, and where we differ from others in our ordering of duties. Similarly, utilitarians differ among themselves about goods such that if a group of utilitarians were asked to list goods in their order of goodness we could confidently expect different lists of different goods and of goods listed in different orders. But this would not show that utilitarianism is therefore a theory to be discounted. It shows simply that whatever theory of punishment is adopted, there will be disagreements and uncertainties as to precisely what it dictates. With the utilitarian theory, the uncertainty and doubts arise concerning the assessments of the value of the goods and the determination of which goods should be promoted by punishment. With the retributive theory the difficulties arise in determining the relative gravity of offences; and there, clearly, the appropriate method of seeking to resolve our doubts is neither to look at what punishments arc in fact imposed, nor at what punishments will produce the greatest good, but rather to look at the nature of the offence itself.

III. Teleological Retributivism

St. Thomas Aquinas

Whether Vengeance is Lawful*

Vengeance consists in the infliction of a penal evil on one who has sinned. Accordingly, in the matter of vengeance, we must consider the mind of the avenger. For if his intention is directed chiefly to the evil of the person on whom he takes vengeance and rests there, then his vengeance is altogether unlawful: because to take pleasure in another's evil belongs to hatred, which is contrary to the charity whereby we are bound to love all men. Nor is it an excuse that he intends the evil of one who has unjustly inflicted evil on him, as neither is a man excused for hating one that hates him: for a man may not sin against another just because the latter has already sinned against him, since this is to be overcome by evil, which was forbidden by the Apostle, who says (Rom. xii. 21): *Be not overcome by evil, but overcome evil by good.*

If, however, the avenger's intention be directed chiefly to some good, to be obtained by means of the punishment of the person who has sinned (for instance that the sinner may amend, or at least that he may be restrained and others be not disturbed, that justice may be upheld, and God honored), then vengeance may be lawful, provided other due circumstances be observed.

---

*St. Thomas Aquinas, *Summa Theologica* (New York: Benzinger, Inc., 1947), II, part 2–2, quest. 108, first article.

K. G. Armstrong

The Right to Punish*

But before we leave the question of penalty-fixing it is worth asking why it should be so often thought that Retributive theories in this area are necessarily barbarous. The charge springs from the misconception, which I mentioned before, that there is only one such theory—the *lex talionis*. In fact, all that a Retributive theory of penalty-fixing needs to say to deserve the name is that there should be a proportion between the severity of the crime and the severity of the punishment. It sets an upper limit to the punishment, suggests what is due. But the "repayment" (so to speak) need not be in kind; indeed in some cases it could not be. What would the *lex talionis* prescribe for a blind man who blinded someone else? Even in those cases where repayment in kind of violent crime is possible there is no reason why we should not substitute a more civilized equivalent punishment; the scale of equivalent punishments will, of course, vary from society to society. There is also no reason, having got some idea of the permissible limits of a man's punishment from Retributive considerations, why we should not be guided in our choice of the form of the penalty by Deterrent and Reformatory considerations. . . .

A vital point here is that justice gives the appropriate authority the right to punish offenders up to some limit, but one is not necessarily and invariably obliged to punish to the limit of justice. Similarly, if I lend a man money I have a right, in justice, to have it returned; but if I choose not to take it back I have not done anything unjust. I cannot claim more than is owed to me but I am free to claim less, or even to claim nothing. For a variety of reasons (amongst them the hope of reforming the criminal) the appropriate authority may choose to punish a man less than it is entitled to, but it is never just to punish a man more than he deserves.

---

*K. G. Armstrong, "The Retributivist Hits Back," *Mind* 70 (1961): 486–87. Reprinted by permission of the author and D. W. Hamlyn, the editor of *Mind*.

A. C. Ewing

On "Retributivism"*

It seems to me that Armstrong's defence[1] of the retributive theory can only be described as an evacuation. He reduces the theory to the negative conditions that a man should not be punished unless he is guilty and even if guilty should not be punished excessively out of proportion to the offence. These principles also seem evident to me, but I think that more can be said by way of explanation of them and it is far less clear that a utilitarian explanation is not available than he thinks. But I must first point out that his form of the retributive theory provides no positive reason for punishment at all but merely declares that there is an insuperable objection against punishment unless a certain condition (guilt) is satisfied to an extent proportionate to the punishment. It does not make it a duty in itself or even a prima facie duty to punish. It is still for him only a duty if it serves a utilitarian purpose. The theory is really only utilitarianism with one *vital* reservation supposed not to be justifiable on utilitarian grounds. Thus understood the "retributive theory" is no doubt not open to most of the criticism I and others have brought, which has force only against those who suppose it to be an end in itself that an offender should be made to suffer in proportion to his deserts. Incidentally, the retributive definition, "Punishment is the infliction of pain, by an appropriate authority, on a person because he is guilty of a crime" is ambiguous. If the "because" clause signifies the ultimate reason, then it implies that we ought to punish a man just because he has done wrong and not for the sake of consequences i.e., that the punishment of the guilty is an end in itself; if it is intended to be compatible with "because" not signifying an ultimate reason, it is compatible

---

*A. C. Ewing, "Armstrong on the Retributive Theory," *Mind* 72 (1963): 121–24. Reprinted by permission of the author and D.W. Hamlyn, the editor of *Mind*.

1. *Mind*, Oct. 1961, vol. LXX, p. 471 ff.

with utilitarianism. Armstrong holds that it gives a necessary condition but not any positive reason, I think, let alone a sufficient reason for punishment. Whether we call his theory retributive or not is a question of terminology, but it is certainly not what I and most others who have criticized the "retributive theory" have understood by it, and if so his use of the term seems liable to lead to dangerous confusions. But I agree with what he calls a "retributive definition" of punishment, provided this is not taken to imply that retribution is to be regarded as a positive ultimate reason for punishment. I further agree with him that you cannot reconcile utilitarianism with justice by merely saying that, if the man punished is innocent, it is not really punishment. If we heard an innocent man had been sentenced for the good of others, such an argument, as far as it goes, would enable us to say only—The judge has been incorrect in his terminology, he ought not to have called it a "punishment"—not that it is in any way worse than if a guilty man had been condemned with the same supposedly good consequences. I should, however, prefer not to define "punishment" as "the infliction of pain on a man . . . because he is guilty" but as "the infliction of pain because he is supposed guilty." Then we can properly speak of punishing the innocent.

But I think the utilitarian could do very much more than Armstrong admitted to explain why it is wrong to be unjust. He argues that on the deterrent theory cruel punishments would be justified as more effective deterrents and that we may deter others by punishing the innocent, and that on the reformatory theory it might be justifiable to punish people before they had committed any crime at all. But no utilitarian worth his salt would hold that we need not consider the indirect harm done by punishing the innocent or the sufferings of people who were punished excessively but should just concentrate on the deterrent and reformatory effects and ignore all other results. There are very obvious utilitarian reasons why we should avoid punishing people not guilty of definite offences defined by law or have recourse to a reign of terror. The miserable insecurity produced by such unjust punishment has been sufficiently exemplified in certain states in the last years as well as in earlier history. But, it may be said, this will only apply if such action is taken frequently; there may well be occasional cases where the punishment of the innocent is useful. But the utilitarian has still a possible reply. He may admit that there are cases where this is so but deny that any human authority could be trusted to decide which these cases are. It is all very well to say that the innocence of the man punished might be kept secret, but could the authorities ever be quite sure that they would succeed in doing this (unless at least they imposed an extreme dictatorship, which would be open to other objections)? And, if they recognised that they might punish the innocent sometimes, would not there be a great danger of their going too far in this practice? Against the tangible advantages that they saw or might think they saw have to be set a number of considerations which are very important and yet hardly susceptible of measurement—the psychological effects of being punished when one knew oneself innocent, the risk of discovery, the effects on the relatives of the person punished, the bad psychological effects on the punisher. As with most cases of adopting means generally condemned morally in order to produce good results, we should realize that besides any definitely foreseeable results there is reason to think that the unforeseeable results of such action will tend to be bad rather than good and these ought to be allowed for. I think this generalization is supported by the empirical evidence. But an authority which adopted the practice of making exceptions when it thought more good could be done by this would be liable to be biased in favour of the apparent concrete advantages as against these intangibles because they are easier to be reckoned with, and in any case it would be so hard to decide when the good consequences outweighed the bad, and such a power would be so liable to abuse that it might well be argued on purely utilitarian grounds that it would be best to take it as an absolutely unbreakable rule that the innocent ought never to be punished. For, although there probably are cases where it would do more good than harm to punish an innocent man, authorities who did not make it a general law never to punish the innocent, but allowed the making of exceptions on the ground of consequences, would be likely to do more harm by punishing innocent men when the consequences were really bad, although thought good, than authorities who stuck to the general law did by not punishing innocent people in the rare cases when the consequences would have been good.

Or is this going a little too far? Miss Anscombe expressed the greatest horror at the normal philosophers who suggested that it might ever be justifiable to condemn an innocent man to death even to avoid a war, but suppose the question were not whether he was to be put to death but whether he was to be given a month's imprisonment (or fined £20)? Suppose this were all that was needed to mollify a mad dictator who would otherwise declare war? If we admitted that in such a case it might be right to punish the innocent, that would be sufficient to make us give up the absoluteness of the principle and substitute "almost always" for "always." But this would only show that everybody had in certain cases to agree with the utilitarian.

As for excessive punishment inflicted on deterrent grounds, the pain caused may easily outweigh the evils of the crimes prevented and, in general, over-severe punishments have other detrimental effects besides the sheer suffering. They make people feel sympathy with the suffering offender rather than with the law, they make juries reluctant to convict, and they tend to the brutalization of society. Society may pay too great a price for the diminution of crimes.

The utilitarian may further urge that the reformatory function of punishment, at any rate, is essentially and not only incidentally connected with its justice. For how can punishment as such reform? Only by making a man realize more vividly the wrongness of what he has been doing. A punishment functions as a way of telling a man more emphatically than by mere words that he has done very wrong, and this has no reformatory point if the man has not done wrong. Offenders can, of course, be reformed by other means, e.g., psychological treatment while they are in prison, but, as McTaggart said, we must distinguish between reforming a man while he is being punished and reforming him by punishment. Certain psychological treatments may be unpleasant, but that does not make them punishments, and some may be undesirable because they violate the rights of individuals, but that does not make them unjust punishments. Deterrence is connected more loosely with justice and may occur without it (generally with disastrous effects), but even the deterrent force of punishment commonly depends a good deal on its being considered a disgrace because it implies that the man punished has acted very wrongly.

But I am not satisfied that the objection to unjust punishment lies simply in its effects. Suppose it could be strictly proved that, everything taken into account, the consequences of punishing a particular innocent man would be better than the consequences of acquitting him, I should not necessary think it right to punish him. This is not necessarily incompatible with utilitarianism ("ideal"), though it is with hedonism, because the utilitarian may include among things bad in themselves certain actions and attitudes of mind or will. The action and the attitude of mind inseparable from it might be intrinsically evil, although its effects in a particular instance were on the whole rather good than bad. Why should this be? It is not merely or mainly because it is a case of doing undeserved harm to a man. We must of course avoid harming people as far as possible, but there are many instances where laws harm the interests of some people for the sake of others. It is not unjust or terribly deplorable that the well-to-do have to pay extra taxes for the benefit of the poor, though, unless we say it is wrong to have plenty of money at all, this harm is not deserved by previous wrongdoing. It is not unjust to accept a man's offer to volunteer for a hopelessly dangerous but necessary job in war, though he has not thereby deserved death or the extreme risk of death. Thus what makes punishment of the innocent so wrong seems to be not mainly the fact that it is undeserved, but the pretence of guilt. This brings one back to Quinton's (and my) suggestion that the evil consists in a lying imputation of guilt, and this is certainly a very important, but I should not be prepared to say the only, factor. There is also the breach of faith involved in the violation of the tacit understanding that people will not be punished if they obey the laws. To inflict the worse kinds of harm on an innocent man against his will for the sake of others may be said grossly to violate a principle which perhaps must be taken as ultimate, i.e., the principle which Kant expressed by saying that a man ought never to be treated as a mere means, but it is not clear why this should not be the case even if the man is guilty. I do not know whether there are any other factors involved. Ross (who might have been mentioned, since Armstrong adopts a very similar view to his) also invokes the principle that it is good in itself that a man's happiness or unhappiness should be in proportion to his moral goodness or badness, but for the reasons I have given above I think we can maintain that the punishment of the innocent is intrinsically evil without accepting this (properly retributive) principle, of the truth of which I am very doubtful indeed. But I shall not discuss this matter, for I do not think Armstrong either accepts it as a reason for punishment.

D. Daiches Raphael

Justice*

. . . I agree with the utilitarian theory of punishment to the extent of thinking that where there is an obligation to punish, the obligation arises from utility. The strength of the so-called retributive (or, as I prefer to call it, the desert) theory of punishment lies, not in the justification of a positive obligation to punish the guilty, but in the protection of innocence. The utilitarian theory, taken alone, requires us to say, with Samuel Butler's Erewhonians, that sickness is a crime which deserves the punishment of medicine. It also requires us to say, when "it is expedient that one man should die for the people," that he deserves this as a punishment. It is here that common sense protests against the "injustice" of utilitarianism, and it is here that the "retributive" theory of punishment has greatest force. Punishment is permissible only if it is deserved. But this does not of itself give rise to an obligation to punish. An obligation to inflict punishment, where punishment is permitted by desert, arises from the social utility of its infliction. The desert permits this socially useful action to be taken although it means pain to the particular person concerned. Where there is no guilt, the infliction of pain on a particular person may still be socially useful, but the claim of social utility is opposed by the claim of the individual to be treated as an "end-in-himself" and not merely as a means to the ends of society. Where, however, a person is guilty of having willfully done wrong, he has thereby forfeited part of his claim to be treated as an end-in-himself in acting as a nonmoral being he leaves it open to his fellows to use him as such.[1] Such forfeit of his claim not to be pained does not of itself give rise to an obligation to pain him, for his ill-desert consists in the removal, not the

---

*D. Daiches Raphael, Moral Judgment (London: George Allen & Unwin Ltd., 1955): 70–73. Reprinted by permission of the author and Shaw Maclean, London.

1. Cf. W. G. Maclagan, "Punishment as Retribution," Philosophy, July, 1939, section v.

creation, of a claim with its corresponding obligation. The guilt does not constitute, or give rise to, a claim on the part of the guilty person to be punished i.e., an obligation on the part of others to punish him. It removes, to the degree to which he has infringed another's rights, his normal claim not to be pained; i.e., it removes, to that degree, the obligations of others not to pain him. Where there is a positive obligation to punish him, this is the obligation to the public at large to safeguard their security, and the corresponding claim is the claim of the public to have their security safeguarded.

This obligation to, or claim of, the public at large, exists of course at all times, and if the fulfilment of it involves pain for an innocent individual it still has its force. But the claim of the public in such circumstances conflicts with the claim of the individual not to be pained, to be treated as an end, and sometimes the one claim, sometimes the other, is thought to be paramount in the circumstances. If it should be thought necessary to override the claim of the individual for the sake of the claim of society, our decision is coloured by compunction, which we express by saying that the claim of justice has to give way to that of utility. Where the individual has been guilty of deliberate wrongdoing, however, this claim not to be pained is thought to be removed; there is held to be no conflict of claims now, no moral *obstat*[2] raised by justice to the fulfilment of the claim of utility. This thought is expressed by saying that the individual "deserves" his pain, and the pain is called "punishment," which is simply a way of saying that in this situation the infliction of pain, for the sake of social utility, involves no trespass on the claims of justice, no conflict between utility and justice. What is called "punishment" is not a different sort of *fact* from any other pain inflicted for utilitarian purposes; it receives a different *name* to express the thought that the pain is inflicted in circumstances where it commits no offence against justice. Justice is "satisfied" by the "punishment," for justice has not, in the circumstances of guilt, a countervailing claim that would have been breached by pursuing the path of utility.

---

2. There is always the weaker *obstat* of unfittingness in the infliction of pain. My point is that the *obstat* of a moral claim is not only greater in degree but also different in kind, and the difference of a kind is marked by the use of different language.

In giving this interpretation of the saying that "justice is satisfied by punishment," I do not imply that the statement has always had the meaning which I am now attributing to it (or rather, recommending for it). Clearly it used to have a more positive meaning. No doubt it originally referred to the satisfaction of the desire for vengeance. My point is that our present moral thinking recoils, as opponents of the retributive theory rightly insist, from justifying punishment by mere retaliation, but at the same time it does give an important place to justice in the idea of punishment. This role of justice, I am suggesting, is the protection of innocence, the raising of a moral *obstat* to the infliction of pain on an innocent individual. Where we think that, despite the moral *obstat* of justice, the pain must be inflicted for the sake of utility, we recognize the claim of justice at least to the extent of using different language. It may be *expedient*, but not just, that one man should die for the people. "Expediency" then has the a-moral or anti-moral connotation which it bears when "expediency" is contrasted with "principle." But where the victim of expediency is guilty, he has forfeited the claim of justice; now we may speak of his pain as "punishment," as "deserved." Expediency here does not conflict with "principle," i.e., with justice, but conforms to "principle." Not that the punishment is now *required* by justice. The "principle" that requires the "punishment" is the principle of safeguarding public security, i.e., expediency itself. Justice does not demand the punishment; justice stands aside, for it is satisfied that its claims raise no obstruction. It does demand *reparation*, where possible, for the person wronged, and thereby lays an obligation on the wrongdoer toward the person he has wronged. But it lays no obligation on others to *punish* the wrongdoer. It permits the punishment by withdrawing its protection against the claims of expediency. The obligation to punish comes from expediency.

Of course, expediency does not become "principle" only when justice stands aside. The claim of social utility is always a valid claim. It is the claim of the members of society in general not to be harmed. In denying earlier that there is a moral obligation to produce good as such, I was not denying the partial truth of hedonistic utilitarianism. There is an obligation to relieve and to prevent pain in others. When I say that the utility of punishment gives rise to an obligation, the obligation is to the members of society who will thereby be protected from harm. . . .

H. L. A. Hart

Principles of Punishment*

I. Introductory

The main object of this paper is to provide a framework for the discussion of the mounting perplexities which now surround the institution of criminal punishment, and to show that any morally tolerable account of this institution must exhibit it as a compromise between distinct and partly conflicting principles.

General interest in the topic of punishment has never been greater than it is at present and I doubt if the public discussion of it has ever been more confused. The interest and the confusion are both in part due to relatively modern scepticism about two elements which have figured as essential parts of the traditionally opposed "theories" of punishment. On the one hand, the old Benthamite confidence in fear of the penalties threatened by the law as a powerful deterrent, has waned with the growing realization that the part played by calculation of any sort in antisocial behaviour has been exaggerated. On the other hand a cloud of doubt has settled over the keystone of "retributive" theory. Its advocates can no longer speak with the old confidence that statements of the form "This man who has broken the law could have kept it" had a univocal or agreed meaning; or where scepticism does not attach to the *meaning* of this form of statement, it has shaken the confidence that we are generally able to distinguish the cases where a statement of this form is true from those where it is not.[1]

---

*H. L. A. Hart, "Prolegomenon to the Principles of Punishment," 1959 Inaugural Address to the Aristotelian Society, pub. In *Proc. Arist. Soc.* 60 (1959–60). Reprinted by courtesy of the Editor of the Aristotelian Society: © 1959.

1. See Barbara Wootton, *Social Science and Social Pathology* (1959), for a comprehensive modern statement of these doubts.

Yet quite apart from the uncertainty engendered by these fundamental doubts, which seem to call in question the accounts given of the efficacy, and the morality of punishment by all the old competing theories, the public utterances of those who conceive themselves to be expounding, as plain men for other plain men, orthodox or commonsense principles (untouched by modern psychological doubts) are uneasy. Their words often sound as if the authors had not fully grasped their meaning or did not intend the words to be taken quite literally. A glance at the parliamentary debates or the *Report of the Royal Commission on Capital Punishment*[2] shows that many are now troubled by the suspicion that the view that there is just one supreme value or objective (e.g., Deterrence, Retribution, or Reform) in terms of which *all* questions about the justification of punishment are to be answered, is somehow wrong; yet, from what is said on such occasions no clear account of what the different values or objectives are, or how they fit together in the justification of punishment, can be extracted.[3]

No one expects judges or statesmen occupied in the business of sending people to the gallows or prison, or in making (or unmaking) laws which enable this to be one, to have much time for philosophical discussion of the principles which make it morally tolerable to do these things. A judicial bench is not and should not be a professorial chair. Yet what is said in public debates about punishment by those especially concerned with it as judges or legislators is important. Few are likely to be more circumspect, and if what they say seems, as it often does, unclear, one-sided and easily refutable by pointing to some aspect of things of any punishment is not that it is a deterrent but that it is the emphatic denunciation by the community of

---

2. (1953) Cmd. 8932.

3. In the Lords' debate in July 1956 the Lord Chancellor agreed with Lord Denning that "the ultimate justification of any punishment is not that it is a deterrent but that it Is the emphatic denunciation by the community of a crime" yet also said that "the real crux" of the question at issue is whether capital punishment is a uniquely effective deterrent. See 198 *H. L. Deb* (5th July) 576, 577, 596 (1956). In his article, "An Approach to the Problems of Punishment," *Philosophy* (1958), Mr. S. I. Benn rightly observes of Lord Denning's view that denunciation does not imply the deliberate imposition of suffering which is the feature needing justification (p. 325, n.I).

a crime yet also said that "the real crux" of the question at issue is which they have overlooked, it is likely that in our inherited ways of talking or thinking about punishment there is some persistent drive towards an over-simplification of multiple issues which require separate consideration. To counter this drive what is most needed is *not* the simple admission that instead of a single value or aim (Deterrence, Retribution, Reform, or any other) a plurality of different values and aims should be given as a conjunctive answer to some *single* question concerning the justification of punishment. What is needed is the realization that different principles (each of which may in a sense be called a "justification") are relevant at different points in any morally acceptable account of punishment. What we should look for are answers to a number of different questions such as: What justifies the general practice of punishment? To whom may punishment be applied? How severely may we punish? In dealing with these and other questions concerning punishment we should bear in mind that in this, as in most other social institutions, the pursuit of one aim may be qualified by or provide an opportunity, not to be missed, for the pursuit of others. Till we have developed this sense of the complexity of punishment (and this prolegomenon aims only to do this) we shall be in no fit state to assess the extent to which the whole institution has been eroded by, or needs to be adapted to, new beliefs about the human mind.

II. Justifying Aims and Principles of Distribution

There is, I think, an analogy worth considering between the concept of punishment and that of property. In both cases we have to do with a social institution of which the centrally important form is a structure of *legal* rules, even if it would be dogmatic to deny the names of punishment or property to the similar though more rudimentary rule-regulated practices within groups such as a family, or a school, or in customary societies whose customs may lack some of the standard or salient features of law (e.g., legislation, organized sanctions, courts). In both cases we are confronted by a complex institution presenting different interrelated features calling for separate explanation; or, if the morality of the institution is challenged, for separate justification.

In both cases failure to distinguish separate questions or attempting to answer them all by reference to a single principle ends in confusion. Thus in the case of property we should distinguish between the question of the *definition* of property, the question why and in what circumstance it is a *good* institution to maintain, and the questions in what ways individuals may become *entitled* to acquire property and *how much* they should be allowed to acquire. These we may call questions of *Definition, General Justifying Aim,* and *Distribution* with the last subdivided into questions of *Title* and *Amount.* It is salutary to take some classical exposition of the idea of property, say Locke's chapter "Of Property" in the *Second Treatise,*[4] and to observe how much darkness is spread by the use of a single notion (in this case "the labour of [a man's] body and the work of his hands") to answer all these different questions which press upon us when we reflect on the institution of property. In the case of punishment the beginning of wisdom (though by no means its end) is to distinguish similar questions and confront them separately.

(A) DEFINITION

Here I shall simply draw upon the recent admirable work scattered through English philosophical[5] journals and add to it only an admonition of my own against the abuse of definition in the philosophical discussion of punishment. So with Mr. Benn and Professor Flew I shall define the standard or central case of "punishment" in terms of five elements:

(i)   It must involve pain or other consequences normally considered unpleasant.

(ii) It must be for an offence against legal rules.

(iii) It must be of an actual or supposed offender for his offence.

---

4. Chapter IV.

5. K. Baier, "Is Punishment Retributive?" *Analysis*, March 16, (1955):26. A. Flew, "The Justification of Punishment," *Philosophy* (1954): 291–307. S.I. Benn, *op. cit.*, pp. 325–26.

(iv)   It must be intentionally administered by human beings other than the offender.

(v)   It must be imposed and administered by an authority constituted by a legal system against which the offence is committed.

In calling this the standard or central case of punishment I shall relegate to the position of substandard or secondary cases the following among many other possibilities:

(a)   Punishments for breaches of legal rules imposed or administered otherwise than by officials (decentralised sanctions).

(b)   Punishments for breaches of nonlegal rules or orders (punishments in a family or school).

(c)   Vicarious or collective punishment of some member of a social group for actions done by others without the former's authorization, encouragement, control or permission.

(d)   Punishment of persons (otherwise than under (c)) who neither are in fact nor supposed to be offenders.

The chief importance of listing these substandard cases is to prevent the use of what I shall call the "definitional stop" in discussions of punishment. This is an abuse of definition especially tempting when use is made of conditions (ii) and (iii) of the standard case in arguing against the utilitarian claim that the practice of punishment is justified by the beneficial consequences resulting from the observance of the laws which it secures. Here the stock "retributive" argument[6] is: If *this* is the justification of punishment, why not apply it, when it pays to do so, to those innocent of any crime, chosen at random, or to the wife and children of the offender? And here the wrong reply is: *That*, by definition, would not be punishment' and it is the justification of

---

6. A. C. Ewing, *The Morality of Punishment,* D. J. B. Hawkins, *Punishment and Moral Responsibility* (The King's Good Servant, p. 92), J. D. Mabbott, "Punishment," *Mind* (1939): 153.

punishment which is in issue.[7] Not only will this definitional stop fail to satisfy the advocate of "Retribution," it would prevent us from investigating the very thing which modern scepticism most calls in question: namely the rational and moral status of our preference for a system of punishment under which measures painful to individuals are to be taken against them only when they have committed an offence. Why do we prefer this to other forms of social hygiene which we might employ to prevent antisocial behaviour and which we do employ in special circumstances, sometimes with reluctance? No account of punishment can afford to dismiss this question with a definition.

(B) THE NATURE OF AN OFFENCE

Before we reach any question of justification we must identify a preliminary question to which the answer is so simple that the question may not appear worth asking; yet it is clear that some curious "theories" of punishment gain their only plausibility from ignoring it, and others from confusing it with other questions. This question is: Why are certain kinds of action forbidden by law and so made crimes or offences? The answer is: To announce to society that these actions are not to be done and to secure that fewer of them are done. These are the common immediate aims of making any conduct a criminal offence and until we have laws made with these primary aims we shall lack the notion of a "crime" and so of a "criminal." Without recourse to the simple idea that the criminal law sets up, in its rules, standards of behaviour to encourage certain types of conduct and discourage others we cannot distinguish a punishment in the form of a fine from a tax on a course of conduct.[8] This indeed is one grave

---

7. Mr. Benn seemed to succumb at times to the temptation to give "The short answer to the critics of utilitarian theories of punishment—that they are theories of *punishment* not of any sort of technique involving suffering" (*op. cit.*, p. 322). He has since told me that he does not now rely on the definitional stop.

8. This generally clear distinction may be blurred. Taxes may be imposed to discourage the activities taxed though the law does not announce this as it does when it makes them criminal. Conversely fines payable for some criminal offences because of a depreciation of currency, became so small that they are cheerfully paid and offences are frequent. They are then felt to be mere taxes because the sense is lost that the rule is meant to be taken seriously as a standard of behaviour.

objection to those theories of law which in the interests of simplicity or uniformity obscure the distinction between primary laws setting standards for behaviour and secondary laws specifying what officials must or may do when they are broken. Such theories insist that all legal rules are "really" directions to officials to exact "sanctions" under certain conditions, e.g., if people kill.[9] Yet only if we keep alive the distinction (which such theories thus obscure) between the primary objective of the law in encouraging or discouraging certain kinds of behaviour, and its merely ancillary sanction or remedial steps, can we give sense to the notion of a crime or offence.

It is important however to stress the fact that in thus identifying the immediate aims of the criminal law we have not reached the stage of justification. There are indeed many forms of undesirable behaviour which it would be foolish (because ineffective or too costly) to attempt to inhibit by use of the law and some of these may be better left to educators, trades unions, churches, marriage guidance councils or other non-legal agencies. Conversely there are some forms of conduct which we believe cannot be effectively inhibited without use of the law. But it is only too plain that in fact the law may make activities criminal which it is morally important to promote and the suppression of these may be quite unjustifiable. Yet confusion between the simple immediate aim of any criminal legislation and the justification of punishment seems to be the most charitable explanation of the claim that punishment is *justified* as an "emphatic denunciation by the community of a crime." Lord Denning's dictum that this is the ultimate justification of punishment[10] can be saved from Mr. Benn's criticism, noted above, only if it is treated as a blurred statement of the truth that the aim not of punishment, but of criminal legislation is indeed to denounce certain types of conduct as something not to be practised. Conversely the immediate aim of criminal legislation cannot be any of the things which are usually mentioned as justifying punishment: for until it is settled what conduct is to be legally denounced and discouraged we have not settled from what we are

---

9. cf. Kelsen, *General Theory of Law and State* (1946), pp. 30–33, 33–34, 143–4. "Law is the primary norm, which stipulates the sanction . . ." (id. 61).

10. In evidence to the Royal Commission on Capital Punishment, Cmd. 8932. para. 53 (1953). *Supra*, p. 3, n. 2.

to *deter* people, or who are to be considered *criminals* from whom we are to exact *retribution*, or on whom we are to wreak *vengeance*, or whom we are to *reform*.

Even those who look upon human law as a mere instrument for enforcing "morality as such" (itself conceived as the law of God or Nature) and who at the stage of justifying punishment wish to appeal not to socially beneficial consequences but simply to the intrinsic value of inflicting suffering on wrongdoers who have disturbed by their offence the moral order, would not deny that the aim of criminal legislation is to set up types of behaviour (in this case conformity with a pre-existing moral law) as legal standards of behaviour and to secure conformity with them. No doubt in all communities certain moral offences, e.g., killing, will always be selected for suppression as crimes and it is conceivable that this may be done not to protect human beings from being killed but to save the potential murderer from sin; but it would be paradoxical to look upon the law as designed not to discourage murder at all (even conceived as sin rather than harm) but simply to extract the penalty from the murderer.

(C) GENERAL JUSTIFYING AIM

I shall not here criticize the intelligibility or consistency or adequacy of those theories that are united in denying that the practice of a system of punishment is justified by its beneficial consequences and claim instead that the main justification of the practice lies in the fact that when breach of the law involves moral guilt the application to the offender of the pain of punishment is itself a thing of value. A great variety of claims of this character, designating "Retribution" or "Expiation" or "Reprobation" as the justifying aim, fall in spite of differences under this rough general description. Though in fact I agree with Mr. Benn[11] in thinking that these all either avoid the question of justification altogether or are in spite of their protestations disguised forms of Utilitarianism, I shall assume that Retribution, defined simply as the application of the pains of punishment to an offender who is morally guilty, may figure among the conceivable justifying aims

---

11. *Op. cit.*, pp. 326–35.

of a system of punishment. Here I shall merely insist that it is one thing to use the word Retribution *at this point* in an account of the principle of punishment in order to designate the General Justifying Aim of the system, and quite another to use it to secure that to the question "To whom may punishment be applied?" (the question of Distribution), the answer given is "Only to an offender for an offence." Failure to distinguish Retribution as a General Justifying Aim from retribution as the simple insistence that only those who have broken the law—and voluntarily broken it—may be punished, may be traced in many writers: even perhaps in Mr. J. D. Mabbott's[12] otherwise most illuminating essay. We shall distinguish the latter from Retribution in General Aim as "retribution in Distribution." Much confusing shadow-fighting between utilitarians and their opponents may be avoided if it is recognized that it is perfectly consistent to assert *both* that the General Justifying Aim of the practice of punishment is its beneficial consequences *and* that the pursuit of this General Aim should be qualified or restricted out of deference to principles of Distribution which require that punishment should be only of an offender for an offence. Conversely it does not in the least follow from the admission of the latter principle of retribution in Distribution that the General Justifying Aim of punishment is Retribution though of course Retribution in General Aim entails retribution in Distribution.

We shall consider later the principles of justice lying at the root of retribution in Distribution. Meanwhile it is worth observing that both the old fashioned Retributionist (in General Aim) and the most modern sceptic often make the same (and, I think, wholly mistaken) assumption that sense can only be made of the restrictive principle that punishment be applied only to an offender for an offence if the General Justifying Aim of the practice of punishment is Retribution. The sceptic consequently imputes to all systems of punishment (when they are restricted by the principle of retribution in Distribution) all the irrationality he finds in the idea of Retribution as a General Justifying Aim; conversely the advocates of the latter think the admission of retribution in Distribution is a refutation of the utilitarian claim that the social consequences of punishment are its Justifying Aim.

---

12. *Op. cit. supra* p. 5, n. 6. It is not always quite clear what he considers a "retributive" theory to be.

The most general lesson to be learnt from this extends beyond the topic of punishment. It is, that in relation to any social institution, after stating what general aim or value its maintenance fosters we should enquire whether there are any and if so what principles limiting the unqualified pursuit of that aim or value. Just because the pursuit of any single social aim always has its restrictive qualifier, our main social institutions always possess a plurality of features which can only be understood as a compromise between partly discrepant principles. This is true even of relatively minor legal institutions like that of a contract. In general this is designed to enable individuals to give effect to their wishes to create structures of legal rights and duties, and so to change, in certain ways, their legal position. Yet at the same time there is need to protect those who, in good faith, understand a verbal offer made to them to mean what it would ordinarily mean, accept it, and then act on the footing that a valid contract has been concluded. As against them, it would be unfair to allow the other party to say that the words he used in his verbal offer or the interpretation put on them did not express his real wishes or intention. Hence principles of "estoppel" or doctrines of the "objective sense" of a contract are introduced to prevent this and to qualify the principle that the law enforces contracts in order to give effect to the joint wishes of the contracting parties.

(D) DISTRIBUTION

This as in the case of property has two aspects (i) Liability (Who may be punished?) and (ii) Amount. In this section I shall chiefly be concerned with the first of these.[13]

From the foregoing discussions two things emerge. First, though we may be clear as to what value the practice of punishment is to promote, we have still to answer as a question of Distribution "Who may be punished?" Secondly, if in answer to this question we say "only an offender for an offence" this admission of retribution in Distribution is not a principle from which anything follows as to the severity or

---

13. Amount is considered below in Section III (in connexion with Mitigation) and Section V.

amount of punishment; in particular it neither licenses nor requires, as Retribution in General Aim does, more severe punishments than deterrence or other utilitarian criteria would require.

The root question to be considered is, however, why we attach the moral importance which we do to retribution in Distribution. Here I shall consider the efforts made to show that restriction of punishment to offenders is a simple consequence of whatever principles (Retributive or Utilitarian) constitute the Justifying Aim of punishment.

The standard example used by philosophers to bring out the importance of retribution in Distribution is that of a wholly innocent person who has not even unintentionally done anything which the law punishes if done intentionally. It is supposed that in order to avert some social catastrophe officials of the system fabricate evidence on which he is charged, tried, convicted and sent to prison or death. Or it is supposed that without resort to any fraud more persons may be deterred from crime if wives and children of offenders were punished vicariously for their crimes. In some forms this kind of thing may be ruled out by a consistent sufficiently comprehensive utilitarianism.[14] Certainly expedients involving fraud or faked charges might be very difficult to justify on utilitarian grounds. We can of course imagine that a negro might be sent to prison or executed on a false charge of rape in order to avoid widespread lynching of many others; but a *system* which openly empowered authorities to do this kind of thing, even if it succeeded in averting specific evils like lynching, would awaken such apprehension and insecurity that any gain from the exercise of these powers would by any utilitarian calculation be offset by the misery caused by their existence. But official resort to this kind of fraud on a particular occasion in breach of the rules and the subsequent indemnification of the officials responsible might save many lives and so be thought to yield a clear surplus of value. Certainly vicarious punishment of an offender's family might do so and legal systems have occasionally though exceptionally resorted to this. An example of it is the Roman *Lex Quisquis* providing for the punishment of the children of those guilty of *majestas*.[15] In extreme

---

14. See J. Rawls, "Two Concepts of Rules," *Philosophical Review* (1955): 4–13.

15. Constitution of emperors Arcadius and Honorius (AD 397).

cases many might still think it right to resort to these expedients but we should do so with the sense of sacrificing an important principle. We should be conscious of choosing the lesser of two evils, and this would be inexplicable if the principle sacrificed to utility were itself only a requirement of utility.

Similarly the moral importance of the restriction of punishment to the offender cannot be explained as merely a consequence of the principle that the General Justifying Aim is Retribution for immorality involved in breaking the law. Retribution in the Distribution of punishment has a value quite independent of Retribution as Justifying Aim. This is shown by the fact that we attach importance to the restrictive principle that only offenders may be punished, even where breach of this law might not be thought immoral. Indeed even where the laws themselves are hideously immoral as in Nazi Germany, e.g., forbidding activities (helping the sick or destitute of some racial group) which might be thought morally obligatory, the absence of the principle restricting punishment to the offender would be a further *special* iniquity; whereas admission of this principle would represent some residual respect for justice shown in the administration of morally bad laws.

J. D. Mabbott

Punishment*

I propose in this paper to defend a retributive theory of punishment and to reject absolutely all utilitarian considerations from its justification. I feel sure that this enterprise must arouse deep suspicion and hostility both among philosophers (who must have felt that the retributive view is the only moral theory except perhaps psychological hedonism, which has been definitely destroyed by criticism) and among practical men (who have welcomed its steady decline in our penal practice).

The question I am asking is this. Under what circumstances is the punishment of some particular person justified and why? The theories of reform and deterrence which are usually considered to be the only alternatives to retribution involve well-known difficulties. These are considered fully and fairly in Dr. Ewing's book, *The Morality of Punishment,* and I need not spend long over them. The central difficulty is that both would on occasion justify the punishment of an innocent man, the deterrent theory if he were believed to have been guilty by those likely to commit the crime in future, and the reformatory theory if he were a bad man though not a criminal. To this may be added the point against the deterrent theory that it is the threat of punishment and not punishment itself which deters, and that when deterrence seems to depend on actual punishment, to implement the threat, it really depends on publication and may be achieved if men believe that punishment has occurred even if in fact it has not. As Bentham saw, for a Utilitarian apparent justice is everything, real justice is irrelevant.

Dr. Ewing and other moralists would be inclined to compromise with retribution in the face of the above difficulties. They would

---

*J. D. Mabbott, "Punishment," *Mind* 48 (1939): 150–67. Reprinted by permission of the author and D. W. Hamlyn, the editor of *Mind*.

admit that one fact and one fact only can justify the punishment of this man, and that is a past fact, that he has committed a crime. To this extent reform and deterrence theories, which look only to the consequences, are wrong. But they would add that retribution can determine only that a man should be punished. It cannot determine how or how much, and here reform and deterrence may come in. Even Bradley, the fiercest retributionist of modern times, says "Having once the right to punish we may modify the punishment according to the useful and the pleasant, but these are external to the matter; they cannot give us a right to punish and nothing can do that but criminal desert." Dr. Ewing would maintain that the whole estimate of the amount and nature of a punishment may be effected by considerations of reform and deterrence. It seems to me that this is a surrender which the upholders of retribution dare not make. As I said above, it is publicity and not punishment which deters, and the publicity though often spoken of as "part of a man's punishment" is no more part of it than his arrest or his detention prior to trial, though both these may be also unpleasant and bring him into disrepute. A judge sentences a man to three years' imprisonment not to three years plus three columns in the press. Similarly with reform. The visit of the prison chaplain is not part of a man's punishment nor is the visit of Miss Fields or Mickey Mouse.

The truth is that while punishing a man and punishing him justly, it is possible to deter others, and also to attempt to reform him, and if these additional goods are achieved the total state of affairs is better than it would be with the just punishment alone. But reform and deterrence are not modifications of the punishment, still less reasons for it. A parallel may be found in the case of tact and truth. If you have to tell a friend an unpleasant truth you may do all you can to put him at his ease and spare his feelings as much as possible, while still making sure that he understands your meaning. In such a case no one would say that your offer of a cigarette beforehand or your apology afterwards are modifications of the truth still less reasons for telling it. You do not tell the truth in order to spare his feelings, but having to tell the truth you also spare his feelings. So Bradley was right when he said that reform and deterrence were "external to the matter," but therefore wrong when he said that they may "modify the punishment." Reporters are admitted to our trials so that punishments may become public and help to deter others. But the punishment would be no less just were reporters excluded and deterrence not achieved. Prison authorities may make it possible that a convict may become physically or morally better. They cannot ensure either result; and the punishment would still be just if the criminal took no advantage of their arrangements and their efforts failed. Some moralists see this and exclude these "extra" arrangements for deterrence and reform. They say that it must be the punishment *itself* which reforms and deters. But it is just my point that the punishment *itself* seldom reforms the criminal and never deters others. It is only "extra" arrangements which have any chance of achieving either result. As this is the central point of my paper, at the cost of labored repetition I would ask the upholders of reform and deterrence two questions. Suppose it could be shown that a particular criminal had not been improved by a punishment and also that no other would-be criminal had been deterred by it, would that prove that the punishment was unjust? Suppose it were discovered that a particular criminal had lived a much better life after his release and that many would-be criminals believing him to have been guilty were influenced by his fate, but yet that the "criminal" was punished for something he had never done, would these excellent results prove the punishment just?

It will be observed that I have throughout treated punishment as a purely legal matter. A "criminal" means a man who has broken a law, not a bad man; an "innocent" man is a man who has not broken the law in connection with which he is being punished, though he may be a bad man and have broken other laws. Here I dissent from most upholders of the retributive theory—from Hegel, from Bradley, and from Dr. Ross. They maintain that the essential connection is one between punishment and moral or social wrongdoing.

My fundamental difficulty with their theory is the question of status. It takes two to make a punishment, and for a moral or social wrong I can find no punisher. We may be tempted to say when we hear of some brutal action "that ought to be punished"; but I cannot see how there can be duties which are nobody's duties. If I see a man ill-treating a horse in a country where cruelty to animals is not a legal offence, and I say to him "I shall now punish you," he will reply, rightly, "What has it to do with you? Who made you a judge and a ruler over me?" I may have a duty to try to stop him and one way of stopping him may be to hit him, but another way may be to buy the horse. Neither the blow nor the price is a punishment. For a moral offence, God alone has the status necessary to punish the offender; and the theologians are becoming more and more doubtful whether even God has a duty to punish wrongdoing.

Dr. Ross would hold that not all wrongdoing is punishable, but only invasion of the rights of others; and in such a case it might be thought that the injured party had a right to punish. His right, however, is rather a right to reparation, and should not be confused with punishment proper.

This connection, on which I insist, between punishment and crime, not between punishment and moral or social wrong, alone accounts for some of our beliefs about punishment, and also meets many objections to the retributive theory as stated in its ordinary form. The first point on which it helps us is with regard to retrospective legislation. Our objection to this practice is unaccountable on reform and deterrent theories. For a man who commits a wrong before the date on which a law against it is passed, is as much in need of reform as a man who commits it afterwards; nor is deterrence likely to suffer because of additional punishments for the same offence. But the orthodox retributive theory is equally at a loss here, for if punishment is given for moral wrongdoing or for invasion of the rights of others, that immorality or invasion existed as certainly before the passing of the law as after it.

My theory also explains, where it seems to me an others do not, the case of punishment imposed by an authority who believes the law in question is a bad law. I was myself for some time disciplinary officer of a college whose rules included a rule compelling attendance at chapel. Many of those who broke this rule broke it on principle. I punished them. I certainly did not want to reform them; I respected their characters and their views. I certainly did not want to drive others into chapel through fear of penalties. Nor did I think there had been a wrong done which merited retribution. I wished I could have believed that I would have done the same myself. My position was clear. They had broken a rule; they knew it and I knew it. Nothing more was necessary to make punishment proper.

I know that the usual answer to this is that the judge enforces a bad law because otherwise law in general would suffer and good laws would be broken. The effect of punishing good men for breaking bad laws is that fewer bad men break good laws.

[*Excursus on Indirect Utilitarianism.* The above argument is a particular instance of a general utilitarian solution of all similar problems. When I am in funds and consider whether I should pay my debts or give the same amount to charity, I must choose the former because repayment not only benefits my creditor (for the benefit to him might be less than the good done through charity) but also upholds the general credit system. I tell the truth when a lie might do more good to the parties directly concerned, because I thus increase general trust and confidence. I keep a promise when it might do more immediate good to break it, because indirectly I bring it about that promises will be more readily made in future and this will outweigh the immediate loss involved. Dr. Ross has pointed out that the effect on the credit system of my refusal to pay a debt is greatly exaggerated. But I have a more serious objection of principle. It is that in all these cases the indirect effects do not result from my wrong action — my lie or defalcation or bad faith — but from the publication of these actions. If in any instance the breaking of the rule were to remain unknown then I could consider only the direct or immediate consequences. Thus in my "compulsory chapel" case I could have considered which of my culprits were law-abiding men generally and unlikely to break any other college rule. Then I could have sent for each of these separately and said "I shall let you off if you will tell no one I have done so." By these means the general keeping of rules would not have suffered. Would this course have been correct? It must be remembered that the proceedings need not deceive everybody. So long as they deceive would-be lawbreakers the good is achieved.

As this point is of crucial importance and as it has an interest beyond the immediate issue, and gives a clue to what I regard as the true general nature of law and punishment, I may be excused for expanding and illustrating it by an example or two from other fields. Dr. Ross says that two men dying on a desert island would have duties to keep promises to each other even though their breaking them would not affect the future general confidence in promises at all. Here is certainly the same point. But as I find that desert-island morality always rouses suspicion among ordinary men I should like to quote two instances from my own experience which also illustrate the problem.

(i) A man alone with his father at his death promises him a private and quiet funeral. He finds later that both directly and indirectly the keeping of this promise will cause pain and misunderstanding. He can see no particular positive good that the quiet funeral will achieve. No one yet knows that he has made the promise nor need anyone ever know. Should he therefore act as though it had never been made?

(ii) A college has a fund given to it for the encouragement of a subject which is now expiring. Other expanding subjects are in great need of endowment. Should the authorities divert the money? Those who oppose the diversion have previously stood on the past, the promise. But one day one of them discovers the "real reason" for this slavery to a dead donor. He says "We must consider not only the value of this money for these purposes, since on all direct consequences it should be diverted at once. We must remember the effect of this diversion on the general system of benefactions. We know that benefactors like to endow special objects, and this act of ours would discourage such benefactors in future and leave learning worse off." Here again is the indirect utilitarian reason for choosing the alternative which direct utilitarianism would reject. But the immediate answer to this from the most ingenious member of the opposition was crushing and final. He said, "Divert the money but keep it dark." This is obviously correct. It is not the act of diversion which would diminish the stream of benefactions but the news of it reaching the ears of benefactors. Provided that no possible benefactor got to hear of it no indirect loss would result. But the justification of our action would depend entirely on the success of the measures for "keeping it dark." I remember how I felt and how others felt that whatever answer was right this result was certainly wrong. But it follows that indirect utilitarianism is wrong in all such cases. For its argument can always be met by "Keep it dark."]

The view, then, that a judge upholds a bad law in order that law in general should not suffer is indefensible. He upholds it simply because he has no right to dispense from punishment.

The connection of punishment with law-breaking and not with wrongdoing also escapes moral objections to the retributive theory as held by Kant and Hegel or by Bradley and Ross. It is asked how we can measure moral wrong or balance it with pain, and how pain can wipe out moral wrong. Retributivists have been pushed into holding that pain *ipso facto* represses the worse self and frees the better, when this is contrary to the vast majority of observed cases. But if punishment is not intended to measure or balance or negate moral wrong then all this is beside the mark. There is the further difficulty of reconciling punishment with repentance and with forgiveness. Repentance is the reaction morally appropriate to moral wrong and punishment added to remorse is an unnecessary evil. But if punishment is associated with lawbreaking and not with moral evil the punisher is not entitled to consider whether the criminal is penitent any more than he may consider whether the law is good. So, too, with forgiveness. Forgiveness is not appropriate to law-breaking. (It is noteworthy that when, in divorce cases, the law has to recognize forgiveness it calls it "condonation," which is symptomatic of the difference of attitude.) Nor is forgiveness appropriate to moral evil. It is appropriate to personal injury. No one has any right to forgive me except the person I have injured. No judge or jury can do so. But the person I have injured has no right to punish me. Therefore there is no clash between punishment and forgiveness since these two duties do not fall on the same person nor in connection with the same characteristic of my act. (It is the weakness of vendetta that it tends to confuse this line, though even there it is only by personifying the family that the injured party and the avenger are identified. Similarly we must guard against the plausible fallacy of personifying society and regarding the criminal as "injuring society," for then once more the old dilemma about forgiveness would be insoluble.) A clergyman friend of mine catching a burglar red-handed was puzzled about his duty. In the end he ensured the man's punishment by information and evidence, and at the same time showed his own forgiveness by visiting the man in prison and employing him when he came out. I believe any "good Christian" would accept this as representing his duty. But obviously, if the punishment is thought of as imposed by the victim or for the injury or immorality, then the contradiction with forgiveness is hopeless.

So far as the question of the actual punishment of any individual is concerned this paper could stop here. No punishment is morally retributive or reformative or deterrent. Any criminal punished for any one of these reasons is certainly unjustly punished. The only justification for punishing any man is that he has broken a law.

In a book which has already left its mark on prison administration I have found a criminal himself confirming these views. *Walls Have Mouths*, by W. F. R. Macartney, is prefaced, and provided with appendices to each chapter, by Compton Mackenzie. It is interesting to notice how the novelist maintains that the proper object of penal servitude should be reformation,[1] whereas the prisoner himself accepts the view I have set out above. Macartney says "To punish a man is to treat him as an equal. To be punished for an *offence against rules* is a sane man's right."[2] It is striking also that he never uses "injustice" to describe the brutality or provocation which he experienced. He makes it clear that there were only two types of prisoner who were *unjustly* imprisoned, those who were insane and not responsible for the acts for which they were punished[3] and those who were innocent and had broken no law.[4] It is irrelevant, as he rightly observes, that some of these innocent men were, like Steinie Morrison, dangerous and violent characters, who on utilitarian grounds might well have been restrained. That made their punishment no whit less unjust.[5] To these general types may be added two specific instances of injustice. First, the sentences on the Dartmoor mutineers. "The Penal Servitude Act . . . lays down specific punishments for mutiny and incitement to mutiny, which include flogging. . . . Yet on the occasion of the only big mutiny in an English prison, men are not dealt with by the Act specially passed to meet mutiny in prison, but are taken out of gaol and tried under an Act expressly passed to curb and curtail the Chartists—a revolutionary movement."[6] Here again the injustice does not lie in the actual effect the sentences are likely to have on the prisoners (though Macartney has some searching suggestions

---

1. p. 97.

2. p. 165. My italics.

3. pp. 165–166.

4. p. 298.

5. p. 301.

6. p. 255.

about that also) but in condemning men for breaking a law they did not break and not for breaking the law they did break. The second specific instance is that of Coulton, who served his twenty years and then was brought back to prison to do another eight years and to die. This is due to the "unjust order that no lifer shall be released unless he has either relations or a job to whom he can go: and it is actually suggested that this is really for the lifer's own good. Just fancy, you admit that the man in doing years upon years in prison had expiated his crime: but, instead of releasing him, you keep him a further time—perhaps another three years—because you say he has nowhere to go. Better a ditch and hedge than prison! True, there are abnormal cases who want to stay in prison, but Lawrence wanted to be a private soldier, and men go into monasteries. Because occasionally a man wants to stay in prison, must every lifer who has lost his family during his sentence (I was doing only ten years and I lost all my family) be kept indefinitely in gaol after he has paid his debt?"[7] Why is it unjust? Because he has paid his debt. When that is over it is for the man himself to decide what is for his own good. Once again the reform and utilitarian arguments are summarily swept aside. Injustice lies not in bad treatment or treatment which is not in the man's own interest, but in restriction which, according to the law, he has not merited.

It is true that Macartney writes, in one place, a paragraph of general reflection on punishment in which he confuses, as does Compton Mackenzie, retribution with revenge and in which he seems to hold that the retributive theory has some peculiar connection with private property. "Indeed it is difficult to see how, in society as it is today constituted, a humane prison system could function. All property is sacred, although the proceeds of property may well be reprehensible, therefore any offence against property is sacrilege and must be punished. Till a system eventuates which is based not on exploitation of man by man and class by class, prisons must be dreadful places, but at least there might be an effort to ameliorate the more savage side of the retaliation, and this could be done very easily."[8] The alternative system

---

7. p. 400.

8. pp. 166, 167.

of which no doubt he is thinking is the Russian system described in his quotations from A *Physician's Tour in Soviet Russia*, by Sir James Purves-Stewart, the system of "correctional colonies" providing curative "treatment" for the different types of criminal.[9] There are two confusions here, to one of which we shall return later. First, Macartney confuses the retributive system with the punishment of one particular type of crime, offences against property, when he must have known that the majority of offenders against property do not find themselves in Dartmoor or even in Wandsworth. After all his own offence was not one against property—it was traffic with a foreign power—and it was one for which in the classless society of Russia the punishment is death. It is surely clear that a retributive system may be adopted for any class of crime. Secondly, Macartney confuses injustice within a penal system with the wrongfulness of a penal system. When he pleads for "humane prisons" as if the essence of the prison should be humanity, or when Compton Mackenzie says the object of penal servitude should be reform, both of them are giving up punishment altogether, not altering it. A Russian "correctional colony," if its real object is curative treatment, is no more a "prison" than is an isolation hospital or a lunatic asylum. To this distinction between abolishing injustice in punishment and abolishing punishment altogether we must now turn.

It will be objected that my original question "Why ought X to be punished?" is an illegitimate isolation of the issue. I have treated the whole set of circumstances as determined. X is a citizen of a state. About his citizenship, whether willing or unwilling, I have asked no questions. About the government, whether it is good or bad, I do not enquire. X has broken a law. Concerning the law, whether it is well-devised or not, I have not asked. Yet all these questions are surely relevant before it can be decided whether a particular punishment is just. It is the essence of my position that none of these questions is relevant. Punishment is a corollary of lawbreaking by a member of the society whose law is broken. This is a static and an abstract view but I see no escape from it. Considerations of utility come in on two quite different issues. Should there be laws, and what laws should

_____

9. p. 229.

there be? As a legislator I may ask what general types of action would benefit the community, and, among these, which can be "standard-ized" without loss, or should be standardized to achieve their full value. This, however, is not the primary question since particular laws may be altered or repealed. The choice which is the essential *prius* of punishment is the choice that there should be laws. The choice is not Hobson's. Other methods may be considered. A government might attempt to standardize certain modes of action by means of advice. It might proclaim its view and say "Citizens are requested" to follow this or that procedure. Or again it might decide to deal with each case as it arose in the manner most effective for the common welfare. Anarchists have wavered between these two alternatives and a third—that of doing nothing to enforce a standard of behavior but merely giving arbitrational decisions between conflicting parties, deci-sions binding only by consent.

I think it can be seen without detailed examination of particular laws that the method of law-making has its own advantages. Its orders are explicit and general. It makes behaviour reliable and predictable. Its threat of punishment may be so effective as to make punishment unnecessary. It promises to the good citizen a certain security in his life. When I have talked to business men about some inequity in the law of liability they have usually said "Better a bad law than no law, for then we know where we are."

Someone may say I am drawing an impossible line. I deny that punishment is utilitarian; yet now I say that punishment is a corol-lary of law and we decide whether to have laws and which laws to have on utilitarian grounds. And surely it is only this corollary which distinguishes law from good advice or exhortation. This is a misunder-standing. Punishment is a corollary not of law but of lawbreaking. Leg-islators do not choose to punish. They hope no punishment will be needed. Their laws would succeed even if no punishment occurred. The criminal makes the essential choice: he "brings it on himself." Other men obey the law because they see its order is reasonable, because of inertia, because of fear. In this whole area, and it may be the major part of the state, law achieves its ends without punishment. Clearly, then, punishment is not a corollary of law.

We may return for a moment to the question of amount and nature of punishment. It may be thought that this also is automatic.

The law will include its own penalties and the judge will have no option. This, however, is again an initial choice of principle. If the laws do include their own penalties then the judge has no option. But the legislature might adopt a system which left complete or partial freedom to the judge, as we do except in the case of murder. Once again, what are the merits (regardless of particular laws, still more of particular cases) of fixed penalties and variable penalties? At first sight it would seem that all the advantages are with the variable penalties; for men who have broken the same law differ widely in degree of wickedness and responsibility. When, however, we remember that punishment is not an attempt to balance moral guilt this advantage is diminished. But there are still degrees of responsibility; I do not mean degrees of freedom of will but, for instance, degrees of complicity in a crime. The danger of allowing complete freedom to the judicature in fixing penalties is not merely that it lays too heavy a tax on human nature but that it would lead to the judge expressing in his penalty the degree of his own moral aversion to the crime. Or he might tend on deterrent grounds to punish more heavily a crime which was spreading and for which temptation and opportunity were frequent. Or again on deterrent grounds he might "make examples" by punishing ten times as heavily those criminals who are detected in cases in which time nine out of ten evade detection. Yet we should revolt from all such punishments if they involved punishing theft more heavily than blackmail or negligence more heavily than premeditated assault. The death penalty for sheep-stealing might have been defended on such deterrent grounds. But we should dislike equating sheep-stealing with murder. Fixed penalties enable us to draw these distinctions between crimes. It is not that we can say how much imprisonment is right for a sheep-stealer. But we can grade crimes in a rough scale and penalties in a rough scale, and keep our heaviest penalties for what are socially the most serious wrongs regardless of whether these penalties will reform the criminal or whether they are exactly what deterrence would require. The compromise of laying down maximum penalties and allowing judges freedom below these limits allows for the arguments on both sides.

To return to the main issue, the position I am defending is that it is essential to a legal system that the infliction of a particular punishment should not be determined by the good that particular punishment will do either to the criminal or to "society." In exactly the same way it is essential to a credit system that the repayment of a particular debt should not be determined by the good that particular payment will do. One may consider the merits of a legal system or of a credit system, but the acceptance of either involves the surrender of utilitarian considerations in particular cases as they arise. This is in effect admitted by Ewing in one place where he says "It is the penal system as a whole which deters and not the punishment of any individual offender."[10]

To show that the choice between a legal system and its alternatives is one we do and must make, I may quote an early work of Lenin in which he was defending the Marxist tenet that the state is bound to "wither away" with the establishment of a classless society. He considers the possible objection that some wrongs by man against man are not economic and therefore that the abolition of classes would not ipso facto eliminate crime. But he sticks to the thesis that these surviving crimes should not be dealt with by law and judicature. "We are not Utopians and do not in the least deny the possibility and inevitability of excesses by *individual persons*, and equally the need to suppress such excesses. But for this no special machine, no special instrument of repression is needed. This will be done by the armed nation itself as simply and as readily as any crowd of civilized people even in modern society parts a pair of combatants or does not allow a woman to be outraged."[11] This alternative to law and punishment has obvious demerits. Any injury not committed in the presence of the crowd, any wrong which required skill to detect or pertinacity to bring home would go untouched. The lynching mob, which is Lenin's instrument of justice, is liable to error and easily deflected from its purpose or driven to extremes. It must be a mob, for there is to be no "machine." I do not say that no alternative machine to ours could be devised but it does seem certain that the absence of all "machines" would be intolerable. An alternative machine might be based on the view that "society" is responsible for all criminality, and a curative and protective system developed. This is the system

---

10. *The Morality of Punishment,* p. 66.

11. *The State and Revolution* (Eng. trans.), p. 93. Original italics.

of Butler's "Erewhon" and something like it seems to be growing up in Russia except for cases of "sedition."

We choose, then, or we acquiesce in and adopt the choice of others of, a legal system as one of our instruments for the establishment of the conditions of a good life. This choice is logically prior to and independent of the actual punishment of any particular persons or the passing of any particular laws. The legislators choose particular laws within the framework of this predetermined system. Once again a small society may illustrate the reality of these choices and the distinction between them. A headmaster launching a new school must explicitly make both decisions. First, shall he have any rules at all? Second, what rules shall he have? The first decision is a genuine one and one of great importance. Would it not be better to have an "honour" system, by which public opinion in each house or form dealt with any offence? (This is the Lenin method.) Or would complete freedom be better? Or should he issue appeals and advice? Or should he personally deal with each malefactor individually, as the case arises, in the way most likely to improve his conduct? I can well imagine an idealistic headmaster attempting to run a school with one of these methods or with a combination of several of them and therefore without punishment. I can even imagine that with a small school of, say, twenty pupils all open to direct personal psychological pressure from authority and from each other, these methods involving no "rules" would work. The pupils would of course grow up without two very useful habits, the habit of having some regular habits and the habit of obeying rules. But I suspect that most headmasters, especially those of large schools, would either decide at once, or quickly be driven, to realize that some rules were necessary. This decision would be "utilitarian" in the sense that it would be determined by consideration of consequences. The question "what rules?" would then arise and again the issue is utilitarian. What action must be regularized for the school to work efficiently? The hours of arrival and departure, for instance, in a day school. But the one choice which is now no longer open to the headmaster is whether he shall punish those who break the rules. For if he were to try to avoid this he would in fact simply be returning to the discarded method of appeals and good advice. Yet the headmaster does not decide to punish. The pupils make the decision there. He decides actually to have rules and to threaten, but only hypothetically, to punish. The one essential condition which makes actual punishment just is a condition he *cannot* fulfil—namely that a rule should be broken.

I shall add a final word of consolation to the practical reformer. Nothing that I have said is meant to counter any movement for "penal reform" but only to insist that none of these reforms have anything to do with punishment. The only type of reformer who can claim to be reforming the system of punishment is a follower of Lenin or of Samuel Butler who is genuinely attacking the system and who believes there should be no laws and no punishments. But our great British reformers have been concerned not with punishment but with its accessories. When a man is sentenced to imprisonment he is not sentenced also to partial starvation, to physical brutality, to pneumonia from damp cells and so on. And any movement which makes his food sufficient to sustain health, which counters the permanent tendency to brutality on the part of his warders, which gives him a dry or even a light and well-aired cell, is pure gain and does not touch the theory of punishment. Reformatory influences and prisoners' aid arrangements are also entirely unaffected by what I have said. I believe myself that it would be best if all such arrangements were made optional for the prisoner, so as to leave him in these cases a freedom of choice which would make it clear that they are not part of his punishment. If it is said that every such reform lessens a man's punishment, I think that is simply muddled thinking which, if it were clear, would be mere brutality. For instance, a prisoners' aid society is said to lighten his punishment, because otherwise he would suffer not merely imprison-ment but also unemployment on release. But he was sentenced to imprisonment, not imprisonment *plus* unemployment. If I promise to help a friend and through special circumstances I find that keeping my promise will involve upsetting my day's work, I do not say that I really promised to help him and to ruin my day's work. And if another friend carries on my work for me I do not regard him as carrying out part of my promise, nor as stopping me from carrying it out myself. He merely removes an indirect and regrettable consequence of my keeping my promise. So with punishment. The Prisoners' Aid Society does not alter a man's punishment nor diminish it, but merely removes an indirect and regrettable consequence of it. And anyone who thinks that a criminal cannot make this distinction and will regard all the inconvenience that comes to him as punishment, need only talk to a prisoner or two to find how sharply they resent these wanton additions to a punishment which by itself they will accept as just. Macartney's chapter on "Food" in the book quoted above is a good illustration of this point, as are also his comments on Clayton's administration. "To keep a man in prison for many years at considerable expense and then to free him charged to the eyes with uncontrollable venom and hatred generated by the treatment he has received in gaol, does not appear to be sensible." Clayton "endeavoured to send a man out of prison in a reasonable state of mind. 'Well, I've done my time. They were not too bad to me. Prison is prison and not a bed of roses. Still they didn't rub it in. . . .'"[12] This "reasonable state of mind" is one in which a prisoner on release feels he has been punished but not *additionally* insulted or ill-treated. I feel convinced that penal reformers would meet with even more support if they were clear that they were *not* attempting to alter the system of punishment but to give its victims "fair play." We have no more right to starve a convict than to starve an animal. We have no more right to keep a convict in a Dartmoor cell "down which the water trickles night and day"[13] than we have to keep a child in such a place. If our reformers really want to alter the system of punishment, let them come out clearly with their alternative and preach, for instance, that no human being is responsible for any wrong-doing, that all the blame is on society, that curative or protective measures should be adopted, forcibly if necessary, as they are with infection or insanity. Short of this let them admit that the essence of prison is deprivation of liberty for the breaking of law, and that deprivation of food or of health or of books is unjust. And if our sentimentalists cry "coddling of prisoners," let us ask them also to come out clearly into the open and incorporate whatever starvation and disease and brutality they think necessary *into the sentences they propose*.[14] If it is said that

---

12. p. 152.

13. *Op. cit.*, p. 258.

14. "One of the minor curiosities of jail life was that they quickly provided you with a hundred worries which left you no time or energy for worrying about your sentence, long or short. . . . Rather as if you were thrown into a fire with spikes in it, and the spikes hurt you so badly that you forget about the fire. But then your punishment would *be* the spikes not the fire. Why did they pretend it was only the fire, when they knew very well about the spikes?" (From *Lifer*, by Jim Phelan, p. 40.)

some prisoners will prefer such reformed prisons, with adequate food and aired cells, to the outer world, we may retort that their numbers are probably not greater than those of the masochists who like to be flogged. Yet we do not hear the same "coddling" critics suggest abolition of the lash on the grounds that some criminals may like it. Even if the abolition from our prisons of all maltreatment other than that imposed by law results in a few down-and-outs breaking a window (as O. Henry's hero did) to get a night's lodging, the country will lose less than she does by her present method of sending out her discharged convicts "charged with venom and hatred" because of the additional and uncovenanted "rubbing it in" which they have received.

I hope I have established both the theoretical importance and the practical value of distinguishing between penal reform as we know and approve it—that reform which alters the accompaniments of punishment without touching its essence—and those attacks on punishment itself which are made not only by reformers who regard criminals as irresponsible and in need of treatment, but also by every judge who announces that he is punishing a man to deter others or to protect society, and by every juryman who is moved to his decision by the moral baseness of the accused rather than by his legal guilt.

Chapter Three

The Death Penalty

The Deterrent Value of Capital Punishment*

The Function of Capital Punishment

50. We cannot hope to find reasoned answers to these questions unless we first consider what purpose capital punishment is intended to serve and how far, as now applied in this country, it achieves that purpose. This is a difficult and controversial subject, long and hotly debated; and it evoked strongly conflicting views from our witnesses. It is generally agreed that the scope of this drastic and irrevocable punishment should be no wider than is necessary for the protection of society, but there is no such agreement about how wide a scope the protection of society demands.

51. It is commonly said that punishment has three principal purposes—retribution, deterrence and reformation. The relative importance of these three principles has been differently assessed at different periods and by different authorities; and philosophers and penologists have emphasized one or another of them, sometimes even to the exclusion of the others. For the purposes of our inquiry, however, we may accept this traditional classification, and consider the importance of each of the three principles in relation to capital punishment in Great Britain at the present time.

52. Discussion of the principle of *retribution* is apt to be confused because the word is not always used in the same sense. Sometimes it is intended to mean vengeance, sometimes reprobation. In the first sense the idea is that of satisfaction by the State of a wronged individual's desire to be avenged; in the second it is that of the State's marking its disapproval of the breaking of its laws by a punishment proportionate to the gravity of the offence. Modern penological thought discounts retribution in the sense of vengeance. Lord Templewood[1]

Royal Commission on Capital Punishment 1949–53 Report (London: H.M.S.O., 1953), 17–24. Reprinted by permission of the Controller of Her Britannic Majesty's Stationery Office.

1. Q. 8533.

went so far as to say that recently "the reforming element has come to predominate and that the other two are carried incidentally to the reforming element." Sir John Anderson[2] attached greater importance to deterrence, but agreed in excluding retribution:

> I think there would be general agreement that the justification for the capital sentence, as for other salient features of our penal system, must be sought in the protection of society and that alone. . . . There is no longer in our regard at the criminal law any recognition of such primitive conceptions as atonement or retribution. We have, over the years, fortunately succeeded to a very large extent, it not entirely, in relegating the purely punitive aspect at our criminal law to the background.

53. Lord Templewood and Sir John Anderson had in mind retribution in the sense of vengeance or atonement. But in another sense retribution must always be an essential element in any form of punishment; punishment presupposes an offence and the measure of the punishment must not be greater than the offence deserves. Moreover, we think it must be recognized that there is a strong and widespread demand for retribution in the sense of reprobation—not always unmixed in the popular mind with that of atonement and expiation. As Lord Justice Denning put it:[3]

> The punishment inflicted for grave crimes should adequately reflect the revulsion felt by the great majority of citizens for them. It is a mistake to consider the objects of punishment as being deterrent or reformative or preventive and nothing else. . . . The ultimate justification of any punishment is not that it is a deterrent, but that it is the emphatic denunciation by the community of a crime: and tram this point of view, there are some murders which, in the present state at public

---

2. House of Commons, Official Report, 14th April, 1948, cols. 998–99.

3. p. 207 (1, 3).

opinion, demand the most emphatic denunciation at all, namely the death penalty.

The Archbishop of Canterbury, while expressing no opinion about the ethics of capital punishment, agreed with Lord Justice Denning's view about the ultimate justification of any punishment.[4] By reserving the death penalty for murder the criminal law stigmatises the gravest crime by the gravest punishment; and it may be argued that, by so doing, the law helps to foster in the community a special abhorrence of murder as "the crime of crimes," so that the element of retribution merges into that of deterrence. Whatever weight may be given to this argument, the law cannot ignore the public demand for retribution which heinous crimes undoubtedly provoke; it would be generally agreed that, though reform of the criminal law ought sometimes to give a lead to public opinion, it is dangerous to move too far in advance of it.

54. The *reformation* of the individual offender is usually regarded as an important function of punishment. But it can have no application where the death penalty is exacted, if "reformation" is taken to mean not merely repentance,[5] but reestablishment in normal life as a good citizen.[6] Not that murderers in general are incapable of reformation; the evidence plainly shows the contrary. Indeed, as we shall see later,[7] the experience of countries without capital punishment indicates that the prospects of reformation are at least as favourable

---

4. Fisher, Q. 4087–88.

5. It has sometimes been suggested that the death penalty has a unique value as a stimulus to repentance. The Royal Commission on Capital Punishment of 1864–66 were informed that in the opinion of the Governor, Chaplain and Chief Clerk of Millbank Prison "criminals deserving death generally are not likely to reform with ordinary opportunities, but they do repent before hanging" (Minutes of Evidence, p. 639).

6. It might be argued, as Professor Sellin pointed out that the death sentence, subsequently commuted, has a stronger reformative effect in some cases than an original sentence of life imprisonment would have had; but we received no evidence which might support this hypothesis.

7. Paragraphs 651–52 and Appendix 15.

with murderers as with those who have committed other kinds of serious crimes.

55. Discussion of the value of capital punishment has been largely devoted to the aspect of *deterrence*. This is an issue on which it is extraordinarily difficult to find conclusive arguments either way. Both sides are commonly argued by wide generalisations confidently expressed with little positive evidence to support them. We heard much evidence about it from numerous witnesses, and were furnished with much relevant information, largely statistical. The greater part of this information will be found in our Minutes of Evidence, including the evidence obtained from other countries; but, as much of it is not readily available elsewhere, we have thought it useful to give a full summary of it in an appendix to this Report.[8]

56. Supporters of capital punishment commonly maintain that it has a uniquely deterrent force, which no other form of punishment has or could have. The arguments adduced both in support of this proposition and against it fall into two categories. The first consists of what we may call the common-sense argument from human nature, applicable particularly to certain kinds of murders and certain kinds of murderers. This a priori argument was supported by evidence given by representatives of all ranks of the police and of the prison service. The second comprises various arguments based on examination of statistics.

57. The arguments in the first category are not only the simplest and most obvious, but are perhaps the strongest that can be put forward in favor of the uniquely deterrent power of capital punishment. The case was very clearly stated by Sir James Fitzjames Stephen nearly a hundred years ago:[9]

No other punishment deters men so effectually from committing crimes as the punishment of death. This is one of those propositions which it is difficult to prove, simply because they are in themselves more obvious than any proof can make them. It is possible to display ingenuity in arguing

---

8. Appendix 6 (pp. 328 ff).

9. "Capital Punishments" in *Fraser's Magazine*, Vol. LXIX, June, 1864, p. 753.

against it, but that is all. The whole experience of mankind is in the other direction. The threat of instant death is the one to which resort has always been made when there was an absolute necessity for producing some result. . . . No one goes to certain inevitable death except by compulsion. Put the matter the other way. Was there ever yet a criminal who, when sentenced to death and brought out to die, would refuse the offer at a commutation at his sentence for the severest secondary punishment? Surely not. Why is this? It can only be because 'All that a man has will he give for his life.' In any secondary punishment, however terrible, there is hope; but death is death; its terrors cannot be described more forcibly.

58. It is true, as has often been pointed out in reply to this argument, that capital punishment as applied in Great Britain falls very far short of a threat of instant and certain death to every murderer. This is clearly shown by the figures in Tables 1 and 2 of Appendix 3. During the 50 years 1900–1949, 7,454 murders were known to the police in England and Wales. In 1,674 cases the suspect committed suicide. During the same period 4,173 persons were arrested on a charge of murder and 3,129 were committed for trial at assizes.[10] Of those committed for trial 658 were acquitted or not tried, 428 were found insane on arraignment and 798 were found guilty but insane. Of those convicted of murder 35 were sentenced to penal servitude for life or detention during H. M. pleasure and 1,210 were sentenced to death. Of those sentenced to death 23 had their conviction quashed on appeal, 47 were certified insane and 506 were reprieved. There remain 632 (621 men and 11 women) who were executed for murder. There was therefore only one execution for every 12 murders known to the police. In Scotland the proportion was even lower. In that country during the same period 612 murders were known to the police, 59 persons were convicted of murder and sentenced to death and 23 (22 men and 1 woman) were executed. There was therefore less than one

---

10. Owing to the basis on which the Criminal Statistics are compiled, this figure does not include persons charged with murder and convicted of manslaughter or some other lesser offense; but for the present purpose this defect is immaterial.

execution to every 25 murders known to the police. But these odds against being hanged for murder are probably realised only vaguely, if at all, by would-be murderers. Those who, like Stephen, are convinced that the fear of death cannot fail to have a more potent effect on most men and women than the fear of any other punishment are not likely to be shaken in that conviction by these figures.

59. Capital punishment has obviously failed as a deterrent when a murder is committed. We can number its failures. But we cannot number its successes. No one can ever know how many people have refrained from murder because of the fear of being hanged. For that we have to rely on indirect and inconclusive evidence. We have been told that the first thing a murderer says when he is arrested is often "Shall I be hanged?" or "I did it and I am ready to swing for it," or something of that kind. What is the inference to be drawn from this? Clearly not that the death penalty is an effective deterrent, for he has not been deterred; nor that he consciously considered the risk of the death penalty and accepted it; still less that the death penalty was not so effective a deterrent as some other punishment might have been. The true inference seems to us to be that there is a strong association between murder and the death penalty in the popular imagination. We think it is reasonable to suppose that the deterrent force of capital punishment operates not only by affecting the conscious thoughts of individuals tempted to commit murder, but also by building up in the community, over a long period of time, a deep feeling of peculiar abhorrence for the crime of murder. "The fact that men are hung for murder is one great reason why murder is considered so dreadful a crime." This widely diffused effect on the moral consciousness of society is impossible to assess, but it must be at least as important as any direct part which the death penalty may play as a deterrent in the calculations of potential murderers. It is likely to be especially potent in this country, where the punishment for lesser offences is much more lenient than in many other countries, and the death penalty stands out in the sharper contrast.

60. We have already remarked that the deterrent effect of capital punishment may naturally be expected to operate more strongly to prevent some kinds of murders than others, and to deter some kinds of individuals more than others. To form any idea of the extent to which, and the way in which, this expectation coincides with experi-

ence, it would be necessary to have some classification of murders according to motives or causes. Attempts at such a classification have been made, notably by the Home Office in 1905 and by the Home Office and Scottish Home Department in 1949. But these are inevitably very general and tentative and for several reasons can hardly fail to be misleading if they are taken as more than a rough guide. Such a classification can only be framed in somewhat crude categories. If it is in terms of motives, it is unsatisfactory, because many murders are prompted by a combination of motives, or by hidden motives, or have no obvious motive. If, like the tables prepared for us by the Home Office and Scottish Home Department, they classify murders in terms of the relationship between the murderer and his victim, they can give only an approximate indication of the motive that inspired the crime. Although the murder of a wife, for example, will in many cases be committed for reasons which may broadly be described as of a sexual character, it may be inspired by the widest range of motives— jealousy, boredom, pity, exasperation, revenge, a wish to be free to marry another woman or a desire to dispose of the wife's fortune. Such analyses can do no more than lend some support to conclusions that can be reached by commonsense, namely that capital punishment is likely to act as a deterrent more of premeditated murders than of impulsive ones, and on normal persons more than on the mentally abnormal. Even these generalisations are subject to many exceptions. Premeditated murders are committed in spite of the existence of the death penalty—in them the offender will often calculate on escaping detection—and it can hardly be doubted that impulsive murders are prevented by it. Mentally normal persons do commit murder, and, though the deterrent effect of capital punishment will certainly be negligible on the severely deranged, the question how far persons suffering from lesser forms of mental abnormality, and especially that difficult and amorphous category known as psychopaths, are capable of being deterred by the fear of punishment is far from clear. Our evidence was that some are and some are not. It was even suggested that in some very rare cases the existence of capital punishment may act as an incitement to murder on the mentally abnormal.[11]

11. Howard League, p. 279 (4), Calvert, Q. 3561–62; Henderson, p. 462** (17); Institute of Pyscho-Analysis, p. 546 (6(ii)(e)); Sellin, Q. 8888.

61. Of more importance was the evidence of the representatives of the police and prison service. From them we received virtually unanimous evidence in both England and Scotland, to the effect that they were convinced of the uniquely deterrent value of capital punishment in its effect on professional criminals. On these the fear of the death penalty may not only have the direct effect of deterring them from using lethal violence to accomplish their purpose, or to avoid detection by silencing the victim of their crime, or to resist arrest. It may also have the indirect effect of deterring them from carrying a weapon lest the temptation to use it in a tight corner should prove irresistible. These witnesses had no doubt that the existence of the death penalty was the main reason why lethal violence was not more often used and why criminals in this country do not usually carry firearms or other weapons. They thought that, if there were no capital punishment, criminals would take to using violence and carrying weapons; and the police, who are now unarmed, might be compelled to retaliate. It is in the nature of the case that little could be adduced in the way of specific evidence that criminals had been deterred by the death penalty. What an offender says on his arrest, probably some time after the commission of the crime, is not necessarily a valid indication of what was in his mind when he committed it; nor is it certain that a man who tells the police that he refrained from committing a murder because he might have to "swing for it" was in fact deterred wholly or mainly by that fear. Moreover we received no evidence that the abolition of capital punishment in other countries had in fact led to the consequences apprehended by our witnesses in this country; though it is fair to add that any comparison between Great Britain and most of these countries, with the exception of Belgium, is vitiated by the differences in social and industrial conditions and in density of population. But we cannot treat lightly the considered and unanimous views of these experienced witnesses, who have had many years of contact with criminals. Some of our most distinguished judicial witnesses—notably the Lord Chief Justice, Mr. Justice Humphreys and the Lord Justice General—felt no doubt that they were right.[12] It seems to us inherently probable that, if capital

---

12. Goddard, Q. 3109; Humphreys, p. 260 (2); Cooper, Q. 5370–71.

punishment has any unique value as a deterrent, it is here that its effect would be chiefly felt and here that its value to the community would be greatest. For the professional criminal imprisonment is a normal professional risk, of which the idea is familiar, if not the experience, and which for him carries no stigma. It is natural to suppose that for such people (except the rare gangster, who constantly risks his life in affrays with the police and other gangs) the death penalty comes into an entirely different category from other forms of punishment. The Commissioner of Police of the Metropolis told us[13] of a gang of armed shop-breakers who continued their operations after one of their members had been sentenced to death for murder and reprieved, but broke up and disappeared when, on a later occasion, two others were convicted of another murder and hanged. He thought it "a reasonable inference" that this was evidence of the uniquely deterrent effect of the death penalty; and that was the opinion of the police officers who dealt with the gang. It is also contended that in the case of a violent prisoner undergoing a life sentence the death penalty may be the only effective deterrent against his making a murderous assault on a fellow prisoner or a member of the prison staff.

62. We must now turn to the statistical evidence. This has for the most part been assembled by those who would abolish the death penalty; their object has been to disprove the deterrent value claimed for that punishment. Supporters of the death penalty usually counter them by arguing that the figures are susceptible of a different interpretation, or that for one reason or another they are too unreliable and misleading to form a basis for valid argument. The question should be judged, they say, not on statistics but on such considerations as we have been examining in the preceding paragraphs.

63. The arguments drawn by the abolitionists from the statistics fall into two categories. The first, and by far the more important, seeks to prove the case by showing that the abolition of capital punishment in other countries has not led to an increase of murder or of homicidal crime. This may be attempted either by comparing the homicide statistics of countries where capital punishment has been abolished with the

---

13. p. 148 (Appendix B). Extracts from the Commissioner's evidence about this case are printed in Appendix 6, paragraph 15.

statistics for the same period of countries where it has been retained, or by comparing the statistics of a single country, in which capital punishment has been abolished, for periods before and after abolition. The second category is of arguments drawn from a comparison of the number of executions in a country in particular years with the murder or homicide rate in the years immediately succeeding.

64. An initial difficulty is that it is almost impossible to draw valid comparisons between different countries. Any attempt to do so, except within very narrow limits, may always be misleading. Some of the reasons why this is so are more fully developed in Appendix 6.[14] Briefly they amount to this: that owing to differences in the legal definitions of crimes, in the practice of the prosecuting authorities and the courts, in the methods of compiling criminal statistics, in moral standards and customary behavior, and in political, social and economic conditions, it is extremely difficult to compare like with like, and little confidence can be felt in the soundness of the inferences drawn from such comparisons. An exception may legitimately be made where it is possible to find a small group of countries or States, preferably contiguous, and closely similar in composition of population and social and economic conditions generally, in some of which capital punishment has been abolished and in others not. These conditions are satisfied, we think, by certain groups of States in the United States of America, about which we heard evidence from Professor Thorsten Sellin, and perhaps also by New Zealand and the Australian States. In Appendix 6[15] we print a selection from the relevant material. If we take any of these groups we find that the fluctuations in the homicide rate of each of its component members exhibit a striking similarity. We agree with Professor Sellin that the only conclusion which can be drawn from the figures is that there is no clear evidence of any influence of the death penalty on the homicide rates of these States, and that, "whether the death penalty is used or not and whether executions are frequent or not, both death-penalty States and abolition States show rates which suggest that these rates are conditioned by other factors than the death penalty."[16]

---

14. See paragraph 24.

15. See paragraphs 32–36 and 51–54.

16. p. 650 (41, 44).

65. A firmer basis for argument is afforded by the trend of the homicide rate in a country before and after the abolition of capital punishment, and, in a few cases, its reintroduction. The nature of the statistics available differs from one country to another; in a few the number of homicides known to the police are available, but more often there are statistics only of prosecutions for murder or of convictions. The number of homicides known to the police clearly provides the most informative basis and the number of convictions the least: the ratio between crimes committed and convictions may vary widely owing to such factors as the efficiency of the police, the methods of recording crime and the attitude of the courts; moreover juries may sometimes be more ready to return a verdict of guilty when the death penalty has been abolished. But so long as a continuous series of figures compiled on a uniform basis exists for the whole period under review, we think that the fluctuations in these figures can be taken as some index of fluctuations in the homicide rate. Whatever basis is chosen, interpretation of the relevant statistics involves elements of doubt and difficulty. In most countries where capital punishment has been abolished, statutory abolition has come after a long period when the death penalty was in abeyance, and this creates the problem of what date should be taken as the dividing line. Whatever date may be selected, it cannot safely be assumed that variations in the homicide rate after the abolition of capital punishment are in fact due to abolition, and not to other causes, or to a combination of abolition and other causes. There is some evidence[17] that abolition may be followed for a short time by an increase in homicides and crimes of violence, and a fortiori it might be thought likely that a temporary increase of this kind would occur if capital punishment were abolished in a country where it was not previously in abeyance but was regularly applied in practice; but it would appear that, as soon as a country has become accustomed to the new form of the extreme penalty, abolition will not in the long run lead to an increase of crime. The general conclusion which we have reached is that there is no clear evidence in any of the figures we have examined that the abolition of capital punishment has led to an increase in the homicide rate, or that its reintroduction has led to a fall.

---

17. See Appendix 6, paragraphs 69–73.

66. We also review in Appendix 6 such evidence as has been submitted to us about the possible relation between the number of executions in particular years and the incidence of murder in succeeding years.[18] We need not here consider the evidence in detail; it is sufficient to say that we are satisfied that no such relationship can be established. (It was suggested to us by some Scottish witnesses that a fall in the number of murders and crimes of violence in Glasgow in 1946 was due, or mainly due, to the carrying out of three executions in that year after capital punishment had been in abeyance for 17 years, but the available evidence does not support this conclusion).[19] We have suggested (paragraph 59) that any deterrent effect of capital punishment is likely to reside primarily in its long-term effect on the attitude of society to murder rather than in the conscious calculations of potential criminals. If this is so, it cannot be expected that variations in the number of executions from year to year would be directly reflected in a rise or fall of the murder rate, and a failure to find any such correlations cannot properly be used as an argument against the view that the death penalty is a unique deterrent.

67. The negative conclusion we draw from the figures does not of course imply a conclusion that the deterrent effect of the death penalty cannot be greater than that of any other punishment. It means only that the figures afford no reliable evidence one way or the other. It would no doubt be equally difficult to find statistical evidence of any direct relationship between the severity of any other punishment and the rise or fall of the crime to which it relates. Too many other factors come into the question. All we can say is that the deterrent value of punishment in general is probably liable to be exaggerated, and the effect of capital punishment especially so because of its drastic and sensational character. The conclusion of Professor Sellin, who has made a profound study of this subject, is summarised in the answers to four of the questions we put to him:

8916. We cannot conclude from your statistics . . . that capital punishment has no deterrent effect?—No, there is no such conclusion.

---

18. See Appendix 6, paragraphs 74–87.

19. See Appendix 6, paragraphs 78–80.

8917. But can we not conclude that if it has a deterrent effect it must be rather small?—I can make no such conclusion, because I can find no answer one way or another in these data. . . . It is impossible to draw any inferences from the material that is in my possession, that there is any relationship . . . between a large number of executions, small number of executions, continuous executions, no executions, and what happens to the murder rates.

8918. . . . I think you have already agreed that capital punishment cannot, on the basis of your figures, be exercising an overwhelmingly deterrent effect?—That is correct.

8919. . . . But you would not like to go any further than that?—No. . . .

68. We recognise that it is impossible to arrive confidently at firm conclusions about the deterrent effect of the death penalty, or indeed of any form of punishment. The general conclusion which we reach, after careful review of all the evidence we have been able to obtain as to the deterrent effect of capital punishment, may be stated as follows. Prima facie the penalty of death is likely to have a stronger effect as a deterrent to normal human beings than any other form of punishment, and there is some evidence (though no convincing statistical evidence) that this is in fact so. But this effect does not operate universally or uniformly, and there are many offenders on whom it is limited and may often be negligible. It is accordingly important to view this question in a just perspective and not to base a penal policy in relation to murder on exaggerated estimates of the uniquely deterrent force of the death penalty.

Gilpin Versus Mill*

The Honorable Mr. Gilpin
Speech Against Capital Punishment 1868
Capital Punishment Within Prisons Bill—[Bill 36.]
(*Mr. Secretary Gathorne Hardy, Mr. Walpole, Mr. Attorney General.*)

COMMITTEE

Order for Committee read.
Motion made, and Question proposed, "That Mr. Speaker do now
leave the Chair."

Mr. Gilpin said, he rose to move the Amendment of which he had
given notice—

> *That, in the opinion of this House, it is expedient, instead*
> *of carrying out the punishment of death within prisons, that*
> *Capital Punishment should be abolished.*

He felt some difficulty and hesitation in asking the attention of the
House to the Motion of which he had given notice. In the first
instance, he would express his extreme regret at the absence of his
hon. Friend the Member for Dumfries (Mr. Ewart), whose name
had been so closely connected with the amelioration of the criminal
law, and who had done so much to abolish capital punishment. His
reason for bringing forward this Motion now was, that he had a strong
conviction that capital punishment was inexpedient and unnecessary;
that it did not ensure the purposes for which it was enacted; that it
was unjust in principle; that it involved not unfrequently the sacrifice
of innocent human life; and further, that it afforded an escape for

---

*The Honorable Mr. Gilpin, "Parliamentary Debate on Capital Punishment
Within Prisons Bill," in *Hansard's Parliamentary Debates*, 3rd series, April 21,
1868 (London: Hansard, 1868).

many guilty of atrocious crimes. Holding these opinions, he could not permit to pass an Act which proposed to re-enact the punishment of death without entering his solemn protest against it, and submitting the reasons why he thought it inexpedient that capital punishment should be inflicted. The late division on this question was no test whatever of the feeling of the House on the question of capital punishment. He was now asked, "Will you bring forward a Motion for the abolition of capital punishment in the face of the frequent murders, of the increase of the crime of murder—at a time when no doubt there are influences at work"—to which he would not particularly allude— "which aggravate the crime to an extent almost unprecedented?" He unhesitatingly replied, "Yes; I will bring it forward now, because, if my principle is good for anything, it is good at all times and under all circumstances." He would remind the House that the atrocious murders which were now being committed, and which they all so much deplored, were murders which were committed under the present law, and he believed would not be committed under the altered state of the law which he desired to introduce. The question he had to deal with was—by what means could they best stop the crime of murder? He disavowed emphatically any sympathy with crime—he disavowed any maudlin sentimentality with respect to this question. He was sure his right hon. Friend opposite (Mr. Gathorne Hardy) would agree with him that the question between them was, how best to prevent the crime of murder. He said, without fear of contradiction, that almost in every instance in which capital punishment had ceased to be inflicted for certain crimes those crimes had lessened in frequency and enormity since its abolition; yet, as regarded murder, where the punishment of death was still retained, the crime had increased not only in number but enormity. In proof of that allegation he might quote statistics; but the fact was well known, and he would not take up the time of the House by doing so. It was also not to be denied that this was a question upon which there had been a very considerable change in public opinion within a comparatively short period of time. Some of those who had the administration of the law in their hands, and some of those who had occupied the position of the right hon. Gentleman opposite (Mr. Gathorne Hardy), had come to the conclusion, at which he arrived many years ago, that capital punishment was undesirable—that it was unnecessary—and that the time had arrived when some other system ought to be adopted. Surely they were not succeeding in putting down murder. They had for centuries tried the *lex talionis*—the life for life principle—and they had miserably failed, and murder still stalked abroad. Earl Russell, in the introduction to the new edition of his work on the *English Constitution*, thus expressed himself as being favourable to the abolition of capital punishment—

> For my own part, I do not doubt for a moment either the right of a community to inflict the punishment of death, or the expediency of exercising that right in certain states of society. But when I turn from that abstract right and that abstract expediency to our own state of society—when I consider how difficult it is for any Judge to separate the case which requires inflexible justice from that which admits the force of mitigating circumstances—how invidious the task of the Secretary of State in dispensing the mercy of the Crown—how critical the comments made by the public—how soon the object of general horror becomes the theme of sympathy and pity—how narrow and how limited the examples given by this condign and awful punishment—how brutal the scene of execution—I come to the conclusion that nothing would be lost to justice, nothing lost in the preservation of innocent life, if the punishment of death were altogether abolished. In that case a sentence of a long term of separate confinement, followed by another term of hard labour and hard fare, would cease to be considered as an extension of mercy. If the sentence of the Judge were to that effect, there would scarcely ever be a petition for remission of punishment, in cases of murder, sent to the Home Office. The guilty, unpitied, would have time and opportunity to turn repentant to the Throne of Mercy.

Now, the first objection which he (Mr. Gilpin) had to the punishment of death was its essential injustice. They gave the same punishment to the crime of a Rush or a Manning as they did to that of a Samuel Wright, and other less guilty persons. They had, under the present law, constant occurrences in which the feeling, intellect, judgment, and Christianity of the public were against carrying out the extreme penalty, even in cases where the law was clear and unmistakable as to the matter and there was every reason to believe that it had been justly administered by the Judge who had condemned the criminal. Take, for instance, the case of the woman Charlotte Harris. She was sentenced to death, being *enceinte* at the time. According to custom she was reprieved until her babe was born, and then if the sentence of the law had taken its course she would have been hanged; but public opinion in the meantime had become so strong that the Home Office, even, he believed, in opposition to the judgment of the Secretary of State, had to give way, though the case was a fearful and atrocious one, and her life was spared. Richard Cobden, writing to him (Mr. Gilpin) with reference to this case, said—

> You are right. It is truly horrible to think of nursing a woman through her confinement, and then with her first returning strength to walk her to the scaffold! What is to become of the baby at its birth? is it to lie upon the mother's breast until removed by the hand of Calcraft? Oh, horrible! horrible! Could you not have a meeting to shame the authorities.

Well, there were several meetings—one of 40,000 women, headed by Mary Howitt—and they petitioned the Throne for mercy, and mercy was extended. Then there was the case of Alice Holt. She, too, was pregnant; but the Home Office, having got wiser by this time, would not bring her to trial until after the birth of her child. Then they brought her to trial, sentenced her to death, and carried out the execution. Against the injustice of such a proceeding he had at the time most earnestly protested. A practical point most serious to the interests of society was this: numbers of criminals had escaped from the punishment due to their crimes, because of the unwillingness of juries to incur the possibility of convicting the innocent. He believed it was on this ground that Mr. Waddington, the former Under Secretary at the Home Office, came almost to the opinions that he (Mr. Gilpin) entertained. He knew it did not appear in his evidence before the Royal Commission; but Mr. Waddington told him though looking at the matter from a different standpoint and urged by different arguments, still he had very nearly come to his (Mr. Gilpin's) opinions that it would be desirable for the interests of society at large that the abolition of capital punishment should take place. He (Mr. Gilpin) believed it was not too much to say that there were men and women walking about red-handed amongst us—persons unquestionably guilty of the most atrocious murders—who, had the punishment for their crimes been other than capital, would be now immured in prison, utterly unable to repeat such crimes as those for which they had been already tried. This arose from the unwillingness of juries to convict—an unwillingness which did them honour—unless they had evidence positive and indisputable. It was right that evidence which would suffice to convict a man where the punishment would be fourteen years, or imprisonment for life, should be regarded as utterly insufficient to convict a man when the sentence would send him out of the world. Some twenty years ago Charles Dickens wrote a series of letters in *The Daily News* on the subject of capital punishment; and in one, headed "How Jurymen Feel," he said—

> Juries, like society, are not stricken foolish or motionless. They have, for the most part, an objection to the punishment of death; and they will, for the most part, assert it by such verdicts. As jurymen in the forgery cases (where jurors found a £10 note to be worth 39s., so as not to come under capital punishment) would probably reconcile their verdict to their consciences by calling to mind that the intrinsic value of a bank-note was almost nothing; so jurymen, in cases of murder, probably argue that grave doctors have said all men are more or less mad, and therefore they believe the prisoner mad. This is a great wrong to society: but it arises out of the punishment of death. And the question will always suggest itself in jurors' minds, however earnestly the learned Judge presiding may discharge his duty—which is the greater wrong to society?—to give this man the benefit of the possibility of his being mad, or to have another public execution, with all its depraving and hardening influences? Imagining myself a juror, in a case of life or death, and supposing that the evidence had forced me from every other ground of opposition to this punishment in the particular case than a possibility of immediate mistake or otherwise, I would go over it again

on this ground, and, if I could by any reasonable special pleading with myself find him mad rather than hang him, I think I would.

He had alluded to the numbers of persons who had escaped justice altogether, because juries could not make up their minds to convict under such circumstances; but there was another view of the case, and that was the execution of innocent persons, and when he said innocent persons, he meant persons innocent of the crimes with which they were charged. He would not delay the House by quoting what he quoted on a former occasion—the evidence of Daniel O'Connell, or the evidence of the present Lord Chief Baron, as to the frequency of the execution of innocent persons. But he would call the attention of the House to a case which occurred in 1865—that was the Italian Pollizzioni, who was tried for the Saffron Hill murder, when one of the most humane of our Judges expressed his entire belief that the conviction was right. Pollizzioni was sentenced, and was within a few days of being hanged. Law had done its best and its worst, when Mr. Negretti—of the firm of Negretti and Zambra—heard of the case, and became convinced that the man was innocent. He busied himself in getting evidence, which at last satisfied the Home Secretary, not that the prisoner deserved secondary punishment, but that he was absolutely innocent, and then he was taken out of the condemned cell. But for the interference of a private individual this man would have been hanged. It might be said that a case like this was very exceptional, and God forbid that it should be frequent; but within a few months there was the case of another man at Swansea, Giardinieri—oddly enough, also an Italian—who was sentenced to death, and was within a short time of being hanged. Evidence was, however, procured which showed him to be innocent. These were solemn facts. Charles Dickens said—

> I entreat all who may chance to read this letter to pause for an instant, and ask themselves whether they can remember any occasion on which they have in the broad day, and under circumstances the most favourable to recognition, mistaken one person for another, and believed that in a perfect stranger they have seen going away from them, or coming towards them, a familiar friend.

Hence there should be a reasonable hesitation as to an irrevocable verdict. The frequency of cases of mistaken identity were notorious. Mr. Visschers, who held a high position in the Government of the King of the Belgians, stated that in his experience three men convicted of murder appealed to the Court of Cassation, when the conviction was confirmed. The King, however, commuted their sentence into one of perpetual imprisonment; but their innocence being afterwards established, they were liberated, and granted annuities for life. Mr. Serjeant Parry stated, in reply to a Question by Mr. Waddington—

> I could mention six or eight instances within my own knowledge in which men have been acquitted, purely upon the ground that the punishment was capital.

And in reply to Mr. Bright, the learned gentleman said—

> I know that juries have acquitted men clearly and beyond all doubt guilty of murder, and some of the very worst murders that have ever been committed in this country, and have done so simply because the punishment has been the punishment of death. They would have convicted if the punishment had been imprisonment for life, or any punishment short of taking the life of the man, and they have seized hold of any excuse rather than be agents in putting capital punishment into operation.

This was not unreasonable; because a man, if wrongly transported, as in the case of Mr. Barber, the solicitor, could have compensation made to him, but not so if wrongly hanged. Many years ago Sir James Mackintosh stated before a Committee on the Criminal Laws that during a long cycle of years an average of one person was executed every three years whose innocence was afterwards proved. And Sir Fitz Roy Kelly stated, in 1839, that there were no less than fourteen innocent persons within the first forty years of this century who had been convicted, and whose innocence since their death had been fully established. And doubtless the average of one innocent person every three years was much too low, because it should be remembered that after the person was executed there was no motive to discover whether he or she were innocent or not. It was only necessary again to refer to the well-known case of Samuel Wright, a working carpenter in Southwark, to show the inequality of the law, and that, too, resulting simply from the character of the punishment. He believed no jury would have found Wright guilty on the charge of murder, and that no Judge but one would have left him for execution. The prisoner, it was true, pleaded guilty to the crime, and neither the counsel nor the Court could induce him to retract the plea; but it was clear from the facts of the case that this was not a case of willful murder. The man was awoke in the night, and was dragged out of bed by a violent woman with whom he lived. He struggled with her, and seizing his razor, which was lying in his way, without premeditation he killed her. He was brought up for trial, and he pleaded guilty. They could not expect a carpenter to be trained to the niceties of the law, and it could not be wondered at that he, a conscientious man, determined to plead guilty. Almost at the last moment a very large body of his fellow-working men came up to the Home Office to plead that his life might be spared. The present Government was not then in office. [Mr. Buxton: Who was the Home Secretary?] His right hon. Friend the Member for Morpeth (Sir George Grey). It was thought, most unwisely in his opinion, that the appearance of so large a body of working men on such a subject was an attempt to terrorise the Home Office, and a deaf ear was turned to their pleadings, which might wisely have been granted. Samuel Wright was executed, and that in the face of Charlotte Windsor, the hired murderess of babies, who, to solve some of the subtleties of law, was brought from one part of England to another, and after all was only imprisoned for life. He could never forget the morning of that execution. The people in the neighbourhood, instead of rushing to see the execution, had their blinds drawn down. It was a case which it would take a long time to wipe out from the memories of the people of that neighbourhood. That happened about the time that Townley, another murderer, was acquitted on the ground of insanity—a plea which his subsequent suicide showed to be true. But the question of insanity was one of the most uncertain character; the dividing line was disputed by doctors, and even by doctors in divinity; and the result was that in the case of men who were executed no time was allowed to show whether the crime was the result of a diseased brain, or of that moral obliquity which was rightly the subject of punishment. He felt grateful to the House for the indulgence they had shown him on a subject which had occupied his attention for twenty years. Now, he would ask, what was capital punishment? The punishment of death? No, it was not that. The sentence of death was decreed upon all of us by a higher than a mortal Judge. We but antedated the sentence, and by how much this was done no man could know. A man might be sent to the gallows who, according to medical opinion, could not live three months—and, in fact, a man had been recently executed, of whom the medical man said he could not live three months if he died in course of nature, and another man with a prospect of a long life. But what was the punishment? It was not death; it was antedating the sentence passed upon us all by the Most High. From ten thousand pulpits in the land, they were told, and rightly told, that for the repentant sinner the gates of Heaven were open, whether his death was a violent one or not; and yet in the face of those sermons they said—he did not mean that the Judges say it in so many words—"Your crime is so great that there can be no forgiveness with man; but appeal unto God and he may forgive you if you appeal in the right way and pay due attention to your religious advisers." We told the criminal in one breath that his crime was too great for man to forgive—that he was not fit to live on earth, but we commended him to the mercy of the Highest. We said, in effect, that those feet "which would leave no stain on the pure pavements of the New Jerusalem would leave the polluting mark of blood upon the ground that mortals tread." He knew not how to escape from this argument. If criminals were fit to die the time of their going to Heaven was hastened; and if not fit to die, they were allowed to go with all their unexpiated crimes on their heads before their final Judge. If we believed that faith which we professed, then the greater the sin the greater the need for repentance; and it was something monstrous that we should set ourselves up to decide that a fortnight from the date of his sentence was enough time for the worst murderer to make his peace with God. If we believed there was need for that peacemaking, let us give the murderer the time which God would give him to make his peace with Him. If we wanted to teach mercy, let us set an example of that mercy, and at all events stop short of shedding human blood. And if we would teach reverence for human life, let us not attempt to teach it by showing how it may be speedily taken away. He therefore moved the Amendment of which he had given notice, convinced that by the entire abolition of capital punishment, and the removal from their criminal code of the principle of revenge—the life for life principle—they would inaugurate an era in which the sanctity of human life would be regarded more highly than it had hitherto been, and in which the sense of that sanctity, permeating through society, would result in a great lessening of the crime of murder, and consequently in increased security to the public of this country.

John Stuart Mill

Speech In Favor of Capital Punishment 1868*

It would be a great satisfaction to me if I were able to support this Motion. It is always a matter of regret to me to find myself, on a public question, opposed to those who are called—sometimes in the way of honour, and sometimes in what is intended for ridicule—the philanthropists. Of all persons who take part in public affairs, they are those for whom, on the whole, I feel the greatest amount of respect; for their characteristic is, that they devote their time, their labour, and much of their money to objects purely public, with a less admixture of either personal or class selfishness, than any other class of politicians whatever. On almost all the great questions, scarcely any politicians are so steadily and almost uniformly to be found on the side of right; and they seldom err, but by an exaggerated application of some just and highly important principle. On the very subject that is now occupying us we all know what signal service they have rendered. It is through their efforts that our criminal laws—which within my memory hanged people for stealing in a dwelling house to the value of 40s.—laws by virtue of which rows of human beings might be seen suspended in front of Newgate by those who ascended or descended Ludgate Hill—have so greatly relaxed their most revolting and most impolitic ferocity, that aggravated murder is now practically the only crime which is punished with death by any of our lawful tribunals; and we are even now deliberating whether the extreme penalty should be retained in that solitary case. This vast gain, not only to humanity, but to the ends of penal justice, we owe to the philanthropists; and if they are mistaken, as I cannot but think they are, in the present instance, it is only in not perceiving the right

---

*John Stuart Mill, "Parliamentary Debate on Capital Punishment Within Prisons Bill," in *Hansard's Parliamentary Debates*, 3rd series, April 21, 1868 (London: Hansard, 1868).

time and place for stopping in a career hitherto so eminently beneficial. Sir, there is a point at which, I conceive, that career ought to
stop. When there has been brought home to any one, by conclusive
evidence, the greatest crime known to the law; and when the attendant circumstances suggest no palliation of the guilt, no hope that
the culprit may even yet not be unworthy to live among mankind,
nothing to make it probable that the crime was an exception to his
general character rather than a consequence of it, then I confess it
appears to me that to deprive the criminal of the life of which he
has proved himself to be unworthy—solemnly to blot him out from
the fellowship of mankind and from the catalogue of the living—is
the most appropriate as it is certainly the most impressive, mode in
which society can attach to so great a crime the penal consequences
which for the security of life it is indispensable to annex to it. I defend
this penalty, when confined to atrocious cases, on the very ground
on which it is commonly attacked—on that of humanity to the criminal; as beyond comparison the least cruel mode in which it is possible
adequately to deter from the crime. If, in our horror of inflicting
death, we endeavour to devise some punishment for the living criminal which shall act on the human mind with a deterrent force at all
comparable to that of death, we are driven to inflictions less severe
indeed in appearance, and therefore less efficacious, but far more
cruel in reality. Few, I think, would venture to propose, as a punishment for aggravated murder, less than imprisonment with hard labor
for life; that is the fate to which a murderer would be consigned by
the mercy which shrinks from putting him to death. But has it been
sufficiently considered what sort of a mercy this is, and what kind of
life it leaves to him? If, indeed, the punishment is not really inflicted—if it becomes the sham which a few years ago such punishments
were rapidly becoming—then, indeed, its adoption would be almost
tantamount to giving up the attempt to repress murder altogether.
But if it really is what it professes to be, and if it is realized in all its
rigour by the popular imagination, as it very probably would not be,
but as it must be if it is to be efficacious, it will be so shocking that
when the memory of the crime is no longer fresh, there will be almost
insuperable difficulty in executing it. What comparison can there
really be, in point of severity, between consigning a man to the short
pang of a rapid death, and immuring him in a living tomb, there to

linger out what may be a long life in the hardest and most monotonous toil, without any of its alleviations or rewards—debarred from all pleasant sights and sounds, and cut off from all earthly hope, except a slight mitigation of bodily restraint, or a small improvement of diet? Yet even such a lot as this, because there is no one moment at which the suffering is of terrifying intensity, and, above all, because it does not contain the element, so imposing to the imagination, of the unknown, is universally reputed a milder punishment than death—stands in all codes as a mitigation of the capital penalty, and is thankfully accepted as such. For it is characteristic of all punishments which depend on duration for their efficacy—all, therefore, which are not corporal or pecuniary—that they are more rigorous than they seem; while it is, on the contrary, one of the strongest recommendations a punishment can have, that it should seem more rigorous than it is; for its practical power depends far less on what it is than on what it seems. There is not, I should think, any human infliction which makes an impression on the imagination so entirely out of proportion to its real severity as the punishment of death. The punishment must be mild indeed which does not add more to the sum of human misery than is necessarily or directly added by the execution of a criminal. As my hon. Friend the Member for Northampton (Mr. Gilpin) has himself remarked, the most that human laws can do to anyone in the matter of death is to hasten it; the man would have died at any rate; not so very much later, and on the average, I fear, with a considerably greater amount of bodily suffering. Society is asked, then, to denude itself of an instrument of punishment which, in the grave cases to which alone it is suitable, effects its purposes at a less cost of human suffering than any other; which, while it inspires more terror, is less cruel in actual fact than any punishment that we should think of substituting for it. My hon. Friend says that it does not inspire terror, and that experience proves it to be a failure. But the influence of a punishment is not to be estimated by its effect on hardened criminals. Those whose habitual way of life keeps them, so to speak, at all times within sight of the gallows, do grow to care less about it; as, to compare good things with bad, an old soldier is not much affected by the chance of dying in battle. I can afford to admit all that is often said about the indifference of professional criminals to the gallows. Though of that indifference one-third is probably bravado and another third confidence that they shall have the luck to escape, it is quite probable that the remaining third is real. But the efficacy of a punishment which acts principally through the imagination, is chiefly to be measured by the impression it makes on those who are still innocent; by the horror with which it surrounds the first promptings of guilt; the restraining influence it exercises over the beginning of the thought which, if indulged, would become a temptation; the check which it exerts over the graded declension towards the state—never suddenly attained—in which crime no longer revolts, and punishment no longer terrifies. As for what is called the failure of death punishment, who is able to judge of that? We partly know who those are whom it has not deterred; but who is there who knows whom it has deterred, or how many human beings it has saved who would have lived to be murderers if that awful association had not been thrown round the idea of murder from their earliest infancy? Let us not forget that the most imposing fact loses its power over the imagination if it is made too cheap. When a punishment fit only for the most atrocious crimes is lavished on small offences until human feeling recoils from it, then, indeed, it ceases to intimidate, because it ceases to be believed in. The failure of capital punishment in cases of theft is easily accounted for; the thief did not believe that it would be inflicted. He had learnt by experience that jurors would perjure themselves rather than find him guilty; that Judges would seize any excuse for not sentencing him to death, or for recommending him to mercy; and that if neither jurors nor Judges were merciful, there were still hopes from an authority above both. When things had come to this pass it was high time to give up the vain attempt. When it is impossible to inflict a punishment, or when its infliction becomes a public scandal, the idle threat cannot too soon disappear from the statute book. And in the case of the host of offences which were formerly capital, I heartily rejoice that it did become impracticable to execute the law. If the same state of public feeling comes to exist in the case of murder; if the time comes when jurors refuse to find a murderer guilty; when Judges will not sentence him to death, or will recommend him to mercy; or when, if juries and Judges do not flinch from their duty, Home Secretaries, under pressure of deputations and memorials, shrink from theirs, and the threat becomes, as it became in the other cases, a mere *brutum fulmen*; then, indeed, it may become necessary to do in this case what has been done in those—to abrogate the penalty. That time may come—my hon. Friend thinks that it has nearly come. I hardly know whether he lamented it or boasted of it; but he and his Friends are entitled to the boast; for if it comes it will be their doing, and they will have gained what I cannot but call a fatal victory, for they will have achieved it by bringing about, if they will forgive me for saying so, an enervation, an effeminancy, in the general mind of the country. For what else than effeminancy is it to be so much more shocked by taking a man's life than by depriving him of all that makes life desirable or valuable? Is death, then, the greatest of all earthly ills? *Usque adeone mori miserum est?* Is it, indeed, so dreadful a thing to die? Has it not been from of old one chief part of a manly education to make us despise death—teaching us to account it, if an evil at all, by no means high in the list of evils; at all events, as an inevitable one, and to hold, as it were, our lives in our hands, ready to be given or risked at any moment, for a sufficiently worthy object? I am sure that my hon. Friends know all this as well, and have as much of all these feelings as any of the rest of us; possibly more. But I cannot think that this is likely to be the effect of their teaching on the general mind. I cannot think that the cultivating of a peculiar sensitiveness of conscience on this one point, over and above what results from the general cultivation of the moral sentiments, is permanently consistent with assigning in our own minds to the fact of death no more than the degree of relative importance which belongs to it among the other incidents of our humanity. The men of old cared too little about death, and gave their own lives or took those of others with equal recklessness. Our danger is of the opposite kind, lest we should be so much shocked by death, in general and in the abstract, as to care too much about it in individual cases, both those of other people and our own, which call for its being risked. And I am not putting things at the worst, for it is proved by the experience of other countries that horror of the executioner by no means necessarily implies horror of the assassin. The stronghold, as we all know, of hired assassination in the 18th century was Italy; yet it is said that in some of the Italian populations the infliction of death by sentence of law was in the highest degree offensive and revolting to popular feeling. Much has been said of the sanctity of human life, and the absurdity of supposing that we can teach respect for life by ourselves destroying it. But I am surprised at the employment of this argument, for it is one which might be brought against any punishment whatever. It is not human life only, not human life as such, that ought to be sacred to us, but human feelings. The human capacity of suffering is what we should cause to be respected, not the mere capacity of existing. And we may imagine somebody asking how we can teach people not to inflict suffering by ourselves inflicting it? But to this I should answer—all of us would answer—that to deter by suffering from inflicting suffering is not only possible, but the very purpose of penal justice. Does fining a criminal show want of respect for property, or imprisoning him, for personal freedom? Just as unreasonable is it to think that to take the life of a man who has taken that of another is to show want of regard for human life. We show, on the contrary, most emphatically our regard for it, by the adoption of a rule that he who violates that right in another forfeits it for himself, and that while no other crime that he can commit deprives him of his right to live, this shall. There is one argument against capital punishment, even in extreme cases, which I cannot deny to have weight—on which my hon. Friend justly laid great stress, and which never can be entirely got rid of. It is this—that if by an error of justice an innocent person is put to death, the mistake can never be corrected; all compensation, all reparation for the wrong is impossible. This would be indeed a serious objection if these miserable mistakes—among the most tragical occurrences in the whole round of human affairs—could not be made extremely rare. The argument is invincible where the mode of criminal procedure is dangerous to the innocent, or where the Courts of Justice are not trusted. And this probably is the reason why the objection to an irreparable punishment began (as I believe it did) earlier, and is more intense and more widely diffused, in some parts of the Continent of Europe than it is here. There are on the Continent great and enlightened countries, in which the criminal procedure is not so favorable to innocence, does not afford the same security against erroneous conviction, as it does among us; countries where the Courts of Justice seem to think they fail in their duty unless they find somebody guilty; and in their really laudable desire to hunt guilt from its hiding places, expose themselves to a serious danger of condemning the innocent. If our own procedure and Courts of Justice afforded ground for similar apprehension, I should be the first to join in withdrawing the power of inflicting irreparable punishment from such tribunals. But we all know that the defects of our procedure are the very opposite. Our rules of evidence are even too favorable to the prisoner; and juries and Judges carry out the maxim, "It is better that ten guilty should escape than that one innocent person should suffer," not only to the letter, but beyond the letter. Judges are most anxious to point out, and juries to allow for, the barest possibility of the prisoner's innocence. No human judgment is infallible; such sad cases as my hon. Friend cited will sometimes occur; but in so grave a case as that of murder, the accused, in our system, has always the benefit of the merest shadow of a doubt. And this suggests another consideration very germane to the question. The very fact that death punishment is more shocking than any other to the imagination, necessarily renders the Courts of Justice more scrupulous in requiring the fullest evidence of guilt. Even that which is the greatest objection to capital punishment, the impossibility of correcting an error once committed, must make, and does make, juries and Judges more careful in forming their opinion, and more jealous in their scrutiny of the evidence. If the substitution of penal servitude for death in cases of murder should cause any declaration in this conscientious scrupulosity, there would be a great evil to set against the real, but I hope rare, advantage of being able to make reparation to a condemned person who was afterwards discovered to be innocent. In order that the possibility of correction may be kept open wherever the chance of this sad contingency is more than infinitesimal, it is quite right that the Judge should recommend to the Crown a commutation of the sentence, not solely when the proof of guilt is open to the smallest suspicion, but whenever there remains anything unexplained and mysterious in the case, raising a desire for more light, or making it likely that further information may at some future time be obtained. I would also suggest that whenever the sentence is commuted the grounds of the commutation should, in some authentic form, be made known to the public. Thus much I willingly concede to my hon. Friend; but on the question of total abolition I am inclined to hope that the feeling of the country is not with him, and that the limitation of death punishment to the cases referred to in the Bill of last year will be generally considered sufficient. The mania which existed a short time ago for paring down all our punishments seems to have reached its limits, and not before it was time. We were in danger of being left without any effectual punishment, except for small of offences. What was formerly our chief secondary punishment—transportation—before it was abolished, had become almost a reward. Penal servitude, the substitute for it, was becoming, to the classes who were principally subject to it, almost nominal, so comfortable did we make our prisons, and so easy had it become to get quickly out of them. Flogging—a most objectionable punishment in ordinary cases, but a particularly appropriate one for crimes of brutality, especially crimes against women—we would not hear of, except, to be sure, in the case of garrotters, for whose peculiar benefit we reestablished it in a hurry, immediately after a Member of Parliament had been garrotted. With this exception, offences, even of an atrocious kind, against the person, as my hon. and learned Friend the Member for Oxford (Mr.Neate) well remarked, not only were, but still are, visited with penalties so ludicrously inadequate, as to be almost an encouragement to the crime. I think, Sir, that in the case of most offences, except those against property, there is more need of strengthening our punishments than of weakening them; and that severer sentences, with an apportionment of them to the different kinds of offences which shall approve itself better than at present to the moral sentiments of the community, are the kind of reform of which our penal system now stands in need. I shall therefore vote against the Amendment.

Clarence Darrow

Negative Presentation Address*

THE CHAIRMAN: It is only because the next speaker happens for some unknown reason not to live in the City of New York that this Lochinvar has been obliged to come out of the West for the purpose of trying to prove to you that the steed that he rides today is the best. Mr. Darrow has a national reputation. He is known from the Atlantic to the Pacific as a lawyer, as a defender of unpopular causes (laughter), as an essayist and as a great orator. I need not say more. He will prove to you that what I have said so far is pretty nearly correct. (Applause.)

MR. DARROW: I had this stand moved up so I could get next to the audience. (Laughter.)

I hope I will not be obliged to spend too much time on my friend's address. I don't think I shall need to.

First, I deny his statement that every man's heart tells him it is wrong to kill. I think every man's heart desires killing. Personally, I never killed anybody that I know of. But I have had a great deal of satisfaction now and then reading obituary notices (laughter), and I used to delight, with the rest of my hundred percent patriotic friends, when I saw ten or fifteen thousand Germans being killed in a day.

Everybody loves killing. Some of them think it is too mussy for them. Every human being that believes in capital punishment loves killing, and the only reason they believe in capital punishment is because they get a kick out of it. (Laughter and applause.) Nobody kills anyone for love, unless they get over it temporarily or otherwise. But they kill the one they hate. And before you can get a trial to hang somebody or electrocute him, you must first hate him and then get a satisfaction over his death.

---

*Clarence Darrow, "Negative Presentation Address," in *Clarence Darrow on Capital Punishment*. (Chicago: Chicago Historical Bookworks, 1991), pp. 29–41.

There is no emotion in any human being that is not in every single human being. The degree is different, that is all. And the degree is not always different in different people. It depends likewise on the circumstances, on time and on place.

I shall not follow my friend into the labyrinth of statistics. Statistics are a pleasant indoor sport—not so good as cross-word puzzles (laughter)—and they prove nothing to any sensible person who is familiar with statistics. (Applause.)

I might just observe, in passing, that in all of these states where the mortality by homicide is great, they have capital punishment and always have had it. (Applause.) A logical man, when he found out that the death rate increased under capital punishment, would suggest some other way of dealing with it. (Applause.)

I undertake to say—and you can look them up yourselves, for I haven't time to bother with it (and there is nothing that lies like statistics)—I will guarantee to take any set of statistics and take a little time to it and prove they mean directly the opposite for what is claimed. But I will undertake to say that you can show by statistics that the States in which there was no capital punishment have a very much smaller percentage of homicides. (Applause.)

I know it is true. That doesn't prove anything, because, as a rule, they are States with a less divers [sic] population, without as many large cities, without as much mixtures of all sorts of elements which go to add to the general gayety—and homicide is a product of that. There is no sort of question but what those States in the United States where there is no capital punishment have a lower percentage than the others. But that doesn't prove the question. It is a question that cannot be proven one way or the other by statistics. It rests upon things, upon feelings and emotions and arguments much deeper than statistics.

The death rate in Memphis and in some other Southern cities is high from homicide. Why? Well, it is an afternoon's pleasure to kill a Negro—that is about all. (Applause.) Everybody knows it.

The death rate recently in the United States and all over the world has increased. Why? The same thing has happened that has happened in every country in the world since time began. A great war always increases death rates.

We teach people to kill, and the State is the one that teaches them. (Applause.) If a State wishes that its citizens respect human life, then the State should stop killing. It can be done in no other way, and it will perhaps not be fully done that way. There are infinite reasons for killing. There are infinite circumstances under which there are more or less deaths. It never did depend and never can depend upon the severity of the punishment.

He talks about the United States being a lawless country. Well, the people somehow prefer it. (Laughter.) There is such a thing as a people being too servile to law. You may take China with her caste system and much of Europe, which has much more caste than we. It may be full of homicides, but there is less bread and there is less fun; there is less opportunity for the poor. In any new country, homicide is more frequent than in an old country, because there is a higher degree of equality. It is always true wherever you go. And in the older countries, as a general rule, there are fewer homicides because nobody ever thinks of getting out of his class; nobody ever dreams of such a thing.

But let's see what there is in this argument. He says, "Everybody who kills, dreads hanging." Well, he has had experience as a lawyer on both sides. I have experience on one side. I know that everybody who is taken into court on a murder charge desires to live, and they do not want to be hanged or electrocuted. Even a thing as alluring as being cooked with electricity doesn't appeal to them.

But that hasn't anything to do with it. What was the state of mind when the homicide was committed? The state of mind is one thing when a homicide is committed and another thing weeks or months afterward, when every reason for committing it is gone. There is no comparison between it.

We might ask why people kill. I don't want to dispute with him about the right of the State to kill people. Of course, they have got a right to kill them. That is about all we do. The great industry of the world for four long years was killing. They have got a right to kill, of course. That is, they have got the power. And you have got a right to do what you get away with. (Applause.) The words power and right, so far as this is concerned, mean exactly the same thing. So nobody who has any knowledge of philosophy would pretend to say that the State had not the right to kill.

But why not do a good job of it? (Laughter.) If you want to get rid of killings by hanging people or electrocuting them because these are so terrible, why not make a punishment that is terrible? This isn't so much. It lasts but a short time. There is no physical torture in it. Why not boil them in oil, as they used to do? Why not burn them at the stake? Why not sew them into a bag with serpents and throw them out to sea? Why not take them out on the sand and let them be eaten by ants? Why not break every bone in their body on the wrack [sic], as has been done for such serious offenses as heresy and witchcraft?

Those were the good old days in which the Judge should have held court. (Laughter and applause.) Glorious days, when you could kill them by the million because they worshipped God in a different way from that which the State provided, or when you could kill old women for witchcraft! There might be some sense in it if you could kill young ones, but not old ones. (Laughter.) Those were the glorious days to talk of capital punishment. And there wasn't a Judge or a preacher who didn't think that the life of the State depended upon their right to hang old women for witchcraft and to persecute others for worshipping God in the wrong way.

Why, our capital punishment isn't worth talking about, so far as it is being a preventative is concerned. (Applause.) It isn't worth discussing. Why not call back from the dead and barbarous past the hundred and sixty or seventy odd crimes that were punishable by death in England? Why not once more reenact the Blue Laws of our own country and kill people right? Why not resort to all the tortures that the world has always restored to keep men in the straight and narrow path? Why reduce it to a paltry question of murder?

Everybody in this world has some pet aversion to something, and on account of that pet aversion they would like to hang somebody. If the prohibitionists made the law, they would be in favor of hanging you for taking a drink, or certainly for bootlegging, because to them that is the most heinous crime there is.

Some men slay for murder. Why? As a matter of fact, murder as murder is very rare; and the people who commit it, as a rule, are of a much higher type than others. You may go to any penitentiary and, as a rule those who have been convicted of murder become the trustees; whereas, if you are punishing somebody as a sneak thief or a counterfeiter or a confidence man, they never get over it—never.

Now, I don't know how injustice is administered in New York. (Laughter.) I just know about Chicago. But I am glad to learn from the gentlemen that if a man is so poor in New York that he can't hire a lawyer, that he has a first-class lawyer appointed to defend him. (Laughter.) Don't take a chance and go out and kill anybody on the statement made by my friend. (Laughter.)

I suppose anybody can go out and kill somebody and ask to have my friend, Sam Untermyer, appointed. (Laughter) There never was such a thing. Here and there, a good lawyer may have defended people for nothing. But no court ever interferes with a good lawyer's business by calling him in and compelling him to give him time. They have been lawyers too recently themselves to ever work a trick like that on a lawyer. (Laughter.) As a rule, it is the poor and the weak and the friendless who furnish the victims of the law. (Applause.)

Let me take another statement of my friend. He said, "Oh, we don't hang anybody if they kill when they are angry; it is only when they act premeditatedly." Yes, I have been in courts and heard Judges instruct people on this premeditated act. It is only when they act under their judgment and with due consideration. He would also say that if a man is moved by anger, but if he doesn't strike the deadly blow until such time as reason and judgment has a chance to possess him, even if it is a second—how many times have I heard Judges say, "Even if it is a second?" What does anybody know about it? How many people are there in this world that can premeditate on anything? I will strike out the "pre" and say how many people are there that can meditate? (Laughter.)

How long does it take the angry man for his passions to cool when he is in the presence of the thing that angers him? There never was a premeditated murder in any sense of psychology or of science. There are planned murders—planned, yes—but back of every murder and back of every human act are sufficient causes that move the human machine beyond their control.

The other view is an outworn, outlawed, unscientific theory of metaphysicians. Does anybody ever act in this world without a motive? Did they ever act without a sufficient motive? And who am I to say that John Smith premeditated? I might premeditate a good deal quicker than John Smith did. My judgment might have a chance to act quicker than John Smith's judgment had a chance to act.

We have heard talk of justice. Is there anybody who knows what justice is? No one on earth can measure out justice. Can you look at any man and say what he deserves—whether he deserves hanging by the neck until dead or life in prison or thirty days in prison or a medal? The human mind is blind to all who seek to look in at it and to most of us that look out from it. Justice is something that man knows little about. He may know something about charity and understanding and mercy, and he should cling to these as far as he can. (Applause.)

Now, let me see if I am right about my statement that no man believes in hanging, except for a kick or for revenge. How about my friend, Judge Talley, here. He criticizes the State of New York because a prisoner may be shown moving pictures. What do you think about it—those of you who think? What do you feel about it—those of you who have passed the hyena age? I know what they think. What do you think about shutting up a man in a penitentiary for twenty years, mind!—and complaining because he had a chance now and then to go out and see a moving picture—go out of his cell?

A body of people who feels that way could never get rid of capital punishment. If you really felt it, you would feel like the Indian who used the tomahawk on his enemy and who burned him and embalmed his face with ashes.

But what is punishment about anyway? I put a man in prison for the purpose of getting rid of him and for such example as there might be. Is it up to you to torture him while he is in there? Supposing you provided that every man who went to prison should be compelled to wear a nail half an inch long in his shoe. I suppose some of you would do it. I don't know whether the Judge would or not, from what he said. (Laughter.)

Is there any reason for torturing someone who happens to be in prison? Is there any reason why an actor or even an actress might not go there and sing? There is no objection to a preacher going there. Why not give him a little pleasure? (Laughter.)

And they really get food there—what do you know about that? (Laughter.) Now, when I heard him tell about what wonderful food they get—dietary food—did you ever know anybody that liked dietary food? (Laughter.) I supposed the Constitution of the State of New York contains the ordinary provision against cruel and inhuman punishment, and yet you send them up there and feed them on dietary food. (Laughter.)

And you can take your meals out! Now, some of you might not have noticed that I walked over and asked the Warden about it. The reason I did that is because I am stopping over here at the Belmont, and I didn't know but I'd rather go up and board with him. (Laughter.)

Now, this is what I find out: That for those who have gained consideration by good conduct over a considerable period—how long, Mr. Lawes?

WARDEN LAWES: One year.

MR. DARROW: One year—they may spend three dollars a week for board. I pay more than that over here. (Laughter) They ought to pass some law in New York to prevent the inmates getting dyspepsia. And for those who attain the second class, they may spend a dollar and a half a week. And for those below the second class, nothing can come from outside—nothing. A pure matter of prison discipline!

Why, I wonder if the Judge ever took pains to go up there. I will tell you. I have had some experience with people that know them pretty well. I never saw a man who wanted to go to prison, even to see the movies. (Laughter.) I never saw a man in my life who didn't want to get out.

I wonder what you would have. Of course, I live in Chicago, where people are fairly human—I don't know, maybe I don't understand the New York people. What would you have? Suppose you could tell yourselves how a person was to be treated while in prison—and it doesn't require a great amount of imagination. Most people can think of some relative or some friends who are there. If you can't most of you can think of a good many that ought to be there. (Laughter.) How would you have them treated—something worse than being shut up in a cell, four by seven, and given light work—like being a Judge or practicing law (laughter)—something worse than dietary food?

I will tell you. There is just one thing in all this question. It is a question of how you feel, that is all. It is all inside of you. If you love the thought of somebody being killed, why, you're for it. If you hate the thought of somebody being killed, you are against it. (Applause.)

Let me just take a little brief review of what has happened in this world. They used to hang people on the cross-ways and on a high hill, so that everybody would be awed into goodness by the sight.

They have tortured them in every way that the brain of man could conceive. They have provided every torture known or that could be imagined for one who believed differently from his fellow-man—and still the belief persisted. They have maimed and scarred and starved and killed human beings since man began penning his fellow-man. Why? Because we hate him. And what has added to it is that they have done it under the false ideal of self-righteousness.

I have heard parents punish their children and tell their children it hurt the parent more than it did the child. I don't believe it. (Laughter.) I have tried it both ways, and I don't believe it. (Laughter.) I know better.

Gradually, the world has been lopping off these punishments. Why? Because we have grown a little more sensitive, a little more imaginative, a little kindlier, that is all.

Why not reenact the code of Blackstone's day? Why, the Judges were all for it—every one of them—and the only way we got rid of those laws was because Juries were too humane to obey the courts. (Applause.)

That is the only way we got rid of punishing old women, of hanging old women in New England—because, in spite of the courts, the Juries would no longer convict them for a crime that never existed. And in that way they have cut down the crimes in England for punishment by death from one hundred and seventy two. What is going to happen if we get rid of them? Is the world coming to an end? The earth has been here ages and ages before man came. It will be here ages and ages after he disappears, and the amount of people you hang won't make the slightest difference with it.

Now, why am I opposed to capital punishment? It is too horrible a thing for a State to undertake. We are told by my friend, "Oh, the killer does it; why shouldn't the State?" I would hate to live in a state that I didn't think was better than a murderer. (Applause.)

But I told you the real reason. The people of the State kill a man because he killed someone else—that is all—without the slightest logic, without the slightest application to life simply from anger, nothing else!

I am against it because I believe it is inhuman, because I believe that as the hearts of men have softened they have gradually gotten rid of brutal punishment, because I believe that it will only be a few years until it will be banished forever from very civilized country—even New York—because I believe that it has no effect whatever to stop murder. (Applause.)

Now let's make that simple and see. Where do the murders come from? I would say the second largest class of what we call murders grow out of domestic relations. They follow those deep and profound feelings that are the basis of life—and the feelings which give the greatest joy are susceptible of the greatest pain when they go a-riot.

Can you imagine a woman following a man around with a pistol to kill him that would stop if you said, "Oh, you will be hanged!" Nothing doing—not if the world was coming to an end! Can you imagine a man doing it? Not at all. They think of it afterwards, but not before.

They come from acts like burglary and robbery. A man goes out to rob or to burglarize. Somebody catches him or stops him or recognizes him, and he kills to save himself. Do you suppose there was ever a burglar or robber since the world began who would not kill to save himself? Is there anybody who wouldn't? It doesn't make any difference who. Wouldn't he take a chance shooting. Anyone would do it. Why, my friend himself said he would kill in self-defense. That is what they do. If you are going to stop them, you ought to hang them for robbery—which would be a good plan—and then, of course, if one started out to rob, he would kill the victim before he robbed him. (Laughter.)

There isn't, I submit, a single admissible argument in favor of capital punishment. Nature loves life. We believe that life should be protected and preserved. The thing that keeps one from killing is the emotion they have against it; and the greater the sanctity that the State pays to life, the greater the feeling of sanctity the individual has for life. (Applause.)

There is nothing in the history of the world that ever cheapened human life like our great war; next to that, the indiscriminate killing of men by the States.

My friend says a man must be proven guilty first. Does anybody know whether anybody is guilty? There is a great deal implied in that. For me to do something or for you to do something is one thing; for some other man to do something is quite another. To know what one deserves, requires infinite study, which no one can give to it. No one can determine the condition of the brain that did the act. It is out of the question.

All people are products of two things, and two things only—their heredity and their environment. And they act in exact accord with the heredity which they took from all the past, and for which they are in no wise responsible, and the environment, which reaches out to the farthest limit of all life that can influence them. We all act from the same way. And it ought to teach us to be charitable and kindly and understanding of our fellow-man. (Applause.)

Ernest Van den Haag

The Death Penalty Once More*

People concerned with capital punishment disagree on essentially three questions: (1) Is it constitutional? (2) Does the death penalty deter crime more than life imprisonment? (3) Is the death penalty morally justifiable?

I. Is The Death Penalty Constitutional?

The fifth amendment, passed in 1791, states that "no person shall be deprived of life, liberty, or property, without due process of law." Thus, with "due process of law," the Constitution authorizes depriving persons "of life, liberty or property." The fourteenth amendment, passed in 1868, applies an identical provision to the states. The Constitution, then, authorizes the death penalty. It is left to elected bodies to decide whether or not to retain it.

The eighth amendment, reproducing almost verbatim a passage from the English Bill of Rights of 1689, prohibits "cruel and unusual punishments." This prohibition was not meant to repeal the fifth amendment since the amendments were passed simultaneously. "Cruel" punishment is not prohibited unless "unusual" as well, that is, new, rare, not legislated, or disproportionate to the crime punished. Neither the English Bill of Rights, nor the eighth amendment, hitherto has been found inconsistent with capital punishment.

---

*Ernest Van Den Haag, "The Death Penalty Once More," *The Death Penalty in America Current Controversies* ed. by Hugo Adam Bedau (New York: Oxford University Press, 1997), 445–56. Reprinted by permission of the publisher, from *University of California-Davis Law Review*, 18, no. 4 summer 1985): 957–72; permission conveyed through Copyright Clearance Center, Inc.

Some commentators argue that, in *Trop v. Dulles*, the Supreme Court indicated that "evolving standards of decency that mark the progress of a maturing society" allow courts to declare "cruel and unusual," punishments authorized by the Constitution. However, *Trop* was concerned with expatriation, a punishment that is not specifically authorized by the Constitution. The death penalty is. *Trop* did not suggest that "evolving standards" could de-authorize what the Constitution repeatedly authorizes. Indeed, Chief Justice Warren, writing for the majority in *Trop*, declared that "the death penalty . . . cannot be said to violate the constitutional concept of cruelty."[1] Furthermore, the argument based on "evolving standards" is paradoxical: the Constitution would be redundant if current views, enacted by judicial fiat, could supersede what it plainly says. If "standards of decency" currently invented or evolved could, without formal amendment, replace or repeal the standards authorized by the Constitution, the Constitution would be superfluous.

It must be remembered that the Constitution does not force capital punishment on the population but merely authorizes it. Elected bodies are left to decide whether to use the authorization. As for "evolving standards," how could courts detect them without popular consensus as a guide? Moral revelations accepted by judges, religious leaders, sociologists, or academic elites, but not by the majority of voters, cannot suffice. The opinions of the most organized, most articulate, or most vocal might receive unjustified deference. Surely the eighth amendment was meant to limit, but was not meant to replace, decisions by the legislative branch, or to enable the judiciary do what the voters won't do. The general consensus on which the courts would have to rely could be registered only by elected bodies. They favor capital punishment. Indeed, at present, more than seventy percent of the voters approve of the death penalty. The state legislatures reflect as much. Wherefore, the Supreme Court, albeit reluctantly, rejected abolition of the death penalty by judicial fiat. This decision was subsequently qualified by a finding that the death

---

1. 356 U.S. 86 (1958) at 99.

penalty for rape is disproportionate to the crime,[2] and by rejecting all mandatory capital punishment.[3]

B. CAPRICE

Laws that allowed courts too much latitude to decide, perhaps capriciously, whether to actually impose the death penalty in capital cases also were found unconstitutional. In response, more than two-thirds of the states have modified their death penalty statutes, listing aggravating and mitigating factors, and imposing capital punishment only when the former outweigh the latter. The Supreme Court is satisfied that this procedure meets the constitutional requirements of noncapriciousness. However, abolitionists are not.

In *Capital Punishment: The Inevitability of Caprice and Mistake*, Professor Charles Black contends that the death penalty is necessarily imposed capriciously, for irremediable reasons. If he is right, he has proved too much, unless capital punishment is imposed more capriciously now than it was in 1791 or 1868, when the fifth and fourteenth amendments were enacted. He does not contend that it is. Professor Black also stresses that the elements of chance, unavoidable in all penalizations, are least tolerable when capital punishment is involved. But the irreducible chanciness inherent in human efforts does not constitutionally require the abolition of capital punishment, unless the framers were less aware of chance and human frailty than Professor Black is. (I shall turn to the moral as distinguished from the legal bearing of chanciness anon.)

---

2. The courts have sometimes confirmed the obsolescence of non-repealed laws or punishments. But here they are asked to invent it.

3. In *Coker v. Georgia*, 433 U.S. 584, 592 (1977), the Court concluded that the eighth amendment prohibits punishments that are " 'excessive' in relation to the crime committed." I am not sure about this disproportion. However, threatening execution would tempt rapists to murder their victims who, after all, are potential witnesses. By murdering their victims, rapists would increase their chances of escaping execution without adding to their risk. Therefore, I agree with the court's conclusion, though not with its argument.

Sociologists have demonstrated that the death penalty has been distributed in a discriminatory pattern in the past: black or poor defendants were more likely to be executed than equally guilty others. This argues for correction of the distributive process, but not for abolition of the penalty it distributes, unless constitutionally excessive maldistribution ineluctably inheres in the penalty. There is no evidence to that effect. Actually, although we cannot be sure that it has disappeared altogether, discrimination has greatly decreased compared to the past.[4]

However, recently the debate on discrimination has taken a new turn. Statistical studies have found that, *ceteris paribus*, a black man who murders a white has a much greater chance to be executed than he would have had, had his victim been black.[5] This discriminates against black *victims* of murder: they are not as fully, or as often, vindicated as are white victims. However, although unjustified per se, discrimination against a class of victims need not, and here does not, amount to discrimination against their victimizers. The pattern discriminates *against* black murderers of whites and *for* black murderers of blacks. One may describe it as discrimination for, or discrimination against, just as one may describe a glass of water as half full or half empty. Discrimination against one group (here, blacks who kill whites) is necessarily discrimination in favor of another (here, blacks who kill blacks).

Most black victims are killed by black murderers, and a disproportionate number of murder victims is black. Wherefore the discrimination in favor of murderers of victims more than offsets, numerically, any remaining discrimination against other black murderers.[6]

---

4. See *Woodson v. North Carolina*, 428 U.S. 280 (1976); *Roberts v. Louisiana*, 428 U.S. 325 (1976). Once more I disagree with the reasoning, at least in part, but welcome the conclusion, since mandatory capital punishment risks jury cancellations.

5. For a survey of the statistical literature, see, e.g., Bowers, *The Pervasiveness of Arbitrariness and Discrimination Under Post-Furman Capital Statutes*, 74 J. CRIM. L. & CRIMINOLOGY 1067 (1983). His article is part of a "Symposium on Current Death Penalty Issues" compiled by death penalty opponents.

6. Those who demonstrated the pattern seem to have been under the impression that they had shown discrimination against black murderers. They were wrong. However, the discrimination against black victims is invidious and should be corrected.

Recently lawyers have argued that the death penalty is unconstitutionally disproportionate if defendants, elsewhere in the state, received lesser sentences for comparable crimes. But the Constitution only requires that penalties be appropriate to the gravity of the crime, not that they cannot exceed penalties imposed elsewhere. Although some states have adopted "comparative excessiveness" reviews, there is no constitutional requirement to do so.

Unavoidably, different courts, prosecutors, defense lawyers, judges and juries produce different penalties even when crimes seem comparable. Chance plays a great role in human affairs. Some offenders are never caught or convicted, while others are executed; some are punished more than others guilty of worse crimes. Thus, a guilty person, or group of persons, may get away with no punishment, or with a light punishment, while others receive the punishment they deserve. Should we let these others go too, or punish them less severely? Should we abolish the penalty applied unequally or discriminatorily?[7]

The late Justice Douglas suggested an answer to these questions:

> A law that . . . said that blacks, those who never went beyond the fifth grade in school, those who made less than $3,000 a year, or those who were unpopular or unstable should be the only people executed [would be wrong]. A law which in the overall view reaches that result in practice has no more sanctity than a law which in terms provides the same.[8]

Justice Douglas's answer here conflates an imagined discriminatory law with the discriminatory application of a non-discriminatory law. His imagined law would be inconsistent with the "equal protection of the laws" demanded by the fourteenth amendment, and the Court

---

7. The capriciousness argument is undermined when capriciousness is conceded to be unavoidable. But even when capriciousness is thought reducible, one wonders whether releasing or retrying one guilty defendant, because another equally guilty defendant was not punished as much, would help reduce capriciousness. It does not seem a logical remedy.

8. *Furman v. Georgia*, 408 U.S. 238, 256 (1972) (Douglas, J., concurring).

would have to invalidate it ipso facto. But discrimination caused by uneven application of non-discriminatory death penalty laws may be remedied by means other than abolition, as long as the discrimination is not intrinsic to the laws.

Consider now, albeit fleetingly, the moral as distinguished from the constitutional bearing of discrimination. Suppose guilty defendants are justly executed, but only if poor, or black and not otherwise. This unequal justice would be morally offensive for what may be called tautological reasons:[9] if any punishment for a given crime is just, then a greater or lesser punishment is not. Only one punishment can be just for all persons equally guilty of the same crime.[10] Therefore, different punishments for equally guilty persons or group members are unjust: some offenders are punished more than they deserve, or others less.

Still, equality and justice are not the same. "Equal justice" is not a redundant phrase. Rather, we strive for two distinct ideals, justice and equality. Neither can replace the other. We want to have justice and, having it, we want to extend it equally to all. We would not want equal injustice. Yet, sometimes, we must choose between equal injustice and unequal justice. What should we prefer? Unequal justice is justice still, even if only for some, whereas equal injustice is injustice for all. If not every equally guilty person is punished equally, we have unequal justice. It seems preferable to equal injustice—having no guilty person punished as deserved.[11] Since it is never possible to

---

9. I shall not consider here the actual psychological motives that power our unending thirst for equality.

10. If courts impose different punishments on different persons, we may not be able to establish in all cases whether the punishment is just, or (it amounts to the same) whether the different persons were equally guilty of the same crime, or whether their crimes were identical in all relevant respects. Thus, we may not be able to tell which of two unequal punishments is just. Both may be, or neither may be. Inequality may not entail more injustice than equality, and equality would entail justice only if we were sure that the punishment meted out was the just punishment.

11. Similarly, it is better that only some innocents suffer undeserved punishment than that all suffer it equally.

punish equally all equally guilty murderers, we should punish, as they deserve, as many of those we apprehend and convict as possible. Thus, even if the death penalty were inherently discriminatory—which is not the case—but deserved by those who receive it, it would be morally just to impose it on them. If, as I contend, capital punishment is just and not inherently discriminatory, it remains desirable to eliminate inequality in distribution, to apply the penalty to all who deserve it, sparing no racial or economic class. But if a guilty person or group escaped the penalty through our porous system, wherein is this an argument for sparing others?

If one does not believe capital punishment can be just, discrimination becomes a subordinate argument, since one would object to capital punishment even if it were distributed equally to all the guilty. If one does believe that capital punishment for murderers is deserved, discrimination against guilty black murderers and in favor of equally guilty white murderers is wrong, not because blacks receive the deserved punishment, but because whites escape it.

Consider a less emotionally charged analogy. Suppose traffic police ticketed all drivers who violated the rules, except drivers of luxury cars. Should we abolish tickets? Should we decide that the ticketed drivers of nonluxury cars were unjustly punished and ought not to pay their fines? Would they become innocent of the violation they are guilty of because others have not been ticketed? Surely the drivers of luxury cars should not be exempted. But the fact that they were is no reason to exempt drivers of nonluxury cars as well. Laws could never be applied if the escape of one person, or group, were accepted as ground for not punishing another. To do justice is primarily to punish as deserved, and only secondarily to punish equally.

Guilt is personal. No one becomes less guilty or less deserving of punishment because another was punished leniently or not at all. That justice does not catch up with all guilty persons understandably is resented by those caught. But it does not affect their guilt. If some, or all, white and rich murderers escape the death penalty, how does that reduce the guilt of black or poor murderers, or make them less deserving of punishment, or deserving of a lesser punishment?

Some lawyers have insisted that the death penalty is distributed among those guilty of murder as though by a lottery and that the worst may escape it.[12] They exaggerate, but suppose one grants the point. How do those among the guilty selected for execution by lottery become less deserving of punishment because others escaped it? What is wrong is that these others escaped, not that those among the guilty who were selected by the lottery did not.

Those among the guilty actually punished by a criminal justice system unavoidably are selected by chance, not because we want to so select them, but because the outcome of our efforts largely depends on chance. No murderer is punished unless he is unlucky enough both to be caught and to have convinced a court of his guilt. And courts consider evidence not truth. They find truth only when the evidence establishes it. Thus they may have reasonable doubts about the guilt of actually guilty person. Although we may strive to make justice as equal as possible, unequal justice will remain our lot in this world. We should not give up justice, or the death penalty, because we cannot extend it as equally to all the guilty as we wish. If we were not to punish one offender because another got away because of caprice or discrimination, we would give up justice for the sake of equality. We would reverse the proper order of priorities.

II. Is the Death Penalty More Deterrent Than Other Punishments?

Whether or not the death penalty deters the crimes it punishes more than alternative penalties—in this case life imprisonment with or without parole—has been widely debated since Isaac Ehrlich broke the abolitionist ranks by finding that from 1933–65 "an additional execution per year . . . may have resulted on the average in seven

---

12. It would be desirable that all of the worst murderers be sentenced to death. However, since murderers are tried in different courts, this is unlikely. Further, sometimes the testimony of one murderer is needed to convict another, and cannot be obtained except by leniency. Morally, and legally it is enough that those sentenced to death deserve the penalty for their crimes, even if others, who may deserve it as much, or more, were not sentenced to death.

or eight fewer murders."[13] Since his article appeared, a whole cottage industry devoted to refuting his findings has arisen. Ehrlich, no slouch, has been refuting those who refuted him.[14] The result seems inconclusive.[15] Statistics have not proved conclusively that the death penalty does or does not deter murder more than other penalties. Still, Ehrlich has the merit of being the first to use a sophisticated statistical analysis to tackle the problem, and of defending his analysis, although it showed deterrence. (Ehrlich started as an abolitionist.) His predecessors cannot be accused of mathematical sophistication. Yet the academic community uncritically accepted their abolitionist results. I myself have no contribution to make to the mathematical analyses of deterrent effects. Perhaps this is why I have come to believe that they may becloud the issue, leading us to rely on demonstrable deterrence as though decisive.

Most abolitionists believe that the death penalty does not deter more than other penalties. But most abolitionists would abolish it, even if it did.[16] I have discussed this matter with prominent abolitionists such as Charles Black, Henry Schwarzschild, Hugo Adam Bedau, Ramsey Clark, and many others. Each told me that, even if every execution were to deter a hundred murders, he would oppose it. I infer that, to these abolitionist leaders, the life of every murderer is more valuable than the lives of a hundred prospective victims, for these abolitionists would spare the murderer, even if doing so would cost a hundred future victims their lives.

---

13. Ehrlich, *The Deterrent Effect of Capital Punishment: A Question of Life or Death*, 65 Am. Econ. Rev. 397,414 (1975).

14. Ehrlich, *Fear of Deterrence*, 6 J. LEGAL STUD. 293 (1977); Ehrlich & Gibbons, *On the Measurement of the Deterrent Effect of Capital Punishment and the Theory of Deterrence*, 6 J. LEGAL STUD. 35 (1977).

15. At present there is no agreement even on whether the short run effects of executions delay or accelerate homicides. See Phillips, *The Deterrent Effect of Capital Punishment: New Evidence on an Old Controversy*, 86 AM. J. SOC. 139 (1980).

16. Jeffrey Reiman is an honorable exception. See Reiman, *Justice, Civilization, and the Death Penalty: Answering van den Haag*, 14 PHIL. & PUB. AFF. 115 (1985).

Obviously, deterrence cannot be the decisive issue for these abolitionists. It is not necessarily for me either, since I would be for capital punishment on grounds of justice alone. On the other hand, I should favor the death penalty for murderers, if probably deterrent, or even just possibly deterrent. To me, the life of any innocent victim who might be spared has great value; the life of a convicted murderer does not. This is why I would not take the risk of sacrificing innocents by not executing murderers.

Even though statistical demonstrations are not conclusive, and perhaps cannot be, I believe that capital punishment is likely to deter more than other punishments because people fear death more than anything else. They fear most death deliberately inflicted by law and scheduled by the courts. Whatever people fear most is likely to deter most. Hence, I believe that the threat of the death penalty may deter some murderers who otherwise might not have been deterred. And surely the death penalty is the only penalty that could deter prisoners already serving a life sentence and tempted to kill a guard, or offenders about to be arrested and facing a life sentence. Perhaps they will not be deterred. But they would certainly not be deterred by anything else. We owe all the protection we can give to law enforcers exposed to special risks.

Many murders are "crimes of passion" that, perhaps, cannot be deterred by any threat. Whether or not they can be would depend on the degree of passion; it is unlikely to be always so extreme as to make the person seized by it totally undeterrable. At any rate, offenders sentenced to death ordinarily are guilty of premeditated murder, felony murder, or multiple murders. Some are rape murderers, or hit men, but, to my knowledge, no one convicted of a "crime of passion" is on death row. Whatever the motive, some prospective offenders are not deterrable at all, others are easily deterred, and most are in between. Even if only some murders were, or could be, deterred by capital punishment, it would be worthwhile.

Sometimes an anecdote, invented in the 19th Century, is told to suggest that the threat of the death penalty does not deter. Some pickpockets are said to have gone eagerly about their business in a crowd assembled to see one of them hang. We are not told what the level of their activity was, compared to the level in crowds of similar size assembled for different purposes. Thus, the anecdote merely shows that the death penalty does not deter some criminals. This never was contested.

Almost all convicted murderers try to avoid the death penalty by appeals for commutation to life imprisonment. However, a minuscule proportion of convicted murderers prefer execution. It is sometimes argued that they murdered for the sake of being executed, of committing suicide via execution. More likely, they prefer execution to life imprisonment. Although shared by few, this preference is not irrational per se. It is also possible that these convicts accept the verdict of the court, and feel that they deserve the death penalty for the crimes they committed, although the modern mind finds it hard to imagine such feelings. But not all murderers are ACLU humanists.

Because those sentenced to death tend to sedulously appeal the verdict of the trial courts, executions are correctly said to be costly. It is doubtful, however, that they are more costly than life imprisonment. Contrary to widely shared assumptions, life prisoners spend much of their time preparing habeas corpus appeals (not to speak of other lawsuits) just as prisoners condemned to death do.[17] But even if execution were more costly than life imprisonment, it should not be abandoned if it is just. If unjust, execution should not occur, even if it were cheap and imprisonment costly. But execution probably is less costly than life imprisonment.

III. Is the Death Penalty Moral?

A. MISCARRIAGES

Miscarriages of justice are rare, but do occur. Over a long enough time they lead to the execution of some innocents.[18] Does this make

---

17. Often the marginal cost of appeals is erroneously compared to the average cost of imprisonment. See, e.g., Kaplan, *The Problem of Capital Punishment*, 1983 U. ILL.L. REV. 555.

18. Life imprisonment avoids the problem of executing innocent persons to some extent. It can be revoked. But the convict also may die in prison before his innocence is discovered.

irrevocable punishments morally wrong? Hardly. Our government employs trucks. They run over innocent bystanders more frequently than courts sentence innocents to death. We do not give up trucks because the benefits they produce outweigh the harm, including the death of innocents. Many human activities, even quite trivial ones, foreseeably cause wrongful deaths. Courts may cause fewer wrongful deaths than golf. Whether one sees the benefit of doing justice by imposing capital punishment as moral, or as material, or both, it outweighs the loss of innocent lives through miscarriages, which are as unintended as traffic accidents.

B. VENGEANCE

Some abolitionists feel that the motive for the death penalty is an un-Christian and unacceptable desire for vengeance. But though vengeance be the motive, it is not the purpose of the death penalty. Doing justice and deterring crime are the purposes, whatever the motive. Purpose (let alone effect) and motive are not the same.

The Lord is often quoted as saying "Vengeance is mine." He did not condemn vengeance. He merely reserved it to Himself—and to the government. For, in the same epistle He is also quoted as saying that the ruler is "the minister of God, a revenger, to execute wrath upon him that doeth evil." The religious notion of hell indicates that the biblical God favored harsh and everlasting punishment for some. However, particularly in a secular society, we cannot wait for the day of judgment to see murderers consigned to hell. Our courts must "execute wrath upon him that doeth evil" here and now.

C. CHARITY AND JUSTICE

Today many religious leaders oppose capital punishment. This is surprising, because there is no biblical warrant for their opposition. The Roman Catholic Church and most Protestant denominations traditionally have supported capital punishment. Why have their moral views changed? When sharing secular power, the churches clearly distinguished between justice, including penalization as deserved, a function of the secular power, and charity, which, according to religious doctrine, we should feel for all those who suffer for whatever reasons. Currently, religious leaders seem to conflate justice and charity, to conclude that the death penalty and, perhaps, all punishment, is wrong because uncharitable. Churches no longer share secular power. Perhaps bystanders are more ready to replace justice with charity than are those responsible for governing.

D. HUMAN DIGNITY

Let me return to the morality of execution. Many abolitionists believe that capital punishment is "degrading to human dignity" and inconsistent with the "sanctity of life." Justice Brennan, concurring in *Furman*, stressed these phrases repeatedly. He did not explain what he meant.

Why would execution degrade human dignity more than life imprisonment? One may prefer the latter; but it seems at least as degrading as execution. Philosophers, such as Immanuel Kant and G. F. W. Hegel, thought capital punishment indispensable to redeem, or restore, the human dignity of the executed. Perhaps they were wrong. But they argued their case, whereas no one has explained why capital punishment degrades. Apparently those who argue that it does degrade dignity simply define the death penalty as degrading. If so, degradation (or dehumanization) merely is a disguised synonym for their disapproval. Assertion, reassertion, or definition do not constitute evidence or argument, nor do they otherwise justify, or even explain, disapproval of capital punishment.

Writers, such as Albert Camus, have suggested that murderers have a miserable time waiting for execution and anticipating it.[19] I do not doubt that. But punishments are not meant to be pleasant. Other people suffer greatly waiting for the end, in hospitals, under circumstances that, I am afraid, are at least as degrading to their dignity as execution. These sufferers have not deserved their suffering

---

19. In *Reflections on the Guillotine*, Camus stated that "[t]he parcel [the condemned person] is no longer subject to the laws of chance that hang over the living creature but to mechanical laws that allow him to foresee accurately the day of his beheading. . . . The Greeks, after all, were more humane with their hemlock." A. Camus, RESISTANCE, REBELLION AND DEATH 175, 202 (1960).

by committing crimes, whereas murderers have. Yet, murderers suffer less on death row, unless their consciences bother them.

E. LEX TALIONIS

Some writers insist that the suffering the death penalty imposes on murderers exceeds the suffering of their victims. This is hard to determine, but probably true in some cases and not in other cases. However, the comparison is irrelevant. Murderers are punished, as are all offenders, not just for the suffering they caused their victims, but for the harm they do to society by making life insecure, by threatening everyone, and by requiring protective measures. Punishment, ultimately, is a vindication of the moral and legal order of society and not limited by the *Lex Talionis*, meant to limit private retaliation for harms originally regarded as private.

F. SANCTITY OF LIFE

We are enjoined by the Declaration of Independence to secure life. How can this best be achieved? The Constitution authorizes us to secure innocent life by taking the life of murderers, so that anyone who deliberately wants to take an innocent life will know that he risks forfeiting his own. The framers did not think that taking the life of a murderer is inconsistent with the "sanctity of life" which Justice Brennan champions. He has not indicated why they were wrong.[20]

G. LEGALIZED MURDER?

Ever since Cesare Bonesana, Marchese di Beccaria, wrote *Dei Delitti e Delle Pene*, abolitionists have contended that executing murderers

---

20. "Sanctity of life" may mean that we should not take, and should punish taking innocent life: "*homo homini res sacra.*" In the past this meant that we should take the life of a murderer to secure innocent life, and stress its sacredness. Justice Brennan seems to mean that the life of the murderer should be sacred too-but no argument is given for this premise.

legitimizes murder by doing to the murderer what he did to his victim. Indeed, capital punishment retributes, or pays back the offender. Occasionally we do punish offenders by doing to them what they did to their victims. We may lock away a kidnapper who wrongfully locked away his victim, and we may kill the murderer who wrongfully killed his victim. To lawfully do to the offender what he unlawfully did to his victim in no way legitimizes his crime. It legitimizes (some) killing, and not murder. An act does not become a crime because of its physical character, which, indeed, it may share with the legal punishment, but because of its social, or, better, antisocial, character—because it is an unlawful act.

H. SEVERITY

Is the death penalty too severe? It stands in a class by itself. But so does murder. Execution is irreparable. So is murder. In contrast, all other crimes and punishments are, at least partly or potentially, reparable. The death penalty thus is congruous with the moral and material gravity of the crime it punishes.[21]

Still, is it repulsive? Torture, however well deserved, now is repulsive to us. But torture is an artifact. Death is not, since nature has placed us all under sentence of death. Capital punishment, in John Stuart Mill's phrase, only "hastens death"—which is what the murderer did to his victim. I find nothing repulsive in hastening the murderer's death, provided it be done in a nontorturous manner. Had he wished to be secure in his life, he could have avoided murder.

To believe that capital punishment is too severe for any act, one must believe that there can be no act horrible enough to deserve death.[22] I find this belief difficult to understand. I should readily

---

21. Capital punishment is not inconsistent with *Weems v. United States*, 217 U.S. 349 (1910), which merely held that punishment cannot be excessive, that is, out of proportion to the gravity of the crime. Indeed, if life imprisonment suffices for anything else, it cannot be appropriate for murder.

22. The notion of deserving is strictly moral, depending exclusively on our sense of justice, unlike the notion of deterrence, which depends on the expected factual consequences of punishment. Whilst deterrence alone would justify most of the punishments we should impose, it may not suffice to justify all those punishments that our sense of justice demands. Wherefore criminal justice must rest on desert as well as deterrence, to be seen as morally justified.

impose the death penalty on a Hitler or a Stalin, or on anyone who does what they did, albeit on a smaller scale.

Conclusion

The death penalty has become a major issue in public debate. This is somewhat, puzzling, because quantitatively it is insignificant. Still, capital punishment has separated the voters as a whole from a small, but influential, abolitionist elite. There are, I believe, two reasons that explain the prominence of the issue.

First, I think, there is a genuine ethical issue. Some philosophers believe that the right to life is equally imprescriptible for all, that the murderer has as much right to live as his victim. Others do not push egalitarianism that far. They believe that there is a vital difference, that one's right to live is lost when one intentionally takes an innocent life, that everyone has just the right to one life, his own. If he unlawfully takes that of another he, *eo ipso*, loses his own right to life.

Second, and perhaps as important, the death penalty has symbolic significance. Those who favor it believe that the major remedy for crime is punishment. Those who do not, in the main, believe that the remedy is anything but punishment. They look at the causes of crime and conflate them with compulsions, or with excuses, and refuse to blame. The majority of the people are less sophisticated, but perhaps they have better judgment. They believe that everyone who can understand the nature and effects of his acts is responsible for them, and should be blamed and punished, if he could know that what he did was wrong. Human beings are human because they can be held responsible, as animals cannot be. In that Kantian sense the death penalty is a symbolic affirmation of the humanity of both victim and murderer.

Chapter Four

Groups Punished

Michelle Alexander

Blacks and Hispanics*

Jarvious Cotton cannot vote. Like his father, grandfather, great-grand-father, and great-great-grandfather, he has been denied the right to participate in our electoral democracy. Cotton's family tree tells the story of several generations of black men who were born in the United States but who were denied the most basic freedom that democracy promises—the freedom to vote for those who will make the rules and laws that govern one's life. Cotton's great-great-grandfather could not vote as a slave. His great-grandfather was beaten to death by the Ku Klux Klan for attempting to vote. His grandfather was prevented from voting by Klan intimidation. His father was barred from voting by poll taxes and literacy tests. Today, Jarvious Cotton cannot vote because he, like many black men in the United States, has been labeled a felon and is currently on parole.[1]

Cotton's story illustrates, in many respects, the old adage "The more things change, the more they remain the same." In each gen-eration, new tactics have been used for achieving the same goals—goals shared by the Founding Fathers. Denying African Americans citizenship was deemed essential to the formation of the original union. Hundreds of years later, America is still not an egalitarian

---

*Michelle Alexander, *The New Jim Crow Mass Incarceration in the Age of Colorblindness* (New York: New Press, 2010), 1–16. Excerpt from *The New Jim Crow*. © 2010, 2012 by Michelle Alexander. Reprinted by permission of The New Press. www.thenewpress.com

1. Jarvious Cotton was a plaintiff in *Cotton v. Fordice*, 157 F.3d 388 (5th Cir. 1998), which held that Mississippi's felon disenfranchisement provision had lost its racially discriminatory taint. The information regarding Cotton's family tree was obtained by Emily Bolton on March 29, 1999, when she interviewed Cotton at Mississippi State Prison. Jarvious Cotton was released on parole in Mississippi, a state that denies voting rights to parolees.

democracy. The arguments and rationalizations that have been trotted out in support of racial exclusion and discrimination in its various forms have changed and evolved, but the outcome has remained largely the same. An extraordinary percentage of black men in the United States are legally barred from voting today, just as they have been throughout most of American history. They are also subject to legalized discrimination in employment, housing, education, public benefits, and jury service, just as their parents, grandparents, and great-grandparents once were.

What has changed since the collapse of Jim Crow has less to do with the basic structure of our society than with the language we use to justify it. In the era of colorblindness, it is no longer socially permissible to use race, explicitly, as a justification for discrimination, exclusion, and social contempt. So we don't. Rather than rely on race, we use our criminal justice system to label people of color "criminals" and then engage in all the practices we supposedly left behind. Today it is perfectly legal to discriminate against criminals in nearly all the ways that it was once legal to discriminate against African Americans. Once you're labeled a felon, the old forms of discrimination—employment discrimination, housing discrimination, denial of the right to vote, denial of educational opportunity, denial of food stamps and other public benefits, and exclusion from jury service—are suddenly legal. As a criminal, you have scarcely more rights, and arguably less respect, than a black man living in Alabama at the height of Jim Crow. We have not ended racial caste in America; we have merely redesigned it.

I reached the conclusions presented in this book reluctantly. Ten years ago, I would have argued strenuously against the central claim made here—namely, that something akin to a racial caste system currently exists in the United States. Indeed, if Barack Obama had been elected president back then, I would have argued that his election marked the nation's triumph over racial caste—the final nail in the coffin of Jim Crow. My elation would have been tempered by the distance yet to be traveled to reach the promised land of racial justice in America, but my conviction that nothing remotely similar to Jim Crow exists in this country would have been steadfast.

Today my elation over Obama's election is tempered by a far more sobering awareness. As an African-American woman, with three young children who will never know a world in which a black man could not be president of the United States, I was beyond thrilled on election night. Yet when I walked out of the election night party, full of hope and enthusiasm, I was immediately reminded of the harsh realities of the New Jim Crow. A black man was on his knees in the gutter, hands cuffed behind his back, as several police officers stood around him talking, joking, and ignoring his human existence. People poured out of the building; many stared for a moment at the black man cowering in the street, and then averted their gaze. What did the election of Barack Obama mean for him?

Like many civil rights lawyers, I was inspired to attend law school by the civil rights victories of the 1950s and 1960s. Even in the face of growing social and political opposition to remedial policies such as affirmative action, I clung to the notion that the evils of Jim Crow are behind us and that, while we have a long way to go to fulfill the dream of an egalitarian, multiracial democracy, we have made real progress and are now struggling to hold on to the gains of the past. I thought my job as a civil rights lawyer was to join with the allies of racial progress to resist attacks on affirmative action and to eliminate the vestiges of Jim Crow segregation, including our still separate and unequal system of education. I understood the problems plaguing poor communities of color, including problems associated with crime and rising incarceration rates, to be a function of poverty and lack of access to quality education—the continuing legacy of slavery and Jim Crow. Never did I seriously consider the possibility that a new racial caste system was operating in this country. The new system had been developed and implemented swiftly, and it was largely invisible, even to people, like me, who spent most of their waking hours fighting for justice.

I first encountered the idea of a new racial caste system more than a decade ago, when a bright orange poster caught my eye. I was rushing to catch the bus, and I noticed a sign stapled to a telephone pole that screamed in large bold print: \stet caps-small caps\THE DRUG WAR IS THE NEW JIM CROW. I paused for a moment and skimmed the text of the flyer. Some radical group was holding a community meeting about police brutality, the new three-strikes law in California, and the expansion of America's prison system. The meeting was being held at a small community church a few blocks away; it had seating capacity for no more than fifty people. I sighed, and muttered to myself something like, "Yeah, the criminal justice system is racist in many ways, but it really doesn't help to make such an absurd comparison. People will just think you're crazy." I then crossed the street and hopped on the bus. I was headed to my new job, director of the Racial Justice Project of the American Civil Liberties Union (ACLU) in Northern California.

When I began my work at the ACLU, I assumed that the criminal justice system had problems of racial bias, much in the same way that all major institutions in our society are plagued with problems associated with conscious and unconscious bias. As a lawyer who had litigated numerous class-action employment-discrimination cases, I understood well the many ways in which racial stereotyping can permeate subjective decision-making processes at all levels of an organization, with devastating consequences. I was familiar with the challenges associated with reforming institutions in which racial stratification is thought to be normal—the natural consequence of differences in education, culture, motivation, and, some still believe, innate ability. While at the ACLU, I shifted my focus from employment discrimination to criminal justice reform and dedicated myself to the task of working with others to identify and eliminate racial bias whenever and wherever it reared its ugly head.

By the time I left the ACLU, I had come to suspect that I was wrong about the criminal justice system. It was not just another institution infected with racial bias but rather a different beast entirely. The activists who posted the sign on the telephone pole were not crazy; nor were the smattering of lawyers and advocates around the country who were beginning to connect the dots between our current system of mass incarceration and earlier forms of social control. Quite belatedly, I came to see that mass incarceration in the United States had, in fact, emerged as a stunningly comprehensive and well-disguised system of racialized social control that functions in a manner strikingly similar to Jim Crow.

In my experience, people who have been incarcerated rarely have difficulty identifying the parallels between these systems of social control. Once they are released, they are often denied the right to vote, excluded from juries, and relegated to a racially segregated and subordinated existence. Through a web of laws, regulations, and informal rules, all of which are powerfully reinforced by social stigma, they are confined to the margins of mainstream society and denied access to the mainstream economy. They are legally denied the ability to obtain employment, housing, and public benefits—much as African Americans were once forced into a segregated, second-class citizenship in the Jim Crow era.

Those of us who have viewed that world from a comfortable distance—yet sympathize with the plight of the so-called underclass—tend to interpret the experience of those caught up in the criminal justice system primarily through the lens of popularized social science, attributing the staggering increase in incarceration rates in communities of color to the predictable, though unfortunate, consequences of poverty, racial segregation, unequal educational opportunities, and the presumed realities of the drug market, including the mistaken belief that most drug dealers are black or brown. Occasionally, in the course of my work, someone would make a remark suggesting that perhaps the War on Drugs is a racist conspiracy to put blacks back in their place. This type of remark was invariably accompanied by nervous laughter, intended to convey the impression that although the idea had crossed their minds, it was not an idea a reasonable person would take seriously.

Most people assume the War on Drugs was launched in response to the crisis caused by crack cocaine in inner-city neighborhoods. This view holds that the racial disparities in drug convictions and sentences, as well as the rapid explosion of the prison population, reflect nothing more than the government's zealous—but benign—efforts to address rampant drug crime in poor, minority neighborhoods. This view, while understandable, given the sensational media coverage of crack in the 1980s and 1990s, is simply wrong.

While it is true that the publicity surrounding crack cocaine led to a dramatic increase in funding for the drug war (as well as to sentencing policies that greatly exacerbated racial disparities in incarceration rates), there is no truth to the notion that the War on Drugs was launched in response to crack cocaine. President Ronald Reagan officially announced the current drug war in 1982, before crack became an issue in the media or a crisis in poor black neighborhoods. A few years after the drug war was declared, crack began to spread rapidly in the poor black neighborhoods of Los Angeles and later emerged in cities across the country.[2] The Reagan administration hired staff to publicize the emergence of crack cocaine in 1985 as part of a strategic effort to build public and legislative support for the war.[3] The media campaign was an extraordinary success. Almost overnight, the media was saturated with images of black "crack whores," "crack dealers," and "crack babies"—images that seemed to confirm the worst negative racial stereotypes about impoverished inner-city residents. The media bonanza surrounding the "new demon drug" helped to catapult the War on Drugs from an ambitious federal policy to an actual war.

The timing of the crack crisis helped to fuel conspiracy theories and general speculation in poor black communities that the War on Drugs was part of a genocidal plan by the government to destroy black people in the United States. From the outset, stories circulated on the street that crack and other drugs were being brought into black neighborhoods by the CIA. Eventually, even the Urban League came to take the claims of genocide seriously. In its 1990 report "The State of Black America," it stated: "There is at least one concept that must be recognized if one is to see the pervasive and insidious nature of the drug problem for the African American community. Though difficult to accept, that is the concept of genocide."[4] While the conspiracy theories were initially dismissed as far-fetched, if not downright loony, the word on the street turned out to be right, at least to a point. The CIA admitted in 1998 that guerilla armies it actively supported in Nicaragua were smuggling illegal drugs into the United States—

---

2. The *New York Times* made the national media's first specific reference to crack in a story published in late 1985. Crack became known in a few impoverished neighborhoods in Los Angeles, New York, and Miami in early 1986. See Craig Reinarman and Harry Levine, "The Crack Attack: America's Latest Drug Scare, 1986–1992," in *Images of Issues: Typifying Contemporary Social Problems* (New York: Aldine De Gruyter, 1995), 152.

3. The Reagan administration's decision to publicize crack "horror stories" is discussed in more depth in chapter I.

4. Clarence Page, "'The Plan': A Paranoid View of Black Problems," *Dover (Delaware) Herald*, Feb. 23, 1990. See also Manning Marable, *Race, Reform, and Rebellion: The Second Reconstruction in Black America, 1945–1990* (Jackson: University Press of Mississippi, 1991), 212–13.

drugs that were making their way onto the streets of inner-city black neighborhoods in the form of crack cocaine. The CIA also admitted that, in the midst of the War on Drugs, it blocked law enforcement efforts to investigate illegal drug networks that were helping to fund its covert war in Nicaragua.[5]

It bears emphasis that the CIA never admitted (nor has any evidence been revealed to support the claim) that it intentionally sought the destruction of the black community by allowing illegal drugs to be smuggled into the United States. Nonetheless, conspiracy theorists surely must be forgiven for their bold accusation of genocide, in light of the devastation wrought by crack cocaine and the drug war, and the odd coincidence that an illegal drug crisis suddenly appeared in the black community after—not before—a drug war had been declared. In fact, the War on Drugs began at a time when illegal drug use was on the decline.[6] During this same time period, however, a war was declared, causing arrests and convictions for drug offenses to skyrocket, especially among people of color.

The impact of the drug war has been astounding. In less than thirty years, the U.S. penal population exploded from around 300,000 to more than 2 million, with drug convictions accounting for the majority of the increase.[7] The United States now has the highest rate of incarceration in the world, dwarfing the rates of nearly every developed country, even surpassing those in highly repressive regimes like Russia, China, and Iran. In Germany, 93 people are in prison for every 100,000 adults and children. In the United States, the rate is roughly eight times that, or 750 per 100,000.[8]

---

5. See Alexander Cockburn and Jeffrey St. Clair, *Whiteout: The CIA, Drugs, and the Press* (New York: Verso, 1999). See also Nick Shou, "The Truth in 'Dark Alliance,'" *Los Angeles Times*, Aug. 18, 2006; Peter Kornbluh, "CIA's Challenge in South Central," *Los Angeles Times* (Washington edition) Nov. IS, 1996; and Alexander Cockburn, "Why They Hated Gary Webb," *The Nation*, Dec. 16, 2004.

6. Katherine Beckett and Theodore Sasson, *The Politics of Injustice: Crime and Punishment in America*, (Thousand Oaks, CA: Sage Publications, 2004), 163.

7. Marc Mauer, *Race to Incarcerate*. rev. ed. (New York: The New Press, 2006), 33.

8. PEW Center on the States, *One in 100: Behind Bars in America* 2008 (Washington, DC: PEW Center, Feb. 2008), 5.

The racial dimension of mass incarceration is its most striking feature. No other country in the world imprisons so many of its racial or ethnic minorities. The United States imprisons a larger percentage of its black population than South Africa did at the height of apartheid. In Washington, D.C., our nation's capital, it is estimated that three out of four young black men (and nearly all those in the poorest neighborhoods) can expect to serve time in prison.[9] Similar rates of incarceration can be found in black communities across America.

These stark racial disparities cannot be explained by rates of drug crime. Studies show that people of all colors *use and sell* illegal drugs at remarkably similar rates.[10] If there are significant differences in the surveys to be found, they frequently suggest that whites, particularly white youth, are more likely to engage in drug crime than people of color.[11] That is not what one would guess, however, when entering

---

9. Donald Braman, *Doing Time on the Outside: Incarceration and Family Life in Urban America* (Ann Arbor: University of Michigan Press, 2004), 3, citing D.C. Department of Corrections data for 2000.

10. See, e.g., U.S. Department of Health and Human Services, Substance Abuse and Mental Health Services Administration, *Summary of Findings from the 2000 National Household Survey on Drug Abuse*, NHSDA series H-I3, DHHS pub. no. SMA 01-3549 (Rockville, MD: 2001), reporting that 6.4 percent of whites, 6.4 percent of blacks, and 5.3 percent of Hispanics were current users of illegal drugs in 2000; *Results from the 2002 National Survey on Drug Use and Health: National Findings*, NHSDA series H-22, DHHS pub. no. SMA 03-3836 (2003), revealing nearly identical rates of illegal drug use among whites and blacks, only a single percentage point between them; and *Results from the 2007 National Survey on Drug Use and Health: National Findings*, NSDUH series H-34, DHHS pub. no. SMA 08-4343 (2007), showing essentially the same finding. See also Marc Mauer and Ryan S. King, *A 25-Year Quagmire: The "War on Drugs" and Its Impact on American Society* (Washington, DC: Sentencing Project, Sept. 2007), 19, citing a study suggesting that African Americans have slightly higher rates of illegal drug use than whites.

11. See, e.g., Howard N. Snyder and Melissa Sickman, *Juvenile Offenders and Victims: 2006 National Report*, U.S. Department of Justice, Office of Justice Programs, Office of Juvenile Justice and Delinquency Prevention (Washington, DC: U.S. Department of Justice, 2006), reporting that white youth are more likely than black youth to engage in illegal drug sales. See also Lloyd D. Johnston, Patrick M. O'Malley, Jerald G. Bachman, and John E. Schulenberg, *Monitoring the Future, National Survey Results on Drug Use, 1975–2006, vol. 1, Secondary School Students*, U.S. Department of Health and Human Services,

our nation's prisons and jails, which are overflowing with black and brown drug offenders. In some states, black men have been admitted to prison on drug charges at rates twenty to fifty times greater than those of white men.[12] And in major cities wracked by the drug war, as many as 80 percent of young African-American men now have criminal records and are thus subject to legalized discrimination for the rest of their lives.[13] These young men are part of a growing under-caste, permanently locked up and locked out of mainstream society.

It may be surprising to some that drug crime was declining, not rising, when a drug war was declared. From a historical perspective, however, the lack of correlation between crime and punishment is nothing new. Sociologists have frequently observed that governments use punishment primarily as a tool of social control, and thus the extent or severity of punishment is often unrelated to actual crime patterns. Michael Tonry explains in *Thinking About Crime*: "Governments decide how much punishment they want, and these decisions are in no simple way related to crime rates."[14] This fact, he points out, can be seen most clearly by putting crime and punishment in comparative perspective. Although crime rates in the United States have not been markedly higher than those of other Western countries, the rate of incarceration has soared in the United States while it has remained stable or declined in other countries. Between 1960 and

---

National Institute on Drug Abuse, NIH pub. no. 07-6205 (Bethesda, MD: 2007), 32, "African American 12th graders have consistently shown lower usage rates than White 12th graders for most drugs, both licit and illicit"; and Lloyd D. Johnston, Patrick M. O'Malley, and Jerald G. Bachman, *Monitoring the Future: National Results on Adolescent Drug Use: Overview of Key Findings 2002*, U.S. Department of Health and Human Services, National Institute on Drug Abuse, NIH pub. no. 03-5374 (Bethesda, MD: 2003), presenting data showing that African American adolescents have slightly lower rates of illicit drug use than their white counterparts.

12. Human Rights Watch, *Punishment and Prejudice: Racial Disparities in the War on Drugs*, HRW Reports vol. 12, no. 2 (New York, 2000).

13. See, e.g., Paul Street, *The Vicious Circle: Race, Prison, Jobs, and Community in Chicago, Illinois, and the Nation* (Chicago Urban League, Department of Research and Planning, 2002).

14. Michael Tonry, *Thinking About Crime: Sense and Sensibility in American Penal Culture* (New York: Oxford University Press, 2004), 14.

1990, for example, official crime rates in Finland, Germany, and the United States were close to identical. Yet the U.S. incarceration rate quadrupled, the Finnish rate fell by 60 percent, and the German rate was stable in that period.[15] Despite similar crime rates, each government chose to impose different levels of punishment.

Today, due to recent declines, U.S. crime rates have dipped below the international norm. Nevertheless, the United States now boasts an incarceration rate that is six to ten times greater than that of other industrialized nations[16]—a development directly traceable to the drug war. The only country in the world that even comes close to the American rate of incarceration is Russia, and no other country in the world incarcerates such an astonishing percentage of its racial or ethnic minorities.

The stark and sobering reality is that, for reasons largely unrelated to actual crime trends, the American penal system has emerged as a system of social control unparalleled in world history. And while the size of the system alone might suggest that it would touch the lives of most Americans, the primary targets of its control can be defined largely by race. This is an astonishing development, especially given that as recently as the mid-1970s, the most well-respected criminologists were predicting that the prison system would soon fade away. Prison did not deter crime significantly, many experts concluded. Those who had meaningful economic and social opportunities were unlikely to commit crimes regardless of the penalty, while those who went to prison were far more likely to commit crimes again in the future. The growing consensus among experts was perhaps best reflected by the National Advisory Commission on Criminal Justice Standards and Goals, which issued a recommendation in 1973 that "no new institutions for adults should be built and existing institutions for juveniles should be closed."[17] This recommendation was based on their finding that "the prison, the reformatory and the jail have

---

15. Ibid.

16. Ibid., 20.

17. National Advisory Commission on Criminal Justice Standards and Goals, *Task Force Report on Corrections* (Washington, DC: Government Printing Office, 1973), 358.

achieved only a shocking record of failure. There is overwhelming evidence that these institutions create crime rather than prevent it."[18]

These days, activists who advocate "a world without prisons" are often dismissed as quacks, but only a few decades ago, the notion that our society would be much better off without prisons—and that the end of prisons was more or less inevitable—not only dominated mainstream academic discourse in the field of criminology but also inspired a national campaign by reformers demanding a moratorium on prison construction. Marc Mauer, the executive director of the Sentencing Project, notes that what is most remarkable about the moratorium campaign in retrospect is the context of imprisonment at the time. In 1972, fewer than 350,000 people were being held in prisons and jails nationwide, compared with more than 2 million people today. The rate of incarceration in 1972 was at a level so low that it no longer seems in the realm of possibility, but for moratorium supporters, that magnitude of imprisonment was egregiously high. "Supporters of the moratorium effort can be forgiven for being so naive," Mauer suggests, "since the prison expansion that was about to take place was unprecedented in human history."[19] No one imagined that the prison population would more than quintuple in their lifetime. It seemed far more likely that prisons would fade away.

Far from fading away, it appears that prisons are here to stay. And despite the unprecedented levels of incarceration in the African-American community, the civil rights community is oddly quiet. One in three young African-American men is currently under the control of the criminal justice system—in prison, in jail, on probation, or on parole—yet mass incarceration tends to be categorized as a criminal justice issue as opposed to a racial justice or civil rights issue (or crisis).

The attention of civil rights advocates has been largely devoted to other issues, such as affirmative action. During the past twenty years, virtually every progressive, national civil rights organization in the country has mobilized and rallied in defense of affirmative action. The struggle to preserve affirmative action in higher education, and

---

18. Ibid., 597.

19. Mauer, *Race to Incarcerate*, 17–18.

thus maintain diversity in the nation's most elite colleges and universities, has consumed much of the attention and resources of the civil rights community and dominated racial justice discourse in the mainstream media, leading the general public to believe that affirmative action is the main battlefront in U.S. race relations—even as our prisons fill with black and brown men.

My own experience reflects this dynamic. When I first joined the ACLU, no one imagined that the Racial Justice Project would focus its attention on criminal justice reform. The ACLU was engaged in important criminal justice reform work, but no one suspected that work would eventually become central to the agenda of the Racial Justice Project. The assumption was that the project would concentrate its efforts on defending affirmative action. Shortly after leaving the ACLU, I joined the board of directors of the Lawyers' Committee for Civil Rights of the San Francisco Bay Area. Although the organization included racial justice among its core priorities, reform of the criminal justice system was not (and still is not) a major part of its racial justice work. The Lawyers' Committee is not alone.

In January 2008, the Leadership Conference on Civil Rights—an organization composed of the leadership of more than 180 civil rights organizations—sent a letter to its allies and supporters informing them of a major initiative to document the voting record of members of Congress. The letter explained that its forthcoming report would show "how each representative and senator cast his or her vote on some of the most important civil rights issues of 2007, including voting rights, affirmative action, immigration, nominations, education, hate crimes, employment, health, housing, and poverty." Criminal justice issues did not make the list. That same broad-based coalition organized a major conference in October 2007, entitled Why We Can't Wait: Reversing the Retreat on Civil Rights, which included panels discussing school integration, employment discrimination, housing and lending discrimination, economic justice, environmental justice, disability rights, age discrimination, and immigrants' rights. Not a single panel was devoted to criminal justice reform.

The elected leaders of the African-American community have a much broader mandate than civil rights groups, but they, too, frequently overlook criminal justice. In January 2009, for example, the Congressional Black Caucus sent a letter to hundreds of community and organization leaders who have worked with the caucus over the years, soliciting general information about them and requesting that they identify their priorities. More than thirty-five topics were listed as areas of potential special interest, including taxes, defense, immigration, agriculture, housing, banking, higher education, multimedia, transportation and infrastructure, women, seniors, nutrition, faith initiatives, civil rights, census, economic security, and emerging leaders. No mention was made of criminal justice. "Re-entry" was listed, but a community leader who was interested in criminal justice reform had to check the box labeled "other."

This is not to say that important criminal justice reform work has not been done. Civil rights advocates have organized vigorous challenges to specific aspects of the new caste system. One notable example is the successful challenge led by the NAACP Legal Defense Fund to a racist drug sting operation in Tulia, Texas. The 1999 drug bust incarcerated almost 15 percent of the black population of the town, based on the uncorroborated false testimony of a single informant hired by the sheriff of Tulia. More recently, civil rights groups around the country have helped to launch legal attacks and vibrant grassroots campaigns against felon disenfranchisement laws and have strenuously opposed discriminatory crack sentencing laws and guidelines, as well as "zero tolerance" policies that effectively funnel youth of color from schools to jails. The national ACLU recently developed a racial justice program that includes criminal justice issues among its core priorities and has created a promising Drug Law Reform Project. And thanks to the aggressive advocacy of the ACLU, NAACP, and other civil rights organizations around the country, racial profiling is widely condemned, even by members of law enforcement who once openly embraced the practice.

Still, despite these significant developments, there seems to be a lack of appreciation for the enormity of the crisis at hand. There is no broad-based movement brewing to end mass incarceration and no advocacy effort that approaches in scale the fight to preserve affirmative action. There also remains a persistent tendency in the civil rights community to treat the criminal justice system as just another institution infected with lingering racial bias. The NAACP's Web site offers one example. As recently as May 2008, one could find a brief introduction to the organization's criminal justice work in the section entitled Legal Department. The introduction explained that "despite the civil rights victories of our past, racial prejudice still pervades the criminal justice system." Visitors to the Web site were urged to join the NAACP in order to "protect the hard-earned civil rights gains of the past three decades." No one visiting the Web site would learn that the mass incarceration of African Americans had already eviscerated many of the hard-earned gains it urged its members to protect.

Imagine if civil rights organizations and African-American leaders in the 1940s had not placed Jim Crow segregation at the forefront of their racial justice agenda. It would have seemed absurd, given that racial segregation was the primary vehicle of racialized social control in the United States during that period. This book argues that mass incarceration is, metaphorically, the New Jim Crow and that all those who care about social justice should fully commit themselves to dismantling this new racial caste system. Mass incarceration—not attacks on affirmative action or lax civil rights enforcement—is the most damaging manifestation of the backlash against the Civil Rights Movement. The popular narrative that emphasizes the death of slavery and Jim Crow and celebrates the nation's "triumph over race" with the election of Barack Obama, is dangerously misguided. The colorblind public consensus that prevails in America today—i.e., the widespread belief that race no longer matters—has blinded us to the realities of race in our society and facilitated the emergence of a new caste system.

Clearly, much has changed in my thinking about the criminal justice system since I passed that bright orange poster stapled to a telephone pole ten years ago. For me, the new caste system is now as obvious as my own face in the mirror. Like an optical illusion—one in which the embedded image is impossible to see until its outline is identified—the new caste system lurks invisibly within the maze of rationalizations we have developed for persistent racial inequality. It is possible—quite easy, in fact—never to see the embedded reality. Only after years of working on criminal justice reform did my own focus finally shift, and then the rigid caste system slowly came into view. Eventually it became obvious. Now it seems odd that I could not see it before.

Knowing as I do the difficulty of seeing what most everyone insists does not exist, I anticipate that this book will be met with skepticism or something worse. For some, the characterization of mass incarceration as a "racial caste system" may seem like a gross exaggeration, if not hyperbole. Yes, we may have "classes" in the United States—vaguely defined upper, middle, and lower classes—and we may even have an "underclass" (a group so estranged from mainstream society that it is no longer in reach of the mythical ladder of opportunity), but we do not, many will insist, have anything in this country that resembles a "caste."

The aim of this book is not to venture into the long-running, vigorous debate in the scholarly literature regarding what does and does not constitute a caste system. I use the term *racial caste* in this book the way it is used in common parlance to denote a stigmatized racial group locked into an inferior position by law and custom. Jim Crow and slavery were caste systems. So is our current system of mass incarceration.

It may be helpful, in attempting to understand the basic nature of the new caste system, to think of the criminal justice system—the entire collection of institutions and practices that comprise it—not as an independent system but rather as a *gateway* into a much larger system of racial stigmatization and permanent marginalization. This larger system, referred to here as mass incarceration, is a system that locks people not only behind actual bars in actual prisons, but also behind virtual bars and virtual walls—walls that are invisible to the naked eye but function nearly as effectively as Jim Crow laws *once* did at locking people of color into a permanent second-class citizenship. The term *mass incarceration* refers not only to the criminal justice system but also to the larger web of laws, rules, policies, and customs that control those labeled criminals both in and out of prison. Once released, former prisoners enter a hidden underworld of legalized discrimination and permanent social exclusion. They are members of America's new undercaste.

The language of caste may well seem foreign or unfamiliar to some. Public discussions about racial caste in America are relatively rare. We avoid talking about caste in our society because we are ashamed of our racial history. We also avoid talking about race. We even avoid talking about class. Conversations about class are resisted in part because there is a tendency to imagine that one's class reflects upon one's character. What is key to America's understanding of class is the persistent belief—despite all evidence to the contrary—that anyone, with the proper discipline and drive, can move from a lower class to a higher class. We recognize that mobility may be difficult, but the key to our collective self-image is the assumption that mobility is always possible, so failure to move up reflects on one's character. By extension, the failure of a race or ethnic group to move up reflects very poorly on the group as a whole.

What is completely missed in the rare public debates today about the plight of African Americans is that a huge percentage of them are not free to move up at all. It is not just that they lack opportunity, attend poor schools, or are plagued by poverty. They are barred by law from doing so. And the major institutions with which they come into contact are designed to prevent their mobility. To put the matter starkly: The current system of control permanently locks a huge percentage of the African American community out of the mainstream society and economy. The system operates through our criminal justice institutions, but it functions more like a caste system than a system of crime control. Viewed from this perspective, the so-called underclass is better understood as an *undercaste*—a lower caste of individuals who are permanently barred by law and custom from mainstream society. Although this new system of racialized social control purports to be colorblind, it creates and maintains racial hierarchy much as earlier systems of control did. Like Jim Crow (and slavery), mass incarceration operates as a tightly networked system of laws, policies, customs, and institutions that operate collectively to ensure the subordinate status of a group defined largely by race.

This argument may be particularly hard to swallow given the election of Barack Obama. Many will wonder how a nation that just elected its first black president could possibly have a racial caste system. It's a fair question. But as discussed in chapter 6, there is no inconsistency whatsoever between the election of Barack Obama to the highest office in the land and the existence of a racial caste system in the era of colorblindness. The current system of control depends on black exceptionalism; it is not disproved or undermined by it. Others may wonder how a racial caste system could exist when most Americans—of all colors—oppose race discrimination and endorse colorblindness. Yet as we shall see in the pages that follow, racial caste systems do not require racial hostility or overt bigotry to thrive.

They need only racial indifference, as Martin Luther King Jr. warned more than forty-five years ago.

The recent decisions by some state legislatures, most notably New York's, to repeal or reduce mandatory drug sentencing laws have led some to believe that the system of racial control described in this book is already fading away. Such a conclusion, I believe, is a serious mistake. Many of the states that have reconsidered their harsh sentencing schemes have done so not out of concern for the lives and families that have been destroyed by these laws or the racial dimensions of the drug war, but out of concern for bursting state budgets in a time of economic recession. In other words, the racial ideology that gave rise to these laws remains largely undisturbed. Changing economic conditions or rising crime rates could easily result in a reversal of fortunes for those who commit drug crimes, particularly if the drug criminals are perceived to be black and brown. Equally important to understand is this: Merely reducing sentence length, by itself, does not disturb the basic architecture of the New Jim Crow. So long as large numbers of African Americans continue to be arrested and labeled drug criminals, they will continue to be relegated to a permanent second-class status upon their release, no matter how much (or how little) time they spend behind bars. The system of mass incarceration is based on the prison label, not prison time.

Skepticism about the claims made here is warranted. There are important differences, to be sure, among mass incarceration, Jim Crow, and slavery—the three major racialized systems of control adopted in the United States to date. Failure to acknowledge the relevant differences, as well as their implications, would be a disservice to racial justice discourse. Many of the differences are not as dramatic as they initially appear, however; others serve to illustrate the ways in which systems of racialized social control have managed to morph, evolve, and adapt to changes in the political, social, and legal context over time. Ultimately, I believe that the similarities between these systems of control overwhelm the differences and that mass incarceration, like its predecessors, has been largely immunized from legal challenge. If this claim is substantially correct, the implications for racial justice advocacy are profound.

With the benefit of hindsight, surely we can see that piecemeal policy reform or litigation alone would have been a futile approach to dismantling Jim Crow segregation. While those strategies certainly had their place, the Civil Rights Act of 1964 and the concomitant cultural shift would never have occurred without the cultivation of a critical political consciousness in the African-American community and the widespread, strategic activism that flowed from it. Likewise, the notion that the *New* Jim Crow can ever be dismantled through traditional litigation and policy-reform strategies that are wholly disconnected from a major social movement seems fundamentally misguided.

Such a movement is impossible, though, if those most committed to abolishing racial hierarchy continue to talk and behave as if a state-sponsored racial caste system no longer exists. If we continue to tell ourselves the popular myths about racial progress or, worse yet, if we say to ourselves that the problem of mass incarceration is just too big, too daunting for us to do anything about and that we should instead direct our energies to battles that might be more easily won, history will judge us harshly. A human rights nightmare is occurring on our watch.

A new social consensus must be forged about race and the role of race in defining the basic structure of our society, if we hope ever to abolish the New Jim Crow. This new consensus must begin with dialogue, a conversation that fosters a critical consciousness, a key prerequisite to effective social action. This book is an attempt to ensure that the conversation does not end with nervous laughter.

It is not possible to write a relatively short book that explores all aspects of the phenomenon of mass incarceration and its implications for racial justice. No attempt has been made to do so here. This book paints with a broad brush, and as a result, many important issues have not received the attention they deserve. For example, relatively little is said here about the unique experience of women, Latinos, and immigrants in the criminal justice system, though these groups are particularly vulnerable to the worst abuses and suffer in ways that are important and distinct. This book focuses on the experience of African-American men in the new caste system. I hope other scholars and advocates will pick up where the book leaves off and develop the critique more fully or apply the themes sketched here to other groups and other contexts.

What this book is intended to do—the only thing it is intended to do—is to stimulate a much-needed conversation about the role of the criminal justice system in creating and perpetuating racial hierarchy in the United States. The fate of millions of people—indeed the future of the black community itself—may depend on the willingness of those who care about racial justice to re-examine their basic assumptions about the role of the criminal justice system in our society. The fact that more than half of the young black men in many large American cities are currently under the control of the criminal justice system (or saddled with criminal records) is not—as many argue—just a symptom of poverty or poor choices, but rather evidence of a new racial caste system at work.

Michael Tonry

Blacks and Hispanics*

"Three findings about race, crime, and punishment stand out concerning blacks. First, at every criminal justice system stage from arrest through incarceration, blacks are present in numbers greatly out of proportion to their presence in the general population. In 1991, for example, blacks made up a bit under 13 percent of the general population but 44.8 percent of those arrested for violent felonies and nearly 50 percent of those in prison on an average day. Second, although black disproportions in the front of the system—as offenders and arrestees—are essential stable, since the early 1980s they have steadily grown worse at the back. Between 1979 and 1990, for example, the percentage of blacks among persons admitted to state and federal prisons grew from 39 to 53 percent. By contrast, 44.1 percent of violent crime arrests in 1979 were of blacks, virtually the same as the 1992 figure. Third, perhaps surprisingly, for nearly a decade there has been a near consensus among scholars and policy analysts that most of the black punishment disproportions result not from racial bias or discrimination within the system but from patterns of black offending and of blacks' criminal records. Drug law enforcement is the conspicuous exception. Blacks are arrested and confined in numbers grossly out of line with their use or sale of drugs" (p. 49).

". . . [B]lack incarceration rates in recent years have been six to seven times than white incarceration rates" (p. 61).

The Foreseeable Disparate Impact on Blacks

The crucial question is whether the architects of the War on Drugs should be held morally accountable for the havoc they have wrought

---

*Michael Tonry, *Malign Neglect, Race, Crime and Punishment in America* (New York: Oxford University Press, 1995), 49, 61, 104–115, 151.

among disadvantaged members of minority groups. The answer is that they should, and this section explains why. Three sets of issues arise. First, were the disparate impacts on black Americans foreseeable? The only possible answer, as the data presented in the following sections demonstrate beyond peradventure of doubt, is yes, they knew what they were doing. Second, putting aside its disparate impact implications, were there valid grounds for believing that the war's prohibitionistic approach would diminish drug trafficking and drug use? Third, is there any arguable basis for justifying the war's foreseeable effects on black Americans? In particular, what should be made of the standard defense of the war's racial effects—almost a confession in avoidance—that most crime is intraracial and that the war's strategies were devised not to damage blacks but to protect black victims and communities? The answers to these questions are that there were no valid bases for believing that the war would accomplish its ostensible objectives, that the claim to protect black victims was disingenuous, and that there is no arguable basis for justifying the war's malign neglect of its implications for black Americans.

Urban black Americans have borne the brunt of the War on Drugs. They have been arrested, prosecuted, convicted, and imprisoned at increasing rates since the early 1980s, and grossly out of proportion to their numbers in the general population or among drug users. By every standard, the war has been harder on blacks than whites; that this was predictable makes it no less regrettable.

Cocaine and, more recently, crack have been the drugs primarily targeted, and they, particularly crack, are notoriously used and distributed in the inner city. The political symbolism of cocaine has been high since the mid-1980s. The United States invaded Panama in part because Manuel Noriega was believed to be cooperating with Colombian drug lords. In the United States, the Medellín and Cali cartels were for many years among the best-known foreign business enterprises. Newspapers, television, and movies regularly portray trafficking in cocaine and crack as characteristic of inner-city minority neighborhoods. Any mildly informed person in the late 1980s knew that the major fronts in the drug wars were located in minority neighborhoods.

The institutional character of urban police departments led to a tactical focus on disadvantaged minority neighborhoods. For a variety of reasons it is easier to make arrests in socially disorganized neighborhoods, as contrasted with urban blue-collar and urban or suburban white-collar neighborhoods. First, more of the routine activities of life, including retail drug dealing, occur on the streets and alleys in poor neighborhoods. In working-class and middle-class neighborhoods, many activities, including drug deals, are likelier to occur indoors. This makes it much easier to find dealers from whom to make an undercover buy in a disadvantaged urban neighborhood than elsewhere.

Second, it is easier for undercover narcotics officers to penetrate networks of friends and acquaintances in poor urban minority neighborhoods than in more stable and closely knit working-class and middle-class neighborhoods. The stranger buying drugs on the urban street corner or in an alley or overcoming local suspicions by hanging around for a few days and then buying drugs, is commonplace. The substantial increases in the numbers of black and Hispanic police officers in recent decades make undercover narcotics work in such neighborhoods easier. An undercover policeman of Irish or Polish descent in the 1960s was much less likely to be successful working undercover in a minority neighborhood than is a black policeman today in Chicago's Woodlawn or an Hispanic policeman in South-Central Los Angeles.

A stranger trying to buy drugs in the working-class Highland Park neighborhood around the Ford plant in St. Paul, Minnesota, or in Highland Park, Illinois, a middle-class suburb of Chicago, is likely to have much less success. Drugs are used and sold in both places, but rarely in the streets and not to strangers. Police undercover operations can succeed in such places but they take longer, cost more, and are less likely to succeed.

Both of these differences between socially disorganized urban neighborhoods and other neighborhoods make extensive drug-law enforcement operations in the inner city more likely and, by police standards, more successful. Because urban drug dealing is often visible, individual citizens, the media, and elected officials more often pressure police to take action against drugs in poor urban neighborhoods than in other kinds of neighborhoods. Although wholesale drug arrests are seldom strategically successful in reducing drug use or trafficking, they briefly disrupt the drug markets and so win media and public approval.

There is another more powerful reason that the police focus their attention on the inner city. Both for individual officers and for departments, numbers of arrests made have long been a measure of productivity and effectiveness. If it takes more work and longer to make a single drug arrest in either Highland Park than in Woodlawn, the trade-off may be between two arrests per month of an officer's time in Highland Park and six arrests per month in Woodlawn. From the perspectives of the individual officer's personnel record and the department's year-to-year statistical comparisons, arrests are fungible, and six arrests count for more than two.

Thus, a major reason that relatively more drug arrests are made in minority communities than elsewhere is that they are easier to make. Somewhat surprisingly, I am told by leading drug policy experts that there is no literature that confirms or contradicts this analysis or that considers why police target drug-law enforcement on minority communities. There are ethnographic and economic literatures on urban drug markets, and it and the economic literature explain why arrested dealers are nearly always quickly replaced by successors willing to accept the risks, but neither sheds light on police tactics. The police and policy literatures explain how and why narcotics enforcement operates but shed no light on why the emphasis is so much more often on the Woodlawns than on the Highland Parks.

Experienced police officials and prosecutors confirm my analysis. Former Kansas City prosecutor Albert Riederer, for example, is one person who offered this analysis to me. The police chief in Charlottesville, Virginia, justifying police targeting of casual drug dealing in University of Virginia fraternities, observed that "local civil rights advocates had a good point when they argued that anti-drug efforts were directed mainly toward the poor and members of minorities." In a 1993 article on drug policy in *Criminology*, Alfred Blumstein offers a similar analysis and, because of the absence of a literature, cites "personal communication with several individuals involved in drug-related police work."

No matter why it happens, the police emphasis on disorganized minority neighborhoods produces racial proportions in arrests that do not mirror racial proportions in drug use. . . . [According to the] percentages of blacks and whites among drug arrestees reported in the FBI's *Uniform Crime Reports* for the years 1976 to 1992 . . .

[t]he black percentage climbed steadily throughout the period and by two-fifths—from 30 to 42 percent—between 1985 and 1989. Since the absolute number of arrests was also rising, the number of arrests of blacks grew even faster. . . . [B]etween 1985 and 1989 the number of black arrests more than doubled, from 210,298 to 452,574. The number of white arrests grew only by 27 percent.

The arrest percentages by race bear no relation to drug use percentages. . . . Black Americans are less likely to have used drugs than whites are, for all major drugs of abuse except heroin. In 1990, for example, a year in which 41 percent of drug arrestees were black, NIDA's national household survey on drug abuse indicated that only 10 percent of blacks reported that they had *ever* used cocaine (compared with 11.7 percent of whites and 11.5 percent of Hispanics), 1.7 percent reported *ever* using heroin (compared with 0.7 percent of whites and 1.2 percent Hispanics), 31.7 percent reported *ever* using marijuana (34.2 percent whites, 29.6 percent Hispanics), 3.0 percent *ever* reported using hallucinogens (8.7 percent whites, 5.2 percent Hispanics), and 76.6 percent *ever* reported using alcohol (85.2 percent whites, 78.6 percent Hispanics).

. . . [W]hether the questions concerned drug use within the previous year or within the previous month, the comparative black, white, and Hispanic patterns were much the same. The only data . . . showing higher levels of black drug use are for marijuana and cocaine use in the last 30 days and the "ever used" data on heroin. Although in percentage terms, blacks' reports of cocaine use in the preceding 30 days or heroin use ever are three times the white levels (1.7 to 0.7), in absolute terms these differences are insignificant. There were, after all, 213 million white Americans in 1991, compared with 30 million blacks.

Drug arrests are a principal reason that the proportions of blacks in prison and more generally under criminal justice system control have risen rapidly in recent years to the extraordinary levels . . . , which show the percentages of blacks and whites among persons admitted to prisons and in prison and jail on survey dates over extended periods. The black percentages climbed slowly for several decades but rapidly after 1980.

The pattern of increasing black percentages is apparent in the aggregate national data on arrests and in state data. . . . [T]he national arrest rates per 100,000 population for whites and nonwhites from

1965 to 1991. Nonwhite rates were higher than white rates, usually at least double, throughout that period. From the early 1970s onward, white drug arrest rates were basically stable, fluctuating around 300 per 100,000. After 1980, nonwhite states rose steadily and then skyrocketed: By 1988 they were five times higher than white rates.

A more striking pattern of racial difference is revealed when juvenile drug arrests by race are examined. Alfred Blumstein, longtime dean of the Heinz School of Public Policy and Management, and America's leading authority on racial trends in criminal justice statistics, presented [a Figure on Arrest Rates of Juveniles for Drug Offenses, by Race, 1965–91] as part of his 1992 presidential address to the American Society of Criminology. White arrest rates for juvenile drug offenses were higher than those for black juveniles from the late 1960s to the early 1980s, though both rates fell sharply after 1974. After the early 1980s, white arrest rates continued to drop. Black rates shot up until the late 1980s when they were four to five times higher than white rates. Blumstein's "our kids, their kids" explanation for those trends is that drug use in the 1970s was a middle-income, principally white, phenomenon, which is why enforcement severity dropped, whereas in the late 1980s, drug use was a low-income, principally minority, phenomenon, which is why enforcement was uncompromisingly aggressive:

> The decline after the 1974 peak was undoubtedly a consequence of the general trend toward decriminalization of marihuana in the United States. A major factor contributing to that decriminalization was undoubtedly a realization that the arrestees were much too often the children of individuals, mostly white, in positions of power and influence. These parents certainly did not want the consequences of a drug arrest to be visited on their children, and so they used their leverage to achieve a significant degree of decriminalization.

One irony attending the data on arrests is their juxtaposition with drug use patterns. They are out of synch. During the late 1970s and early 1980s when arrests were falling or essentially stable, . . . drug use climbed to its modern peaks and began falling, well before arrests and arrest rates began their steep climb.

Blumstein's analysis of national drug arrest trends by race is mirrored in the states. Stephens Clarke of the Institute of Government of the University of North Carolina at Chapel Hill, the preeminent scholar of North Carolina's criminal justice trends, reports that drug arrests of nonwhites in that state climbed five times faster than white rates between 1984 and 1989. Nonwhite drug arrests increased from 5,021 in 1984 to 14,192 in 1989, a 183 percent increase. White drug arrests increased from 10,269 in 1984, twice the nonwhite number, to 14,007 in 1989, less than the nonwhite number and an increase of only 36 percent. Similar patterns can be found in other states, as of course they must, since the respective increases nationally in black and white arrests between 1985 and 1989 were 115 and 27 percent, respectively. In Minnesota, drug arrests of blacks grew by 500 percent during the 1980s, compared with 22 percent for whites, according to Debra Dailey, director of the Minnesota Sentencing Guidelines Commission.

The drug war's effect on prison populations has been substantial, and since the mid-1980s it has been the single most important cause of population increases. Twenty-five percent of state prisoners in 1991 had been convicted of drug charges, as had 56 percent of those in federal prisons. Twelve years earlier, in 1979, a year for which a special population profile makes detailed state data available, 6.4 percent of state and 25 percent of federal inmates had been convicted of drug crimes.

At every level of the criminal justice system, empirical analyses demonstrate that an increasing black disproportion has resulted from the War on Drugs—in jails, state and federal prisons, and juvenile institutions. The title of a 1990 publication of the Department of Justice's Office of Juvenile Justice and Delinquency Prevention captures the juvenile story: "Growth in Minority Detentions Attributed to Drug Law Violators." The experience in several state prison systems is illustrative. . . . [N]onwhite and white admissions per 100,000 same-race population to North Carolina prisons from 1970 to 1990. White rates held steady during the entire period. Nonwhite rates doubled between 1980 and 1990 from a higher starting point, growing most rapidly after 1987, the period when nonwhite drug arrests more than doubled.

. . . [I]ncreases in prison commitments in Pennsylvania between 1980 and 1990 for drug and other offenses by race and sex. Drug commitments of nonwhite males rose by 1613 percent during the decade; white males by 477 percent. The pattern for females was similar, though the differences were less dramatic. In 1990, 11 percent of Pennsylvanians were white; 58 percent of state prisoners were nonwhite.

. . . [W]hite and nonwhite drug commitments to Virginia prisons from 1983 to 1989: sixty-two percent of drug offenders committed in 1983 were white, and 38 percent were nonwhite. By 1989, those percentages had more than reversed; 65 percent of drug commitments were nonwhite, and 35 percent were white. Drug commitments have continued to rise since 1989; current data would show worse racial disproportion.

These figures are illustrative of prison admission and population trends across the country. Phrased most charitably to the officials who launched and conducted America's latest War on Drugs, worsening of racial incarceration patterns was a foreseen but not an intended consequence. Less charitably, the recent blackening of America's prison population is the product of malign neglect of the war's effects on black Americans.

"There are two major reasons why a just system of punishment would take account of offenders' disadvantaged backgrounds. First, from a consequentialist perspective, by mitigating disadvantaged offenders' punishments when feasible, we would do less harm to them as individuals and to disadvantaged black Americans as a class, without significantly diminishing public safety. Recent punishment policies, to the contrary, have destabilized disadvantaged inner-city communities, without significantly reducing crime or achieving their ostensible objectives" (p. 151).

Correctional Association

Women in Prison*

When "Free" Means Losing Your Mother: The Collision of Child Welfare and the Incarceration of Women in New York State

Executive Summary

Mary, a mother of two young children, is sentenced to three to six years in prison after being convicted of larceny for using her ex-boyfriend's debit card. She is incarcerated at a medium-security prison eight hours away from her home, which is in New York City. Mary has no family in New York, so a friend takes her children after Mary is arrested. Unfortunately, the friend cannot afford to continue caring for both her own children and Mary's, and eventually Mary's children are placed in foster care. Acting under state law, the child welfare agency files a petition to terminate Mary's parental rights 15 months after her children enter foster care. Termination of rights was not part of Mary's sentence, yet she now faces the prospect of being cut off from her children forever.

In 1973, about 380 women were incarcerated in New York State correctional facilities. Driven by policies like New York's harsh Rockefeller Drug Laws, today that number has increased by nearly 630%, a rate of growth significantly higher than the rate for men. Although New

---

*http://www.correctionalassociation.org/publications/download/wipp/reports/
When_Free_Rpt_Feb_2006.pdf

York's female prison population—along with the total prison population—has been steadily decreasing since 2000, there are currently still more than 2,800 women in state custody. Women of color are disproportionately represented: nearly three-quarters of New York State women prisoners are African American or Latina. Almost 75% are mothers; most were primary caretakers of their children before their arrest, many as single parents. More than 11,000 children have a mother incarcerated in a New York correctional facility, either in a state prison or city or county jail.

When a mother is sent to prison, she becomes part of a stigmatized and invisible community. She often receives substandard health care and deficient rehabilitation services, has minimal access to effective vocational and educational programs, and faces significant barriers to maintaining stable relationships with—and sometimes parental rights to—her children. These obstacles include limited visiting and family reunification services, inadequate or nonexistent legal representation in Family Court, and insufficient coordination between corrections departments, child welfare agencies, and the courts.

A mother's incarceration has a pernicious effect on her family and community. The removal of a primary caretaker disrupts family structures, while relatives who may assume responsibility for minor children must grapple with added financial burdens.

Separation and dislocation cause children significant mental distress. These repercussions are concentrated within a handful of low-income communities of color in New York City, where more than half of the state's women prisoners lived before their incarceration.

Social, emotional and economic harm to families and communities is a defining legacy of female imprisonment.

This picture need not be so grim. Research and experience have shown that maintaining family ties can mitigate the destructive aspects of parental incarceration by helping children process their mother's absence, easing family reunification when a mother returns home, bolstering children's well-being and healthy development, and decreasing the likelihood that a mother will return to prison.

Visits play a critical role in preserving and building family ties, but consistent visiting between incarcerated parents and their children at most New York State prisons is the exception rather than the rule. Albion Correctional Facility, New York's largest women's prison, which houses more than 40% of the state's female inmates, is roughly 370 miles from New York City. The associated travel expenses can be prohibitive for families typically struggling with poverty, while the long distances are extremely taxing on young children and the older relatives with whom they often live. Child welfare agencies often fail to arrange regular prison visits and the handful of private organizations that facilitate visits do not have sufficient resources to provide services for most children of incarcerated parents who need them. A government study published in 2000 found that more than half of mothers in state prisons nationwide have never had a visit with their children.

Incarceration adversely affects families regardless of whether the children are living in foster care or in a private custody arrangement. Changes in New York's child welfare policies, however, have exacerbated the risks for incarcerated mothers with children in foster care. In 1999, New York State enacted a law modeled on the federal Adoption and Safe Families Act (ASFA) that requires a child welfare agency to file a petition to terminate parental rights if a child has been in foster care for 15 of the last 22 months. Although ASFA has laudable goals—to prevent children from lingering in foster care and to find permanent homes quickly for children who cannot be reunified with their families—in practice it is a blunt instrument that often causes serious damage.

No comprehensive data exist on termination of parental rights proceedings filed against incarcerated parents. A recent study, however, indicates that termination proceedings involving incarcerated parents nationwide increased by an estimated 108% from ASFA's enactment in 1997 to 2002. In contrast, in the five years preceding the implementation of ASFA, the number of termination proceedings involving incarcerated parents increased by about 67%. New York State's ASFA laws make no exception for incarcerated parents. Because the median minimum sentence for women in New York (36 months) far exceeds ASFA's 15-month timeline, mothers in prison—including mothers whose children remain in foster care solely because they can find no alternative temporary home—face increased danger of being separated from their children forever.

ASFA does have limited exceptions, one of which allows a foster care agency to waive filing a termination proceeding if it has documented a "compelling reason" why termination would not be in the "best interest of the child." This exception is critical for incarcerated mothers with children in foster care. A caseworker who observes firsthand that a child's relationship with her mother is integral to the child's well-being is more likely to exercise his or her discretion and reconsider filing a termination proceeding after ASFA's 15-month deadline has been reached. Unfortunately, most child welfare agencies do not provide caseworkers with adequate training, resources, or support to facilitate regular prison visits, and New York State corrections' policies and practices often make visiting difficult and unpleasant even for the most experienced visitor. These realities, along with the courts' frequent unwillingness to hold foster care agencies and correctional facilities accountable, lead many already overworked caseworkers to disregard their legally mandated responsibilities to arrange for child-parent prison visits at least once per month. Without visits and the chance to witness interactions between a mother and her child, a caseworker would be hard pressed to find a "compelling reason" not to petition the court to terminate parental rights.

ASFA's time limits intensify the challenges facing incarcerated mothers. State law mandates that parents with children in foster care—including incarcerated parents—maintain consistent contact with and "plan for the future" of their children, which includes finding a stable, non-foster care home placement within a reasonable period of time. Failure to fulfill these obligations can trigger allegations of "abandonment" or "permanent neglect" which can serve as grounds to terminate parental rights and "free" a child for adoption. Unlike other parents, an incarcerated mother confronts serious impediments to maintaining contact with the outside world: she can only place extremely expensive collect calls which many foster care agencies, foster families, relatives, and friends do not or cannot accept; she is rarely able to participate in important planning meetings with her child's caseworker; and she often faces difficulty being produced for Family Court hearings where she might meet her child's lawyer or caseworker and the judge.

An incarcerated mother's limited access to legal representation and the courts jeopardizes her fundamental rights as a parent. Even though New York State law provides indigent parents with the right to assigned counsel in Family Court proceedings, generally an attorney will be initially assigned only if the parent is physically produced in court—sometimes an insurmountable hurdle for an incarcerated mother. Additionally, even if an incarcerated mother is produced and assigned counsel during one phase of her case, the representation can end with that phase. Recently passed legislation designed to provide indigent parents with continuity of counsel may improve this situation, although the practical impact of these statutory changes remains to be seen. Even an incarcerated mother who retains the same lawyer will likely have little or no time to discuss her case with counsel before she appears in front of the judge for the first time and will have continuing difficulty meeting and communicating with her lawyer outside of court to prepare for trial.

ASFA's timeframes also ignore a child's right to have a relationship with his or her mother. Many children would rather reunify with their mother when she is released, even if that means remaining in foster care for a longer period of time. Children, especially very young children, are unlikely to comprehend the implications of having their relationship with their mother "terminated" or being "freed" to be adopted by someone else. Moreover, many children continue to languish in foster care even after being "freed" for adoption. Cutting children's ties to their mothers without a likely prospect of providing them with a permanent and stable home not only seems precipitous, but also contrary to the sound child welfare policy espoused by ASFA's stated goals.

Whatever their living circumstances, children of incarcerated parents have committed no crime, yet are punished by the loss of their parents and the accompanying emotional hardship, including feelings of anxiety, guilt, fear, and depression. Beyond experiencing short-term damage to their well-being, children of incarcerated mothers are more likely than their peers to become involved in illegal activity, to abuse substances, and to have difficulties in school. For many who are in foster care, being "freed" for adoption does not bring relief from a troubled family situation: it simply means losing their mother forever.

The overwhelming majority of people interviewed for this report felt that visits are vital to maintaining familial relationships and reducing the trauma of separation. Also prevalent was the strong conviction that current prison conditions discourage visiting by creating undue hardships for adult visitors and children alike. Interviewees described the long distances visitors must travel to some women's facilities as expensive and exhausting, security procedures as burdensome and humiliating, and treatment by some correction officers as disrespectful. Although certain visiting facilities were singled out for praise, interviewees criticized most facilities as having few, if any, age-appropriate activities for children, limited space, and little to eat. Interview participants also described the need for more programs to assist families separated by incarceration.

ON THE IMPORTANCE OF VISITS

CAREGIVER: "The best way to have a relationship is through talking. She wants to see that her mother is okay, and my daughter wants to see that my granddaughter is okay. We make the best of the situation."

CASEWORKER: "Once you see the bond between the mother and the child, it becomes rewarding."

INCARCERATED MOTHER: "Children need to see their mother. Even if it's painful, you need to have the connection. By seeing her I could still be her mother. . . . You need to have contact with the kids all the time."

INCARCERATED MOTHER: "I needed them to know that mommy didn't abandon them. They needed to understand that. Mommy made a mistake . . . and I am coming back for you and I'm fighting for you."

CHILD OF AN INCARCERATED MOTHER: "[Y]ou never had enough time. Just when you were beginning to feel a connection it was time to leave, and the sense of disappointment and loss would reappear . . . the visit gave a sense of comfort to be with my mom. After not being with her and being with so many strangers it felt safe and complete."

ON VISITING CONDITIONS

CAREGIVER: "By the time you get in [to Albion Correctional Facility], you gotta turn around and come back. . . . Right when you get in the door, it's already time to leave. Just a hug, then back on the bus at 12:30 [p.m.]."

CHILD OF AN INCARCERATED MOTHER: "I was treated just like the prisoner. Humiliated, violated and stripped [of my] dignity. After all the security points and searches it doesn't make you even want to ever go back."

ON THE NEED FOR MORE PROGRAMS

INCARCERATED MOTHER: "Maybe if I had started seeing him in prison, he might have been through that anger by the time I was out."

INCARCERATED MOTHER: "Me and my children could have been bonding since I was in Bayview, so that way, when I came home, it wouldn't have been so new for me trying to reunite and interact with them."

A Fair Chance for Families Separated by Prison

Incarcerated parents and their children receive long sought-after, critical support in efforts to maintain ties to each other and to protect parental rights.

June 15, 2010—After years of advocacy by the Correctional Association of New York's Women in Prison Project, the Coalition for Women Prisoners, and allies statewide, Governor David Paterson signed into law the Adoption and Safe Families Act (ASFA) Expanded Discretion Bill.

This bill amends New York's ASFA law, which almost always requires foster care agencies to file termination of parental rights papers if a child has been in care for 15 of the last 22 months. The median sentence for women in New York's prisons is 36 months, far exceeding ASFA's timeline. Incarcerated parents often face barriers in meeting legal responsibilities required to preserve their parental rights, like maintaining contact and finding children a non-foster care home while they are away. The result? ASFA inadvertently tips the scales in favor of terminating parental rights of incarcerated parents, even when such an action is not necessarily in the long-term best interests of the child and family.

The new law—which applies to both mothers and fathers—allows foster care agencies to refrain from filing for termination if a parent is in prison or a residential drug treatment program or if a parent's prior incarceration or program participation is a significant factor in why the child has been in foster care for 15 of the last 22 months.

For the first time, foster care agencies will be required to inform parents in prison and residential drug treatment of their rights and responsibilities and to provide referrals to social services and family visiting programs. Because mothers in prison are much more likely to report having children in foster care than fathers, the new law has particular importance for incarcerated women.

Working with bill sponsor Assembly member Jeffrion Aubry and expert advisors, the Project drafted the bill and, with the determined advocacy of members of the Coalition for Women Prisoners and its Incarcerated Mothers Committee, secured its passage in the Assembly every year since 2007. With strong sponsorship by Senator Velmanette Montgomery, the Coalition and community partners mounted an intensified campaign for the bill in the State Senate, including: organizing a series of advocacy days in Albany; creating a user-friendly, one-pager and photo slideshow; securing support from key organizations and the State Office of Children and Family Services; stepping up efforts to facilitate the leadership of women directly affected by ASFA; and providing opportunities for mothers to share their experiences in written documents, public forums, and press conferences.

One-by-one, the Project garnered the commitment of senators. By April, all but four of the majority needed to secure passage of the bill had pledged their support. Coalition members, including many formerly incarcerated mothers, traveled to Albany to meet with the remaining holdouts. The action was a success. Two legislators pledged their support that day and two others agreed shortly after. After a vigorous floor debate, the Senate passed the bill three weeks later.

The new law places New York among the most progressive states in the country for child welfare policies that recognize the special circumstances of families separated by incarceration. In the months to come, the Women in Prison Project and the Coalition for Women Prisoners will work to ensure that the new law is implemented effectively and helps to prevent the devastating, permanent separation of families—families who can, if given a fair chance, rebuild safe, loving and life-long relationships.

Jeffrey Reiman and Paul Leighton

Poor More Likely to be Punished for Same Crime?*

This chapter has mainly tried to document that, *even among those dangerous acts that our criminal justice system labels as crimes,* the system works to make it more likely that those who end up in jail or prison will be from the bottom of society. This works in two broad ways:

1. *For the same crime,* the system is more likely to investigate and detect, arrest and charge, convict and sentence, and sentence to prison (and for a longer time) a lower-class individual than a middle- or upper-class individual. To support this, we reviewed a large number of studies performed over a long period of time comparing the treatment of high- and low-socioeconomic status offenders and of white and nonwhite offenders, from arrest through sentencing for the same crimes.

2. *Between crimes that are characteristically committed by poor people (street crimes) and those characteristically committed by the well-off (white-collar corporate crimes),* the system treats the former much more harshly than the latter, even when the crimes of the well-off take far more money from the public or cause far more death and injury than the crimes of the poor. To support this, we compared the sentences meted out for robbery with those for embezzlement, grand theft, and Medicaid-provider fraud, and we looked at the treatment of those responsible for death and destruction in the workplace as well as those responsible for S&L scandal and the recent financial cheating at Enron and other major corporations.

---

*Reiman, Jeffrey, and Paul Leighton. *The Rich Get Richer and the Poor Get Prison: Ideology, Class, and Criminal Justice,* 9th ed., © 2010. Printed and electronically reproduced by permission of Pearson Education, Inc., Upper Saddle River, NJ. p. 158.

Chapter Five

Prison Labor

| Rania Khalek | Prison Labor |
| Paul Wright | Slaves of the State |

Rania Khalek

Prison Labor*

Taking account of offenders disadvantaged background does less harm to individuals without diminishing public safety.

21st-Century Slaves: How Corporations Exploit Prison Labor

> In the eyes of the corporation, inmate labor is a brilliant strategy in the eternal quest to maximize profit.
>
> —July 21, 2011

There is one group of American workers so disenfranchised that corporations are able to get away with paying them wages that rival those of third-world sweatshops. These laborers have been legally stripped of their political, economic, and social rights and ultimately relegated to second-class citizens. They are banned from unionizing, violently silenced from speaking out, and forced to work for little to no wages. This marginalization renders them practically invisible, as they are kept hidden from society with no available recourse to improve their circumstances or change their plight.

They are the 2.3 million American prisoners locked behind bars where we cannot see or hear them. And they are modern-day slaves of the 21st century.

---

*Rania Khalek, "Prison Labor: 21st Century Slaves: How Corporations Exploit Prison Labor." *Alternet*, accessed July 21, 2011.

Incarceration Nation

It's no secret that America imprisons more of its citizens than any other nation in history. With just 5 percent of the world's population, the United States currently holds 25 percent of the world's prisoners. "In 2008, over 2.3 million Americans were in prison or jail, with one of every 48 working-age men behind bars," according to a study by the Center for Economic and Policy Research (CEPR). That doesn't include the tens of thousands of detained undocumented immigrants facing deportation, prisoners awaiting sentencing, or juveniles caught up in the school-to-prison pipeline. Perhaps it's reassuring to some that the U.S. still holds the number one title in at least one arena, but needless to say the hyper-incarceration plaguing America has had a damaging effect on society at large.

The CEPR study observes that U.S. prison rates are not just excessive in comparison to the rest of the world, they are also "substantially higher than our own longstanding history." The study finds that incarceration rates between 1880 and 1970 ranged from about "100 to 200 prisoners per 100,000 people." After 1980, the inmate population "began to grow much more rapidly than the overall population" and the rate climbed from "about 220 in 1980 to 458 in 1990, 683 in 2000, and 753 in 2008."

The costs of this incarceration industry are far from evenly distributed, with the impact of excessive incarceration falling predominantly on African-American communities. Although black people make up just 13 percent of the overall population, they account for 40 percent of U.S. prisoners. According to the Bureau of Justice Statistics (BJS), black males are incarcerated at a rate "more than 6.5 times that of white males and 2.5 that of Hispanic males" and "black females are incarcerated at approximately three times the rate of white females and twice that of Hispanic females."

Michelle Alexander points out in her book, *The New Jim Crow*, that more black men "are in prison or jail, on probation or on parole than were enslaved in 1850." Higher rates of black drug arrests do not reflect higher rates of black drug offenses. In fact, whites and blacks engage in drug offenses, possession and sales at roughly comparable rates.

Incentivizing Incarceration

Clearly, the U.S. prison system is riddled with racism and classism, but it gets worse. As it turns out, private companies have a cheap, easy labor market, and it isn't in China, Indonesia, Haiti, or Mexico. It's right here in the land of the free, where large corporations increasingly employ prisoners as a source of cheap and sometimes free labor.

In the eyes of the corporation, inmate labor is a brilliant strategy in the eternal quest to maximize profit. By dipping into the prison labor pool, companies have their pick of workers who are not only cheap but are also easily controlled. Companies are free to avoid providing benefits like health insurance or sick days, while simultaneously paying little to no wages. They don't need to worry about unions or demands for vacation time or raises. Inmates work full-time and are never late or absent because of family problems.

"If they refuse to work, they are moved to disciplinary housing and lose canteen privileges" along with "good time credit that reduces their sentences," reports Chris Levister. To top it off, Abe Louise Young reports in *The Nation* that the federal government subsidizes the use of inmate labor by private companies through lucrative tax write-offs. Under the Work Opportunity Tax Credit (WOTC), private-sector employers receive a tax credit of $2,400 for every work release inmate they employ as a reward for hiring "risky target groups" and they can "earn back up to 40 percent of the wages they pay annually to target group workers."

Study after study demonstrates the wastefulness of America's prison-industrial complex, in both taxpayer dollars and innocent lives, yet rolling back imprisonment rates is proving to be more challenging than ever. Meanwhile, the use of private prisons and now privately contracted inmate labor has created a system that does not exactly incentivize leaner sentencing.

The disturbing implications of such a system mean that skyrocketing imprisonment for the possession of miniscule amounts of marijuana and the expansion of severe mandatory sentencing laws regardless of the conviction, are policies that have the potential to increase corporate profits. As are the "three strikes laws" that require courts to hand down mandatory and extended sentences to people who have been convicted of felonies on three or more separate occasions. People have literally been sentenced to life for minor crimes like shoplifting.

The Reinvention of Slavery

The exploitation of prison labor is by no means a new phenomenon. Jaron Browne, an organizer with People Organized to Win Employment Rights (POWER), maps out how the exploitation of prison labor in America is rooted in slavery. The abolition of slavery dealt a devastating economic blow to the South following the loss of free labor after the Civil War. So in the late 19th century, "an extensive prison system was created in the South in order to maintain the racial and economic relationship of slavery," a mechanism responsible for re-enslaving black workers. Browne describes Louisiana's famous Angola Prison to illustrate the intentional transformation from slave to inmate:

> In 1880, this 8000-acre family plantation was purchased by the state of Louisiana and converted into a prison. Slave quarters became cell units. Now expanded to 18,000 acres, the Angola plantation is tilled by prisoners working the land—a chilling picture of modern day chattel slavery.

The abolition of slavery quickly gave rise to the Black Codes and Convict Leasing, which together worked wonders at perpetuating African-American servitude by exploiting a loophole in the 13th Amendment to the U.S. Constitution, which reads:

> Neither slavery nor involuntary servitude, except as a punishment for crime whereof the party shall have been duly convicted, shall exist within the United States, or any place subject to their jurisdiction.

The Black Codes were a set of laws that "criminalized legal activity for African Americans" and provided a pretext for the arrest and mass imprisonment of newly freed blacks, which caused the rate of African-

Americans prisoners to "surpass whites for the first time," according to Randall G. Sheldon in the *Black Commentator*. Convict leasing involved leasing out prisoners to private companies that paid the state a certain fee in return. Convicts worked for the companies during the day outside the prison and returned to their cells at night. The system provided revenue for the state and profits for plantation owners and wasn't abolished until the 1930s.

Unfortunately, convict leasing was quickly replaced with equally despicable state-run chain gangs. Once again, stories of vicious abuse created enough public anger to abolish chain gangs by the 1950s. Nevertheless, the systems of prisoner exploitation never actually disappeared.

Today's corporations can lease factories in prisons, as well as lease prisoners out to their factories. In many cases, private corporations are running prisons-for-profit, further incentivizing their stake in locking people up. The government is profiting as well, by running prison factories that operate as "multibillion-dollar industries in every state, and throughout the federal prison system," where prisoners are contracted out to major corporations by the state.

In the most extreme cases, we are even witnessing the reemergence of the chain gang. In Arizona, the self-proclaimed "toughest sheriff in America," Joe Arpaio, requires his Maricopa County inmates to enroll in chain gangs to perform various community services or face lockdown with three other inmates in an 8-by-12-foot cell, for 23 hours a day. In June of this year, Arpaio started a female-only chain gang made up of women convicted of driving under the influence. In a press release he boasted that the inmates would be wearing pink T-shirts emblazoned with messages about drinking and driving.

The modern-day version of convict leasing was recently spotted in Georgia, where Governor Nathan Deal proposed sending unemployed probationers to work in Georgia's fields as a solution to a perceived labor shortage following the passage of the country's most draconian anti-immigrant law. But his plan backfired when some of the probationers began walking off their jobs because the fieldwork was too strenuous.

There has also been a disturbing reemergence of the debtors' prison, which should serve as an ominous sign of our dangerous reliance on prisons to manage any and all of society's problems. According to the *Wall Street Journal*, "more than a third of all U.S. states allow borrowers who can't or won't pay to be jailed." They found that judges "signed off on more than 5,000 such warrants since the start of 2010 in nine counties." It appears that any act that can be criminalized in the era of private prisons and inmate labor will certainly end in jail time, further increasing the ranks of the captive workforce.

Who Profits?

Prior to the 1970s, private corporations were prohibited from using prison labor as a result of the chain gang and convict leasing scandals. But in 1979, the U.S. Department of Justice admits that congress began a process of deregulation to "restore private sector involvement in prison industries to its former status, provided certain conditions of the labor market were met." Over the last 30 years, at least 37 states have enacted laws permitting the use of convict labor by private enterprise, with an average pay of $0.93 to $4.73 per day.

Federal prisoners receive more generous wages that range from $0.23 to $1.25 per hour, and are employed by Unicor, a wholly owned government corporation established by Congress in 1934. Its principal customer is the Department of Defense, from which Unicor derives approximately 53 percent of its sales. Some 21,836 inmates work in Unicor programs. Subsequently, the nation's prison industry—prison labor programs producing goods or services sold to other government agencies or to the private sector—now employs more people than any Fortune 500 company (besides General Motors), and generates about $2.4 billion in revenue annually. Noah Zatz of UCLA law school estimates that:

> Well over 600,000, and probably close to a million, inmates are working full-time in jails and prisons throughout the United States. Perhaps some of them built your desk chair: office furniture, especially in state universities and the federal government, is a major prison labor product. Inmates also take hotel reservations at corporate call centers, make body armor for the U.S. military, and manufacture prison chic

fashion accessories, in addition to the iconic task of stamping license plates.

Some of the largest and most powerful corporations have a stake in the expansion of the prison labor market, including but not limited to IBM, Boeing, Motorola, Microsoft, AT&T, Wireless, Texas Instrument, Dell, Compaq, Honeywell, Hewlett-Packard, Nortel, Lucent Technologies, 3Com, Intel, Northern Telecom, TWA, Nordstrom's, Revlon, Macy's, Pierre Cardin, Target Stores, and many more. Between 1980 and 1994 alone, profits went up from $392 million to $1.31 billion. Since the prison labor force has likely grown since then, it is safe to assume that the profits accrued from the use of prison labor have reached even higher levels.

In an article for *Mother Jones*, Caroline Winter details a number of mega-corporations that have profited off of inmates:

> In the 1990s, subcontractor Third Generation hired 35 female South Carolina inmates to sew lingerie and leisure wear for Victoria's Secret and JCPenney. In 1997, a California prison put two men in solitary for telling journalists they were ordered to replace "Made in Honduras" labels on garments with "Made in the USA."

According to Winter, the defense industry is a large part of the equation as well:

> Unicor, says that in addition to soldiers' uniforms, bedding, shoes, helmets, and flak vests, inmates have "produced missile cables (including those used on the Patriot missiles during the Gulf War)" and "wiring harnesses for jets and tanks." In 1997, according to *Prison Legal News*, Boeing subcontractor MicroJet had prisoners cutting airplane components, paying $7 an hour for work that paid union wages of $30 on the outside.

Oil companies have been known to exploit prison labor as well. Following the explosion of the Deepwater Horizon rig that killed 11 workers and irreparably damaged the Gulf of Mexico for generations to come, BP elected to hire Louisiana prison inmates to clean up its mess. Louisiana has the highest incarceration rate of any state in the nation, 70 percent of which are African-American men. Coastal residents desperate for work, whose livelihoods had been destroyed by BP's negligence, were outraged at BP's use of free prison labor.

In the *Nation* article that exposed BP's hiring of inmates, Abe Louise Young details how BP tried to cover up its use of prisoners by changing the inmates' clothing to give the illusion of civilian workers. But nine out of 10 residents of Grand Isle, Louisiana are white, while the cleanup workers were almost exclusively black, so BP's ruse fooled very few people.

Private companies have long understood that prison labor can be as profitable as sweatshop workers in third-world countries with the added benefit of staying closer to home. Take Escod Industries, which in the 1990s abandoned plans to open operations in Mexico and instead "moved to South Carolina, because the wages of American prisoners undercut those of de-unionized Mexican sweatshop workers," reports Josh Levine in a 1999 article that appeared in *Perspective Magazine*. The move was fueled by the state, which gave a $250,000 "equipment subsidy" to Escod along with industrial space at below-market rent. Other examples listed by Gordon Lafer in the American Prospect include Ohio's Honda supplier, which "pays its prison workers $2 an hour for the same work for which the UAW has fought for decades to be paid $20 to $30 an hour. Konica, which has hired prisoners to repair its copiers for less than 50 cents an hour. And in Oregon, where private companies can 'lease' prisoners at a bargain price of $3 a day."

Even politicians have been known to tap into prison labor for their own personal use. In 1994, a contractor for GOP congressional candidate Jack Metcalf hired Washington state prisoners to call and remind voters he was pro-death penalty. After winning his campaign, he claimed to have no knowledge of the scandal. Perhaps this is why Senator John Ensign (R-NV) introduced a bill earlier this year to "require all low-security prisoners to work 50 hours a week." After all, the *New York Times* reminds us that "creating a national prison labor force has been a goal of his since he went to Congress in 1995."

In an unsettling turn of events lawmakers have begun ditching public employees in favor of free prison labor. The *New York Times* recently reported that states are "enlisting prison labor to close budget gaps" to offset cuts in "federal financing and dwindling tax revenue." At a time of record unemployment, inmates are being hired to "paint vehicles, clean courthouses, sweep campsites and perform many other services done before the recession by private contractors or government employees." In Wisconsin, prisoners are now taking up jobs that were once held by unionized workers, as a result of Governor Scott Walker's contentious anti-union law.

Why You Should Care

Those who argue in favor of prison labor claim it is a useful tool for rehabilitation and preparation for post-jail employment. But this has only been shown to be true in cases where prisoners are exposed to meaningful employment, where they learn new skills, not the labor-intensive, menial, and often dangerous work they are being tasked with. While little if any evidence exists to suggests that the current prison labor system decreases recidivism or leads to better employment prospects outside of prison, there are a number of solutions that have been proven to be useful.

According to a study by the Pew Charitable Trusts, "having a history of incarceration itself impedes subsequent economic success." Pew found that "past incarceration reduced subsequent wages by 11 percent, cut annual employment by nine weeks and reduced yearly earnings by 40 percent." The study suggests that the best approach is for state and federal authorities to "invest in programs that reconnect inmates to the labor market," as well as "provide training and job placement services around the time of release." Most importantly, Pew suggests that in the long term, America must move toward alternative sentencing programs for low-level and nonviolent offenders, and issuing penalties that are actually proportionate with real public safety concerns.

The exploitation of any workforce is detrimental to all workers. Cheap and free labor pushes down wages for everyone. Just as American workers cannot compete with sweatshop labor, the same goes for prison labor. Many jobs that come into prison are taken from free citizens. The American labor movement must demand that prison labor be allowed the right to unionize, the right to a fair and living wage, and the right to a safe and healthy work environment. That is what prisoners are demanding, but they can only do so much from inside a prison cell.

As unemployment on the outside increases, so too will crime and incarceration rates, and our 21st-century version of corporate slavery will continue to expand unless we do something about it.

Editor's Note: *This article has been corrected since its original publication for more accurate attribution to original sources.*

Paul Wright

Slaves of the State*

Many people have the mistaken impression that slavery was outlawed or abolished in the United States after the civil war by the passage of the Thirteenth Amendment. Unfortunately, that was not the case. The Thirteenth Amendment reads: "Neither slavery nor involuntary servitude except as punishment for crimes whereof the party shall have been duly convicted, shall exist within the United States, or any place subject to their jurisdiction." The effect of the Thirteenth Amendment was not to abolish slavery but to limit it to those who had been convicted of a crime.

The reality was made apparent in the aftermath of the civil war when large numbers of newly freed Black slaves found themselves "duly convicted" of crimes and in state prisons where, once again, they labored without pay. It was common practice for state prisons to "lease" prison labor out to private contractors in a modern form of chattel slavery. This situation led the Virginia Supreme Court to remark in an 1871 case, *Ruffin v. Commonwealth*, that prisoners were "slaves of the state." All that has changed since then is that the state is less honest about its slaveholding practices.

Until the 1930s most state and federal prisons were largely self-sufficient, producing most of the goods and food they consumed and even producing a surplus, for sale, of food and some industrial products. In many states prisoners even served as armed guards (until the mid-1970s the state of Arkansas held some 3,000 prisoners with only 27 civilian employees) and many other functions which required minimal investment by the state. Prison self-sufficiency and excess production for profit largely ended during the mid-1930s when the U.S. was in the midst of the depression and both unions and manufacturers

*Paul Wright, "Slaves of the State." *The Celling of America*, ed. by Daniel Burton-Rose, Dan Pens, and Paul Wright, 1998, pp. 102–06.

complained about competing against prison-made products on the open market.

One of the laws passed was the Ashurst-Sumners Act (1935) which prohibited the transport in interstate commerce of prison-made goods unless the prisoners were paid at least minimum wage.

Prison labor did not start to become a major issue again until the 1980s. Until then most prison-produced goods were either for use within the prison system or sold to other state agencies, license plates being the most familiar example. This began to change with the massive prison building and incarceration binge. In a 1986 study designed to reduce the cost to the government of its prison policies, former Supreme Court Justice Warren Burger issued the call for transforming prisons into "factories with fences." In essence, prisons should once again become self-sustaining, even profit-producing, entities requiring minimal financial input from the state.

While some think that slavery—i.e., unpaid, forced labor—offers enormous profit potential for the slave owner, there are historical reasons slavery is no longer the dominant mode of economic production. First, the slave owner has a capital investment in his slave: regardless of whether the slave is working or producing profit he must be fed, housed, and so on, in minimal conditions to ensure the slave's value as a labor producer remains. With the rise of industrial capitalism in the 18th and 19th century, capitalists discovered that capitalism has its boom and bust cycles characterized by over-production. Thus, idle slaves would become a drain on the owner's finance because they would still require feeding, housing, etc., regardless of whether they were working. However, if the slave were "free" he could be employed at low wages and then laid off when not producing profit for the employee, the wage slave was free to starve, free to be homeless, and so on, with no consequences for the owner.

Another reason chattel slavery was inefficient compared to wage slavery was that the slaves would occasionally revolt, destroying the means of production and/or killing the slave owner. More common and less dramatic were the acts of sabotage and destruction that made machinery, with its attendant capital investment, impractical for use by slaves. So by the middle of the 19th century wage slaves employing machines could out produce, at greater profit for the factory owner, chattel slaves using less easily damaged, more primitive machinery.

The problem slave owners of old faced was what to do with non-producing slaves. Today's slave owner—the state—faces the opposite problem of having idle slaves who must be fed, clothed, and housed whether or not they produce anything of value. The current thinking goes that any potential profit produced by prison slaves is better than none.

Some of the proponents of prison slavery try to disguise it as a "rehabilitation" or "vocational" program designed to give prisoners job skills or a trade which can be used upon their release. This is not the case. First, almost without exception the jobs available in prison industries are labor intensive, menial, low-skill jobs which tend to be performed by exploited workers in three places: Third World dictatorships, and in the U.S. by illegal immigrants or prisoners. Clothes and textile manufacturing are the biggest example of this. Second, because the jobs don't exist in the first place the job skills acquired are hardly useful. Does anyone expect a released prisoner to go to Guatemala or El Salvador to get a job sewing clothes for the U.S. market at a dollar a day? Third, if it is rehabilitation, then why not pay the prisoner at least minimum wage for his/her work? Fourth, it ignores the reality that the U.S. has at least 8 or 9 million unemployed workers at any given time, many of them highly skilled, who cannot find jobs that pay a meaningful wage to support themselves. So-called "job retraining" programs are a failure because all the training in the world won't create jobs with decent wages. In pursuit of higher profits—by paying lower salaries—U.S. and transnational corporations have transferred virtually all labor-intensive production jobs to Third World countries.

The U.S. has little problem condemning the export of prison-made goods from China. What makes this blatant hypocrisy is the fact that the same criticisms leveled by the U.S. government against Chinese prison-made goods can be leveled at U.S. prison-made goods. Prison-made goods from California and Oregon are being exported for retail sales. In a supreme irony, the California DOC is marketing its clothing lines in Asia, competing against the sweatshops of Indonesia, Hong Kong, Thailand, and, of course, China. The Prison Blues brand of clothes, made by prisoners in Oregon has annual projected sales of over $1.2 million in export revenues. U.S. State Department officials were quoted saying they wished prison-made goods were not exported by state DOC's because it is being raised as an issue by other governments: namely the Chinese, which have cited U.S. practices in response to criticisms. For their part, the Chinese have announced a ban on their export of prison-made goods while the U.S. is stepping up to such exports.

California prisoners making clothes for export are paid between 35 cents and $1 an hour. The Oregon prisoners are paid between $6 to $8 an hour, but have to pay back up to 80 percent of that to cover the cost of their captivity. As they are employed by a DOC-owned company, this is essentially an accounting exercise where the prisoners' real wages are between $1.20 and $1.80 an hour. Still competitive with the wages paid to illegal immigrant sweatshop workers here in the U.S. and wages paid to garment workers in the Far East and Central America.

Fred Nichols, the administrator of Unigroup, the Oregon DOC prison industries, has said: "We want them to work in the same environment as on the outside" in terms of hiring interviews and such. Yet obviously this does not include the right to collective bargaining and union representation.

While the particulars may change, the trend continues towards increased exploitation of prison slave labor. Some sates, especially those in the South—such as Texas, Arkansas, Louisiana—still have unpaid prisoners laboring in fields supervised by armed guards on horseback, with no pretense of "rehabilitation" or "job training." In those states the labor is mandatory; refusal to work brings harsh punishment and increases in prison sentences served.

In 1977 the Supreme Court decided *Jones v. North Carolina Prisoner's Labor Union*, which removed court protection for prison union organizing. Efforts to obtain the minimum wage for prisoners through litigation have been largely unsuccessful, with courts bending over backwards to read exemptions (which are not written) into the federal Fair Labor and Standards Act (FLSA).

In Washington the state offers a lot of incentives for private businesses to employ prison slaves. Class I venture industries pay no rent, electricity, water, or similar costs. They are exempt from state and federal workplace safety standards and pay no medical, unemployment, or vacation/sick leave to slaves who have no right to collective organizing or bargaining. In a case like this we are seeing welfare capitalism where private business is getting a handout from the state at taxpayer expense. One which will largely swallow the profit paid back to the state under guise of taxes, room and board, etc., by the prisoner. To the extent that prison slaves are forced to pay state and federal taxes there arises the question, aligned to the right to vote, of taxation without representation. If forced to pay taxes like any other citizen, under the guise of rehabilitative or vocational employment, then why not the right to vote given to other workers and taxpayers?

Workers on the outside should also be aware of the consequences that prison slave labor poses for their jobs. Ironically, as unemployment on the outside increases, crime and the concomitant incarceration rate increases. It may be that before too long people can only find menial labor-intensive production jobs in prisons or Third World countries where people labor under similar conditions. The factory with fences meets the prison without walls.

Chapter Six

Solitary Confinement

Human Rights Watch	Teens in Solitary Confinement
Sasha Abramsky	Supermaximum Security Prisons are Inhumane

Human Rights Watch

Teens in Solitary Confinement*

Youths Suffer Serious Harm from Weeks, Months in "Lock-Down"

October 10, 2012

A cell at the Pinellas County jail, an adult facility where young people are held in solitary confinement. One girl interviewed for the report said she spent four months in isolation there.

~

(Washington, DC)—Young people are held in solitary confinement in jails and prisons across the United States, often for weeks or months at a time, Human Rights Watch and the American Civil Liberties Union (ACLU) said in a report released today.

The 141-page report, "Growing Up Locked Down: Youth in Solitary Confinement in Jails and Prisons Across the United States," is based on research in both U.S. jails and prisons in five states— Colorado, Florida, Michigan, New York, and Pennsylvania—and correspondence with young people in 14 others. The isolation of solitary confinement causes anguish, provokes serious mental and physical health problems, and works against rehabilitation for teenagers, Human Rights Watch and the ACLU found.

"Locking kids in solitary confinement with little or no contact with other people is cruel, harmful, and unnecessary," said Ian Kysel, Aryeh Neier Fellow with Human Rights Watch and the ACLU and author of the report. "Normal human interaction is essential to the

*Human Rights Watch, "US: Teens in Solitary Confinement." (http://www.hrw. org/news/2012/10/10/us-teens-solitary-confinement). © Human Rights Watch.

healthy development and rehabilitation of young people; to cut that off helps nobody."

The report is based on interviews and correspondence with more than 125 young people in 19 states who spent time in solitary confinement while under age 18, as well as with jail and/or prison officials in 10 states.

Human Rights Watch and the ACLU estimate that, in 2011, more than 95,000 young people under age 18 were held in prisons and jails. A significant number of these facilities use solitary confinement—for days, weeks, months, or even years—to punish, protect, house, or treat some of the young people held there.

Because young people are still developing, traumatic experiences like solitary confinement may have a profound effect on their chance to rehabilitate and grow, the groups found. Solitary confinement can exacerbate short- and long-term mental health problems or make it more likely that such problems will develop. Young people in solitary confinement are routinely denied access to treatment, services, and programming required to meet their medical, psychological, developmental, social, and rehabilitative needs.

The New York City Department of Corrections, for example, reported that in fiscal year 2012, which ended in June, more than 14 percent of all adolescents were held in at least one period of solitary confinement while detained. The average length of time young people spent in solitary confinement at Rikers Island was 43 days. More than 48 percent of adolescents at Rikers have diagnosed mental health problems.

"Being in isolation to me felt like I was on an island all alone, dying a slow death from the inside out," said "Kyle B.," from California, who spent time in solitary confinement while under age 18.

Young people interviewed for the report repeatedly described how solitary confinement compounded the stress of being in jail or prison. They spoke about cutting themselves with staples or razors while in solitary confinement, having hallucinations, and losing touch with reality. Several said they had attempted suicide multiple times in solitary confinement.

Those allowed outside described only being allowed to exercise in small metal cages, alone, a few times a week. Several said they could not get books, magazines, paper, pens, or pencils, or attend any classes or programming. For some, the hardest part about solitary confinement was being denied visits and not being able to hug their mother or father.

The solitary confinement of young people under age 18 is itself a serious human rights violation and can constitute cruel, inhuman, or degrading treatment under international human rights law, Human Rights Watch and the ACLU said. Conditions that compound the harm of solitary confinement, such as denial of educational programming, exercise, or family visits, often constitute independent, serious human rights violations.

A number of corrections officials have begun to recognize and speak against the use of solitary confinement, saying that it is costly, ineffective, and harmful.

There are alternative ways to address the problems—whether disciplinary, administrative, protective, or medical—that officials typically cite to justify using solitary confinement, while taking into account the rights and special needs of adolescents, Human Rights Watch and the ACLU said. Youth could be housed in specialized facilities organized to encourage positive behavior. And punishment should be proportional to the infraction, using any short-term isolation as a rare exception.

The federal and state governments should ban placing youth in solitary confinement, Human Rights Watch and the ACLU said. They should also prohibit housing adolescents with adults or in jails and prisons designed to house adults, and strictly regulate and monitor all forms of isolation of young people.

"No one believes that locking a teenager in a closet is an effective way to improve either their behavior or their character, much less to protect them long term," Kysel said. "Young people have rights and needs that are different from adults; jail and prison practices should reflect those differences and promote their ability to grow and change—we should invest in youth, not banish them."

Selected quotes from young people interviewed:

In seg[regation] you either implode or explode; you lose touch with reality, hear voices, hallucinate and think for hours about killing yourself, others or both. The anger and hurt gets so intense that you suspect everyone and trust no one and when someone does something nice for you, you don't understand it.

—"Douglas C." Colorado, April 2012

The hardest thing about isolation is that you are trapped in such a small room by yourself. There is nothing to do so you start talking to yourself and getting lost in your own little world. It is crushing. You get depressed and wonder if it is even worth living. Your thoughts turn over to the more death-oriented side of life . . . I want[ed] to kill myself.

—"Paul K.," Michigan, March 2012

I just felt I wanted to die, like there was no way out—I was stressed out. I hung up the first day. I took a sheet and tied it to my light and they came around . . . The officer when she was doing rounds found me. She was banging on the window—"Are you alive? Are you alive?" I could hear her but I felt like I was going to die. I couldn't breathe.

—"Luz M.," New York, April 2012

Me? I cut myself. I started doing it because it is the only release of my pain. I'd see the blood and I'd be happy . . . I did it with staples, not razors. When I see the blood and it makes me want to keep going. I showed the officers and they didn't do anything . . . I wanted [the staff] to talk to me. I wanted them to understand what was going on with me.

—"Alyssa E.," Florida, April 2012

If I would describe isolation to another person I would tell them it's bad. We didn't do anything wrong to be put in isolation. They say it's to protect us but I think it puts us in more danger . . . [H]ow could we be charged as men but be separated from men. It makes no sense. If that's the case, keep our cases at juvenile if they want to protect us.

—"Charles O.," Pennsylvania, April 2012

Sasha Abramsky

Supermax Security Prisons are Inhumane*

Last summer [2001], some 600 inmates in the notorious supermaxi-mum-security unit at California's Pelican Bay State Prison [in north-ern California] stopped eating. They were protesting the conditions in which the state says it must hold its most difficult prisoners: locked up for 23 hours out of every 24 in a barren concrete cell measuring 7½ by 11 feet. One wall of these cells is perforated steel; inmates can squint out through the holes, but there's nothing to see outside either. In Pelican Bay's supermax unit, as in most supermax pris-ons around the country, the cells are arranged in lines radiating out like spokes from a control hub, so that no prisoner can see another human being—except for those who are double-bunked. Last year [2001], the average population of the Pelican Bay supermax unit was 1,200 inmates, and on average, 288 men shared their tiny space with a "cellie." Since 1995, 12 double-bunked prisoners in the Pelican Bay supermax unit have been murdered by their cell mates. But near-total isolation is the more typical condition.

Extreme Deprivation

Meals are slid to the inmates through a slot in the steel wall. Some prisoners are kept in isolation even for the one hour per day that they're allowed out to exercise; all are shackled whenever they are taken out of their cells. And many are forced to live this way for years on end.

Such extreme deprivation, the food strikers said, literally drives people crazy. Many experts agree. But the protest died out after two weeks, according to the jailhouse lawyer who organized it; and

---

*Sasha Abramsky, "Supermaximum Security Prisons are Inhumane." *Prison*, ed. by James Haley, 2005, pp. 75–86.

though a state senator promised that he would look into the strikers' complaints, so far conditions [as of 2001] at Pelican Bay remain unchanged.

All told, more than 8,000 prisoners in California and at least 42,000 around the country, by the conservative estimate of the *Corrections Yearbook*, are currently held in similar conditions of extreme confinement. As of 2000, Texas alone boasted 16 supermax prisons and supermax units, housing some 10,000 inmates. In Florida, more than 7,000 inmates were double-bunked in such facilities and the corrections department was lobbying to build another one (at an estimated cost of nearly $50 million) to house an additional 1,000 offenders.

Seven years ago, in January 1995, inmates at Pelican Bay won a class-action lawsuit, *Madrid v Gomez*, against the California Department of Corrections. Among other constitutional violations, U.S. District Court Judge Thelton Henderson found that the staff had systematically brutalized inmates, particularly mentally ill inmates. "The Eighth Amendment's restraint on using excessive force has been repeatedly violated at Pelican Bay, leading to a conspicuous pattern of excessive force," Henderson wrote in describing the severe beatings then common at the facility, the third-degree burns inflicted on one mentally ill inmate who was thrown into boiling water after he smeared himself with feces, and the routine use of painful restraining weapons against others. The judge ordered California to remove any seriously mentally ill or retarded inmates from the supermax unit, and he appointed a special master to overhaul the prison.

What Henderson didn't rule, however, was that the supermax model, per se, amounted to cruel and unusual punishment in violation of the Eighth Amendment. And so, while a new warden and new rules were brought to Pelican Bay, the basic conditions of sensory deprivation in its supermax unit have remained intact. Extremely mentally ill inmates are now held elsewhere; but critics say that less severe cases are still send to the unit, where they often deteriorate drastically, for the same reasons that Judge Henderson originally identified: "The physical environment reinforces a sense of isolation and detachment from the outside world, and helps create a palpable distance from the ordinary compunctions, inhibitions and community norms."

Meanwhile, the prescribed method for dealing with uncoopera-
tive inmates who "act out" in a supermax is still to send a team of
guards into the cell with batons, stun guns, Mace, and tear gas. Thus,
say critics, the chances for guard-on-inmate violence remain high at
Pelican Bay, just as at other supermaxes around the country.

Roots of the Supermax Model

The supermax model emerged out of the prison violence of the
1970s and the early 1980s, when dozens of guards around the country, including two at the maximum-security federal prison at Marion,
Illinois, were murdered by prisoners. First, prison authorities developed procedures to minimize inmate-staff contact; then they took to
"locking down" entire prisons for indefinite periods, keeping inmates
in their cells all day and closing down communal dining rooms and
exercise yards. Eventually, they began to explore the idea of making the general prison population safer by creating entirely separate
high-tech, supermax prisons in which "the worst of the worst" gang
leaders and sociopaths would be incarcerated in permanent lockdown
conditions. In the late 1980s, several states and the federal government
began constructing supermax units. California—which had seen 11
guards murdered by inmates between 1970 and 1973, and a staggering
32 prisoners killed by other inmates in 1972 alone—opened Corcoran
State Prison and its supermax unit in 1988 and Pelican Bay the year
following. In 1994, the first federal supermax opened, in Florence,
Colorado. Soon, dozens of correctional systems across the country
were embracing this model.

Indeed, throughout the 1990s, despite year-by-year declines in
crime, one state after another pumped tens of millions of dollars
into building supermax prisons and supermax facilities within existing prisons—sections that are usually called "secure housing units,"
or SHUs. Defenders of supermaxes, like Todd Ishee, warden of Ohio
State Penitentiary (OSP), a supermax in Youngstown, argue that their
restrictions provide a way to establish control in what is still—and
inherently—an extremely dangerous environment. "In 1993," he says,
"our maximum security prison at Southern Ohio Correctional Facility
was host to a riot. One correctional officer was killed. A number

of inmates were killed and several injured. Following the riot, the department made a decision that a 500-bed facility of this nature was needed to control the most dangerous inmates."

Overusing Supermax Facilities

But while it may be necessary to maintain such restricted facilities as prisons of last resort for some inmates, critics point out that far less troublesome inmates end up being sent to them. In Ohio, for example, a special legislative committee appointed to inspect the state's prisons in 1999 concluded that fewer than half of the inmates at OSP met the state's own supermax guidelines. State correctional-department data indicate that of the more than 350 inmates currently incarcerated at OSP, 20 were ringleaders of the 1993 riot and 31 had killed either an inmate or a correctional officer while living among the general prison population; but the rest had been sent there for much less serious offenses (often little more than a fistfight with another inmate).

And Ohio isn't alone in this practice. According to a study issued by the state of Florida, fully one-third of the correctional departments across the country that operate supermax prisons report placing inmates in them simply because they don't have enough short-term disciplinary housing in lower-security prisons—this is hardly an economically efficient arrangement.

Yet the available numbers suggest that casual overuse of these facilities is common. For in tough-on-crime America, imposing grim conditions on prisoners is all too often seen as a good in itself, regardless of the long-term costs. The U.S. Department of Justice's 1997 report on supermax housing . . . found Mississippi officials insisting that they needed to house fully 20 percent of their prison inmates in separate supermax-type prisons and another 35 percent in similar units within existing prisons. Arizona claimed that it needed to house 8 percent of its inmates in supermax prisons and another 20 percent in SHUs. In Virginia, after Jim Austin, the state's nationally renowned consultant on prisoner classification, told officials that they needed to put more of their inmates into medium-security prisons, the state instead spent approximately $150 million to build Red Onion and

Wallens Ridge, two supermax prisons with a combined capacity to house 2,400 prisoners.

Proponents of the supermax system claim that its introduction has reduced violence in the general prison population—both by removing the most hard-core miscreants and also by introducing a fearsome deterrent to misbehavior. But the data on this are, at best, mixed. Among Ohio's total prison population, for example, there were more inmate-on-inmate assaults serious enough to be written up by officials in 2000 that there were in 1997, the year before the OSP supermax opened for business (8 assaults for every 1,000 prisoners in 1997 compared with 10 for every 1,000 in 2000). And even where lower-security prisons have been made somewhat safer, that safety has been purchased at a staggering financial and, ultimately, social cost.

Mental Illness

Even the best-run of the supermax facilities seem to see high rates of mental illness among their inmates. For example, a study carried out by the Washington State Department of Corrections, which is known as one of the more humane, rehabilitation-focused prison systems in the country, found that approximately 30 percent of inmates in its supermax units show evidence of serious psychiatric disorders—at least twice the rate in the overall prison population.

In Connecticut's Northern Correctional Institution (NCI), Warden Larry Myers presides over an inmate population just shy of 500 and a staff of just over 300. With six mental-health profession-als, a gradated three-phase program offering inmates the possibility of returning to the general prison population within one year, and relatively calm inmate-staff relations. Myers prides himself on run-ning a tight ship. Unlike the staffers at many other supermaxes, once those at NCI identify an inmate as psychotic, they remove him to an institution that caters to mentally ill prisoners. Myers says that to avoid a "ping-pong effect," with inmates bouncing back and forth between NCI and mental health institutions, the prison has not accepted severely disturbed inmates since 1999.

Yet even in Myers's prison, psychiatrist Paul Chaplin estimates that 10 percent of the inmates are on antidepressants or antipsychotic drugs, and several times a month an inmate gets violent enough to be placed in four-point restraints. Last September [2001], guards had to subdue prisoners with Mace on 12 occasions. As I toured the pink-painted steel tiers of level one, dozens of inmates began screaming out their often incoherent complaints in a bone-jarring cacophony of despair.

"This is shitty," shouted one of the more intelligible of them. "We ain't got no recreations, no space. If I try to sit back and motivate, you got people yelling." He said he sleeps for more than 10 hours a day, does push-ups, and sits around. "I have trouble concentrating," he yelled. Through the narrow Plexiglas window in the door of his cell, a 21-year-old shouted: "I'm in jail for behavior problems. My cellie has behavior problems. Why put two people with behavior problems in the same cell?"

The greatly disputed chicken-and-egg question is: Do previously healthy inmates go mad under these extreme conditions of confinement, or do inmates who are already mentally unstable and impulsive commit disciplinary infractions that get them shipped off to SHUs or supermax prisons, where they are then likely to further decompensate?

Some psychiatrists, including Harvard University professor Stuart Grassian, have testified in the court that the sensory deprivation in a supermax frequently leads otherwise healthy individuals to develop extreme manifestations of psychosis, such as hallucinations, uncontrollable rage, paranoia, and nearly catatonic depressions. Grassian and others have also documented examples of extreme self-mutilation: supermax inmates gouging out their eyes or cutting off their genitals. Using the tools of the supermax prison, writes James Gilligan in his book *Violence*, "does not protect the public; it only sends a human time bomb into the community" when the inmate is eventually released.

Other psychiatrists are more cautious, arguing that while some perfectly healthy people are driven insane by these dehumanizing prison settings, the more common problem is that mildly mentally ill inmates are often precisely the ones who find it hardest to control their behavior while in the general prison population and who therefore get sent to the supermax or SHU. Judge Henderson acknowledged this in his Pelican Bay ruling; and *Ruiz v. Johnson*, a 1999 case involving Texas's use of long-term inmate-segregation fatalities in its prisons, another federal court likewise found that "inmates, obviously in need of medical help, are instead inappropriately managed merely as miscreants."

Dehumanizing Treatment

In the large supermaxes of Texas, correctional bureaucrats have devised a systematically humiliating and, indeed, dehumanizing regimen of punishments for prisoners who elsewhere would more likely be considered disturbed: no real meals, only a "food loaf" of all the day's food ground together, for prisoners who don't return their food trays; paper gowns forced on those who won't wear their clothes. I myself have heard guards joking about "the mutilators" who slash their own veins to get attention. According to Thomas Conklin, the psychiatrist and medical director at the Hampden County Jail in Massachusetts who was called on to evaluate mental-health care in one Texas supermax, "All suicide gestures by inmates [were] seen as manipulating the correctional system with the conscious intent of secondary gain. In not one case was the inmate's behavior seen as reflecting mental pathology that could be treated." In most supermaxes, this kind of thinking still seems to be the norm.

Although prison authorities say that they provide mental-health care to their supermax inmates, prisoner advocates tend to dismiss these claims. Documentary filmmaker Jim Lipscomb, who has interviewed scores of inmates in Ohio's most secure prisons, reports that mental-health programs there often consist of little more than in-cell videos offering such platitudes as, "If you feel angry at one of the guards, try not to curse and shout at him."

"That's called mental health!" Lipscomb says in amazement.

"The forceful rushes of this isolational perversion has pulled my essence into a cesspool," wrote one inmate from a supermax in Pennsylvania to Bonnie Kerness of the American Friends Service Committee (AFSC). "This just ain't life, pathologized in a subsumed litany of steel and cement codes preoccupied with the disturbing thrust of death." Accompanying the florid words was a penciled image of a grown man curled into a fetal position against a brick wall.

Challenging the Conditions

The American Civil Liberties Union's National Prison Project is currently spearheading three class action lawsuits against supermaxes in Illinois, Ohio, and Wisconsin. In the Wisconsin case, U.S. District Court Judge Barbara Crabb issued a preliminary ruling in October [2001] against the Supermax Correctional Institute in Boscobel after hearing the testimony of various health experts, including Dr. Terry Kupers, a Berkeley psychiatrist and author of the book *Prison Madness*. Kupers, who had been to Boscobel, told me that "there're a lot of crazy people in here, and they need to be removed on an emergency basis because it's not safe." In court, he testified that he had interviewed inmates who had been diagnosed with a paranoid schizophrenia and who continued to hallucinate despite being given high doses of Thorazine.

Judge Crabb ordered prison authorities to remove five mentally ill inmates from the facility immediately and to provide an independent mental-health assessment to any inmate with symptoms of mental illness. "The conditions at Supermax are so severe and restrictive," Crabb wrote, "that they exacerbate the symptoms that mentally ill inmates exhibit. Many of the severe conditions serve no legitimate penological interest; they can only be considered punishment for punishment's sake." She also set a trial date in July 2002 to hear evidence on the lawsuit's larger claim that the stringent conditions of confinement at the supermax—the extreme isolation, extraordinary levels of surveillance, and tight restrictions on personal property—constitute cruel and unusual punishment.

For advocates of prisoners' rights, this is the Holy Grail: a broad new reading of the Eighth Amendment that would prohibit supermax-style incarceration. And a broad reading is warranted, they say, by the international conventions that the United States has signed—such as the International Covenant on Civil Treatment of Prisoners, which prohibit torture and regulate prison conditions much more stringently than does U.S. case law. It's also a manner of human decency, says attorney Jamie Fellner of Human Rights Watch. "The moral critique is this: Secure-housing units have been designed, at the best, with utter disregard for human misery. At the worst, it's a deliberate use of human misery for deterrence and punishment."

Pending such a ruling, however, the filing of lawsuits provides virtually the only public accountability for what goes on in the super-maxes. With the exception of the New York Correctional Association, there is no legislatively mandated oversight agency watching the prisons—no civilian review board or independent ombudsman—in any state with supermax facilities. And over the past few years, in response to a rash of critical media coverage and unfavorable reports by human-rights organizations, many prison authorities have stopped allowing outside observers to visit these prisons or interview their inmates. (In the past, I have visited supermax sites in California, Texas, and Illinois to report on them. For this [viewpoint], only Connecticut opened its supermax doors to me; Arizona, New Jersey, Pennsylvania, Texas, and Virginia all refused to do so.) Says Human Rights Watch's Fellner: "It is incredible that it's sometimes easier to get access to prisons in closed regimes in third-world countries than it is in the U.S."

Breeding Violence

If nothing else, the lawsuits are keeping the human-rights questions on the table. Supermax critics are also trying to call attention to the pubic costs, which are not just financial. Tens of thousands of inmates are now being held in supermax facilities, and almost all of them will be released one day. Indeed, many states are releasing such inmates directly from the SHUs to the streets after their sentence is up, without even reacclimatizing them to a social environment.

Although no national tracking surveys of ex-supermax and ex-SHU inmates have been carried out, anecdotal evidence suggests that many prisoners have been made more violent by their long-term spells of extreme deprivation and isolation. Bonnie Kerness of the AFSC talks about a whole new generation of cons coming out of supermax prisons with hair-trigger tempers. One former inmate at Rikers Island jail in New York City, who now participates in a rehabilitation program run by the Manhattan-based Fortune Society, recalls that prisoners routinely to "Bing monsters." (The Bing is the nickname for the Rikers Island version of the SHU.)

"The impact on society could be devastating," says Steve Rigg, a former correctional officer who worked at California's supermax prison in Corcoran during the mid-1990s and blew the whistle on his fellow officers for organizing fights between rival prison-gang members. Corcoran's administration was overhauled after this, but Rigg warns that the underlying dangers in undermonitored supermaxes remain. "There's more [inmate] recidivism," he says of SHUs. "They breed the worst."

Chapter Seven

Possible Alternatives to Punishment

Bernard Shaw

Imprisonment*

Preface

THE SPIRIT IN WHICH TO READ THIS BOOK

Imprisonment as it exists today, and as it is described hereafter in these two volumes: *English Prisons under Local Government* and *English Prisons To-day*, is a worse crime than any of those committed by its victims; for no single criminal can be as powerful for evil, or as unrestrained in its exercise, as an organized nation. Therefore, if any person is addressing himself to the perusal of these dreadful books in the spirit of a philanthropist bent on reforming a necessary and beneficent public institution, I beg him to put it down and go about some other business. It is just such reformers who have in the past made the neglect, oppression, corruption, and physical torture of the old common goal the pretext for transforming it into that diabolical den of torment, mischief, and damnation, the modern model prison.

If, on the contrary, the reader comes to the books as a repentant sinner, let him read on.

The Obstacle of Vindictiveness

The difficulty in finding repentant sinners when this crime is in question has two roots. The first is that we are all brought up to believe that we may inflict injuries on anyone against whom we can make

---

*George Bernard Shaw, "Imprisonment," preface to S. and B. Webb, *English Prisons Under Local Government* (London: Longmans Green, 1922). Reprinted by permission of the Society of Authors as the Literary Representative of the Estate of Bernard Shaw.

out a case of moral inferiority. We have this thrashed into us in our childhood by the infliction on ourselves of such injuries by our parents and teachers, or indeed by any elder who happens to be in charge of us. The second is that we are all brought up to believe, not now that the king can do no wrong, because kings have been unable to keep up that pretence, but that society can do no wrong. Now not only does society commit more frightful crimes than any individual, king or commoner: it legalizes its crimes, and forges certificates of righteousness for them, besides torturing anyone who dares expose their true character. A society like ours, which will, without remorse, ruin a boy body and soul for life for trying to sell newspapers in a railway station, is not likely to be very tender to people who venture to tell it that its laws would shock the Prince of Darkness himself if he had not been taught from his earliest childhood to respect as well as fear them.

Consequently these two volumes go to a desperately sophisticated public, as well as to a quite frankly vindictive one. Judges spend their lives consigning their fellow creatures to prison; and when some whisper reaches them that prisons are horribly cruel and destructive places, and that no creature fit to live should be sent there, they only remark calmly that prisons are not meant to be comfortable, which is no doubt the consideration that reconciled Pontius Pilate to the practice of crucifixion.

The Obstacle of Stupidity

Another difficulty is the sort of stupidity that comes from lack of imagination. When I tell people that I have seen with these eyes a man (no less a man than Richard Wagner, by the way) who once met a crowd going to see a soldier broken on the wheel by the crueller of the two legalized methods of carrying out that hideous sentence, they shudder, and are amazed to hear that what they call medieval torture was used in civilized Europe so recently. They forget that the punishment of half-hanging, unmentionably mutilating, drawing and quartering, was on the British statute book within my own memory. The same people will read of a burglar being sentenced to ten years' penal servitude without turning a hair. They are like Ibsen's Peer

Gynt, who was greatly reassured when he was told that the pains of hell are mental: he thought they could not be so very bad if there was no actual burning brimstone. When such people are terrified by an outburst of robbery with violence, or sadistically excited by reports of the White Slave traffic, they clamor to have sentences of two years' hard labor supplemented by a flogging, which is a joke by comparison. They will try to lynch a criminal who illtreats a child in some sensationally cruel manner; but on the most trifling provocation they will inflict on the child the prison demoralization and the prison stigma which condemn it to crime for the rest of its life as the only employment open to a prison child. The public conscience would be far more active if the punishment of imprisonment were abolished, and we went back to the rack, the stake, the pillory, and the lash at the cart's tail.

Blood Sports Disguised as Punishment are Less Cruel Than Imprisonment but More Demoralizing to the Public

The objection to retrogression is not that such punishments are more cruel than imprisonment. They are less cruel, and far less permanently injurious. The decisive objection to them is that they are sports in disguise. The pleasure to the spectators, and not the pain to the criminal, condemns them. People will go to see Titus Oates flogged or Joan of Arc burnt with equal zest as an entertainment. They will pay high prices for a good view. They will reluctantly admit that they must not torture one another as long as certain rules are observed; but they will hail a breach of the rules with delight as an excuse for a bout of cruelty. Yet they can be shamed at last into recognizing that such exhibitions are degrading and demoralizing; that the executioner is a wretch whose hand no decent person cares to take; and that the enjoyment of the spectators is fiendish. We have then to find some form of torment which can give no sensual satisfaction to the tormentor, and which is hidden from public view. That is how imprisonment, being just such a torment, became the normal penalty. The fact that it may be worse for the criminal is not taken into account. The public is seeking its own salvation, not that of the lawbreaker. It would be far better for him to suffer in the public eye;

for among the crowd of sightseers there might be a Victor Hugo or a Dickens, able and willing to make the sightseers think of what they are doing and ashamed of it. The prisoner has no such chance. He envies the unfortunate animals in the Zoo, watched daily by thousands of disinterested observers who never try to convert a tiger into a Quaker by solitary confinement, and would set up a resounding agitation in the papers if even the most ferocious man-eater were made to suffer what the most docile convict suffers. Not only has the convict no such protection: the secrecy of his prison makes it hard to convince the public that he is suffering at all.

How We All Become Inured to Imprisonment

There is another reason for this incredulity. The vast majority of our city populations are inured to imprisonment from their childhood. The school is a prison. The office and the factory are prisons. The home is a prison. To the young who have the misfortune to be what is called well brought up it is sometimes a prison of inhuman severity. The children of John Howard, as far as their liberty was concerned, were treated very much as he insisted criminals should be treated, with the result that his children were morally disabled, like criminals. This imprisonment in the home, the school, the office, and the factory is kept up by browbeating, scolding, bullying, punishing, disbelief of the prisoner's statements and acceptance of those of the official, essentially as in a criminal prison. The freedom given by the adult's right to walk out of his prison is only a freedom to go into another or starve: he can choose the prison where he is best treated: that is all. On the other hand, the imprisoned criminal is free from care as to his board, lodging, and clothing: he pays no taxes, and has no responsibilities. Nobody expects him to work as an unconvicted man must work if he is to keep his job: nobody expects him to do his work well, or cares twopence whether it is well done or not.

Under such circumstances it is very hard to convince the ordinary citizen that the criminal is not better off than he deserves to be, and indeed on the verge of being positively pampered. Judges, magistrates, and Home Secretaries are so commonly under the same delusion that people who have ascertained the truth about prisons have been driven to declare that the most urgent necessity of the situation is that every judge, magistrate and Home Secretary should serve a six months' sentence incognito; so that when he is dealing out and enforcing sentences he should at least know what he is doing.

Competition in Evil Between Prison and Slum

When we get down to the poorest and most oppressed of our population we find the conditions of their life so wretched that it would be impossible to conduct a prison humanely without making the lot of the criminal more eligible than that of many free citizens. If the prison does not underbid the slum in human misery, the slum will empty and the prison will fill. This does in fact take place to a small extent at present, because slum life at its worst is so atrocious that its victims, when they are intelligent enough to study alternatives instead of taking their lot blindly, conclude that prison is the most comfortable place to spend the winter in, and qualify themselves accordingly by committing an offence for which they will get six months. But this consideration affects only those people whose condition is not defended by any responsible publicist: the remedy is admittedly not to make the prison worse but the slum better. Unfortunately the admitted claims of the poor on life are pitifully modest. The moment the treatment of the criminal is decent and merciful enough to give him a chance of moral recovery, or, in incorrigible cases, to avoid making bad worse, the official descriptions of his lot become so rosy that a clamor arises against thieves and murderers being better off than honest and kindly men; for the official reports tell us only of the care that is taken of the prisoner and the advantages he enjoys, or can earn by good conduct, never of his sufferings; and the public is not imaginative or thoughtful enough to supply the deficiency.

What sane man, I ask the clamorers, would accept an offer of free board, lodging, clothing, waiters in attendance at a touch of the bell, medical treatment, spiritual advice, scientific ventilation and sanitation, technical instruction, liberal education, and the use of a carefully selected library, with regular exercise daily and sacred music at frequent intervals, even at the Ritz Hotel, if the conditions were that he should never speak, never sing, never laugh, never see a newspaper, and write only one sternly censored letter and have one miserable interview at long intervals through the bars of a cage under the eye of a warder? And when the prison is not the Ritz Hotel, when the lodging, the food, the bed, are all deliberately made so uncomfortable as to be instruments of torture, when the clothes are rags promiscuously worn by all your fellow prisoners in turn with yourself, when the exercise is that of a turnspit, when the ventilation and sanitation are noisome, when the instruction is a sham, the education a fraud, when the doctor is a bully to whom your ailments are all malingerings, and the chaplain a moral snob with no time for anything but the distribution of unreadable books, when the waiters are bound by penalties not to speak to you except to give you an order or a rebuke, and then to address you as you would not dream of addressing your dog, when the manager holds over your head a continual threat of starvation and confinement in a punishment cell (as if your own cell were not punishment enough), then what man in his senses would voluntarily exchange even the most harassed freedom for such a life, much less wallow luxuriously in it, as the *Punch* burglar always does on paper the moment anyone suggests the slightest alleviation of the pain of imprisonment?

Giving Them Hell

Yet people cannot be brought to see this. They ask, first, what right the convict has to complain when he brought it on himself by his own misconduct, and second, what he has to complain of. You reply that his grievances are silence, solitude, idleness, waste of time, and irresponsibility. The retort is, "Why call that torture, as if it were boiling oil or red hot irons or something like that? Why, I have taken a cottage in the country for the sake of silence and solitude; and I should be only too glad to get rid of my responsibilities and waste my time in idleness like a real gentleman. A jolly sight too well off, the fellows are. I should give them hell."

Thus imprisonment is at once the most cruel of punishments and the one that those who inflict it without having ever experienced it cannot believe to be cruel. A country gentleman with a big hunting stable will indignantly discharge a groom and refuse him a reference for cruelly thrashing a horse. But it never occurs to him that his stables are horse prisons, and the stall a cell in which it is quite unnatural for the horse to be immured. In my youth I saw the great Italian actress Ristori play Mary Stuart; and nothing in her performance remains more vividly with me than her representation of the relief of Mary at finding herself in the open air after months of imprisonment. When I first saw a stud of hunters turned out to grass, they reminded me so strongly of Ristori that I at once understood that they had been prisoners in their stables, a fact which, obvious as it was, I had not thought of before. And this sort of thoughtlessness, being continuous and unconscious, inflicts more suffering than all the malice and passion in the world. In prison you get one piled on the other: to the cruelty that is intended and contrived, that grudges you even the inevitable relief of sleep and tries to make that a misery by plank beds and the like, is added the worse cruelty that is not intended as cruelty, and, when its perpetrators can be made conscious of it at all, deludes them by a ghastly semblance of pampered indulgence.

The Three Official Aims of Imprisonment

And now comes a further complication. When people are at last compelled to think about what they are doing to our unfortunate convicts, they think so unsuccessfully and confusedly that they only make matters worse. Take for example the official list of the results aimed at by the Prison Commissioners. First, imprisonment must be "retributory" (the word vindictive is not in official use). Second, it must be deterrent. Third, it must be reformative.

The Retribution Muddle

Now if you are to punish a man retributively, you must injure him. If you are to reform him, you must improve him. And men are not improved by injuries. To propose to punish and reform people — by the same operation is exactly as if you were to take a man suffering from pneumonia, and attempt to combine punitive and curative treatment. Arguing that a man with pneumonia is a danger to the community, and that he need not catch it if he takes proper care of his health, you resolve that he shall have a severe lesson, both to punish him for his negligence and pulmonary weakness and to deter others from following his example. You therefore strip him naked, and in that condition stand him all night in the snow. But as you admit the duty of restoring him to health if possible, and discharging him with sound lungs, you engage a doctor to superintend the punishment and administer cough lozenges, made as unpleasant to the taste as possible so as not to pamper the culprit. A Board of Commissioners ordering such treatment would prove thereby that either they were imbeciles or else they were hotly in earnest about punishing the patient and not in the least in earnest about curing him.

When our Prison Commissioners pretend to combine punishment with moral reformation they are in the same dilemma. We are told that the reformation of the criminal is kept constantly in view; yet the destruction of the prisoner's self-respect by systematic humiliation is deliberately ordered and practised, and we learn from a chaplain that he "does not think it is good to give opportunity for the exercise of Christian and social virtues one towards another" among prisoners. The only consolation for such contradictions is their demonstration that, as the tormentor instinctively feels that he must be a liar and a hypocrite on the subject, his conscience cannot be very easy about the torment. The contradictions are obvious enough here, because I put them on the same page. The Prison Commissioners keep them a few pages apart; and the average reader's memory, it seems, is not long enough to span the gap when his personal interests are not at stake.

Plausibility of the Deterrence Delusion

Deterrence, which is the real object of the courts, has much more to be said for it, because it is neither simply and directly wicked like retribution, nor a false excuse for wickedness like reformation. It is an unquestionable fact that, by making rules and forcing those who break them to suffer so severely that others like them become afraid to break them, discipline can be maintained to a certain extent among creatures without sense enough to understand its necessity, or, if they do understand it, without conscience enough to refrain from violating it. This is the crude basis of all our disciplines, home discipline, school discipline, factory discipline, army and navy discipline, as well as prison discipline and the whole fabric of criminal law. It is imposed not only by cruel rulers, but by unquestionably humane ones, the only difference being that the cruel rulers impose it with alacrity and gloat over its execution, and the humane rulers are driven to it reluctantly by the failure of their appeals to the conscience of people who have no conscience. Thus we find Mahomet, a conspicuously humane and conscientious Arab, keeping his fierce staff in order, not by unusual punishments, but by threats of a hell after death which he invented for the purpose in revolting detail of a kind which suggests that Mahomet had perhaps too much of the woman and the artist in him to know what would frighten a Bedouin most. Wellington, a general so humane that he sacrificed the exercise of a military genius of the first order to his moral horror of war and his freedom from its illusions, nevertheless hanged and flogged his soldiers mercilessly because he had learnt from experience that, as he put it, nothing is worse than impunity. All revolutions have been the work of men who, like Robespierre, were sentimental humanitarians and conscientious objectors to capital punishment and the severities of military and prison discipline; yet all the revolutions have after a very brief practical experience been driven to Terrorism (the proper name of Deterrence) as ruthless as the Counter-Revolutionary Terror of Sulla, the latest example being that of the Russian revolution now in progress. Whether it is Sulla, Robespierre, Trotsky, or the fighting mate of a sailing ship with a crew of loafers and wastrels, the result is the same: there are people to be dealt with who will not obey the law unless they are afraid to disobey it, and whose disobedience means disaster.

Crime Cannot Be Killed by Kindness

It is useless for humanitarians to shirk this hard fact, and proclaim their conviction that all lawbreakers can be cured by kindness. That may be true of most cases, provided you can find a very gifted practitioner to take the worst ones in hand, with unlimited time, and means to treat them. But if these conditions are not available, and a policeman and an executioner who will disable the wrongdoer instantaneously are available, the police remedy is the only practicable one, even for rulers filled with the spirit of the Sermon on the Mount. The late G. V. Foote, a strong humanitarian, once had to persuade a very intimate friend of his, a much smaller and weaker man, to allow himself to be taken to an asylum for lunatics. It took four hours of humanitarian persuasion to get the patient from the first floor of his house to the cab door. Foote told me that he not only recognized at once that no asylum attendant, with several patients to attend to, could possibly spend four hours in getting each of them downstairs, but found his temper so intolerably strained by the unnatural tax on his patience that if the breaking point had been reached, as it certainly would have been in the case of a warder or asylum attendant, he would have been far more violent, not to say savage, than if he had resorted to force at once, and finished the job in five minutes.

From taking this rational and practically compulsory use of kindly physical coercion to making it so painful that the victim will be afraid to give any trouble next time is a pretty certain step. In prisons, the warders have to protect themselves against violence from prisoners, of which there is a constant risk and very well founded dread, as there are always ungovernably savage criminals who have little more power of refraining from furious assaults than some animals, including quite carefully bred dogs and horses, have of refraining from biting and savaging. The official punishment is flogging and putting in irons for months. But the immediate rescue of the assaulted warder has to be effected by the whole body of warders within reach; and whoever supposes that the prisoner suffers nothing more at their hands than the minimum of force necessary to restrain him knows nothing of prison life and less of human nature.

Any criticism of the deterrent theory of our prison system which ignores the existence of ungovernable savages will be discredited by the citation of actual cases. I should be dismissed as a sentimentalist if I lost sight of them for a moment. On any other subject I could dispose of the matter by reminding my critics that hard cases make bad law. On this subject I recognize that the hard cases are of such a nature that provision must be made for them. Indeed hard cases may be said to be the whole subject matter of criminal law; for the normal human case is not that of the criminal, but of the law-abiding person on whose collar the grip of the policeman never closes. Only, it does not follow that the hardest cases should dictate the treatment of the relatively soft ones.

The Seamy Side of Deterrence

Let us now see what are the objections to the Deterrent or Terrorist system.

It necessarily leaves the interests of the victim wholly out of account. It injures and degrades him; destroys the reputation without which he cannot get employment; and when the punishment is imprisonment under our system, atrophies his powers of fending for himself in the world. Now this would not materially hurt anyone but himself if, when he had been duly made an example of, he were killed like a vivisected dog. But he is not killed. He is, at the expiration of his sentence, flung out of the prison into the streets to earn his living in a labor market where nobody will employ an ex-prisoner, betraying himself at every turn by his ignorance of the common news of the months or years he has passed without newspapers, lamed in speech, and terrified at the unaccustomed task of providing food and lodging for himself. There is only one lucrative occupation available for him; and that is crime. He has no compunction as to society: why should he have any? Society, for its own selfish protection, having done its worst to him, he has no feeling about it except a desire to get a bit of his own back. He seeks the only xix company in which he is welcome: the society of criminals; and sooner or later, according to his luck, he finds himself in prison again. The figures of recidivism show that the exceptions to this routine are so few as to be negligible for the purposes of this argument. The criminal, far from being deterred from crime, is forced into it; and the citizen whom his punishment was meant to protect suffers from his depredations.

Our Plague of Unrestrained Crime

It is, in fact, admitted that the deterrent system does not deter the convicted criminal. Its real efficacy is sought in the deterrent effect on the free citizens who would commit crimes but for their fear of punishment. The Terrorist can point to the wide range of evil-doing which, not being punished by law, is rampant among us; for though a man can get himself hanged for a momentary lapse of self-control under intolerable provocation by a nagging woman, or into prison for putting the precepts of Christ above the orders of a Competent Military Authority, he can be a quite infernal scoundrel without breaking any penal law. If it be true, as it certainly is, that it is conscience and not the fear of punishment that makes civilized life possible, and that Dr. Johnson's

> How small, of all that human hearts endure
> That part that laws or kings can cause or cure!

is as applicable to crime as to human activity in general, it is none the less true that commercial civilization presents an appalling spectacle of pillage and parasitism, of corruption in the press and in the pulpit, of lying advertisements which make people buy rank poisons in the belief that they are health restorers, of traps to catch the provision for the widow and the fatherless and divert it to the pockets of company promoting rogues, of villainous oppression of the poor and cruelty to the defenceless; and it is arguable that most of this could, like burglary and forgery, be kept within bearable bounds if its perpetrators were dealt with as burglars and forgers are dealt with today. It is, of course, equally arguable that if we can afford to leave so much villainy unpunished we can afford to leave all villainy unpunished. Unfortunately, we cannot afford it: our toleration is threatening our civilization. The prosperity that consists in the wicked nourishing like a green bay tree, and the humble and contrite hearts being thoroughly despised, is a commercial delusion. Facts must be looked in the face, rascals told what they are, and all men called on to justify their ways to God and Man up to the point at which the full discharge of their social duties leaves them free to exercise their individual fancies. Restraint from evil-doing is within the rights as well as within the powers of organized society over its members; and it cannot be denied that the execution of these powers, as far as it could be made inevitable, would incidentally deter from crime a certain number of people with a marginal conscience or none at all, and that their

codification would create fresh social conscience by enlarging the list
of things which law-abiding people make it a point of honor not to
do, besides calling the attention of the community to grave matters
in which they have hitherto erred through thoughtlessness.

Deterrence a Function of Certainty, Not of Severity

But there is all the difference in the world between deterrence as an
incident of the operation of criminal law, and deterrence as its sole
object and justification. In a purely deterrent system, for instance, it
matters not a jot who is punished provided somebody is punished
and the public persuaded that he is guilty. The effect of hanging or
imprisoning the wrong man is as deterrent as hanging or imprisoning
the right one. This is the fundamental explanation of the extreme
and apparently fiendish reluctance of the Home Office to release a
prisoner when, as in the Beck case, the evidence on which he was
convicted has become discredited to a point at which no jury would
maintain its verdict of guilty. The reluctance is not to confess that an
innocent man is being punished, but to proclaim that a guilty man
has escaped. For if escape is possible, deterrence shrinks almost to
nothing. There is no better established rule of criminology than that
it is not the severity of punishment that deters, but its certainty. And
the flaw in the case for Terrorism is that it is impossible to obtain
enough certainty to deter. The police are compelled to confess every
year, when they publish their statistics, that against the list of crimes
reported to them they can set only a percentage of detections and
convictions. And the list of reported crimes can form only a percentage, how large or small it is impossible to say, but probably small, of
the crimes actually committed; for it is the greatest mistake to suppose
that everyone who is robbed runs to the police: on the contrary, only
foolish and ignorant or very angry people do so without very serious
consideration and great reluctance. In most cases it costs nothing
to let the thief off, and a good deal to prosecute him. The burglar
in Heartbreak House, who makes his living by robbing people, and
then blackmailing them by threatening to give himself up to the
police and put them to the expense and discomfort of attending his
trial and giving evidence after enduring all the worry of the police

enquiries, is not a joke: he is a comic dramatization of a process that is going on every day. As to the black sheep of respectable families who blackmail them by offering them the alternative of making good their thefts and frauds or having the family name disgraced, ask any experienced family solicitor.

Beside the chance of not being prosecuted, there are chances of acquittal; but I doubt whether the chances of acquittal count for very much except with very attractive women; but it is worth mentioning that juries will snatch at the flimsiest pretexts for refusing to send people who engage their sympathy to the gallows or to penal servitude, even on evidence of murder or theft which would make short work of a repulsive person.

Some Personal Experiences

Take my own experience as probably common enough. Fifty years ago a friend of mine, hearing that a legacy had been left him, lent himself the expected sum out of his employers' cash; concealed the defalcation by falsifying his accounts; and was detected before he could repay. His employers naturally resented the fraud, and had no desire to spare the culprit. But a public exposure of the affair would have involved shock to their clients' sense of security, loss of time and consequently of money, and the unpleasantness of attendance in court at the trial. All this put any recourse to the police out of the question; and the delinquent obtained another post after a very brief interval during which he supported himself as a church organist. This, by the way, was a quite desirable conclusion, as he was for most practical purposes an honest man. It would have been pure mischief to make him a criminal; but that is not the present point. He serves here as an illustration of the fact that our criminal law, far from inviting prosecution, attaches serious losses and inconveniences to it.

It may be said that whatever the losses and inconveniences may be, it is a public duty to prosecute. But is it? Is it not a Christian duty not to prosecute? A man stole £500 from me by a trick. He speculated in my character with subtlety and success; and yet he ran risks of detection which no quite sensible man would have ventured on. It was assumed that I would resort to the police. I asked why.

The answer was that he should be punished to deter others from similar crimes. I naturally said, "You have been punishing people cruelly for more than a century for this kind of fraud; and the result is that I am robbed of £500. Evidently your deterrence does not deter. What it does do is to torment the swindler for years, and then throw him back, a worse man in every respect, upon society with no other employment open to him except that of fresh swindling. However, your elaborate arrangements to deter me from prosecuting are convincing and effective. I could earn £500 by useful work in the time it would take me to prosecute this man vindictively and worse than uselessly. So I wish him joy of his booty, and invite him to swindle me again if he can." Now this was not sentimentality. I am not a bit fonder of being swindled than other people; and if society would treat swindlers properly I should denounce them without the slightest remorse, and not grudge a reasonable expenditure of time and energy in the business. But to throw good money after bad in setting to work a wicked and mischievous process like the one described in this book would be to stamp myself as a worse man than the swindler, who earned the money more energetically, and appropriated it no more unjustly, than I earn and appropriate my dividends.

I must however warn our thieves that I can promise them no immunity from police pursuit if they rob me. Some time after the operation just recorded, an uninvited guest came to a luncheon party in my house. He (or she) got away with an overcoat and a pocketful of my wife's best table silver. But instead of selecting my overcoat, he took the best overcoat, which was that of one of my guests. My guest was insured against theft; the insurance company had to buy him a new overcoat; and the matter thus passed out of my hands into those of the police. But the result, as far as the thief was concerned, was the same. He was not captured; and he had the social satisfaction of providing employment for others in converting into a strongly fortified obstacle the flimsy gate through which he had effected an entrance, thereby giving my flat the appearance of a private madhouse.

On another occasion a drunken woman obtained admission by presenting an authentic letter from a soft hearted member of the House of Lords. I had no guests at the moment; and as she, too, wanted an overcoat, she took mine, and actually interviewed me with it most perfunctorily concealed under her jacket. When I called her attention to it, she handed it back to me effusively; begged me to shake hands with her; and went her way.

Now these things occur by the dozen every day, in spite of the severity with which they are punished when the thief is captured by the police. I daresay all my readers, if not too young to have completed a representative experience, could add two or three similar stories. What do they go to prove? Just that detection is so uncertain that its consequences have no really effective deterrence for the potential offender, whilst the unpleasant and expensive consequences of prosecution, being absolutely certain, have a very strong deterrent effect indeed on the prosecutor. In short, all the hideous cruelty practised by us for the sake of deterrence is wasted: we are damning our souls at great expense and trouble for nothing.

Judicial Vengeance as an Alternative to Lynch Law

Thus we see that of the three official objects of our prison system: vengeance, deterrence, and reformation of the criminal, only one is achieved; and that is the one which is nakedly abominable. But there is a plea for it which must be taken into account, and which brings us to the root of the matter in our own characters. It is said, and it is in a certain degree true, that if the Government does not lawfully organize and regulate popular vengeance, the populace will rise up and execute this vengeance lawlessly for itself. The standard defence of the Inquisition is that without it no heretic's life would have been safe. In Texas today the people are not satisfied with the prospect of knowing that a murderer and ravisher will be electrocuted inside a jail if a jury can resist the defence put up by his lawyer. They tear him from the hands of the sheriff; pour lamp oil over him; and burn him alive. Now the burning of human beings is not only an expression of outraged public morality: it is also a sport for which a taste can be acquired much more easily and rapidly than a taste for coursing hares, just as a taste for drink can be acquired from brandy and cocktails more easily and rapidly than from beer or sauterne. Lynching mobs begin with [N]egro ravishers and murderers; but they presently go on to any sort of delinquent, provided he is black. Later on, as a white man will burn as amusingly as a black one, and a white woman react to tarring and feathering as thrillingly as a [N]egress, the color line is effaced by what professes to be a rising wave of virtuous indignation, but is in fact an epidemic of Sadism. The defenders of our penal system take advantage of it to assure us that if they did not torment and ruin a boy guilty of sleeping in the open air, the British public would rise and tear that boy limb from limb.

Now the reply to such a plea, from the point of view of civilized law, cannot be too sweeping. The government which cannot restrain a mob from taking the law into its own hands is no government at all. If Landru can go to the guillotine unmolested in France, and his British prototype who drowned all his wives in their baths can be peaceably hanged in England, Texas can protect its criminals by simply bringing its civilization up to the French and British level. But indeed the besetting sin of the mob is a morbid hero worship of great criminals rather than a ferocious abhorrence of them. In any case nobody will have the effrontery to pretend that the number of criminals who excite popular feeling enough to risk lynching is more than a negligible percentage of the whole. The theory that the problem of crime is only one of organizing, regulating, and executing the vengeance of the mob will not bear plain statement, much less discussion. It is only the retributive theory over again in its weakest form.

The Hard Cases That Make Bad Law

Having now disposed of all the official theories as the trash they are, let us return to the facts, and deal with the hard ones first. Everyone who has any extensive experience of domesticated animals, human or other, knows that there are negatively bad specimens who have no conscience, and positively bad ones who are incurably ferocious. The negative ones are often very agreeable and even charming companions; but they beg, borrow, steal, defraud and seduce almost by reflex action: they cannot resist the most trifling temptation. They are indulged and spared to the extreme limit of endurance; but in the end they have to be deprived of their liberty in some way. The positive ones enjoy no such tolerance. Unless they are physically restrained they break people's bones, knock out their eyes, rupture their organs, or kill them.

Then there are the cruel people, not necessarily unable to control their tempers, nor fraudulent, nor in any other way disqualified for ordinary social activity or liberty, possibly even with conspicuous virtues. But by a horrible involution, they lust after the spectacle of suffering, mental and physical, as normal men lust after love. Torture is to them a pleasure except when it is inflicted on themselves. In scores of ways, from the habitual utterance of wounding speeches, and the contriving of sly injuries and humiliations for which they cannot be brought to book legally, to thrashing their wives and children or, as bachelors, paying prostitutes of the hardier sort to submit to floggings, they seek the satisfaction of their desire wherever and however they can.

Possibilities of Therapeutic Treatment

Now in the present state of our knowledge it is folly to talk of reforming these people. By this I do not mean that even now they are all quite incurable. The cases of no conscience are sometimes cases of unawakened conscience. Violent and quarrelsome people are often only energetic people who are underworked: I have known a man cured of wife-beating by setting him to beat the drum in a village band; and the quarrels that make country life so very unarcadian are picked mostly because the quarrelers have not enough friction in their lives to keep them good humored.

Psycho-analysis, too, which is not all quackery and pornography, might conceivably cure a case of Sadism as it might cure any of the phobias. And psychoanalysis is a mere fancy compared to the knowledge we have been gathering recently as to the functions of our glands in relation to our conduct. In the nineteenth century this knowledge was pursued barbarously by crude vivisectors whose notion of finding out what a gland was for was to cut it violently out and see what would happen to the victim, meanwhile trying to bribe the public to tolerate such horrors by promising to make old debauchees young again. This was rightly felt to be a villainous business; besides, who could suppose that the men who did these things would hesitate to lie about the results when there was plenty of money to be made by representing them as cures for dreaded diseases? But to-day we are not asked to infer that because something has happened to a horribly mutilated dog it will happen also to an unmutilated human being. We can now make authentic pictures of internal organs by means of rays to which flesh is transparent. This makes it possible to take a criminal and say authoritatively that he is a case, not of original sin, but of an inefficient, or excessively efficient, thyroid gland, or pituitary gland, or adrenal gland, as the case may be. This of course does not help the police in dealing with a criminal: they must apprehend and bring him to trial all the same. But if the prison doctor were able to say "Put some iodine in this man's skilly, and his character will change," then the notion of punishing instead of curing him would become ridiculous. Of course the matter is not so simple as that; but a considerable case can be made out for at least a conjecture that many cases which are now incurable may be disposed of in the not very remote future by either inducing the patient to produce more thyroxin or pituitrin or adrenalin or what not, or else administering them to him as thyroxin is at present administered in cases of myxo-edema. Yet the reports of the work of our prison medical officers suggest that hardly any of them has ever heard of these discoveries, or regards a convict as anything more interesting scientifically than a malingering rascal.

Samuel Butler

Erewhon and Erewhon Revisited*

This is what I gathered. That in that country if a man falls into ill health, or catches any disorder, or fails bodily in any way before he is seventy years old, he is tried before a jury of his countrymen and if convicted is held up to public scorn and sentenced more or less severely as the case may be. There are subdivisions of illness into crimes and misdemeanors as with offenses amongst ourselves—a man being punished very heavily for serious illness, while failure of eyes or hearing in one over sixty-five, who has had good health hitherto, is dealt with by fine only, or imprisonment in default of payment. But if a man forges a check, or sets his house on fire, or robs with violence from the person, or does any other such things as are criminal in our own country, he is either taken to a hospital and most carefully tended at the public expense, or if he is in good circumstances, he lets it be known to all his friends that he is suffering from a severe fit of immorality, just as we do when we are ill, and they come and visit him with great solicitude, and inquire with interest how it all came about, what symptoms first showed themselves, and so forth—questions which he will answer with perfect unreserve; for bad conduct, though considered no less deplorable than illness with ourselves, and as unquestionably indicating something seriously wrong with the individual who misbehaves, is nevertheless held to be the result of either pre-natal or post-natal misfortune.

The strange part of the story, however, is that though they ascribe moral defects to the effect of misfortune either in character or surroundings, they will not listen to the plea of misfortune in cases that in England meet with sympathy and commiseration only. Ill luck of

---

*Samuel Butler, *Erewhon nd Erewhon Revisited*, intro. Lewis Mumford (New York: Random House, 1927), pp. 88–101.

any kind, or even ill treatment at the hands of others, is considered an offense against society, inasmuch as it makes people uncomfortable to hear of it. Loss of fortune, therefore, or loss of some dear friend on whom another was much dependent, is punished hardly less severely than physical delinquency.

Foreign, indeed, as such ideas are to our own, traces of somewhat similar opinions can be found even in nineteenth-century England. If a person has an abscess, the medical man will say that it contains "peccant" matter, and people say that they have a "bad" arm or finger, or that they are very "bad" all over, when they only mean "diseased." Among foreign nations Erewhonian opinions may be still more clearly noted. The Mahommedans, for example, to this day, send their female prisoners to hospitals, and the New Zealand Maories visit any misfortune with forcible entry into the house of the offender, and the breaking up and burning of all his goods. The Italians, again, use the same word for "disgrace" and "misfortune." I once heard an Italian lady speak of a young friend whom she described as endowed with every virtue under heaven, "ma," she exclaimed, "povero disgraziato, ha ammazzato suo zio." ("Poor unfortunate fellow, he has murdered his uncle.")

On mentioning this, which I heard when taken to Italy as a boy by my father, the person to whom I told it showed no surprise. He said that he had been driven for two or three years in a certain city by a young Sicilian cabdriver of prepossessing manners and appearance, but then lost sight of him. On asking what had become of him, he was told that he was in prison for having shot at his father with intent to kill him—happily without serious results. Some years later my informant again found himself warmly accosted by the prepossessing young cabdriver. "Ah, caro signore," he exclaimed, "sono cinque anni che non lo vedo—tre anni di militare, e due anni di disgrazia," etc. ("My dear sir, it is five years since I saw you—three years of military service, and two of misfortune")—during which last the poor fellow had been in prison. Of moral sense he showed not so much as a trace. He and his father were now on excellent terms, and were likely to remain so unless either of them should again have the misfortune mortally to offend the other.

In the following chapter I will give a few examples of the way in which what we should call misfortune, hardship, or disease are dealt with by the Erewhonians, but for the moment will return to their treatment of cases that with us are criminal. As I have already said, these, though not judicially punishable, are recognized as requiring correction. Accordingly, there exists a class of men trained in soulcraft, whom they call straighteners, as nearly as I can translate a word which literally means "one who bends back the crooked." These men practice much as medical men in England, and receive a quasi-surreptitious fee on every visit. They are treated with the same unreserve, and obeyed as readily, as our own doctors—that is to say, on the whole sufficiently—because people know that it is their interest to get well as soon as they can, and that they will not be scouted as they would be if their bodies were out of order, even though they may have to undergo a very painful course of treatment.

When I say that they will not be scouted, I do not mean that an Erewhonian will suffer no social inconvenience in consequence, we will say, of having committed fraud. Friends will fall away from him because of his being less pleasant company, just as we ourselves are disinclined to make companions of those who are either poor or poorly. No one with any sense of self-respect will place himself on an equality in the matter of affection with those who are less lucky than himself in birth, health, money, good looks, capacity, or anything else. Indeed, that dislike and even disgust should be felt by the fortunate for the unfortunate, or at any rate for those who have been discovered to have met with any of the more serious and less familiar misfortunes, is not only natural, but desirable for any society, whether of man or brute.

The fact, therefore, that the Erewhonians attach none of that guilt to crime which they do to physical ailments, does not prevent the more selfish among them from neglecting a friend who has robbed a bank, for instance, till he has fully recovered; but it does prevent them from even thinking of treating criminals with that contemptuous tone which would seem to say, "I, if I were you, should be a better man than you are," a tone which is held quite reasonable in regard to physical ailment. Hence, though they conceal ill health by every cunning and hypocrisy and artifice which they can devise, they are quite open about the most flagrant mental diseases, should they happen to exist, which to do the people justice is not often. Indeed, there are some who are, so to speak, spiritual valetudinarians, and who make themselves exceedingly ridiculous by their nervous supposition that they are wicked, while they are very tolerable people all the time. This however is exceptional, and on the whole they use much the same reserve or unreserve about the state of their moral welfare as we do about our health.

Hence all the ordinary greetings among ourselves, such as, How do you do? and the like, are considered signs of gross ill-breeding; nor do the politer classes tolerate even such a common complimentary remark as telling a man that he is looking well. They salute each other with, "I hope you are good this morning;" or "I hope you have recovered from the snappishness from which you were suffering when I last saw you"; and if the person saluted has not been good, or is still snappish, he says so at once and is condoled with accordingly. Indeed, the straighteners have gone so far as to give names from the hypothetical language (as taught at the Colleges of Unreason), to all known forms of mental indisposition, and to classify them according to a system of their own, which, though I could not understand it, seemed to work well in practice; for they are always able to tell a man what is the matter with him as soon as they have heard his story, and their familiarity with the long names assures him that they thoroughly understand his case.

The reader will have no difficulty in believing that the laws regarding ill health were frequently evaded by the help of recognized fictions, which everyone understood, but which it would be considered gross ill-breeding to even seem to understand. Thus, a day or two after my arrival at the Nosnibors', one of the many ladies who called on me made excuses for her husband's only sending his card, on the ground that when going through the public market-place that morning he had stolen a pair of socks. I had already been warned that I should never show surprise, so I merely expressed my sympathy, and said that though I had only been in the capital so short time, I had already had a very narrow escape from stealing a clothes-brush, and that though I had resisted temptation so far, I was sadly afraid that if I saw any object of special interest that was neither too hot nor too heavy, I should have to put myself in the straightener's hands.

Mrs. Nosnibor, who had been keeping an ear on all that I had been saying, praised me when the lady had gone. Nothing, she said, could have been more polite according to Erewhonian etiquette. She then explained that to have stolen a pair of socks, or "to have the socks" (in more colloquial language), was a recognized way of saying that the person in question was slightly indisposed.

In spite of all this they have a keen sense of the enjoyment consequent upon what they call being "well." They admire mental health and love it in other people, and take all the pains they can (consistently with their other duties) to secure it for themselves. They have an extreme dislike to marrying into what they consider unhealthy families. They send for the straightener at once whenever they have been guilty of anything seriously flagitious—often even if they think that they are on the point of committing it; and though his remedies are sometimes exceedingly painful, involving close confinement for weeks, and in some cases the most cruel physical tortures, I never heard of a reasonable Erewhonian refusing to do what his straightener told him, any more than of a reasonable Englishman refusing to undergo even the most frightful operation, if his doctors told him it was necessary.

We in England never shrink from telling our doctor what is the matter with us merely through the fear that he will hurt us. We let him do his worst upon us, and stand it without a murmur, because we are not scouted for being ill, and because we know that the doctor is doing his best to cure us, and that he can judge of our case better than we can; but we should conceal all illness if we were treated as the Erewhonians are when they have anything the matter with them; we should do the same as with moral and intellectual diseases—we should feign health with the most consummate art, till we were found out, and should hate a single flogging given in the way of mere punishment more than the amputation of a limb, if it were kindly and courteously performed from a wish to help us out of our difficulty, and with the full consciousness on the part of the doctor that it was only by an accident of constitution that he was not in the like plight himself. So the Erewhonians take a flogging once a week, and a diet of bread and water for two or three months together, whenever their straightener recommends it.

I do not suppose that even my host, on having swindled a confiding widow out of the whole of her property, was put to more actual suffering than a man will readily undergo at the hands of an English doctor. And yet he must have had a very bad time of it. The sounds

I heard were sufficient to show that his pain was exquisite, but he never shrank from undergoing it. He was quite sure that it did him good; and I think he was right. I cannot believe that that man will ever embezzle money again. He may—but it will be a long time before he does so.

During my confinement in prison, and on my journey, I had already discovered a great deal of the above; but it still seemed surpassingly strange, and I was in constant fear of committing some piece of rudeness, through my inability to look at things from the same standpoint as my neighbors; but after a few weeks' stay with the Nosnibors, I got to understand things better, especially on having heard all about my host's illness, of which he told me fully and repeatedly.

It seemed that he had been on the Stock Exchange of the city for many years and had amassed enormous wealth, without exceeding the limits of what was generally considered justifiable, or at any rate, permissible dealing; but at length on several occasions he had become aware of a desire to make money by fraudulent representations, and had actually dealt with two or three sums in a way which had made him rather uncomfortable. He had unfortunately made light of it and pooh-poohed the ailment, until circumstances eventually presented themselves which enabled him to cheat upon a very considerable scale;—he told me what they were, and they were about as bad as anything could be, but I need not detail them;—he seized the opportunity, and became aware, when it was too late, that he must be seriously out of order. He had neglected himself too long.

He drove home at once, broke the news to his wife and daughters as gently as he could, and sent off for one of the most celebrated straighteners of the kingdom to a consultation with the family practitioner, for the case was plainly serious. On the arrival of the straightener he told his story, and expressed his fear that his morals must be permanently impaired.

The eminent man reassured him with a few cheering words, and then proceeded to make a more careful diagnosis of the case. He inquired concerning Mr. Nosnibor's parents—had their moral health been good? He was answered that there had not been anything seriously amiss with them, but that his maternal grandfather, whom he was supposed to resemble somewhat in person, had been a consummate scoundrel and had ended his days in a hospital—while a brother of his father's, after having led a most flagitious life for many years, had been at last cured by a philosopher of a new school, which as far as I could understand it bore much the same relation to the old as homoeopathy to allopathy. The straightener shook his head at this, and laughingly replied that the cure must have been due to nature. After a few more questions he wrote a prescription and departed.

I saw the prescription. It ordered a fine to the State of double the money embezzled; no food but bread and milk for six months, and a severe flogging once a month for twelve. I was surprised to see that no part of the fine was to be paid to the poor woman whose money had been embezzled, but on inquiry I learned that she would have been prosecuted in the Misplaced Confidence Court, if she had not escaped its clutches by dying shortly after she had discovered her loss.

As for Mr. Nosnibor, he had received his eleventh flogging on the day of my arrival. I saw him later on the same afternoon, and he was still twinged; but there had been no escape from following out the straightener's prescription, for the so-called sanitary laws of Erewhon are very rigorous, and unless the straightener was satisfied that his orders had been obeyed, the patient would have been taken to a hospital (as the poor are), and would have been much worse off. Such at least is the law, but it is never necessary to enforce it.

On a subsequent occasion I was present at an interview between Mr. Nosnibor and the family straightener, who was considered competent to watch the completion of the cure. I was struck with the delicacy with which he avoided even the remotest semblance of inquiry after the physical well-being of his patient, though there was a certain yellowness about my host's eyes which argued a bilious habit of body. To have taken notice of this would have been a gross breach of professional etiquette. I was told, however, that a straightener sometimes thinks it right to glance at the possibility of some slight physical disorder if he finds it important in order to assist him in his diagnosis; but the answers which he gets are generally untrue or evasive, and he forms his own conclusions upon the matter as well as he can. Sensible men have been known to say that the straightener should in strict confidence be told of every physical ailment that is likely to bear upon the case; but people are naturally shy of doing this, for they do not like lowering themselves in the opinion of the straightener, and his ignorance of medical science is supreme. I heard of one lady, indeed, who had the hardihood to confess that a furious outbreak of ill-humor and extravagant fancies for which she was seeking advice was possibly the result of indisposition. "You should resist that," said the straightener, in a kind, but grave voice; "we can do nothing for the bodies of our patients; such matters are beyond our province, and I desire that I may hear no further particulars." The lady burst into tears, and promised faithfully that she would never be unwell again.

But to return to Mr. Nosnibor. As the afternoon wore on many carriages drove up with callers to inquire how he had stood his flogging. It had been very severe, but the kind inquiries upon every side gave him great pleasure, and he assured me that he was almost tempted to do wrong again by the solicitude with which his friends had treated him during his recovery: in this I need hardly say that he was not serious.

During the remainder of my stay in the country Mr. Nosnibor was constantly attentive to his business, and largely increased his already great possessions; but I never heard a whisper to the effect of his having been indisposed a second time, or made money by other than the most strictly honorable means. I did hear afterwards in confidence that there had been reason to believe that his health had been not a little affected by the straightener's treatment, but his friends did not choose to be over-curious upon the subject, and on his return to his affairs it was by common consent passed over as hardly criminal in one who was otherwise so much afflicted. For they regard bodily ailments as the more venial in proportion as they have been produced by causes independent of the constitution. Thus if a person ruin his health by excessive indulgence at the table or by drinking, they count it to be almost a part of the mental disease which brought it about, and so it goes for little, but they have no mercy on such illnesses as fevers or catarrhs or lung diseases, which to us appear to be beyond the control of the individual. They are only more lenient towards the diseases of the young—such as measles, which they think to be like sowing one's wild oats—and look over them as pardonable indiscretions if they have not been too serious, and if they are atoned for by complete subsequent recovery.

It is hardly necessary to say that the office of straightener is one which requires long and special training. It stands to reason that he who would cure a moral ailment must be practically acquainted with it in all its bearings. The student for the profession of straightener is required to set apart certain seasons for the practice of each vice in turn as a religious duty. These seasons are called "fasts," and are continued by the student until he finds that he really can subdue all the more usual vices in his own person, and hence can advise his patients from the results of his own experience.

Those who intend to be specialists, rather than general practitioners, devote themselves more particularly to the branch in which their practice will mainly lie. Some students have been obliged to continue their exercises during their whole lives, and some devoted men have actually died as martyrs to the drink, or gluttony, or whatever branch of vice they may have chosen for their especial study. The greater number, however, take no harm by the excursions into the various departments of vice which it is incumbent upon them to study.

For the Erewhonians hold that unalloyed virtue is not a thing to be immoderately indulged in. I was shown more than one case in which the real or supposed virtues of parents were visited upon the children to the third and fourth generation. The straighteners say that the most that can be truly said for virtue is that there is a considerable balance in its favor, and that it is on the whole a good deal better to be on its side than against it; but they urge that there is much pseudovirtue going about, which is apt to let people in very badly before they find it out. Those men, they say, are best who are not remarkable either for vice or virtue. I told them about Hogarth's idle and industrious apprentices, but they did not seem to think that the industrious apprentice was a very nice person.

Karl Marx

Punishment and Society*

Punishment in general has been defended as a means either of ameliorating or of intimidating. Now what right have you to punish me for the amelioration or intimidation of others? And besides, there is history—there is such a thing as statistics—which prove with the most complete evidence that since Cain the world has neither been intimidated nor ameliorated by punishment. Quite the contrary. From the point of view of abstract right, there is only one theory of punishment which recognizes human dignity in the abstract, and that is the theory of Kant, especially in the more rigid formula given to it by Hegel. Hegel says:

> Punishment is the *right* of the criminal. It is an act of his own will. The violation of right has been proclaimed by the criminal as his own right. His crime is the negation of right. Punishment is the negation of this negation, and consequently an affirmation of right, solicited and forced upon the criminal by himself. [Hegel, *Philosophy of Right*]

There is no doubt something specious in this formula, inasmuch as Hegel, instead of looking upon the criminal as the mere object, the slave of justice, elevates him to the position of a free and self-determined being. Looking, however, more closely into the matter, we discover that German idealism here, as in most other instances, has but given a transcendental sanction to the rules of existing society. Is it not a delusion to substitute for the individual with his real motives, with multifarious social circumstances pressing upon him,

---

*Karl Marx, "Capital Punishment," in *Marx and Engels: Basic Writings on Politics and Philosophy*, ed. L. Feuer (Garden City: Anchor Books, 1959), pp. 487–89.

the abstraction of "free-will"—one among the many qualities of man for man himself! This theory, considering punishment as the result of the criminal's own will, is only a metaphysical expression for the old "*jus talionis*" [the right of retaliation by inflicting punishment of the same kind] eye against eye, tooth against tooth, blood against blood. Plainly speaking, and dispensing with all paraphrases, punishment is nothing but a means of society to defend itself against the infraction of its vital conditions, whatever may be their character. Now, what a state of society is that, which knows of no better Instrument for its own defense than the hangman, and which proclaims through the "leading journal of the world" its own brutality as eternal law?

Mr. A. Quételet, in his excellent and learned work, *l'Homme et ses Facultés,* says:

> There is a *budget* which we pay with frightful regularity—it is that of prisons, dungeons and scaffolds. . . . We might even predict how many individuals will stain their hands with the blood of their fellow men, how many will be forgers, how many will deal in poison, pretty nearly the same way as we may foretell the annual births and deaths.

And Mr. Quételet, in a calculation of the probabilities of crime published in 1829, actually predicted with astonishing certainty, not only the amount but all the different kinds of crimes committed in France in 1830. That it is not so much the particular political institutions of a country as the fundamental conditions of modern *bourgeois* society in general, which produce an average amount of crime in a given national fraction of society, may be seen from the following table, communicated by Quételet, for the years 1822–24. We find in a number of one hundred condemned criminals in America and France:

Age	Philadelphia	France
Under twenty-one years	19	19
Twenty-one to thirty	44	35
Thirty to forty	23	23
Above forty	14	23
Total	100	100

Now, if crimes observed on a great scale thus show, in their amount and their classification, the regularity of physical phenomena—if as Mr. Quételet remarks, "it would be difficult to decide in respect to which of the two" (the physical world and the social system) "the acting causes produce their effect with the utmost regularity"—is there not a necessity for deeply reflecting upon an alteration of the system that breeds these crimes, instead of glorifying the hangman who executes a lot of criminals to make room only for the supply of new ones?

Clarence Darrow

The Holdup Man*

The season of the "holdup man" and the "anti-holdup man" is once more at hand. This period comes annually at the same time of year, just after the flower show, the horse show, and along with the college football games. It begins with the season of gaiety, when the days grow short and the nights grow long, when the first sharp, tingling frost of winter drives the people off the streets and huddles them around the fires, and when the price of coal goes up.

The season of the "holdup man" will wane as the winter gaieties fade away—soon after Lent—when the nights again grow short and the days grow long, when the price of coal goes down and the sun comes back once more and warms the poor and homeless, without money and without price.

Lawyers, mayors, doctors, and policemen freely give their advice as to the best way to treat the "holdup man." There is scarcely a topic of the day in which all classes of society so generally agree—one remedy is prescribed by all—more police, more revolvers, more clubs, more jails—this is the remedy for the "holdup man." One able lawyer advises every citizen to carry a revolver and to shoot at every suspected holdup—to aim at the abdomen, presumably the most fatal spot. Why the "holdup man" should be treated differently from other men who transgress the moral law is not quite clear. If all sinners were to be shot at sight few would be left to bury the dead. A doctor, generally humane and wise, declares that the mayor is responsible for all the holdup men, that there is no excuse for a burglary on "Maple Street," and some other street. What the residents of these streets have done to exempt them from the holdup man is not made clear.

---

*Clarence Darrow, "The Holdup Man," *The International Socialist Review* (1909), reprinted in *Verdicts Out of Court* (1963), pp. 220–24. http://darrow.law.umn.edu/documents/Hold_Up_Man_reduced.pdf

It has not occurred to any of these eminent people to find the cause for the "holdup man," and yet most of them know that nothing in this world exists without a cause.

Of course no one but a crank or a fanatic could find any necessary connection between the brilliant costumes of the horse show, the cold blasts of winter, the price of coal and the holdup man; yet after all, many men whom the world has called wise—and even orthodox—have associated these causes and brought not only arguments but long tables of figures to show that there is a law which governs even the actions of the holdup man and relates him to every other living thing upon the earth.

There are many other facts that students have learned while policemen were wielding their brutal clubs.

The number of homeless girls who patrol the streets of our large cities grows greater, they walk more briskly and waste less time negotiating with the prospective customer as the nights grow long and cold—to most people this is an accident like all other things on earth. There are those who know that the rooms where these girls are poor, that they are not all heated with steam, that most of them are cold, and that to say nothing of food, these wanderers must do something to keep warm.

There are other facts, too, which the "crank" and sentimentalist has found out. Our jails and police stations are fuller in winter than in summer. The Salvation Army and other bodies of evangelists who have warm rooms and nice bowls of hot soup make many more converts in winter than in summer. The winter "Christian" is known to all who do this sort of work. Our poorhouses, wood yards, orphan asylums, and even art galleries and public reading rooms are well patronized in winter. This last would teach some profound thinkers that cold weather conduces to literature and art. Pawnshops and secondhand furniture men get better bargains in winter than in summer—but still, what of it?—do not lawyers, doctors, policemen, and clergymen all say that the panacea for all ills is the policeman's club?

There are other facts which dreamers and visionists are wont to note—those people have so little to do with the practical side of life that they must needs dream. In good times tramps are scarce, jails are empty, criminal courts not over busy, streetwalkers few, holdup men very rare.

The early winter is the time that frugal men and frugal beasts lay up their stores for the cold days and nights coming on. The thrifty mine owners lay in their stocks by marking up the price of the coal which the Lord placed in the earth long ages since; the lawyer and merchant telephones his dealer to put twenty tons of coal in his cellar to feed his furnace through the winter months—the poor seamstress works farther into the black night to buy a few bushels to keep her fingers from growing stiff. Old, bent, haggard women take huge sacks upon their shoulders and wander up and down the railroad tracks for the stray lumps that may drive away a portion of the frost, and lean, dirty little boys pull their carts through the streets and sweep up what the rich man leaves; and the holdup man, he, too, goes out to lay in his winter stock against the ice and cold.

The holdup men are not the ones who mark up the price of coal and gas and beef—these would take no such chances as fall to the lot of the holdup man. The holdup man comes from the home of the wretched and the poor. Who think you is this holdup man—was he born this way? If so, don't fire as you meet him on the street, but turn your gun on God Almighty who made him as he is. But he was not born—he was made—he might have been an unsuccessful merchant who could not compete with the department store—or a railroad man whose name is on the black-list because he dared to strike. He grew more and more desperate year after year until he became a "holdup man."

It is fifty years since the great philosopher and historian Buckle gave his monumental work to the world. In this work he showed not alone by reason and logic, but by statistics covering long periods of time, that the suicides, the defalcations, and the crimes of all kinds increased and decreased in England, and have for years, exactly as the price of bread went up and down. This was not new when Buckle wrote it down; it was known before and has been shown by almost every good economist since then.

There are many other facts that cranks often cite. Australia was settled by exported criminals, but they went to a country where land was cheap and opportunity great, and became industrious, hardworking men; the next generation became respected, high-toned citizens. Take a thousand of our low-class crooks and a thousand of our commonest prostitutes, and put them on an island where land is cheap and opportunity great, and in the third generation their descendants will be civilized, well-mannered citizens, with houses and barns, books and pictures, churches, policemen and jails.

The holdup man of today is the same man who lurked around the mansions of the rich in Rome fifteen hundred years ago. He was sent to jail, but he battered away at the civilization of Rome until the rich and poor went down in common ruin and despair. He is the same holdup man that Louis XV and Louis XVI were wont to club and kill in France a hundred years ago, but one day all the disinherited holdup men crept out from the alleys and caverns and marched on the king's palace and took possession of the state. Then these men made the rules of the game, and the nobles and princes went into the back alleys and took the place of the holdup men—that is, those who did not move to the catacombs.

Every increase in the price of coal makes "holdup men." Every time the price of meat goes up, some women go upon the streets, and some men get burglars' tools. Every extortionate penny taken by the gas trust makes holdup men. In their last analysis these despised criminals are men whom our social system has frozen out—who cannot live—who have no place upon the earth. Even the prostitute who plies her trade for the love of the trade, and the criminal who loves crime (if any such there be) have come to their present place through years of misfortune or hard environment, and would surely disappear under fairer conditions and with anything like a decent chance.

The rescue missions save many girls from prostitutes' lives, but they only make room for some other girl whom society is starving and freezing until she takes her place. So you may kill all the holdup men, but back of these are a long line of other men standing on the border, waiting for a chance to take their place.

Chicago is fairly well-to-do for jails and lockups. We have just built a fine, large addition to our county jail—the building has steam heat and electric lights and many boarders are found therein, especially in winter time, but has crime decreased as the jail increased in size? No one seems to expect this—it is taken for granted that this will grow as fast as any other institution of the town. If a pestilence of typhoid fever should break out in town the wise, humane doctors would advise us to build more hospitals—the cranks and visionists would tell us to boil the drinking water and stop the scourge.

Thank God, the practical man has always ruled the world—with clubs!

With a small handful of men controlling all the earth and every opportunity for life, and the great mass forced into hopeless want, it will take more jails, policemen and clubs to keep the disinherited at bay. There is one way, and only one, to treat the holdup men—feed them, or rather let them feed themselves.

But more grim and farcical still than the senseless talk about the holdup man is one other fact. Chicago has hundreds of Christian churches—we are a Christian people. It is nineteen hundred years since Christ's teachings were given to the world—we profess to be the disciples of that lowly man who believed in no jails or clubs—who taught infinite love and infinite mercy—who said if a man asked for your coat, give him also your cloak—and yet today we know nothing better than hatred, repression, brute force, jails, and clubs. We single out a considerable class of our fellow men to shoot on sight. Of course, the world will continue to treat its so-called criminals in this enlightened human way. Therefore would it not be well to rechristen our churches, and stop calling them after Christ?

Bertrand Russell

Roads to Freedom*

Competitiveness is by no means wholly an evil. When it takes the form of emulation in the service of the public, or in discovery or the production of works of art, it may become a very useful stimulus, urging men to profitable effort beyond what they would otherwise make. It is only harmful when it aims at the acquisition of goods which are limited in amount, so that what one man possesses he holds at the expense of another. When competitiveness takes this form it is necessarily attended by fear, and out of fear cruelty is almost inevitably developed. But a social system providing for a more just distribution of material goods might close to the instinct of competitiveness those channels in which it is harmful, and cause it to now instead in channels in which it would become a benefit to mankind. This is one great reason why the communal ownership of land and capital would be likely to have a beneficial effect upon human nature, for human nature, as it exists in adult men and women, is by no means a fixed datum, but a product of circumstances, education and opportunity operating upon a highly malleable native disposition.

What is true of competitiveness is equally true of love of power. Power, in the form in which it is now usually sought, is power of command, power of imposing one's will upon others by force, open or concealed. This form of power consists, in essence, in thwarting others, for it is only displayed when others are compelled to do what they do not wish to do. Such power, we hope, the social system which is to supersede capitalism will reduce to a minimum by the methods which we outlined in the preceding chapter. These methods can be applied in international no less than in national affairs. In international affairs the same formula of federalism will apply: self-

*Russell, B. *Roads to Freedom*, 3rd ed. London: Allen and Unwin Ltd., 1966, 124–28. © The Bertrand Russell Peace Foundation Ltd.

determination for every group in regard to matters which concern it much more vitally than they concern others, and government by a neutral authority embracing rival groups in all matters in which conflicting interests of groups come into play; but always with the fixed principle that the functions of government are to be reduced to the bare minimum compatible with justice and the prevention of private violence. In such a world the present harmful outlets for the love of power would be closed. But the power which consists in persuasion, in teaching, in leading men to a new wisdom or the realization of new possibilities of happiness—this kind of power, which may be wholly beneficial, would remain untouched, and many vigorous men, who in the actual world devote their energies to domination, would in such a world find their energies directed to the creation of new goods rather than the perpetuation of ancient evils.

Envy, the third of the psychological causes to which we attributed what is bad in the actual world, depends in most natures upon that kind of fundamental discontent which springs from a lack of free development, from thwarted instinct, and from the impossibility of realizing an imagined happiness. Envy cannot be cured by preaching; preaching, at the best, will only alter its manifestations and lead it to adopt more subtle forms of concealment. Except in those rare natures in which generosity dominates in spite of circumstances, the only cure for envy is freedom and the joy of life. From populations largely deprived of the simple instinctive pleasures of leisure and love, sunshine and green fields, generosity of outlook and kindliness of dispositions are hardly to be expected. In such populations these qualities are not likely to be found, even among the fortunate few, for these few are aware, however dimly, that they are profiting by an injustice, and that they can only continue to enjoy their good fortune by deliberately ignoring those with whom it is not shared. If generosity and kindliness are to be common, there must be more care than there is at present for the elementary wants of human nature, and more realization that the diffusion of happiness among all who are not the victims of some peculiar misfortune is both possible and imperative. A world full of happiness would not wish to plunge into war, and would not be filled with that grudging hostility which our cramped and narrow existence forces upon average human nature. A world full of happiness is not beyond human power to create; the obstacles imposed by inanimate nature are not insuperable. The real obstacles lie in the heart of man, and the cure for these is a firm hope, informed and fortified by thought.

Chapter VII

SCIENCE AND ART UNDER SOCIALISM

Socialism has been advocated by most of its champions chiefly as a means of increasing the welfare of the wage-earning classes, and more particularly their material welfare. It has seemed accordingly, to some men whose aims are not material, as if it has nothing to offer toward the general advancement of civilization in the way of art and thought. Some of its advocates, moreover—and among these Marx must be included—have written, no doubt not deliberately, as if with the Socialist revolution the millennium would have arrived, and there would be no need of further progress for the human race. I do not know whether our age is more restless than that which preceded it, or whether it has merely become more impregnated with the ideal of evolution, but, for whatever reason, we have grown incapable of believing in a state of static perfection, and we demand, of any social system, which is to have our approval, that it shall contain within itself a stimulus and opportunity for progress toward something still better. The doubts thus raised by Socialist writers make it necessary to inquire whether Socialism would in fact be hostile to art and science, and whether it would be likely to produce a stereotyped society in which progress would become difficult and slow.

It is not enough that men and women should be made comfortable in a material sense. Many members of the well-to-do classes at present, in spite of opportunity, contribute nothing of value to the life of the world, and do not even succeed in securing for themselves any personal happiness worthy to be so called. The multiplication of such individuals would be an achievement of the very minutest value; and if Socialism were merely to bestow upon all the kind of life and outlook which is now enjoyed by the more apathetic among the well-to-do, it would offer little that could inspire enthusiasm in any generous spirit.

"The true role of collective existence," says M. Naquet,[1] ". . . is to learn, to discover, to know. Eating, drinking, sleeping, living, in a word, is a mere accessory. In this respect, we are not distinguished from the brute. Knowledge is the goal. If I were condemned to choose between a humanity materially happy, glutted after the manner of a flock of sheep in a field, and a humanity existing in misery, but from which emanated, here and there, some eternal truth, it is on the latter that my choice would fall."

This statement puts the alternative in a very extreme form in which it is somewhat unreal. It may be said in reply that for those who have had the leisure and the opportunity to enjoy eternal truths it is easy to exalt their importance at the expense of sufferings which fall on others. This is true; but, if it is taken as disposing of the question, it leaves out of account the importance of thought for progress. Viewing the life of mankind as a whole, in the future as well as in the present, there can be no question that a society in which some men pursue knowledge while others endure great poverty offers more hope of ultimate good than a society in which all are sunk in slothful comfort. It is true that poverty is a great evil, but it is not true that material prosperity is in itself a great good. If it is to have any real value to society, it must be made a means to the advancement of those higher goods that belong to the life of the mind. But the life of the mind does not consist of thought and knowledge alone, nor can it be completely healthy unless it has some instinctive contact, however deeply buried, with the general life of the community. Divorced from the social instinct, thought, like art, tends to become finicky and precious. It is the position of such art and thought as is imbued with the instinctive sense of service to mankind that we wish to consider, for it is this alone that makes up the life of the mind in the sense in which, it is a vital part of the life of the community. Will the life of the mind in this sense be helped or hindered by Socialism? And will there still be a sufficient spur to progress to prevent a condition of Byzantine immobility?

In considering this question we are, in a certain sense, passing outside the atmosphere of democracy. The general good of the com-

---

1. Alfred Naquet, *L'Anarchie et le Collectivisme*, p. 114 (Paris, 1904).

munity is realized only in individuals, but it is realized, much more fully in some individuals than in others. Some men have a comprehensive and penetrating intellect, enabling them to appreciate and remember what has been thought and known by their predecessors, and to discover new regions in which they enjoy all the high delights of the mental explorer. Others have the power of creating beauty, giving bodily form to impalpable visions out of which joy comes to many. Such men are more fortunate than the mass, and also more important for the collective life. A larger share of the general sum of good is concentrated in them than in the ordinary man and woman; but also their contribution to the general good is greater. They stand out among men and cannot be wholly fitted into the framework of democratic equality. A social system which would render them unproductive would stand condemned, whatever other merits it might have.

The first thing to realize—though it is difficult in a commercial age—is that what is best in creative mental activity cannot be produced by any system of monetary rewards. Opportunity and the stimulus of an invigorating spiritual atmosphere are important, but, if they are presented, no financial inducements will be required, while if they are absent, material compensations will be of no avail. Recognition, even if it takes the form of money, can bring a certain pleasure in old age to the man of science who has battled all his life against academic prejudice, or to the artist who has endured years of ridicule for not painting in the manner of his predecessors; but it is not by the remote hope of such pleasures that their work has been inspired. All the most important work springs from an uncalculating impulse, and is best promoted, not by rewards after the event, but by circumstances which keep the impulse alive and afford scope for the activities which it inspires. In the creation of such circumstances our present system is much at fault. Will Socialism be better?

I do not think this question can be answered without specifying the kind of Socialism that is intended: some forms of Socialism would, I believe, be even more destructive in this respect than the present capitalist regime, while others would be immeasurably better. Three things which a social system can provide or withhold are helpful to mental creation: first, technical training; second, liberty to follow the creative impulse; third, at least the possibility of ultimate appreciation by some public, whether large or small. We may leave out of our discussion both individual genius and those intangible conditions which make some ages great and others sterile in art and science—not because these are unimportant, but because they are too little understood to be taken account of in economic or political organization. The three conditions we have mentioned seem to cover most of what can be seen to be useful or harmful from our present point of view, and it is therefore to them that we shall confine ourselves.

Jackson Toby

Is Punishment Necessary*

Of 11 contemporary textbooks in criminology written by sociologists, ten have one or more chapters devoted to the punishment of offenders.[1] All ten include a history of methods of punishment in Western society and, more specifically, a discussion of capital punishment. Seven discuss punishment in pre-literate societies. Seven include theoretical or philosophical discussions of the "justification" of punishment—usually in terms of "retribution," "deterrence," and "reformation." These theoretical analyses are at least as much indebted to law and philosophy as to sociology. Thus, in considering the basis for punishment, three textbooks refer both to Jeremy Bentham and to Emile Durkheim; three textbooks refer to Bentham but not to Durkheim; and one textbook refers to Durkheim but not Bentham. Several textbook writers express their opposition to punishment, especially to cruel punishment. This opposition is alleged to be based on an incompatibility of punishment with scientific considerations. The following quotation is a case in point:

> We still punish primarily for vengeance, or to deter, or in the
> interest of a "just" balance of accounts between "deliberate"

---

*This article is a revised version of a paper presented to the 1959 meeting of the Eastern Sociological Society. Jackson Toby, "Is Punishment Necessary?" *The Journal of Criminal Law, Criminology, and Police Science*, Vol. 55, No. 3 (Sept., 1964), 332–37. Reprinted by special permission of Northwestern University School of Law, *The Journal of Criminal Law and Criminology*.

1. Barnes & Teeters, New Horizons in Criminology (3rd ed. 1959); Caldwell, Criminology (1956); Cavan, Criminology (1955); Elliot, Crime in Modern Society (1952); Korn & McCorkle, Criminology and Penology (1959); Reckless, the Crime Problem (2nd ed. 1955); Sutherland & Cressey, Principles of Criminology (5th ed. 1955); Taft, Criminology (3rd ed. 1956); Tappan, Crime, Justice and Correction (1960); von Hentig, Crime: Causes and Conditions (1947); Wood & Waite, Crime and its Treatment (1941).

evildoers on the one hand and an injured and enraged society on the other. We do not yet generally punish or treat as scientific criminology would imply, namely, in order to change antisocial attitudes into social attitudes.[2]

Most of the textbook writers note with satisfaction that "the trend in modern countries has been toward humanizing punishment and toward the reduction of brutalities."[3] They point to the decreased use of capital punishment, the introduction of amenities into the modern prison by enlightened penology, and the increasing emphasis on nonpunitive and individualized methods of dealing with offenders, e.g., probation, parole, psychotherapy. In short, students reading these textbooks might infer that punishment is a vestigial carryover of a barbaric past and will disappear as humanitarianism and rationality spread. Let us examine this inference in terms of the motives underlying punishment and the necessities of social control.

The Urge to Punish

Many crimes have identifiable victims. In the case of crimes against the person, physical or psychic injuries have been visited upon the victim. In the case of crimes against property, someone's property has been stolen or destroyed. In pressing charges against the offender, the victim may express hostility against the person who injured him in a socially acceptable way. Those who identify with the victim—not only his friends and family but those who can imagine the same injury being done to them—may join with him in clamoring for the punishment of the offender. If, as has been argued, the norm of reciprocity is fundamental to human interaction, this hostility of the victim constituency toward offenders is an obstacle to the elimination of punishment from social life.[4] Of course, the size of the group constituted by victims and those who identify with victims may be

---

2. Taft, *op. cit. supra* note 1, at p. 359.

3. Reckless, *op. cit. supra* note 1, at p. 450.

4. Gouldner, The Norm of Reciprocity: A Preliminary Statement, 25 Am. Soc. Rev., p. 161 (1960).

small. Empirical study would probably show that it varies by offense. Thus, it is possible that nearly everyone identifies with the victim of a murderer but relatively few people with the victim of a blackmailer. The greater the size of the victim constituency, the greater the opposition to a nonpunitive reaction to the offender.

It would be interesting indeed to measure the size and the composition of the victim constituencies for various crimes. Take rape as an illustration. Since the victims of rape are females, we might hypothesize that women would express greater punitiveness toward rapists than men and that degrees of hostility would correspond to real or imaginary exposure to rape. Thus, pretty young girls might express more punitiveness toward rapists than homely women. Among males, we might predict that greater punitiveness would be expressed by those with more reason to identify with the victims. Thus, males having sisters or daughters in the late teens or early twenties might express more punitiveness toward rapists than males lacking vulnerable "hostages to fortune."

Such a study might throw considerable light on the wellsprings of punitive motivation, particularly if victimization reactions were distinguished from other reasons for punitiveness. One way to explore such motivation would be to ask the same respondents to express their punitive predispositions toward offenses which do not involve victims at all, e.g., gambling, or which involve victims of a quite different kind. Thus, rape might be balanced by an offense the victims of which are largely male. Survey research of this type is capable of ascertaining the opposition to milder penalties for various offenses. It would incidentally throw light on the comparatively gentle societal reaction to white-collar crime. Perhaps the explanation lies in the difficulty of identifying with the victims of patent infringement or watered hams.[5]

The Social Control Functions of Punishment

Conformists who identify with the victim are motivated to punish the offender out of some combination of rage and fear. Conformists who

---

5. In this connection, it is well to recall that there is less reluctance to steal from corporations than from humans. See A. W. Jones, Life, Liberty and Property (1941).

identify with the offender, albeit unconsciously, may wish to punish him for quite different reasons. Whatever the basis for the motivation to punish, the existence of punitive reactions to deviance is an obstacle to the abolition of punishment. However, it is by no means the sole obstacle. Even though a negligible segment of society felt punitive toward offenders, it might still not be feasible to eliminate punishment if the social control of deviance depended on it. Let us consider, therefore, the consequences of punishing offenders for (a) preventing crime, (b) sustaining the morale of conformists, and (c) rehabilitating offenders.

Punishment as a Means of Crime Prevention

Durkheim defined punishment as an act of vengeance. "What we avenge, what the criminal expiates, is the outrage to morality."[6] But why is vengeance necessary? Not because of the need to deter the bulk of the population from doing likewise. The socialization process prevents most deviant behavior. Those who have introjected the moral norms of their society cannot commit crimes because their self-concepts will not permit them to do so. Only the unsocialized (and therefore amoral) individual fits the model of classical criminology and is deterred from expressing deviant impulses by a nice calculation of pleasures and punishments.[7] Other things being equal, the anticipation of punishment would seem to have more deterrent value for inadequately socialized members of the group. It is difficult to investigate this proposition empirically because other motivationally relevant factors are usually varying simultaneously, e.g., the situational temptations confronting various individuals, their optimism about the chances of escaping detection, and the differential impact of the same punishment on individuals of different status.[8] Clearly, though, the

---

6. Durkheim, *The Division of Labor in Society*, p. 89 (1947).

7. Parsons, *The Structure of Social Action*, 402–03 (1949).

8. Toby, Social Disorganization and Stake in Conformity: Complementary Factors in the Predatory Behavior of Young Hoodlums, 48 J. Crim. L., C. & P.S., 12 (1957).

deterrent effect of anticipated punishments is a complex empirical problem, and Durkheim was not interested in it. Feeling as he did that *some* crime is normal in every society, he apparently decided that the crime prevention function of punishment is not crucial. He pointed out that minute gradation in punishment would not be necessary if punishment were simply a means of deterring the potential offender (crime prevention). "Robbers are as strongly inclined to rob as murderers are to murder; the resistance offered by the former is not less than that of the latter, and consequently, to control it, we would have recourse to the same means."[9] Durkheim was factually correct; the offenses punished most severely are not necessarily the ones which present the greatest problem of social defense. Thus, quantitatively speaking, murder is an unimportant cause of death; in the United States it claims only half as many lives annually as does suicide and only one-fifth the toll of automobile accidents. Furthermore, criminologists have been unable to demonstrate a relationship between the murder rate of a community and its use or lack of use of capital punishment.

Most contemporary sociologists would agree with Durkheim that the anticipation of punishment is not the first line of defense against crime. The socialization process keeps most people law abiding, not the police—if for no other reason than the police are not able to catch every offender. This does not mean, however, that the police could be disbanded. During World War II, the Nazis deported all of Denmark's police force, thus providing a natural experiment testing the deterrent efficacy of formal sanctions.[10] Crime increased greatly. Even though punishment is uncertain, especially under contemporary urban conditions, the possibility of punishment keeps some conformists law-abiding. The empirical question is: *How many* conformists would become deviants if they did not fear punishment?

---

9. *Op. cit, supra* note 6, at p. 88.

10. *Trolle, Syv Maneder Uten Politi* (*Seven Months Without Police*) (Copenhagen, 1945), quoted in Christie, Scandinavian Criminology, 31 Sociological Inquiry, p. 101 (1961).

Punishment as a Means of Sustaining the Morale of Conformists

Durkheim considered punishment indispensable as a means of containing the demoralizing consequences of the crimes that could not be prevented. Punishment was not for Durkheim mere vindictiveness. Without punishment Durkheim anticipated the demoralization of "upright people" in the face of defiance of the collective conscience. He believed that unpunished deviance tends to demoralize the conformist and therefore he talked about punishment as a means of repairing "the wounds made upon collective sentiments."[11] Durkheim was not entirely clear; he expressed his ideas in a metaphorical language. Nonetheless, we can identify the hypothesis that the punishment of offenders promotes the solidarity of conformists.

Durkheim anticipated the psychoanalytic thinking as the following reformulation of his argument shows: One who resists the temptation to do what the group prohibits, to drive his car at 80 miles per hour, to beat up an enemy, to take what he wants without paying for it, would like to feel that these self-imposed abnegations have some meaning. When he sees others defy rules without untoward consequences, he needs some reassurance that his sacrifices were made in a good cause. If "the good die young and the wicked flourish as the green bay tree," the moral scruples which enable conformists to restrain their own deviant inclinations lack social validation. The social significance of punishing offenders is that deviance is thereby defined as unsuccessful in the eyes of conformists, thus making the inhibition or repression of their own deviant impulses seem worthwhile. Righteous indignation is collectively sanctioned reaction formation. The law-abiding person who unconsciously resents restraining his desire to steal and murder has an opportunity, by identifying with the police and the courts, to affect the precarious balance within his own personality between internal controls and the temptation to deviate. A bizarre example of this psychological mechanism is the man who seeks out homosexuals and beats them up mercilessly. Such pathological hostility toward homosexuals is due to the sadist's anxiety

---

11. Durkheim, *op. cit. supra* note 6, at p. 108.

over his own sex-role identification. By "punishing" the homosexual, he denies the latent homosexuality in his own psyche. No doubt, some of the persons involved in the administration of punishment are sadistically motivated. But Durkheim hypothesized that the psychic equilibrium of the *ordinary* member of the group may be threatened by violation of norms; Durkheim was not concerned about psychopathological punitiveness.

Whatever the practical difficulties, Durkheim's hypothesis is, in principle, testable. It should be possible to estimate the demoralizing impact of nonconformity on conformists. Clearly, though, this is no simple matter. The extent of demoralization resulting from the failure to punish may vary with type of crime. The unpunished traffic violator may cause more demoralization than the unpunished exhibitionist—depending on whether or not outwardly confirming members of society are more tempted to exceed the speed limit than to expose themselves. The extent of demoralization may also vary with position in the social structure occupied by the conformist. Thus, Ranulf suggested that the middle class was especially vulnerable:

[T]he disinterested tendency to inflict punishment is a distinctive characteristic of the lower middle class, that is, of a social class living under conditions which force its members to an extraordinarily high degree of self-restraint and subject them to much frustration of natural desires. If a psychological interpretation is to be put on this correlation of facts, it can hardly be to any other effect than that moral indignation is a kind of resentment caused by the repression of instincts.[12]

Once the facts on the rate and the incidence of moral indignation are known, it will become possible to determine whether something must be done to the offender in order to prevent the demoralization of conformists. Suppose that research revealed that a very large proportion of conformists react with moral indignation to most violations of the criminal laws. Does this imply that punishment is a functional necessity? Durkheim apparently thought so, but he might have been

---

12. Ranulf, *Moral Indignation and Middle-Class Psychology*, p. 198 (Copenhagen, 1938).

less dogmatic in his approach to punishment had he specified the functional problem more clearly: making the nonconformist unattractive as a role model. If the norm violation can be defined as unenviable through some other process than by inflicting suffering upon him, punishment is no required by the exigencies of social control.

Punishment can be discussed on three distinct levels: (a) in terms of the motivations of the societal agents administering it, (b) in terms of the definition of the situation on the part of the person being punished, and (c) in terms of its impact on conformists. At this point I am chiefly concerned with the third level, the impact on conformists. Note that punishment of offenders sustains the morale of conformists only under certain conditions. The first has already been discussed, namely that conformists unconsciously wish to violate the rules themselves. The second is that conformists implicitly assume that the nonconformity is a result of *deliberate defiance* of society's norms. For some conformists, this second condition is not met. Under the guidance of psychiatric thinking, some conformists assume that norm violation is the result of illness rather than wickedness.[13] For such conformists, punishment of the offender does not contribute to their morale. Since they assume that the nonconformity is an involuntary symptom of a disordered personality, the offender is automatically unenviable because illness is (by definition) undesirable. Of course, it is an empirical question as to the relative proportions of the conforming members of society who make the "wicked" or the "sick" assumption about the motivation of the offender, but this can be discovered by investigation.

In Western industrial societies, there is an increasing tendency to call contemporary methods of dealing with offenders "treatment" rather than "punishment." Perhaps this means that increasing proportions of the population are willing to accept the "sick" theory of nonconformity. Note, however, that the emphasis on "treatment" may be more a matter of symbolism than of substance. Although the definition of the situation as treatment rather than punishment tends to be humanizing—both to the offender and to the persons who must deal with him—there are still kind guards and cruel nurses.

---

13. Talcott Parsons has repeatedly suggested the analogy between illness and criminality. See also Aubert & Messinger, *The Criminal and the Sick*, 1 Inquiry, p. 137 (1958); and Wootton, *Social Science and Social Pathology*, p. 203, Annals 67 (1959).

Furthermore, it would be an error to suppose that punishment is invariably experienced as painful by the criminal whereas treatment is always experienced as pleasant by the psychopathological offender. Some gang delinquents consider a reformatory sentence an opportunity to renew old acquaintances and to learn new delinquent skills; they resist fiercely the degrading suggestion that they need the services of the "nut doctor." Some mental patients are terrified by shock treatment and embarrassed by group therapy.

What then is the significance of the increasing emphasis on "treatment"? Why call an institution for the criminally insane a "hospital" although it bears a closer resemblance to a prison than to a hospital for the physically ill? In my opinion, the increased emphasis on treatment in penological thinking and practice reflects the existence of a large group of conformists who are undecided as between the "wicked" and the "sick" theories of nonconformity. When they observe that the offender is placed in "treatment," their provisional diagnosis of illness is confirmed and therefore they do not feel that he has "gotten away with it." Note that "treatment" has the capacity to make the offender unenviable to conformists whether or not it is effective in rehabilitation him and whether or not he experiences it as pleasant. Those old-fashioned conformists who are not persuaded by official diagnoses of illness will not be satisfied by "treatment"; they will prefer to see an attempt made to visit physical suffering or mental anguish on the offender. For them, punishment is necessary to prevent demoralization.

Punishment as a Means of Reforming the Offender

Rehabilitation of offenders swells the number of conformists and therefore is regarded both by humanitarians and by scientifically minded penologists as more constructive than punishment. Most of the arguments against imprisonment and other forms of punishment in the correctional literature boil down to the assertion that punishment is incompatible with rehabilitation. The high rate of recidivism for prisons and reformatories is cited as evidence of the irrationality of punishment.[14] What sense is there in subjecting offenders to the frustrations of incarceration? If rehabilitative programs are designed

---

14. Vold, *Does the Prison Reform?* p. 293, Annals 42 (1954).

to help the offender cope with frustrations in his life situation, which presumably were responsible for his nonconformity, imprisoning him hardly seems a good way to begin. To generalize the argument, the status degradation inherent in punishment makes it more difficult to induce the offender to play a legitimate role instead of a nonconforming one. Whatever the offender's original motivations for nonconformity, punishment adds to them by neutralizing this fear of losing the respect of the community; he has already lost it.

Plausible though this argument is, empirical research has not yet verified it. The superior rehabilitative efficacy of "enlightened" prisons is a humanitarian assumption, but brutal correctional systems have, so far as is known, comparable recidivism rates to "enlightened" systems. True, the recidivism rate of offenders who are fined or placed on probation is less than the recidivism rate of offenders who are incarcerated, but this comparison is not merely one of varying degrees of punishment. Presumably, more severe punishment is meted out to criminals who are more deeply committed to a deviant way of life. Until it is demonstrated that the recidivism rates of strictly comparable populations of deviants differ depending on the degree of punitiveness with which they are treated, the empirical incompatibility of punishment and rehabilitation will remain an open question.

Even on theoretical grounds, however, the incompatibility of punishment and rehabilitation can be questioned once it is recognized that one may precede the other. Perhaps, as Lloyd McCorkle and Richard Korn think, some types of deviants become willing to change only if the bankruptcy of their way of live is conclusively demonstrated to them.[15] On this assumption, punishment may be a necessary preliminary to a rehabilitative program in much the same way that shock treatment makes certain types of psychotics accessible to psychotherapy.

It seems to me that the compatibility of punishment and rehabilitation could be clarified (although not settled) if it were considered from the point of view of the *meaning* of punishment to the offender. Those offenders who regard punishment as a deserved deprivation resulting from their own misbehavior are qualitatively different from

---

15. McCorkle & Korn, *Resocialization Within Walls*, p. 293, Annals 88 (1954).

offenders who regard punishment as a misfortune bearing no relationship to morality. Thus, a child who is spanked by his father and the member of a bopping gang who is jailed for carrying concealed weapons are both "punished." But one accepts the deprivation as legitimate, and the other bows before superior force. I would hypothesize that punishment has rehabilitative significance only for the former. If this is so, correctional officials must convince the prisoner that his punishment is just before they can motivate him to change. This is no simple task. It is difficult for several reasons:

1. It is obvious to convicted offenders, if not to correctional officials, that *some* so-called "criminals" are being punished disproportionately for trifling offenses whereas some predatory business men and politicians enjoy prosperity and freedom. To deny that injustices occur confirms the cynical in their belief that "legitimate" people are not only as predatory as criminals but hypocritical to boot. When correctional officials act as though there were no intermediate position between asserting that perfect justice characterizes our society and that it is a jungle, they make it more difficult to persuade persons undergoing punishment that the best approximation of justice is available that imperfect human beings can manage.[16]

2. Of course, the more cases of injustice known to offenders, the harder it is to argue that the contemporary approximation of justice is the best that can be managed. It is difficult to persuade Negro inmates that their incarceration has moral significance if their life experience has demonstrated to them that the police and the courts are less scrupulous of *their* rights than of the rights of white persons. It is difficult to persuade an indigent inmate that his incarceration has moral significance if his poverty resulted in inadequate legal representation.[17]

---

16. See interesting discussions of human fallibility in the works of Reinhold Neibuhr, e.g., *The Children of Light and the Children of Darkness* (1950).

17. Trebach, The Indigent Defendant, 11 Rutgers L. Rev., p. 625 (1957).

3. Finally, the major form of punishment for serious offenders (imprisonment) tends to generate a contraculture which denies that justice has anything to do with legal penalties.[18] That is to say, it is too costly to confine large numbers of people in isolation from one another, yet congregate confinement results in the mutual reinforcement of self-justifications. Even those who enter prison feeling contrite are influenced by the self-righteous inmate climate; this may be part of the reason recidivism rates rise with each successive commitment.[19]

In view of the foregoing considerations, I hypothesize that punishment—as it is now practiced in Western societies—is usually an obstacle to rehabilitation. Some exceptions to this generalization should be noted. A few small treatment institutions have not only prevented the development of a self-righteous contraculture but have managed to establish an inmate climate supportive of changed values.[20] In such institutions punishment has rehabilitative significance for the same reason it has educational significance in the normal family: it is legitimate.

To sum up: The social control functions of punishment include crime prevention, sustaining the morale of conformists, and the rehabilitation of offenders. All of the empirical evidence is not in, but it is quite possible that punishment contributes to some of these and interferes with others. Suppose, for example, that punishment is necessary for crime prevention and to maintain the morale of conformists but is generally an obstacle to the rehabilitation of offenders. Since the proportion of deviants is small in any viable system as compared with the proportion of conformists, the failure to rehabilitate them will not jeopardize the social order. Therefore, under these assump-

---

18. For a discussion of the concept of contraculture, see Yinger, Contraculture and Subculture, 25 Am. Soc. Rev., p. 625 (1960).

19. Sellin, *Recidivism and Maturation*, 4 Nat'l. Probation and Parole A. J., p. 241 (1958).

20. McCorkle, Elias & Bixby, *The Highfields Story* (1958), and Empey & Rabow, Experiment in Delinquency Rehabilitation, 26 Am. Soc. Rev., p. 679 (1961).

tions, sociological counsel would favor the continued employment of punishment.

Conclusion

A member of a social system who violates its cherished rules threatens the stability of that system. Conformists who identify with the victim are motivated to punish the criminal in order to feel safe. Conformists who unconsciously identify with the criminal fear their own ambivalence. If norm violation is defined by conformists as willful, visiting upon the offender some injury or degradation will make him unenviable. If his behavior is defined by conformists as a symptom of pathology they are delighted not to share, putting him into treatment validates their diagnosis of undesirable illness. Whether he is "punished" or "treated," however, the disruptive consequence of his deviance is contained. Thus, from the viewpoint of social control, the alternative outcomes of the punishment or treatment processes, rehabilitation or recidivism, are less important than the deviant's neutralization as a possible role model. Whether the punishment is or is not necessary rests ultimately on empirical questions: (1) the extent to which identification with the victim occurs, (2) the extent to which nonconformity is prevented by the anticipation of punishment, (3) what the consequences are for the morale of conformists of punishing the deviant or treating his imputed pathology, and (4) the compatibility between punishment and rehabilitation.

Michael Hakeem

A Critique of the Psychiatric Approach to Crime and Correction*

I. The Influence of Psychiatrists

The opinion of psychiatrists can have substantial or decisive influence in the determination of whether an offender is fit to stand trial, whether he is responsible for a crime, and whether he is to be executed or given a life sentence. It can play an important part in the decision whether to place him on probation or to send him to a correctional institution. It can, in many instances, affect the duration of the offender's penal servitude, the choice of the particular institution to which he is sent, his subsequent transfer to other institutions, and his activities within the institution. It can sway the estimate of his suitability for parole or pardon.

In jurisdictions having special sex offender laws, the psychiatrist's opinion is usually determinative of whether such an offender is to be dealt with under the customary procedures or under the provisions of these laws. In the latter event, he is released only on the psychiatrist's recommendation, and he can be confined for life. Some psychiatrists have insisted that such procedures should be extended to all offenders. They propose that the law should enable the lifelong incarceration or supervision of any offender, on the recommendation of a psychiatrist, even if his crime were only a minor one. As long ago as 1928, a committee of the American Psychiatric Association, under the chairmanship of Dr. Karl A. Menninger, recommended the "permanent legal detention of the incurably inadequate, incom-

---

*Hakeem, M. "A Critique of the Psychiatric Approach to Crime and Correction," *Law and Contemporary Problems* (1958), 650–81.

1. Menninger, *Medicolegal Proposals of the American Psychiatric Association*, 19 J. XEIM. L. & Criminology 367, p. 376 (1928).

petent, and anti-social offenders irrespective of the particular offense committed. . . ."[1] Not one of the terms used in this grim scheme was defined. It was not even explained how an "antisocial" offender differs from one who is not antisocial. Not a scintilla of evidence was presented that psychiatrists, or anyone else, could distinguish between incurable and curable offenders. Another suggestion on this order has been voiced more recently by a psychiatrist and a law professor in the following statement, which should occasion alarm in any schoolboy who has fully appreciated the implications of his lessons in eighth-grade civics: ". . . [I]f analysis of the convict's personality indicates that he cannot safely be released, he may have to spend the rest of his life under legal supervision of some kind, even though the only crime he has actually committed was a minor one."[2]

The juvenile delinquent is also much at the mercy of psychiatrists. Adjudication as a delinquent, commitment to and release from various institutions, separation from home and family, placement in a foster home, the granting of probation, and a host of other decisions can depend largely on what a psychiatrist advises.

Psychiatrists have been engaged for a long time in a relentless and extensive campaign to extend the scope and power of their influence in the administration of justice, in the disposition of offenders, and in the policies and practices of correctional institutions and agencies. This campaign has now reached reckless and irresponsible proportions, and there has been resort to questionable tactics. Unseemly as it may appear, the profession of psychiatry has even gone so far as to bestow prizes, honors, and unabashed flattery upon judges who have handed down decisions that it views as favorable to its cause. And, in the service of this campaign, psychiatrists have produced a prodigious literature, much of which is propagandistic in nature. It is characterized by incautious and immodest effusions, misrepresentation, extraordinary contradictions, flagrant illogicalities, grossly exaggerated claims, biased selection of data, serious errors of fact and interpretation, ignorance of the distinction between scientific questions and value judgments, lack of sophistication in research methodology, tautological trivialities presented in the guise of technical profundities,

---

2. Manfred S. Guttmacher & Henry Weihofen, *Psychiatry and the Law*, 444–45 (1952).

and language, subject matter, and procedures not bearing the slightest resemblance to anything medical.[3]

Some psychiatrists have insisted that they are still greatly hampered in their forensic work by certain traditional concepts, procedures, and laws governing the prosecution and disposition of offenders, and they have furiously assailed these restraining formalities. They hold that many of the basic tenets of American jurisprudence, which are designed to protect the rights of offenders, and many of the limitations on administrative discretion in the handling of offenders are "stupid" and should yield to make way for psychiatric knowledge. They argue that the law frustrates their desire to deal with offenders in ways they deem best. Menninger puts the general idea as follows: "The scientific attitude as shown in psychiatry must sooner or later totally displace existing legal methods."[4] And he hurls this further challenge: ". . . [M]ust the lawyers still continue solemnly to apply mediaeval stupidities in the name of 'established precedent,' 'public policy,' and other mouthy archaisms?"[5] It is these trends, developments, and pressures that recently prompted a lawyer to suggest: ". . . [I]f the criminal

---

3. A number of psychiatrists have leveled all these criticisms, and others besides, against their colleagues. Wertham, to cite only one, has reviewed some of the literature on forensic psychiatry, and he finds it dangerous, erroneous, misleading, deceptive, highhanded, uninformed, unreliable, confused, unscientific, tautological, biased, and grossly defective in other ways. See the following for references to some of Wertham's reviews in which these criticisms are found: Wertham, *Psychoauthoritarianism and the Law*, 22 U. Chi. L. Rev., p. 336 n. I (1955). For the most brilliant and scholarly appraisal of the literature on forensic psychiatry and of the issues in the question of criminal responsibility, see Jerome Hall, General Principles of Criminal Law CC. 14 (1947); *Psychiatry and Criminal Responsibility*, 65 Yale L. J., p. 761 (1956).

4. Karl A. Menninger, *The Human Mind*, pp. 448–149 (3rd ed. 1945). Since making this statement, Menninger apparently has had some second thoughts. He now confesses that it is "an open professional secret" that psychiatrists do not know how to treat offenders. He also concedes that they cannot predict the possible dangerousness of such offenders. And he points out that psychiatrists are not even available for such work or for even doing research on the problem. See Menninger, *Book Review*, 38 Iowa L. Rev. 697, pp. 701–02 (1953).

5. Karl A. Menninger, *The Human Mind*, p. 449 (3rd ed. 1945).

were in any position to elect between the psychiatrist and the jurist as the future guardian of his liberties, he may be well advised . . . to re-elect the jurist."[6]

During the past several years, psychiatrists have been emboldened to increasing arrogance because some judges and lawyers have finally shown greater disposition to yield to their blandishments and entreaties. No less a person than Supreme Court Justice William O. Douglas recently gave psychiatrists warm encouragement in their efforts to shape the administration of justice. Speaking at the graduation exercises of the William Alanson White Institute of Psychiatry, Psychoanalysis, and Psychology, he reassured them that "recent developments in the law should hearten psychiatrists that their pleas do not always fall on deaf ears."[7] Justice Douglas presented no evidence whatsoever that he had assayed psychiatric knowledge to determine whether its scientific creditability merited such a friendly gesture. In fact, practically all his psychiatric citations were drawn from the propagandistic literature referred to above.

The most important step taken in recent years bearing on the relationship between psychiatry and the law is, of course, the decision in the *Durham* case, handed down in 1954 by the United States Court of Appeals for the District of Columbia.[8] This decision was written by Judge David L. Bazelon and concurred in by Judges Henry W. Edgerton and George T. Washington. It overthrew the existing test of criminal responsibility and adopted a new and broader test similar in type to that for which psychiatrists have long been agitating. There can be no doubt that the basic motivation of this decision was to "recognize" psychiatry. This is precisely what Fortas, who was the court-appointed attorney representing Durham before the Court of Appeals and who advocated the adoption of the new test, sees as its chief significance.[9] Very revealing, from the point of view of the

---

6. De Grazia, *The Distinction of Being Mad*, 22 U. Chi. L. Rev. pp. 339, 352 (1955).

7. William O. Douglass, *Law and Psychiatry*, p, 6 (1956).

8. Durham v. United States, 214 F. 2d 862 (D.C. Cir. 1954).

9. Fortas, *Implications of Durham's Case*; 113 Am. J. Psychiatry, pp. 577, 581 (1957).

motivations operating in some of the champions of psychiatry, is this further observation by Fortas, still referring to the *Durham* decision: "Its importance is that it is a charter, a bill of rights, for psychiatry. . . ."[10] An examination of the *Durham* decision itself leaves no doubt that it was designed to overcome psychiatric objections to the prevailing legal views on criminal responsibility.

Anyone familiar with the psychiatric journals and the literature on forensic psychiatry does not need to have documented the wild elation with which the *Durham* decision was acclaimed. Judge Bazelon himself could not have been idolized more had he discovered the cause and cure of schizophrenia, which, incidentally, is conceded to be the most serious mental disease and one about which, some psychiatrists are frank to admit, knowledge is practically nil.[11] Fulsome praise was certainly heaped upon Judge Bazelon. Forensic psychiatrists said that they were astonished and captivated by the depth and breadth of his medical knowledge and his comprehensive familiarity with medical and psychiatric literature. The following statement, made by a leading forensic psychiatrist, typifies the commentaries of this sort: "To this author, who has had very limited experience in reading legal opinions, it is indeed encouraging to find in this opinion such a wide study of the technical medical literature and such a thorough understanding of it."[12]

Now, an actual examination, item by item, of the citations in the *Durham* decision will show the complete absence of any reference to "technical medical literature" and will show that practically all the psychiatric citations are to the propagandistic literature whose defects have been already noted. Most of this literature contains nothing medical and practically nothing psychiatric. It contains mainly pleas and proposals, based in no small measure on the value judgments of psychiatrists, for changes in the laws, in criminal trial procedures,

---

10. *Id.* at p. 579.

11. Hoch, *The Etiology and Epidemiology of Schizophrenia*, 47 Am. J. Pub. Health, pp. 1071, 1074 (1957); Health, *Psychiatry* in Ann. Rev. Med., p. 230 (1954).

12. Guttmacher, *The Psychiatrist as an Expert Witness*, 22 U. Chi. L. Rev., pp. 325, 330 (1955).

and in correctional policies. The *Durham* decision is not based on a competent and objective appraisal of the truth of psychiatric claims and of the pretensions of psychiatry to scientific knowledge. As a matter of fact, it is a highly biased decision, in as much as it completely disregards the large number of researches and extensive theoretical discussions that have yielded adverse appraisals of psychiatry. But no matter, for the jubilation of psychiatrists was so lasting and unsubduable that more than three years after the *Durham* decision, the American Psychiatric Association officially honored Judge Bazelon. He was presented a "Certificate of Commendation" for what he had done for psychiatry, though it was not put quite that way, of course.[13]

An excellent example of how important and even momentous decisions are sometimes made on the basis of crass naïveté is provided by the deliberations of the American Law Institute on the question of criminal responsibility in connection with its preparation of a Model Penal Code. One would have supposed that before formulating its recommendations regarding the complex and crucial question of psychiatric testimony and the procedures for handling the plea of insanity, the American Law Institute would have tried to come to an independent assessment of the nature, methodological soundness, theoretical coherence, logicality, predictive efficacy, objectivity, reliability, and validity of psychiatric research, contentions, and premises. One would have supposed that, at the very least, the Institute would have wanted to look into the question of the reliability and validity of psychiatric judgments. The course actually followed by the Institute, however, could not have deviated more from this procedure. It sought the advice of three psychiatrists. Two of these have been in the forefront of the assault on the criminal law and have been leaders in the campaign to promote forensic psychiatry. The American Law Institute depended for its recommendations mainly on a brief memorandum prepared by one of these advisers.[14] This memorandum is misleading, grossly exaggerates the scientific status of psychiatric knowledge, does not present the available contradictory or nonconfirmatory data on

---

13. *Judge Bazelon Honored,* 114 Am. J. Psychiatry, p. 565 (1957).

14. Guttmacher, *Principal Difficulties with the Present Criteria of Responsibility and Possible Alternatives,* Model Penal Code app. B (Tent. Draft No. 4, 1955).

various points asserted in it, and fails to make reference to even one of those psychiatrists who have denied that their profession has knowledge that would be of much help in the administration of justice.[15] In addition to this memorandum, there was a "chummy" exchange of correspondence between the psychiatrist who prepared the memorandum and the Chief Reporter of the Institute's Model Penal Code project, by means of which the latter sought to learn about psychiatry and to secure clarification on various issues, particularly, one gets the distinct impression, to determine just what it is the psychiatrists want from lawyers.[16]

In view of the increasing importance of psychiatry in the fields of criminology, law, and corrections, the recent tendency of the law to embrace psychiatry to a greater extent than ever before, the unfortunate practice of some judges and lawyers to embark on this new course without thinking it necessary to inform themselves about psychiatry, and the fact that the glibness of some psychiatrists is in danger of being exceeded by the gullibility of some members of the legal profession, it becomes particularly imperative to scrutinize psychiatric knowledge and contentions. The present paper will review only a limited portion of these—namely, the psychiatric view of delinquency and crime as disease, the reliability of psychiatric diagnosis, and the two mental diseases most often discussed in connection with delinquent and criminal behavior.

II. Delinquency and Crime as Disease

A journal bearing the redoubtable title, *Postgraduate Medicine*, published in one of its volumes such formidable reports as "Atresia of the Esophagus With or Without Tracheo-Esophageal Fistula" and "Herniated Cervical Intervertebral Disk Simulating Angina Pectoris."

---

15. To cite only the latest of these, Szasz says: "I . . . want to suggest, at the very least, that the current popular belief that psychiatry has much to contribute to jurisprudence may be ill-founded and misleading." Szasz, *Psychiatric Expert Testimony—Its Covert Meaning and Social Function*, 20 Psychiatry, pp. 313, 314 (1957).

16. Model Penal Code app. C (Tent. Draft No. 4, 1955).

Among these and other equally weighty disquisitions, in the same volume, appeared an article with this starkly simple tide: "Medical Responsibility for Juvenile Delinquency."[17] This was by a psychiatrist. It contained the usual rebuke of the law for not implementing psychiatric preachments about delinquency, along with an admonition to all who deal with this problem to accept medical concepts regarding it. In the meantime, the medical journals have been carrying an increasing number of articles on delinquency and crime.

In the series of articles on crime that appeared in *Life* several months ago, there was displayed a dramatic photograph of a criminal whose brain waves were being examined by doctors in a clinic. The caption explained that this was done to determine whether the offender needed "surgery" or "psychiatry."[18]

Recently the New York Temporary State Commission on Youth and Delinquency issued a report summarizing a large number of hearings it had held throughout the state to get a public airing of views on all aspects of delinquency. Hundreds of people were heard. The report concluded that the psychiatric orientation emerged as the most popular approach to the understanding, prevention, and treatment of delinquency.[19]

In the course of a symposium on crime, Edwin J. Lukas, who is a lawyer and former executive of a crime prevention agency, stated that if the matter were looked at from the proper perspective, "the

---

17. Blackman, *Medical Responsibility for Juvenile Delinquency*, 10 Postgrad. Med., p. 499 (1951).

18. Life, Oct. 7, 1957, P. 160. Neither the caption nor the story related the experiment in which ten EEG records were submitted to five well-known electroencephalographers for independent interpretation. On only four out of the ten was there agreement on the presence or absence of pathology; on only three out of the ten was there agreement on localization of the pathology; and on only one out of the ten was there agreement on the two factors combined. See Blum, *A Note on the Reliability of Electroencephalographic Judgments*, 4 Neurology 143 (954). No psychiatrist protested this omission, despite the fact that the American Psychiatric Association has been much concerned with securing accurate reporting of news about psychiatry to the public.

19. NY Temporary State Comm'n on Youth and Delinquency, *Youth and Delinquency*, p. 78 (1956).

parallel between crime and physical illness becomes almost exact."[20]

These are all merely incidents exemplifying the operation and impact of an orientation vigorously promoted by psychiatrists: Delinquency and crime are medical problems. Some put the proposition in so many words, simply and tersely, as when one psychiatrist claims that "juvenile delinquency is a medical problem. . . ."[21] Some state it more elaborately: ". . . [T]he whole problem of criminality or criminology is in the field of human behavior psychopathology, the understanding of which requires medical and psychiatric training."[22] Sometimes it is phrased colorfully: "The modern surgical operating amphitheater developed out of dirty public barber-shops. The physicians took surgery away from the barbers a century ago; now they are taking criminology away from jailers and politicians."[23] Sometimes it takes the form of an even more explicit battle cry: "Criminology today, like demonology of yesterday, is a battlefield for the rightful possession of which the psychiatrist is still fighting."[24]

Certain premises underlie the view that delinquency and crime are medical problems. These premises are, of course, that these phenomena constitute disease and that offenders are "sick people." This notion, too, is put in a rich variety of ways. One psychiatrist calls delinquents "seriously sick children."[25] Another says that knowledge of psychopathology is the "only means of preventing crime."[26] Often delinquency is listed along with "neurosis, psychosis, and psychosomatic illness" to underscore the idea that it is just another mental illness

---

20. Lukas, A *Criminologist Looks at Criminal Guilt* in Edmond N. Cahn (ed.), *Criminal Guilt*, p. 145 (Social Meaning of Legal Concepts No. 2, 1950).

21. Eugene Davidoff and Elinor S. Noetzel, *The Child Guidance Approach to Juvenile Delinquency*, p. 150 (1951).

22. Seliger, *Criminal Hygiene*, Fed. Prob. Jan.–March 1946, pp. 16, 19.

23. Karl A. Menninger, *The Human Mind*, p. 451 (3rd ed. 1945).

24. Gregory Zilboorg and George W. Henry, A *History of Medical Psychology*, p. 419 (1941).

25. Eveoleen N. Rexford, in Douglas A. Thom Clinic for Children, Inc., Ann. Rep., p. 17 (1956)

26. Ruth S. Eissler, *Scapegoats of Society*, in K. R. Eissler (ed.) Searchlights on Delinquency, p. 304 (1949).

to be encompassed within the same frame of reference as any other.[27] Another example of this practice is provided by a committee of the House of Representatives. After a "health inquiry" at which psychiatrists testified, the committee issued a report wherein mental illness subsumes delinquency.[28] Sometimes, the point is set forth calmly, as in Glueck's sedate but unconvincing argument that some of the knotty legal issues in criminal responsibility would be eased if crime were viewed as a sickness and not as a moral transgression.[29] More often, it is proclaimed ardently, as in the following statement by Karpman, promulgating the policy of a journal established and edited by him: "The Archives will fight vigorously for the recognition of criminal psychiatry. It will fight for the recognition of the criminal as a very sick person, much sicker than either psychosis [sic] or neurosis [sic]. . . ."[30]

But greatest effectiveness in drumming the ideology that delinquency and crime are disease and offenders are sick is probably not achieved when it is explicitly propounded, whether vociferously or quietly. More persuasive is its exposition unaccompanied by any theoretical elaboration in defense of it, as though there could be no question in the world about the truth of the matter. And resort to the ubiquitous medical analogy clinches this subtle form of presentation. To illustrate, one psychiatrist says:[31]

> Using medical terms delinquency can be described as a very widespread illness, affecting mainly young people and causing gross symptoms [in certain proportions of this population]. . . . [M]ild cases usually are treated at home. . . . The illness,

---

27. George J. Mohr and Marian A. Despres, The Stormy Decade: Adolescence, p. 210 (1958).

28. House Committee on Interstate and Foreign Commerce, *Health Inquiry*, H. R. Rep. No. 1338, 83d Cong. 2d. Sess., p. 123 (1954).

29. Glueck, *Changing Concepts in Forensic Psychiatry*, 45 J. Crim. L., C. & P.S., pp. 123, 127 (1954).

30. Karpman, *Criminal Psychodynamics: A Platform*, Arch. Crim. Psychodyn. 3, p. 95 (1955).

31. Balint, *On Punishing Offenders* in George B. Wilbur and Warner Muensterberger (eds.), Psychoanalysis and Culture, pp. 254, 266 (1951).

on the whole, is benign. Unfortunately [after recovery, in certain proportions of cases] it is followed by relapses. The illness then takes a prolonged course but even then in most cases heals off.

Another says that "theft, like rheumatic fever, is a disease of childhood and adolescence, and, as in rheumatic fever, attacks in later life are frequently in the nature of recurrences."[32] A third puts it as follows: "When a patient goes to the hospital with a physical illness, he receives medication and therapy directed specifically to his ailment . . . We send our children to correctional institutions to be treated for an illness. . . ."[33]

So powerful is the conviction of some psychiatrists that crime stems from mental disease that they have held the commission of crime in itself constitutes conclusive evidence of the presence of mental disease. Again, this aspect of the ideology usually draws on the medical analogy. The thesis runs as follows: Just as fever is a symptom of physical disease, so crime is a symptom of mental disease. The following excerpt provides an example of just such a formulation: ". . . [J]ust as symptoms of physical illness are danger signals that call for remedial measures, a criminal act, in a high percentage of cases, is a signal of psychological distress and a natural appeal for remedy."[34] A like conclusion has been reached by many psychiatrists, another one of whom writes: "It is becoming increasingly apparent that chronic incorrigible criminal behavior is symptomatic of mental disease. . . ."[35] About thirty years ago, Menninger hopefully prophesied that "the time will come when stealing or murder will be thought of as a symptom, indicating the presence of a disease, a personality disease, if you will. . . ."[36] Twenty-five years later, another

---

32. Bowlby, *Forty-Four Juvenile Thieves: Their Characters and Home-Life*, 25 Int'l J. Psycho-Anal., p. 19 (1944).

33. Tarrasch, *Delinquency Is Normal Behavior*, 29 Focus, pp. 97, 101 (1950).

34. Ralph S. Banay, *We Call Them Criminals*, p. 6 (1957).

35. Louis Linn, *A Handbook of Hospital Psychiatry*, p. 331 (1955).

36. Menninger, *Medicolegal Proposals of the American Psychiatric Association*, 19 J. Crim. L. & Criminology, pp. 367, 373 (1928).

psychiatrist expressed the identical sentiment: "One may hope that a day will come when the very fact of having committed a crime will be regarded as evidence of a mental disease. . . ."[37] As early as 1930, the American Medical Association, acting on the recommendations of representatives of medicine, psychiatry, and law, officially went on record in support of the view that a diagnosis of mental disease is permissible "even when the criminal has shown no evidence of mental disease other than his criminal behavior."[38]

In the meantime, some psychiatrists have shown disdain for the legal presumption of sanity, which one dismisses, redundantly, as that "hoary old legal dogma."[39] It has been proposed by more than one psychiatrist that the law should presume not sanity, but insanity. One of these has commented that the legal doctrine of the "reasonable man" does not square with the findings of modern psychiatry. He intimates that the law should replace the presumption of sanity with the presumption of insanity, so confident is he that the offender is more likely to be insane than sane.[40]

However it is put, the irrepressible and irresponsible campaign—for that is what it is—to implant the view that crime and delinquency are disease and offenders are sick people has had great impact. The public, as well as important officials, is more and more coming to actually believe the physicians who tell it that the criminal is a sick person in need of medical treatment. Fortas, who has already been cited, thinks that the *Durham* decision and other decisions which show a greater acceptance of psychiatric doctrines by the courts indicate that the judges involved "suspect that mental disorders may figure in criminal activities with vastly more frequency than is currently recognized by our legal procedures. . . ."[41] If Fortas is correct, then these judges are showing remarkable resoluteness, even if their conclusion

---

37. Benjamin Karpman, *The Sexual Offender and His Offenses*, p. 218 (1954).

38. *Psychiatry in Relation to Crime*, 95 A.M.A.J., p. 346 (1930).

39. Overholser, *The Place of Psychiatry in the Criminal Law*, 16. B.U.L. Rev., pp. 322, 329 (1936).

40. Poindexter, *Mental Illness in a State Penitentiary*, 45 J. Crim. L., C. & P.S., pp. 599, 562 (1955).

41. Fortas, *supra* note 9, at pp. 577–78.

is nothing but a surmise. All the more so because they have presented no scientific evidence to substantiate even a "suspicion," and particularly so in view of the fact that, though these judges may have at least tentatively made up their minds on the matter, psychiatrists are in a state of complete disaccord about it.

For, though it is true that the psychiatric propagandists have gained widespread support for their ideology and have succeeded in getting judges, lawyers, correctional administrators, and others to implement it, the psychiatric profession does not present a united front on this issue. As is true in regard to practically every fundamental postulate in psychiatry, so in regard to this problem, there is vast disagreement, confusion, and contradiction. This can be documented by a few citations, remembering that these constitute an insignificant proportion of those that could be assembled.

One psychiatrist thinks that all offenders show traits differentiating them from nonoffenders,[42] but another says that the great majority do not vary much from the average person.[43] Another psychiatrist advises that "no one would maintain that all criminals are mentally ill or abnormal,"[44] thereby showing unfamiliarity with the writings of Karpman and scores of others who maintain exactly that.[45] Menninger gives the assurance that psychiatrists "do not consider that many offenders in our prisons are mentally sick . . ."[46] thus overlooking a large number of psychiatrists who have contended just the opposite.[47] Schilder maintains that "the majority of criminals are normal . . .";[48]

---

42. Henderson, *Psychopathic Constitution and Criminal Behaviour* in L. Radzinowicz and J. W. C. Turner (eds.), *Mental Abnormality and Crime*, p. 106 (English Studies in Criminal Science No. 2, 1944).

43. Schmideberg, *The Analytic Treatment of Major Criminals: Therapeutic Results and Technical Problems* in Eissler, *op.cit. supra* note 26 at p. 174.

44. David Stafford-Clark, Psychiatry To-Day, p. 221 (1952).

45. Benjamin Karpman, *The Sexual Offender and his Offences*, p. 562 (1954).

46. William C. Menninger, *Psychiatry: Its Evolution and Present Status*, p. 123 (1948).

47. Haugen, Coen, and Dickel, *Possibilities of Psychotherapy in Prisoners*, 31 Focus, p. 83 (1952).

48. Paul Schilder (Arr. by Lauretta Bender), *Psychoanalysis, Man, and Society*, p. 238 (1951).

however, Abrahamsen counters that "the 'normal' offender is a myth. . . ."[49] East has concluded that the "mentally abnormal criminal is the exception and not the rule . . . ,"[50] a view challenged by another psychiatrist who claims that "one does not expect anti-social conduct from normally constituted individuals. . . ."[51] Neustatter decries what he calls the "fallacy" of regarding all criminality as psychological illness,[52] but many psychiatrists share the opinion that "every criminal has a defective personality. . . ."[53] Regarding juvenile delinquents, one psychiatrist is satisfied that "the largest percentage" of serious delinquents is normal,[54] but this is offset by another who is satisfied that all juveniles who are in repeated trouble are "mentally ill."[55] English and Pearson, the well-known child psychiatrists, write that the psychiatrist "does not believe that all delinquents are sick people . . . ,"[56] but they fail to cite Bender, a well-known child psychiatrist, who insists that she does not understand what is meant by "normal delinquency."[57] Regarding murder, Glueck finds that no murderer is normal when he commits his crime,[58] only to be contradicted by another practitioner who finds that there are normal murderers.[59]

---

49. David Abrahamsen, *Who Are the Guilty?*, p. 125 (1952).

50. Norwood East, *Society and the Criminal*, p. 228 (1951).

51. Peskin, *The Modern Approach to Legal Responsibility, the Psychopath and the M'Naghten Rules*, I Forensic Med., pp. 189, 191 (1954).

52. Neustatter, *Psychiatry and Crime*, 170 Practitioner, p. 391 (1953).

53. Banay, *Crime and Aftermath: Results of a Research and on the Individual Offender*, in Nat'l Probation and Parole Ass'n, 1948 Yearbook, p, 35 (1949).

54. Curran, *Specialized Techniques in the Treatment of Juvenile Delinquency*, 157 A.M.A.J., p. 108 (1955).

55. *Juvenile Delinquency (Boston, Mass.) Hearings before the Subcommittee to Investigate Juvenile Delinquency of the Senate Committee on the Judiciary*, 83rd Cong. 2nd Sess. p. 293 (1954).

56. O. Spurgeon English and Gerald H. J. Pearson, *Emotional Problems of Living*, p. 290 (rev. ed. 1955).

57. Bender, cited by Karpman, *Psychodynamics of Child Delinquency: Further Contributions*, 25 Am. J. Orthopsychiatry, pp. 238, 274 (1955).

58. Glueck, *supra* note 29, at pp. 130–31.

59. Royal Comm'n on Capital Punishment, Minutes of Evidence, p. 359 (1949).

One would have supposed that this muddle in itself would have been sufficient to make of psychiatry a profession so utterly humble as practically never to be heard from. At the very least, one would have supposed that psychiatrists would have been too chagrined to prescribe a course of action for society to follow in tackling its crime problem. Quite to the contrary, however, psychiatrists and those convinced by them have moved apace to put their views into effect on many fronts. Changes in the laws and certain court decisions have already been mentioned. All over the country, medically oriented clinics, diagnostic centers, and residential treatment facilities are being established for delinquents and "emotionally disturbed children."[60] An administrator of the New York Department of Mental Hygiene has reported that large numbers of delinquent children are now being certified directly to institutions for the mentally ill in his state. He said that "the line between criminality and mental illness or mental defect is being redrawn."[61] The top administrator of the same department has commented that the psychiatrists have been "singularly successful with the courts," and, increasingly, offenders are being sent to "civil state hospitals instead of hospitals for the criminally insane."[62]

A well-known psychiatrist has revealed that in New York City, Puerto Rican adolescents who become "emotionally disturbed" because of their difficult circumstances have been incorrectly diagnosed as mentally ill and have been wrongly committed to mental hospitals. He has insisted that, despite the fact that "judicial notice has been taken of such falsely committed cases," there has been no improvement in the situation.[63] Recently, a child guidance clinic

---

60. The term "emotionally disturbed" is never operationally defined in the proposals to establish institutions to house children who are said to belong to that category.

61. Hunt, *Mental Hygiene and Correction: An Operational Blueprint* in Proceedings of the Frederick A. Moran Memorial Institute on Delinquency and Crime, p. 21 (1953).

62. Hoch, *The Changing Role of State Mental Hospitals* in 1956 Annual Conference of the Milbank Memorial Fund, Programs for Community and Mental Health, p. 149 (1957).

63. Frederic Wertham, *The Circle of Guilt*, p. 134 (1956).

made a special study of 500 cases referred to it. In only twenty-one percent of these were the referrals regarded as unequivocally justified.[64] An examination of the reported behavior and problems on account of which these children were referred for diagnosis of their mental condition will show that the overwhelming majority were trivialities, universally found in children, and designated "normal" by many psychiatrists, even when manifested in marked degree.

Recently, a psychiatrist issued a very strong warning and protest that there has been an enormous increase in the diagnosis of schizophrenia among children. She pointed out that schizophrenia "is not a disease of childhood."[65] She gave illustrations of delinquents engaged in the customary types of gang activities who were wrongly given diagnoses of the more malignant mental diseases. She commented: "A child who commits a crime is now likely to be diagnosed schizophrenic and sent to a mental hospital."[66] She further pointed out that normal children were being committed to mental hospitals. Finally, she reported on a clinical reevaluation of sixty children "in trouble for many different reasons" who were diagnosed as schizophrenic. It was found that the diagnosis was wrong in practically all cases.[67]

How can psychiatrists tell whether or not a delinquent or a criminal is mentally sick? Psychiatrists, like all other medical practitioners, presumably find this out by a process universally used in medicine— diagnosis. It would be sheer folly to disregard the clamorous insistence of psychiatrists that delinquency and crime are disease and that the offender is mentally sick, if for no reason other than the high authority from which it emanates. On the other hand, surely anyone would agree that it would be equal folly—it would be irresponsible— to encourage it, to advance it, to support it, to act on it, to incorporate it in court decisions and laws without a careful examination of the evidence. Therefore, the first step should be an appraisal of

---

64. Forrest N. Anderson and Helen C. Dean, *Some Aspects of Child Guidance Clinic Intake Policy and Practices*, p. 9 (1956).

65. Mosse, *The Misuse of the Diagnosis Childhood Schizophrenia*, 114 Am. J. Psychiatry, p. 791 (1958).

66. *Ibid.*

67. *Ibid.*

the scientific status of the process of diagnosis by which psychiatrists determine the mental condition of offenders.

III. The Reliability of Psychiatric Diagnosis

Generally, the specific technical diagnosis of an offender's mental condition is not in issue, as such, and does not concern the court or the correctional administrator. The court is interested in the consequences and implications of the defendant's mental condition, in so far as the law gives special effect to these in the judgment and disposition to be made, regardless of the specific diagnostic category. And the correctional administrator is concerned with decisions that can be altered in accordance with the psychiatric counsel he gets regarding the attributes and results thought to be associated with the various types of mental disorders afflicting his charges.

The psychiatrist himself, however, presumably thinks, as do all physicians, in terms of the specific diagnosis. Diagnosis is the process whereby the psychiatrist determines which one or more of the large variety of mental diseases and disorders a subject has. On the basis of the diagnosis, the psychiatrist comes to conclusions regarding the course, symptomatology, prognosis, malignancy, treatment, and other aspects of the subject's ailment that can help determine judicial and correctional decisions. All the decisions that can be affected by psychiatric judgment will ultimately rest on diagnosis, which is the basic instrumentality of medical practice.

A striking example of the importance of diagnosis and of how a specific diagnostic category can have crucial bearing on the disposition of offenders is provided by a recent occurrence. It has been reported that in a certain jurisdiction, the staff of a mental hospital that has been customarily testifying that psychopathic or sociopathic personality is not a mental disease formally announced that henceforth it would testify that this condition does constitute a mental disease.[68] Other psychiatrists, in and outside of hospitals, in this and in other jurisdictions, do not share the view and would not testify that

---

68. *In re* Rosenfield, 157 F. Supp. 18 (D.D.C. 1957).

the condition in question is a mental disease. Thus, the fate—execution, or acquittal on the grounds of insanity—of a murderer, say, can depend in the final analysis on a specific diagnosis and on the value judgment of psychiatrists regarding that diagnosis.

Take, as another example, the question of the malignancy of the various mental diseases. The malignancy ascribed to an offender's mental disease can certainly have a bearing on decisions made about him. It can, in the case of a sex offender, for instance, figure in the determination as to when to release him, if ever. Again, it depends upon the philosophy of psychiatrists whether a mental disease is benign or malignant, and this philosophy differs markedly among different psychiatrists. Take the psychoneuroses, for example. One practitioner describes them as a "relatively benign group of personality disturbances . . . ,"[69] while another reports that "some authorities regard the psychoneuroses as the most serious disease threat of modern civilization."[70]

If so much can depend on psychiatric diagnosis, the question can be raised: How reliable is it?[71] Surely the courts, the correctional administrators, and the welfare officials must be assuming that psychiatric diagnoses have adequate reliability. It is inconceivable that they would embrace psychiatry unless they were convinced that the judgments, diagnoses, and conclusions of its practitioners are reliable.

The literature of the forensic psychiatrists often sets forth implicit and explicit persuasions that psychiatric diagnoses are as reliable as those of any other branch of medicine. Zilboorg, for example, writes: "The clinical judgment of the psychiatrist provided he be properly

---

69. Arthur P. Noyes, *Modern Clinical Psychiatry*, p. 445 (4th ed. 1953).

70. Edward A. Strecker, *Fundamentals of Psychiatry*, p. 38 (5th ed. 1952).

71. Many persons do not understand the meaning of the concept of reliability in scientific methodology. Reliability means agreement by the experts on their theories, observations, and conclusions—agreement not by fiat, but by scientific demonstration of the correctness of any particular proposition. To the extent that a discipline is scientifically established, a question regarding any particular aspect of its subject matter will yield essentially the same answer from all experts. If the same question brings forth widely divergent responses, then it should be clear that the point involved has not been scientifically established.

qualified—must be accepted by the courts to the same extent as the clinical judgment of a surgeon or an internist."[72] More than one psychiatrist has expressed resentment at the proclivity of some observers to raise questions about psychiatric diagnoses and judgments. One of these has called for what looks like unquestioning acceptance of these judgments:[73]

> If society sees fit to appoint neutral experts to determine the sanity of the defendant, then society should demonstrate its faith in these experts and abide fully by their findings. This [apparently referring to noncompliance with psychiatric findings] is tantamount to calling in a physician for a serious medical illness and then not following his advice.

Assurance has been given that "psychiatry has its nosology just as do the other branches of medicine. Psychiatric clinical entities are as discrete as the cardiac or the pulmonary disorders."[74] Statements like the following are often encountered: "Modern psychiatric diagnoses . . . in acute and chronic mental disorders, are as accurate as those in tuberculosis, communicable disease, or other illness."[75]

Time and again, in the face of overwhelming evidence to the contrary, psychiatrists have dismissed as baseless the charge that they

---

72. Zilboorg, *A Step Toward Enlightened Justice*, 22 U. Chi. L. Rev., pp. 331, 335 (1955).

73. *Mental Disorder and Criminal Responsibility: A Symposium*, 3 J. Soc. Therapy 66, pp. 87–88 (1957).

In referring to "neutral experts," this psychiatrist apparently has in mind those jurisdictions and situations in which the expert does not appear as a partisan for the defense or for the prosecution.

74. Guttmacher & Weihofen, *op. cit. supra* note 2, at p. 27. Guttmacher has elsewhere taken a different position: "Psychiatric nosology is, at best, an unsatisfactory business. . . ." See Manfred S. Guttmacher, *Sex Offenses*, p. 102 (1951).

75. A. E. Bennett, Eugene Hargrove, and Bernice Engle, *The Practice of Psychiatry in General Hospitals*, p. 91 (1956).

are frequently in disagreement about their diagnoses, observations, and theories. They insist that they are in agreement on most issues. Overholser makes a daring misrepresentation on this point, typical of many others that could be cited:[76]

> There is general agreement among psychiatrists upon the essential facts and the significance of words and actions, although there are minor differences in theory. The differences and disagreements are much exaggerated by the critics, and constitute one of the alleged reasons for the reluctance of the legal profession to accept any more readily than they do psychiatric concepts and teachings.

If one turns from these writings of the forensic psychiatrists to the writings of leading psychiatrists who have no special interest in forensic work; who address themselves to the problem of diagnosis as a scientific issue to be solved by research; who do not spend an inordinate amount of time haranguing and harassing the legal profession; who are not busily engaged in fighting for changes in the laws which would bring them into greater conformity with their own value position; who do not seize upon every writing and speaking engagement as an opportunity to seduce judges and others about the present status of psychiatric knowledge; who do not pout that the court psychiatrist has as much right as the prosecutor and defense counsel to be heard as to the disposition of defendants;[77] and who, in other ways, are not clamoring to enhance their power to control and decide the destiny of offenders, one gets an entirely different picture of the state of psychiatric diagnosis. As a matter of fact, one arrives at the unmistakable conclusion that psychiatric diagnosis is grossly unreliable, is beset by numerous unsolved complexities, and is, in fact, in a state of chaos.

Take, for example, the report of the 1951 annual meeting of the American Psychopathological Associations.[78] This meeting was devoted to the topic of psychiatric diagnosis and was only incidentally

---

76. Winfred Overholser, *The Psychiatrist and the Law*, p. 23 (1953).

77. Guttmacher, *Adult Court Psychiatric Clinics*, in University of Colorado Conference on Crime, Crimes of Violence, p. 51 (1950).

concerned with forensic matters. By culling certain statements from the report of this meeting, it is possible to show that some psychiatrists' appraisals of the reliability of diagnosis and of the competence of psychiatric research is in striking contrast to the samples of exaggerated claims set forth above. Disregarding the specific authorship of the statements, it was submitted at this meeting that the concept of psychosis is not "definable"[79] and is so fallacious as to have "facilitated loose and unscientific thinking" in psychiatry;[80] that the term schizophrenia means many different things to different people;[81] that "it is hardly necessary to stress the extent to which there is confusion in regard to the diagnosis at the present time"[82] that because there is no agreement on psychodynamics among the different schools of thought at present, "we encounter a complete confusion" in diagnosis;[83] that "the personality and biases of the psychiatrist may also influence his choice of a diagnostic label";[84] that because there is "looseness and ambiguity" in the terms used by psychiatrists, progress in diagnosis and treatment is retarded;[85] that "the psychiatric literature is replete with dissensions and controversies" even on "elementary problems";[86] that diagnosis in child psychiatry "has literally been a 'Tower of Babel' ";[87] that in the military situation, psychiatrists may deliberately make invalid diagnoses in order to comply with administrative exigencies rather than medical dictates;[88] that the extent of agreement among

---

78. Paul H. Hoch and Joseph Zubin (eds.), Current Problems in Psychiatric Diagnosis (1953).

79. *Id.* at p. 25.

80. *Id.* at p. 31.

81. *Id.* at p. 180.

82. *Id.* at p. 41.

83. *Id.* at p. 50.

84. *Id.* at p. 108–09.

85. *Id.* at p. 267.

86. *Id.* at p. 231.

87. *Id.* at p. 220.

88. *Id.* at p. 55.

psychiatrists on specific diagnoses was found through research to be "neither satisfactory nor desirable";[89] that an examination of researches reported in the issues of eleven psychiatric and related journals over a two-year period showed grave defects and serious lack of sophistication in experimental methodology;[90] that psychiatric research is hampered by "an almost total lack of training in terms of scientific disciplines."[91]

It must not be supposed that such strictures are confined to this one report. Far from it; for, although one could never get a true picture of the situation by reading only the highly deceptive literature of the forensic psychiatrists, the unreliability of psychiatric diagnosis is a widely documented fact. Ironically enough, on the very eve of the *Durham* decision, no less a source than the *American Journal of Psychiatry* editorially took to task those psychiatrists who were attacking the existing rules and laws of criminal responsibility and urging their abrogation. The editorial took the position that these psychiatrists had not presented convincing evidence that psychiatry had made the advances claimed by them and on the basis of which they were demanding changes in the laws.[92] The editorial further reminded these doughty fighters that medical experts do not agree even "as to the diagnosis of textbook types of insanity."[93]

Even more recently, a psychiatrist cautioned: "Diagnostic judgments are currently so invalid and unreliable that little weight should be attached to them."[94] And more recently still, Mosse, who has already been cited as expressing alarm at the increasing tendency for psychiatrists readily and wrongly to diagnose delinquents as schizophrenic, stated: "No valid classification of mental diseases in children has yet been- worked out. . . ."[95] Further, she explained: "One of the

---

89. *Id.* at p. 60.

90. *Id.* at p. 20.

91. *Id.* at p. 20.

92. *Criminal Irresponsibility*, 110 Am. J. Psychiatry. pp. 627, 628 (1954).

93. *Ibid.*

94. Thorne, *Psychiatric Responsibilities in the Administration of Criminal Justice*, 2 Arch. Crim. Psychodyn., pp. 226, 236 (1957).

95. Mosse, *supra* note 65, at p. 791.

most important gaps in our knowledge is that the limits of normal for children of different ages have not yet been established,"[96] a view shared by other cautious clinicians. It might be interesting to select the final example from a context as far removed as possible from any immediate forensic concern. A psychiatrist who has done research on the relationship between peptic ulcer and mental disorder has observed that one of the difficulties in such research is the "unreliability of psychiatric diagnosis." He also commented that even the same clinicians are inconsistent with themselves.[97]

Psychiatrists have sought to convince lawyers, correctional administrators, and others not only that their diagnoses are as reliable as those of other branches of medicine, but also that they, like other medical practitioners, have reliable and valid tools, devices, tests, and procedures to augment and confirm their clinical diagnoses and impressions. For example, one psychiatrist has said: "Just as the medical person uses x-ray and laboratory tests in making a physical diagnosis, so are there similar routines to determine the personality structure."[98] A leading forensic psychiatrist has maintained that psychiatrists have "certain physical and psychological tests and well recognized constellations of symptoms, to help guide us in our judgments."[99]

As in regard to the contention about reliability, so in regard to this contention, these writers rarely spoil their positive declarations by referring to quite a different kind of observation that has been made by psychiatrists and other experts about their diagnostic instruments. A psychiatrist in the College of Physicians and Surgeons of Columbia University, for example, has considered the matter of diagnosis and diagnostic tools. He comes to a conclusion that is diametrically opposed to the ones cited. He holds that in contrast to the

---

96. *Id.* at p. 793.

97. Gosling, *Peptic Ulcer and Mental Disorder—II,* 2 J. Psychom. Res., p. 285 (1958).

98. Marie Nyswander, *The Drug Addict as a Patient,* p. 58 (1956).

99. Guttmacher, *Criminal Responsibility in Certain Homicide Cases Involving Family Members* in Paul H. Hoch and Joseph Zubin (eds.) *Psychiatry and the Law,* p. 74 (1955).

physical diseases, the existence of which can be determined on the basis of "a recognizable syndrome" and by the use of certain devices and tests, "in emotional and mental illnesses this is almost never the case; even in the so-called major mental and emotional illnesses, such guides to detection and diagnosis are almost entirely lacking."[100] To cite another example, the New York State Commissioner of Mental Hygiene recently said:[101]

> While other fields of medicine often can augment or even verify clinical diagnoses by other methods—by tests that are independent of the clinical appraisal of the patient this is generally not true in psychiatry. Although I am fully aware of the claims that it can be done, I maintain that it cannot.

Most of the time, there is particular praise for the Rorschach test. One gets the impression that it is regarded by psychiatrists as the most powerful tool at their disposal and one which goes a long way in putting psychiatry on a par with any other medical specialty. Strecker, for example, appearing for the defense in a murder trial in which the life of the defendant was at stake, testified:[102]

> I regard the Rorschach test as very scientific, well-tried, in common use in all good mental hospitals, relied on by the majority of psychiatrists I know, and in my opinion the interpretation has been in agreement with my own opinion and diagnosis in more than 95% of the cases.

---

100. Ginsburg, *The Neuroses*, 286 Annals, p. 55 (1953).

101. Hoch, *The Etiology and Epidemiology of Schizophrenia*, 47 Am. J. Pub. Health, p. 1071 (1957).

102. Richard Gehman, *A Murder in Paradise*, p. 137 (rev. ed. 1956). Dr. Strecker did not reveal whether his own diagnoses were checked for reliability in any way other than by their agreement with the Rorschach test. If diagnoses yielded by the Rorschach test are unreliable and Dr. Strecker's diagnoses are in agreement with them, then Dr. Strecker's diagnoses have to be unreliable. As will be noted shortly, the Rorschach test has been found by some experts to be grossly unreliable.

Wertham has stated, "The Rorschach Test is a valid scientific method."[103] Banay has extolled the Rorschach test.[104] Guttmacher has claimed that the Rorschach test can be "amazingly revealing."[105] Elsewhere, he and a lawyer, writing jointly, say that "definite diagnostic criteria have been established" for it. They are astounded by "how much a skillful Rorschach technician can tell about a patient that he has never seen, merely from analyzing his test responses."[106]

All these misleading effusions fail even to refer to another side of the story. The other side of the story is provided by the experimental researches, theoretical analyses, and methodological observations that have demonstrated the unreliability, invalidity, subjectivity, theoretical weaknesses, illogicalities, and questionable premises of the Rorschach test. It is these considerations that led a psychologist, who is an expert on the construction and validation of personality tests, to conclude that the results secured through the Rorschach test are not superior to the results that would be secured by writing the different diagnoses on the faces of a die and then casting the die to determine the personality of a subject.[107] It is a review of some of these researches and judgments, which need not be repeated here, that also led the present writer to conclude elsewhere: ". . . [T]he results of the Rorschach test should not be used as a basis for reaching decisions about people and they should not be allowed to enter in any serious way into deliberations looking toward the disposition of cases."[108] Testimony regarding a defendant's personality and mental condition which is based in whole or in part on the Rorschach test should certainly not be allowed in court.

---

103. Fredric Wertham, *Seduction of the Innocent*, p. 56 (1954).

104. Banay, *Applications of Clinical Psychology to Crime and Delinquency* in I. Daniel Brower and Lawrence E. Abt (eds.) *Progress in Clinical Psychology*, pp. 459, 463 (1952).

105. Manfred S. Guttmacher, *Sex Offenses*, p. 31 (1951).

106. Guttmacher and Weihofen, *op. cit. supra* note 2, at p. 22.

107. H. J. Eysenck, *Sense and Nonsense in Psychology*, p. 221 (1957).

108. Hakeem, *A Critique of the Psychiatric Approach to the Prevention of Juvenile Delinquency*, 5 Soc. Prob., pp. 194, 196–97 (1958).

The gross unreliability of psychiatric diagnosis—which, in the courts, takes the form of the so-called battle of the experts—has been one of the most painfully embarrassing ordeals for forensic psychiatrists. Indeed, it is one of the leading concerns of the psychiatric profession as a whole that it is in connection with forensic work that the unreliability of diagnosis comes in for the greatest amount of public scrutiny, keeps psychiatry in disrepute with those who have sufficient scientific sophistication to understand its implications, and provides merriment for people. Psychiatrists have tried by every possible means to escape this morass. They have denied the importance of diagnosis. They have even disparaged diagnosis. They have said that a diagnosis is a triviality that cannot encompass the actual object of psychiatric study—"the whole man." But the study of the whole man is philosophy, not medicine. In any event, psychiatrists of this persuasion have been confronted by powerful and even angry reminders from colleagues that if they claim to be physicians, then they must diagnose. They are told that proper treatment depends on it, prognosis depends on it, scientific progress depends on it. The *American Journal of Psychiatry* has issued the following editorial warning on the matter: ". . . [I]n psychiatry, as well as in all medical disciplines, accurate diagnosis is the keystone of appropriate treatment and competent prognosis."[109] A textbook has taken this firm stand: "The contemptuous attitude toward diagnosis, which is so prominent a feature of many contemporary schools [of psychiatry], runs counter to the entire spirit of medicine."[110] One psychiatrist put it very bluntly:[111]

> With really unpardonable ignorance, it is stated by some psychiatrists that the diagnosis of a psychiatric entity is unimportant and that the so-called psychodynamics are the essential object of study. This would be partially excusable,

---

109. *The New Nomenclature*, 109 Am. J. Psychiatry, p. 548 (1953).

110. W. Mayer-Gross, Eliot Slater, and Martin Roth, *Clinical Psychiatry*, p. 6 (1954).

111. Pasamanick, *Patterns of Research in Mental Hygiene*, 26 Psychiatric Q., pp. 577, 578 (1952).

only if they could give the dynamics in more than hypothetical formulation. Such statements display a lamentable lack of insight into the essentials of scientific procedure and do not speak happily for the future of research in the field.

Some psychiatrists have taken refuge from diagnosis by giving a description of personality instead. But Ackerman, as do others, objects to this and points out that what goes into such a description is "too largely determined by subjective emphases in a particular examiner's mind."[112] This, of course, is only another way of saying that descriptions of personality can be as unreliable as diagnostic categorization.

In desperation, forensic psychiatrists have turned to the legal profession for help. They have proposed and vigorously advocated various legal changes the effect of which would be to conceal diagnostic unreliability or to make the diagnosis less accessible to attack. Probably the greatest favor that judges, lawyers, and legislators can do for the profession of psychiatry is to implement its plans to eliminate the "battle of the experts" and to render the psychiatrist's diagnosis unchallengeable. The relentless attempts of the psychiatrists to bring these changes about and the increasing tendency of the legal profession to yield to their entreaties need not be detailed here, since these issues are the subject of a forthcoming paper by the writer. For now, it need only be noted that psychiatrists have insisted that somehow, sometime, the lawyers must find ways to extricate the profession of psychiatry from a very embarrassing state of affairs.

It might be argued that the unreliability of psychiatric diagnoses and judgments is flagrantly evident in the psychiatric literature and cannot be concealed. But the availability of evidence has made no difference to those judges and lawyers who are making momentous decisions and recommendations hospitable to psychiatry.

Furthermore, some judges are not disturbed by the disagreements of physicians. One of these is Judge John Biggs, Jr. He is Chief Judge of the Third Judicial Circuit of the United States. Judge Biggs has been very friendly to psychiatry. His opinions reflect the kind of

---

112. Ackerman, *Psychiatric Disorders in Children—Diagnosis and Etiology in Our Time* in Paul H. Hoch and Joseph Zubin (eds.), *Current Problems in Psychiatric Diagnosis*, p. 221 (1953).

views whose adoption psychiatrists have been urging. These opinions have been widely cited and hailed by psychiatrists. The American Psychiatric Association bestowed the Isaac Ray Award upon Judge Biggs. This is given annually to a member either of the legal or of the psychiatric profession who has contributed notably to the improvement, of the relations between psychiatry and the law. As part of the award, Judge Biggs received one thousand dollars. As another part, he had the privilege of giving a series of lectures on forensic psychiatry at a university of his choice. These lectures have been published in a book.[113] An examination of the notes in this book reveals that it contains almost no citations of psychiatric literature. In the rare instances when such citations do occur in the book, they refer to the propagandistic literature the nature of which has been discussed more than once in this paper. Judge Biggs has said, "Let me make it clear that I am not objecting to even skillful physicians differing in their diagnoses." He further commented, "Heaven knows they differ less than lawyers and judges,"[114] thus overlooking the fundamental differences between medicine and law, the serious implications of the disagreements of physicians, the distinction between scientific questions and value judgments, the fact that the social judgments of psychiatrists are being mistaken by themselves and others for medical judgments, and the methodological and philosophical reasons why it is perfectly legitimate for judges and lawyers to disagree but not permissible for psychiatrists to do so.

It has been seen that psychiatric diagnoses are grossly unreliable. But psychiatrists do diagnose. In the courts, to repeat a point, life or death can depend upon their diagnoses. It is important, therefore, to look into the nature of those diseases and other mental infirmities which psychiatrists diagnose in offenders. Obviously, it will not be possible to discuss all such diseases. Therefore, the two most important ones have been selected for consideration: psychopathic personality and psychoneurosis.

---

113. John Biggs, Jr., *The Guilty Mind* (1955).

114. Biggs, *The Lawyer Looks at the Doctor*, 28 Del. State Med. J., pp. 122, 125 (1956).

IV. Psychopathic Personality

Probably the mental condition most often discussed in connection with delinquency and crime is "psychopathic personality" or "psychopathy."[115] One investigator has listed 202 terms used as equivalents of these,[116] but even this list does not exhaust the number. In 1952, the American Psychiatric Association adopted the new term, "sociopathic personality," for this condition.[117] Since then, the old term continues to be the more widely used one. The old term and its derivative forms will be used here for convenience.

Without exception, on every point regarding psychopathic personality, psychiatrists present varying or contradictory views. There is danger that such a statement will be mistaken for hyperbolic emphasis. Therefore, it should be explicitly made clear that the statement is meant to be taken literally. Not all points can be illustrated here, but a few will be presented, remembering that whenever one authority is

---

115. The words "psychopathic" and "psychopathy" used in the present context should not be confused with one of their dictionary definitions — namely, a generic term meaning mental disorder. "Psychopathic personality" or "psychopathy" is used by psychiatrists to designate a type of mental disease.

Recently, Dr. Albert H. Arenowitz, a juvenile court psychiatrist, speaking before the Ross Club of the University of Wisconsin, misinformed a large audience that the concept of psychopathic personality was no longer used, having been discarded by psychiatrists many years ago. In the few months before and after this disavowal of the concept, a large number of books and many dozens of articles devoted in whole or in part to psychopathic personality were published. The concept has been and is now one of the most important in psychiatry and the most important in forensic psychiatry. Under its newer name, "sociopathic personality," this is the diagnosis a psychiatrist applied to Charles Starkweather in the course of his widely publicized trial in Lincoln, Nebraska, in May 1958, for one of the eleven murders he admittedly committed.

116. Cason, *The Psychopath and the Psychopathic*, 4 J. Crim. Psychopath., p. 522 (1943).

117. The change in terminology has not resulted in any other changes in the concept. Discussions on "sociopathic personality" are identical to discussions on "psychopathic personality." Often, authors using the new term explicitly state that they mean by sociopathic personality what was meant by the old term psychopathic personality.

cited, dozens of others taking a like position on the point in question could be cited.

Psychiatrists are in disagreement on whether they are in agreement or in disagreement on the subject. One investigator questioned seventy-five authorities, sixty-four of whom were psychiatrists, on how much agreement exists among psychiatrists on the concept of sexual psychopathy. Forty-two replied that there is no substantial agreement and twenty-four that there is.[118] Campbell is surprised at "how much conformity exists in the minds of practicing psychiatrists concerning psychopathic personality";[119] Wilson and Pescor, on the other hand, say that "practically every psychiatrist has his own idea of what constitutes a psychopathic personality. . . ."[120] Cleckley, intending to show that great unanimity exists regarding this concept, says: "If a psychiatrist, in speaking to another about a patient, uses the term *psychopath*, there is seldom any misunderstanding as to the sort of patient in question";[121] but Duval states: ". . . [A]ctually I am not sure whether we know what we are talking about when we speak of the psychopath. . . ."[122] Thompson attributes the great amount of agreement among psychiatrists on the concept of psychopathy to the fact that it "is such a well-defined entity that its symptoms and characteristics are as well known to the psychiatrist as the symptoms of measles are known to the pediatrician";[123] but this is countered by Kennard's observation: "Clinicians do not even agree, actually, as to whether such a category exists."[124] Overholser and Richmond express

---

118. Paul W. Tappan, *The Habitual Sex Offender*, p. 57 (1950).

119. John D. Campbell, *Everyday Psychiatry*, p. 67 (2nd ed. 1949).

120. J. G. Wilson and M. J. Pescor, Problems in Prison Psychiatry 134 (1939).

121. Cleckley, *The Psychopath Viewed Practically* in Robert M. Lindner and Robert V. Seliger (eds.), *Handbook of Correctional Psychology*, p. 395 (1947).

122. Daniel Blain (Ed.), *Steps Forward in Mental Hospitals*, p. 178 (1953).

123. George N. Thompson, *The Psychopathic Delinquent and Criminal*, p. 39 (1953).

124. Kennard, in discussion of Hill, *EEG in Episodic, Psychotic and Psychopathic Behaviour: A Classification of Data*, 4 Electroenceph. & Clin. Neurophys., pp. 419, 440 (1952).

the view that "there is no general agreement among psychiatrists as to what type of personality should be designated psychopathic,"[125] only to be contradicted by Guttmacher and Weihofen, who say that while opinion about psychopathy is not unanimous, "there is considerable agreement."[126] Lowrey, referring to the diagnosis of psychopathic personality, thinks that "the important point is that psychiatrists agree there is such a group of abnormal personalities . . .";[127] while Stevenson, writing about the same concept, puts the issue as follows: "There is much disagreement as to the validity of this category as a diagnosis."[128]

Is psychopathic personality a clinical entity? There are contradictory views on this question, varying from those who, after extensive study of the matter, hold that it is "a very definite clinical entity"[129] to those who, after extensive study of the matter, hold that "there is no such entity."[130] Is psychopathic personality a serious condition? Every conceivable shade of opinion is espoused. Wertham is satisfied, as are other clinicians, that psychopathy is a "mild kind of abnormality not gross enough to be called a mental disease"[131] or to be regarded as a "psychosis."[132] But Thorne is satisfied that it is "just as malignant as a psychosis";[133] Carroll explicitly states that it is a "mental disease";[134] and Darling and Sanddal say it is a "psychosis."[135]

---

125. Winfred Overholser and Winifred V. Richmond, *Handbook of Psychiatry*, p. 184 (1947).

126. Guttmacher and Weihofen, *op. cit. supra* note 2, at p. 88.

127. Lawson G. Lowrey, Psychiatry for Social Workers 260 (2nd ed. 1950).

128. George S. Stevenson, Mental Health Planning for Social Action 144 (1956).

129. Hervey Cleckley, *The Mask of Sanity*, p. 210 (3rd ed. 1955).

130. Abrahamsen, *Study of 102 Sex Offenders at Sing Sing*, Fed. Prob., Sept. 1950, pp. 26, 27.

131. Fredric Wertham, *The Show of Violence*, p. 85 (1949).

132. *Id.* at 128.

133. Thorne, *supra* note 94, at p. 235.

134. Royal Comm'n on Capital Punishment, *op. cit. supra* note 59, at p. 551.

135. Darling and Sanddal, *A Psychopathologic Concept of Psychopathic Personality*, 13 J. Clin. & Exper. Psychopath., pp. 175, 178 (1952).

How frequently is psychopathic personality found among offenders? It depends entirely on which psychiatrist is asked, because estimates of the proportion of criminals who are psychopaths and the proportion of psychopaths who are criminals vary from 0 to 100 percent. One psychiatrist holds that the criminal is "rarely" psychopathic.[136] Another claims that criminals are "usually" psychopathic.[137] Two others insist that all psychopathic personalities are pathological criminals.[138] Another counters that many psychopaths are not criminals.[139] One goes so far as to reveal that he has seen "as many psychopathic judges, lawyers, police officers, and psychiatrists as psychopathic criminals."[140] A reception center of a state prison system has reported that only 2.3 percent of prisoners admitted in a twelve-year period were diagnosed as psychopaths by psychiatrists.[141] Three psychiatrists speculate that about five percent of convicted prisoners may be psychopathic.[142] Two others found fourteen percent of prisoners psychopathic.[143] Another holds that one-fourth to one-half of all criminals are psychopathic.[144] Three others are convinced that three-fourths of prisoners under twenty-one years of age are psychopaths.[145] Another testifies that ninety percent or more of incarcerated delinquents are potential, if not actual, psychopaths.[146]

---

136. Hulbert, *Constitutional Psychopathic Inferiority in Relation to Delinquency*, 30 J. Crim. L. & Criminology, pp. 3, 11 (1939).

137. C. S. Bluemel, *The Troubled Mind*, p. 491 (1938).

138. J. M. Nielsen and George N. Thompson, *The Engrammes of Psychiatry*, p. 190 (1947).

139. Lowrey, *op.cit. supra* note 127, at p. 267.

140. Abraham Myerson, *Speaking of Man*, p. 185 (1950).

141. Pennington, *Psychopathic and Criminal Behavior*, in L. A. Pennington and Irwin A. Berg (eds.), *Introduction to Clinical Psychology*, p. 424 (2nd ed. 1954).

142. Stafford-Clark, Pond, and Doust, *The Psychopath in Prison: A Preliminary Report of a Co-Operative Research*, 2 Brit. J. Delinq., pp. 117, 127 (1951).

143. Wilson and Pescor, *op. cit. supra* note 120, at p. 134.

144. Karl A. Menninger, *The Human Mind*, p. 158 (3rd ed. 1945).

145. Haugen, Coen, and Dickel, *supra* note 47, at p. 85.

146. Royal Comm'n on the Laws Relating to Mental Illness and Mental Deficiency, Minutes of Evidence, p. 943 (1954).

What types of crimes do psychopaths commit? No one answer can be given, seeing that different psychiatrists take entirely different positions. One has said that psychopaths "are driven . . . to deeds of violence which are as uncontrollable as a tidal wave."[147] Two others, not even mentioning violence, have stated that the antisocial behavior of psychopaths "consists of every form of petty misdemeanor."[148] Another has explained that a "common feature" of the psychopath is the commission of serious crimes of violence.[149] This is contradicted by the opinion of another, who has concluded that the crimes of psychopaths "generally . . . are not in the category of major crimes."[150] Two psychiatrists have asserted that "crimes of violence such as assault, rape and murder . . . are typical acts of psychopathic criminals,"[151] but this is opposed by the view of another, who has said that the typical psychopath is not likely to commit "major" crimes.[152] One psychiatrist, medically describing the psychopath as an "incorrigible monster,"[153] makes this alarming, and at the same time comforting, observation: "We can thank heaven that the type is rare because the offenses within the range of the genuine psychopath are without limits." "They will," says he, without giving a shred of evidence, "commit profit murder for a sum as low as twenty-five dollars."[154] There is more reassurance in the observation of another psychiatrist, who, while he presents no evidence either, holds that the crimes of the psychopath are "usually . . . relatively minor."[155] In a widely used textbook, three psychiatrists, who are apparently disinclined to get embroiled

---

147. Royal Comm'n on Capital Punishment, *op. cit. supra* note 59, at p. 462.

148. Louis J. Karnosh and Edward M. Zucker, A *Handbook of Psychiatry*, p. 206 (1945).

149. Royal Comm'n on Capital Punishment, *op. cit. supra* note 59, at p. 491.

150. Edward A. Strecker, *Basic Psychiatry*, p. 299 (1952).

151. Nielson and Thompson, *op. cit. supra* note138, at p. 191.

152. Hervey Cleckley, *The Mask of Sanity*, p. 37 (3rd ed. 1955).

153. David Abrahamsen, *Who Are the Guilty?*, p. 212 (1952).

154. *Id.* at 161.

155. Tarumianz, *New State Facilities for Criminally Inclined Psychopaths in Delaware*, 22 Del. State Med. J., pp. 163, 165 (1950).

in these dizzying controversies, have taken refuge in the following sweeping position about the psychopath's behavior: "The behavior of these patients may vary from amiable lying to criminal activity."[156]

What causes psychopathic personality? No single answer would do justice to the large array of factors implicated by different psychiatrists in the causation of this malady. There is no disease like psychopathy in the whole realm of medicine. It is the only disease known for which some practitioners blame conditions in the home and some, conditions in the central nervous system. Birnbaum finds that psychopathy is "constitutional; that is innate and (probably) hereditary";[157] Bender, that it is the purest example of "psychogenic or environmentally determined behavior disorders . . .";[158] Lichtenstein and Small, that in many cases, it is directly attributable to endocrine dysfunction;[159] Greenacre, that it is due to poor parent-child relations;[160] Nielsen and Thompson, that cerebral trauma is the commonest cause;[161] O'Conner, that deprivation of "blood-sugar" has been implicated;[162] and Palmer, that "deprivation of Mother Love" is the basic factor.[163] Two distinguished experts on psychopathy caution that different factors can cause this disease in different patients. They hold that in some cases, the predominating cause will be such factors as poverty, a broken home, and so on; and in other cases, "disturbance of the prefrontal hypothalamic connections," brain injury, and the like.[164] Finally, with refreshing simplicity,

156. Jack R. Ewalt, Edward A. Strecker, and Franklin G. Ebaugh, *Practical Clinical Psychiatry*, p. 258 (8th ed. 1957).

157. Birnbaum, A *Court Psychiatrist's View of Juvenile Delinquents*, 261 Annals, pp. 55, 59 (1949).

158. Lauretta Bender, *Aggression, Hostility and Anxiety in Children*, p. 152 (1953).

159. P. M. Lichtenstein and S. M. Small, A *Handbook of Psychiatry*, p. 88 (1943).

160. Greenacre, *Problems of Patient-Therapist Relationship in the Treatment of Psychopaths* in Lindner and Seliger, *op. cit. supra* note 121, at p. 379.

161. Nielsen and Thompson, *op. cit. supra* note 138, at p. 169.

162. William A. O'Connor, *Psychiatry*, p. 304 (1948).

163. Harold Palmer, *Psychopathic Personalities*, p. 12 (1957).

164. David Henderson and R. D. Gillespie (with Ivor R. C. Batchelor), A *Text-Book of Psychiatry*, p. 388 (8th ed. 1956).

one psychiatrist suggests, in effect, that psychopathic personality results from the failure to train the child to behave himself.[165]

What do psychiatrists say about treatment of psychopaths? Everything, for viewpoints on the treatment of this disease vary markedly from psychiatrist to psychiatrist. Asked by the Royal Commission on Capital Punishment whether any progress had been made toward curing psychopaths, one expert answered, "I am afraid not."[166] A different psychiatrist, answering the same question submitted by the same Commission, said that the curability of the psychopath is "surprisingly large."[167] When it comes to specific treatments that have been proposed or tried, there is rampant diversity. They run the gamut from attempts to incorporate the subject into groups having athletic, cultural, political, or religious interests,[168] to brain surgery.[169] One intriguing type of treatment has been reported in which "the psychopathic delinquent is brought before an awesome *panel* of doctors who literally say *nothing* beyond an initial expression of their desire to help the culprit once he is honestly interested in helping himself." The hazards of this approach are tremendous, judging from one observation that has been made: ". . . [T]he psychopath can sit out the doctors easily enough."[170]

Psychiatrists do not disagree only with each other. Some disagree with themselves. Often it is possible to find one and the same psychiatrist taking contradictory stands on the same question from publication to publication, on different pages of the same publication, and on the same page of the same publication. For example, Banay, a psychiatric consultant to the Federal Bureau of Prisons, has taken curious positions on the psychopath. In a conference on criminal responsibility held in early 1957, he rejected the concept of psycho-

---

165. Wooley, A *Dynamic Approach to Psychopathic Personality*, 35 So. Med. J., p. 926 (1942).

166. Royal Comm'n on Capital Punishment, *op. cit. supra* note 59, at p. 307.

167. *Id.*at 501.

168. Oskar Diethelm, *Treatment in Psychiatry*, p. 426 (2nd ed. 1950).

169. Darling and Sanddal, *supra* note 135, at p. 179.

170. Ruth L. Munroe, *Schools of Psychoanalytic Thought*, p. 293 (1955).

pathic personality, saying: "I am very much in disagreement with the diagnosis of psychopath. Psychopath means we don't know what is wrong with him."[171] Just about the time Banay was making this statement, a book written by him was published. In this book, he describes in detail a treatment for psychopaths:[172]

> Marked success in the treatment of some psychopaths has been obtained through a combination of electrocoma and psychotherapy. The treatment requires hospitalization for eight months to a year and it consists of a series of electrocoma treatments followed by analytically oriented psychotherapy. This is followed by further ambulatory treatment under therapeutic conditions. The procedure has been tested sufficiently to show that many aggressive psychopaths can be guided to adequate social adjustment, over-all change of temperamental trends and freedom from criminal inclinations.

Banay is prescribing drastic and lengthy "therapy" for a diagnostic category he rejects.

Guttmacher took the position in 1951 that "the diagnosis of a psychopathic personality is practically meaningless." He elaborated on the point by urging that the term be discarded or restricted to a type of case described by Cleckley.[173] But in the 1951 annual report of the court clinic of which Guttmacher is Chief Medical Officer, it is recorded that forty-eight cases were diagnosed as psychopaths of a type other than that described by Cleckley.[174] Furthermore, in his memorandum to the American Law Institute, Guttmacher raises no question whatever about the validity of the diagnosis of psychopathic

---

171. *Mental Disorder and Criminal Responsibility: A Symposium, supra* note 73, at p. 82.

172. Ralph S. Banay, *We Call Them Criminals*, p. 170 (1957).

173. Guttmacher, *Diagnosis and Etiology of Psychopathic Personalities as Perceived in Our Time* in Paul H. Hoch and Joseph Zubin (eds.), *Current Problems in Psychiatric Diagnosis*, p. 155 (1953).

174. Medical Officer of the Supreme Bench of Baltimore City, Report, p. 8 (1951).

personality, and, in fact, he favors the institutionalization of psychopaths for an indeterminate period.[175] Guttmacher's clinic is attaching
to offenders a diagnosis which he admits is practically meaningless.
And, in one place, he is recommending possible lifelong custody for
offenders who are diagnosed as having a disease which, in another
place, he says is practically meaningless.

McCarthy and Corrin state that the psychopath "is within normal
limits intellectually . . ."; however, on another page of the same book,
they state that "the psychopath is inferior . . . intellectually. . . ."
Again, these authors hold that the condition of the psychopath is
"clear-cut and uniform in its symptomatology . . ."; but in the very
next paragraph, on the same page, still referring to the same diagnosis,
they assert that "there is no symptom, syndrome or behavior dynamics
upon which one may base a diagnosis."[176]

How is psychopathic personality diagnosed? Numerous psychiatrists have explicitly and implicitly admitted that to diagnose this
disease they do not need to examine the subject's body—which,
incidentally, is universally acknowledged to be the only legitimate
object of investigation in every other branch of medicine. To diagnose
psychopathic personality, the psychiatrist needs to examine only the
subject's FBI record. Numerous psychiatrists have explicitly stated that
they can make this diagnosis if they have access to only the social history of the "patient," particularly a record of his crimes. One example
is Strecker's statement that "since there are no strong and clear-cut
diagnostic criteria, the diagnosis [psychopathic personality] has to be
made retrospectively on the basis of a long history of psychopathic
behavior."[177] An even more pointed example is provided by the following quotation: "For diagnosis of these states [psychopathic personality]
an adequate social history is imperative. The psychopath is not apt

---

175. Guttmacher, *Principal Difficulties with the Present Criteria of Responsibility
and Possible Alternatives*, Model Penal Code app. B, at p. 177 (Tent. Draft No.
4, 1955).

176. Daniel J. McCarthy and Kenneth M. Corrin, *Medical Treatment of Mental
Diseases*, pp. 402, 403, 405 (1955).

177. Edward A. Strecker, *Fundamentals of Psychiatry*, p. 182 (5th ed. 1952).

to reveal his difficulties with the environment voluntarily."[178] One of the newest textbooks on psychiatry teaches that to place a subject in the category of psychopathic personality, "the antisocial behavior of the patient should be the principal manifestation of the disorder."[179] Another textbook advises that "no diagnosis of psychopathic personality should be made in the absence of punishable or censurable acts episodically carried out."[180] Davidson, although discussing psychopathy in witnesses rather than in offenders, makes the following statement, which obviously would apply in any context:[181]

> The diagnosis of psychopathy is not made by examination but by a review of the life history. Examination shows nothing. The life history shows a record of trouble, of shiftlessness, of nomadism, of dishonesty, of nonconformity, of mischief or of some similar trait. When this is the history in a witness of good intelligence and obvious sanity, one has the right to suspect psychopathy.

It is clear what is being admitted in all these excerpts: To be able to diagnose psychopathy, the psychiatrist needs to have evidence that the subject shows a history of psychopathy. A history of psychopathy consists of the subject's record of crime or of other social maladjustment. Given this history, the psychiatrist can diagnose psychopathy. Obviously, a psychiatrist is not needed to diagnose psychopathy. The policeman or the file clerk keeping criminal records could fully measure up to the task.

It should be very clear by now—to all except those who are immovably determined not to allow reason to interfere with their worshipful admiration of psychiatry (an all too common foible)—that

---

178. Dunn, *The Psychopath in the Armed Forces: Review of Literature and Comments*, 4 Psychiatry, pp. 251, 253 (1941).

179. Ewalt, Strecker, and Ebaugh, *op. cit. supra* note 156, at p. 258.

180. O'Connor, *op. cit. supra* note 162, at p. 300.

181. Davidson, *How Trustworthy Is the Witness?*, 2 J. Forensic Med., pp. 14, 18 (1955).

there is no such thing as a medical (psychiatric) "disease" called psychopathic or sociopathic personality. This disease, like so many other in psychiatry, is a figment of the fertile imagination of psychiatrists. Psychopathy is nothing but a synonym for crime and delinquency. Whether or not a person is said to have this disease depends, like so many other diseases in psychiatry, more on what is going on in the head of the psychiatrist than what is going on in the head of the "patient." Just such an observation comes from an unexpected source. Karpman has noted:[182]

> . . . [I]t is perhaps more likely that in studying 100 consecutive cases diagnosed psychopathic personality, what we get is not an understanding of the patient, but a study of the mind of a psychiatrist, that is what he means when he makes a diagnosis of psychopathic personality. It is then discovered that the average psychiatrist calls an individual psychopathic if in some way the individual has gone against the social grain.

Despite all the evidence available, only an insignificant proportion of which has been presented here, despite the disconcerting observation by a psychiatrist that "at present there is no objective proof that they [psychopaths] are ill rather than wicked . . .";[183] despite the fact that Cleckley, one of the foremost proponents of the concept of psychopathy, grants that its "psychopathology . . . is debatable and scarcely to be proved in courts,"[184] despite the angry accusation by Kinberg, the internationally known forensic psychiatrist, that in their approach to psychopathic personality, psychiatrists are practicing something that looks very much more like quackery than medicine,[185] the courts are admitting testimony about this diagnosis and

---

182. Karpman, *Psychopathy as a Form of Social Parasitism—A Comparative Biological Study*, 10 J. Clin. Psychopath., pp. 160, 172 (1949).

183. W. Lindesay Neustatter, *The Mind of the Murderer*, p. 171 (1957).

184. Cleckley, *The Psychopath Viewed Practically* in Robert M. Lindner and Robert V. Seliger (eds.), *Handbook of Correctional Psychology*, p. 412 (1947).

185. Kinberg, *On the Concept of "Psychopathy" and the Treatment of So-called "Psychopaths,"* 93 J. Mental Sci., p. 93 (1947).

are allowing the adjudication and disposition of cases to be influenced by it. This concept and psychiatric testimony about it should not be allowed in court, no disposition of cases should be based on it, and it should not be considered in any serious way in deliberations about defendants. No laws incorporating this concept, in any of its forms or under any of its names, should be passed. Legislation of this type already passed should be repealed. And, it goes without saying, correctional decisions should not be based on such a diagnosis.

In the meantime, society, especially the legal profession, would be wise to keep a very close watch over those courts that allow psychiatrists to testify about this concept. A court that would allow this is just as likely to allow testimony on witchcraft. More heed should be given to those psychiatrists who are capable of at least some sensible judgment about this matter, as illustrated in the following reflection: "Perhaps our psychopathic personality is the heretic or witch in modern guise."[186]

And no special perspicacity is needed to see a statement like the following, made by a psychiatrist in the course of an assault on the law for its reluctance to show greater hospitality to psychiatry, for the fraudulent pretense that it is: ". . . [J]udges have ridden roughshod over perfectly valid scientific discoveries such as the nature of psychopathy. . . ."[187]

V. Psychoneurosis

Another mental condition frequently said to be associated with delinquent and criminal behavior is psychoneurosis, or, to use the equivalent and shorter term, neurosis. It is impossible to state briefly the psychiatric position on the relationship between neurosis and delinquency or crime for two reasons: first, there is endless disagreement

---

186. Roche, *Truth Telling, Psychiatric Expert Testimony and the Impeachment of Witnesses*, 22 Pa. Bar Ass'n. Q., pp. 140, 152 (1951).

187. Glover, *Outline of the Investigation and Treatment of Delinquency in Great Britain: 1912–1948: With Special Reference to Psychoanalytical and Other Psychological Methods*, in Eissler, *op. cit. supra* note 26, at p. 435.

among psychiatrists on every facet of the concept of neurosis; and second, there are as many views on its relation to delinquency and crime as there are psychiatrists.

A psychiatrist who is an outstanding expert on neurosis recently made the following observation:[188]

> Probably nothing has been less conclusively defined than the nature of the neurotic process; and about nothing is there more confusion between laymen and behavioral scientists, among the several varieties of behavioral scientists, and even within the close fraternity of psychiatrists and the even closer fraternity of analysts.

This has been echoed by numerous experts. But it is not only the "nature of the neurotic process" that is in doubt. Usually, many more aspects of the concept are brought into question, as can be seen from the following typical conclusion: "Psychiatric diagnosis of neurosis is not yet standardized; there is variation in the nomenclature and the meaning ascribed to the diagnostic categories. There is widely differing emphasis on phenomenology, and etiology."[189]

Despite this reported state of uncertainty and the apparent divergence in viewpoints, neurosis is usually denominated a "disease." One psychiatrist, for example, counsels that neurosis "is always to be looked upon as a sickness (disease). . . ."[190] Another has pointed out that "mental disease is a term which includes psychosis and neurosis."[191] No psychiatrist who takes the position that neurosis is a disease, however, has ever specified the organ in which it occurs, the type of lesion involved, or the kind of trauma, chemical imbalance, bacteria, virus,

---

188. Kubie, *Social Forces and the Neurotic Process*, in Alexander H. Leighton, John A. Clausen and Robert N. Wilson (eds.), *Explorations in Social Psychiatry*, p. 80 (1957).

189. Freedman and Hollingshead, *Neurosis and Social Class*, 113 Am. J. Psychiatry, pp. 769, 771 (1957).

190. Ginsberg, *supra* note 100, at p. 58.

191. Wertham, *Psychoauthoritarianism and the Law*, 22 U. Chi. L. Rev., pp. 336, 337 (1955).

or other agent thought to be instrumental in its causation. If neurosis is a disease and if psychiatrists proceed in the manner of other medical practitioners—a point on which they unblushingly insist—then it is incumbent upon them to show diseased tissue in neurosis. On the other hand, there are some psychiatrists who say that neurosis is not a disease. Some say that neurosis is the inability to get along with people.[192] But that is not disease; nor is it a medical problem. Another view has it that neurosis, and psychosis, too, for that matter, are not diseases located in the individual, but are problems involving group organization.[193] But this is a concern of sociology, not medicine.

If neurosis is a disease, then it, like psychopathic personality, is one of the strangest kind of disease imaginable. This is certainly the impression one gets from a very recently issued report of a comprehensive and elaborate research on the relationship between mental illness and social class, undertaken by a team of psychiatrists, sociologists, psychologists, and others. Based on their study of the processes out of which psychiatric diagnoses emerge, these investigators were forced to the following observation:[194]

> We take the position that a neurosis is a state of mind not only of the sufferer, but also of the therapist, and it appears likewise to be connected to the class positions of the therapist and the patient. A diagnosis arises from a number of conditioning factors: the experiences of the patient, the training and techniques of the doctor, as well as the social values of the community. Stated otherwise, a diagnosis of neurosis is a resultant of a social interactional process which involves the patient, the doctor, and the patient's position in the status structure of the community.

192. Redlich, *The Concept of Health in Psychiatry*, in Leighton, Clausen, and Wilson, *op. cit. supra* note 188, at p. 144.

193. Ruesch, *Social Factors in Therapy: A Brief Review*, in Ass'n for Research in Nervous and Mental Disease, Psychiatric Treatment, p. 71 (1953).

194. August B. Hollingshead and Fredrick C. Redlich, *Social Class and Mental Illness*, p. 237 (1958).

Apparently, then, the diagnosis of neurosis in a "patient" is dependent on the intricate convergence of a number of factors—the mental condition of the psychiatrist, a process of social—interaction, the relative social class positions of the psychiatrist and the patient, and. the social values prevailing in the community. These researchers also learned that the concept of neurosis can have reference to either a theological dogma, a philosophical premise, or a bodily disturbance: "The sinfulness of the Bible, the *Angst* of the Kierkegaardians, the 'nausea' of the existentialists, and the 'stress' of the internists are all syndromes which may be and have been subsumed under the term neurosis by some experts."[195] It is clear that one cannot be too sure whether an attack of neurosis is a problem calling for the ministrations of the physician or of the preacher.

It should be reiterated that the problems associated with the diagnosis: of neurosis, as is true of other psychiatric diagnoses and concepts, are not matters of mere academic import. The psychiatrist's views on neurosis and all the inferences he draws from them can affect offenders in a multitude of ways. It is obvious that if a psychiatrist considers psychopathic personality to be a mental disease but does not so consider neurosis, or vice versa, and if a criminal act resulting from a mental disease is not punishable, the differential diagnosis of these two conditions becomes a critical matter. Therefore, it is important to take a look at the notions of the psychiatrists on the relationship between neurosis and criminal or delinquent behavior, which, as has been stated and as can be guessed by now, are the subject of abounding controversies.

One psychiatrist includes "the child's delinquent behavior—*all* delinquent behavior—within the framework of the neuroses." He contends that "the delinquent act is but a special type—a syndrome . . . within the group designated 'the neuroses.'"[196] Yet, one psychiatrist found that only twenty-four, or .6 of one percent, out of 4,000 delinquents examined by him gave evidence of a psycho-

---

195. *Id.* at p. 239.

196. Gardner, *The Community and the Aggressive Child: The Expression of Aggressive-Destructive Impulses in Juvenile Delinquent Acts*, 33 Mental Hygiene, pp. 537, 541 (1949).

neurotic reaction.[197] On the other hand, in the well-known study by the Gluecks, it was found that 24.6 percent of 500 delinquents were neurotic—a proportion over forty times larger than that found in the report just cited.[198] It is the observation of a psychiatrist that "most" children with a long history of delinquency referred to child guidance clinics are neurotic.[199] Yet, psychiatrists who examined the more serious delinquents referred to them by a juvenile court during a one-year period diagnosed only 4.4 percent as neurotic.[200] One psychiatrist has expressed the opinion that psychoneurosis "constitutes quite a considerable group of the delinquents."[201] This is contradicted by another, however, who says that it is "rare" for neurosis to be a decisive factor in delinquency.[202]

Into the midst of these ongoing debates and these diligent efforts to settle on the incidence of neurosis among delinquents, one psychiatrist recently interjected what is not a new, but is, nonetheless, a most disconcerting, observation, and one which will be discussed presently. He announced that there is an antithetical relation between psychoneurosis and delinquency![203]—thereby embarrassing all those practitioners who have given sworn testimony before any number of boards, committees, and commissions that neurosis is a cause of delinquency and who, through the years, have been confidently making known publicly the varying proportions of delinquents in whom

---

197. East, cited by Gillespie, *Psychoneurosis and Criminal Behaviour* in Radzinowicz and Turner, *op. cit. supra* note 42, at p. 72.

198. Sheldon & Eleanor T. Glueck, Unraveling Juvenile Delinquency, pp. 239–40 (1950).

199. Lippman, *Difficulties Encountered in the Psychiatric Treatment of Chronic Juvenile Delinquents* in Eissler, *op. cit. supra* note 26, at p. 157.

200. Juvenile Court of Cuyahoga County (Cleveland) Ann. Rep. table 15, at p. 38 (1957).

201. Rees, *Mental Variations and Criminal Behaviour* in Radzinowicz and Turner, *op. cit. supra* note 42, at p. 6.

202. Chess, *Juvenile Delinquency: Whose Problem?*, Fed. Prob., June 1955, pp. 29, 30.

203. Glover, *Psycho-Analysis and Criminology: A Political Survey*, 37 Int'l J. Psycho-Anal., pp. 311, 314 (1956).

they have found neurosis. The issue is further complicated by those psychiatrists who find delinquents to be less neurotic, or less often neurotic, than nondelinquents. Jenkins, as do others, comes to this conclusion. He first dismisses the theory that neurosis can account for all or a major fraction of delinquency as one that "neither rings true nor makes sense." He then reasons that the delinquent is inclined to be less neurotic than the nondelinquent. And he pushes the point even further by describing the delinquent as one who is less prone to manifest neurotic tendencies than are people in general.[204] In the research by the Gluecks, in which a comparison is made between nondelinquents and delinquents, a significantly higher proportion of neurotics was found among the former than among the latter.[205]

But suppose, for purposes of argument, it is granted that a major fraction (or even all) offenders are neurotic. This would not distinguish them from various specified groups in the population, from a large majority of human beings, or even from all the inhabitants of this planet, if the judgment of certain psychiatrists can be trusted. Take, for example, the research on the relationship between mental illness and social class already referred to. One of its findings is that a considerable proportion of the neurotics found in the upper social classes comprised psychiatrists, psychologists, nurses, social workers, artists, other professional workers, and persons in the communication business.[206] In another research, it was discovered that college students are as frequently neurotic as are prison inmates.[207] In a survey of the incidence of mental disorders among a random sample of the residents of a community of three thousand people, it was found that fifty-seven percent were neurotic.[208] One psychiatrist has claimed, "To

---

204. Jenkins, *Adaptive and Maladaptive Delinquency*, II Nervous Child, pp. 9, 11 (1955).

205. Sheldon & Eleanor T. Glueck, *op. cit. supra* note 198.

206. Hollingshead and Redlich, *op. cit. supra* note 194, at p. 337.

207. Levy et al., *The Outstanding Personality Factors Among the Population of a State Penitentiary: A Preliminary Report*, 13 J. Clin. & Exper. Psychopath., pp. 117, 121 (1952).

208. Leighton, *The Distribution of Psychiatric Symptoms in a Small Town*, 112 Am. J. Psychiatry, pp. 716, 722 (1956).

understand the neuroses is to understand the average person. . . ."[209] Another has insisted that few residents of this continent can be called "nonneurotic."[210] Finally, a psychiatrist has gone on record as concurring with another expert whom he paraphrases as saying that "all persons, in all cultures, are victims—whether to a greater or to a lesser extent—of a widely prevalent social neurosis the existence of which is now evident beyond any question . . . ,"[211] thus still leaving unsettled the question whether neurosis is a social or a medical phenomenon.

When it comes to the matter of similarities and differences between neurosis and psychopathic personality, the chaos is complete. Sometimes, one encounters the view that these diseases are worlds apart, and sometimes, that they are one and the same. Thompson holds to the former view, saying that the dissimilarity between the two diseases is "essentially complete."[212] In another source, he joins a colleague in the following elaboration: "The psychopath and psychoneurotic seem to be at opposite extremes with regard to personality function."[213] And they emphasize that when it comes to the traits characterizing the two diagnostic categories, "the incompatibility seems absolute."[214] But this orientation is negated by Federn, who, in speaking of criminal psychopathy, holds that this condition is "usually combined with neurotic symptoms and neurotic character traits."[215] And Schilder says he inclines to the view that the two terms, "psychopathic" and "neurotic," are "equivalent."[216] Guttmacher goes even further toward obliterating the distinction when he writes that criminal psychopaths "suffer from a deep-seated neurosis."[217]

209. Leon J. Saul, Emotional Maturity, p. vii (1947).

210. James Clark Moloney, The Battle for Mental Health, p. 9 (1952).

211. Thornton, Book Review, 41 J. Crim. L., C. & P.S., p. 807 (1951).

212. Thompson, op. cit. supra note 123, at p. 50.

213. Nielsen & Thompson, op. cit. supra note 138, at p. 185.

214. Id. at p. 188.

215. Paul Federn, Ego Psychology and the Psychoses, p. 180 (Edoardo Weiss ed. 1952).

216. Schilder, op. cit. supra note 48, at p. 278.

217. Guttmacher, Medical Aspects of the Causes and Prevention of Crime and the Treatment of Offenders, 2 Bull. WHO, p. 281 (1949).

The opinions just recounted cast serious doubt, to say the least, on the separability of psychopathic personality and neurosis as two distinct and vastly dissimilar disease entities. Any lingering doubt is completely removed by still another theory that has numerous adherents among psychiatrists. This theory makes of psychopathic personality nothing more than a manifestation of neurosis. It is explained by those who identify with this school of thought that psychopathic personality is neurosis expressed in antisocial behavior.[218] Persons are diagnosed as psychopathic, according to this scheme, "when their antisocial behavior is the principle [sic] manifestation of their neurosis."[219] But these definitions are precisely the ones psychiatrists give of neurotic delinquency itself, without reference in any manner or form to psychopathic personality. A typical example is the following: "The essential feature of neurotic delinquency is that it represents behavior directed against society to express a neurotic conflict."[220]

Now, it so happens that such assertions—that psychopathic personality is neurosis manifested in antisocial behavior, that neurotic delinquency is the solution of neurotic conflicts through the commission of aggressive acts, and that the simple assertion that neurotics do commit delinquency and crime—are in complete conflict with another postulate, referred to earlier in passing, often made by psychiatrists. This postulate affirms that it is inherent in the very nature of neurosis that those afflicted with it do not commit offenses. Further, it is contended that the psychopath "acts out" (to use the psychiatric jargon for the commission of aggressive, criminal, or destructive deeds), in contradistinction to the neurotic who does not act out, but rather suffers inwardly or escapes into fantasy. According to Alexander, for example, the very criterion that distinguishes psychopaths from neurotics is that "they [psychopaths] 'act out' their neurotic impulses, in contrast to psychoneurotics whose most important activity is in

---

218. Beulah Chamberlain Bosselman, *Neurosis and Psychosis*, p. 555 (2nd ed. 1956).

219. Edward A. Strecker and others, *Practical Clinical Psychiatry*, p. 310 (7th ed. 1951).

220. Hyman S. Lippman, *Treatment of the Child in Emotional Conflict*, p. 191 (1956).

their fantasy."[221] Sometimes the same point is made in a different way. Abrahamsen, to choose only one example from among many, claims that the offender may get relief from his conflicts through his antisocial actions, but that such an escape is not open to a neurotic because he is "too inhibited."[222] However, Banay declares that just the opposite is true—namely, that one of the means by which offenders get release from neurotic conflicts is to commit delinquencies rather than to remain inhibited.[223] And others go even further and say that a neurotic offender commits crimes "precisely *because* he is over-inhibited. . . ."[224]

Understandably, two psychiatrists recently sought to evade this whole horrendous muddle. Brancale and Heyn reported that those offenders whom they now diagnose as neurotic correspond to those formerly diagnosed as psychopathic.[225] And Karpman, who is Chief Psychotherapist at St. Elizabeth's Hospital, apparently refusing to let this diagnostic fuss stay his therapeutic hand, has solved the problem at least for one category of offenders: "I have developed a rather simple method of dealing with sexual offenders; I merely change the diagnosis from one of psychopathy to one of neurosis and then proceed to treat as any neurosis."[226]

The diagnosis of neurosis obviously is no more reliable or valid than is the diagnosis of psychopathic personality. This and the other criticisms that can be made of the diagnosis of neurosis need not be rehearsed in detail. They are precisely the same as have already been made respecting psychopathic personality.

---

221. Franz Alexander, *Fundamentals of Psychoanalysis*, p. 235 (1948).

222. Abrahamsen, *Family Tension, Basic Cause of Criminal Behavior*, 40 J. Crim. L. & Criminology, pp. 330, 336 (1949).

223. Ralph S. Banay, *Youth in Despair*, p. 141 (1948).

224. Albert Ellis and Ralph Brancale, *The Psychology of Sex Offenders*, p. 39 (1956). [Italics in original.]

225. Brancale and Heyn, *Detection, Classification, and Treatment of the Youthful Offender*, Fed. Prob., March 1957, pp. 33, 36.

226. Benjamin Karpman, *The Sexual Offender and His Offenses*, p. 574 (1954).

VI. Conclusions

Psychiatric testimony should not be admissible in court. The courts have traditionally followed the principle that expert testimony and evidence that purport to be scientific will not be admissible unless their reliability and validity have been amply tested and unless substantial agreement among the appropriate experts has been demonstrated. When it comes to psychiatric testimony, the courts are acting in heedless disregard and flagrant violation of this eminently sound principle. It should be unmistakably clear on the basis of the evidence adduced here—only a tiny part of the available evidence—that psychiatrists have not attained the level of competence and scientific reliability and validity necessary to make their testimony eligible for serious consideration by the courts. Neither should it be looked upon as an objective and sound basis for coercive decisions, judicial or correctional. The courts should not allow psychiatric testimony to be heard, irrespective of whether the psychiatrists are partisan or court-appointed, attached to a court clinic or to a hospital.

Furthermore, the courts and correctional agencies should not persist in giving legal and official support and sanction to the almost universal fallacy of considering psychiatrists to be experts on human behavior, motivation, personality, interpersonal relations, problems of social organization, emotional reactions, crime and delinquency, other social problems, and similar nonmedical topics. It is astounding that judges and correctional officials continue to view psychiatrists as experts on human behavior when there is considerable experimental and other research which shows laymen to be superior to psychiatrists and associated personnel in the judgment of peoples' motives, emotions, abilities, personality traits, and action tendencies.[227]

It is certainly puzzling that the courts insist on admitting psychiatric testimony in spite of the fact that some psychiatrists have repeatedly given candid and pointed warnings against the dogmatism, aggressiveness, dubious tactics, and irresponsibility of some of their colleagues, particularly those who have succeeded in overselling psychiatry to the legal profession and to the general public. Some of the more cautious

---

227. Taft, *The Ability to Judge People*, 52 Psychological Bull. 1 (1955).

practitioners know full well that psychiatry does not have knowledge that would be helpful in the administration of justice. One of these, whose statement to this effect has already been cited,[228] makes the following rejoinder to the claim of some psychiatrists that their success in bringing about changes in the laws of criminal responsibility is due to the increasing knowledge of human behavior accumulated during the past fifty years: "But is this why they have succeeded? I think not. They have succeeded rather because they now possess more social power than they had in the past."[229]

228. See *supra* note 15.

229. Szasz, *supra* note 15, at p. 314.

Bibliography

GENERAL

Beccaria, C. *On Crimes and Punishment*, trans. H. Paolucci, Indianapolis, IN: Bobbs-Merrill, 1963.

Benn, S. "Punishment," in P. Edwards (ed.), *The Encyclopedia of Philosophy*. New York: Macmillan, 1967.

Bentham, J. *The Rationale of Punishment*, in J. Bowring (ed.), *The Works of Jeremy Bentham*. Edinburgh: W. Tait, 1843.

Bentham, J. *An Introduction to the Principles of Morals and Legislation*. Oxford: Basil Blackwell, 1948 (1789).

Durkheim, E. *The Division of Labor in Society*, trans. G. Simpson. New York: Free Press, 1965.

Ewing, A. *The Morality of Punishment*. London: K. Paul, Trench, Trubner and Co. Ltd., 1929.

Fitzgerald, P. *Criminal Law and Punishment*. Oxford: Clarendon Press, 1962.

Fuller, L. "The Case of the Speluncean Explorers," *Harvard Law Review*, 62(1949).

Gerber, J., and P. McAnany (eds.) *Contemporary Punishment*, Views, *Explanations and Justifications*. South Bend: University of Notre Dame, 1972.

Hall, J. *General Principles of Criminal Law*, 2nd ed. Indianapolis, IN: Bobbs-Merrill, 1960.

Hart, H. L. *Punishment and Responsibility*. Oxford: Clarendon Press, 1968.

Hart, H. L. *Law, Liberty and Morality*. New York: Random House, 1963.

Hawkins, G. "Punishment and Deterrence: The Educative, Moralizing and Habituative Effects," *Wisconsin Law Review* (1969).

Hentig, H. *Punishment: Its Origin, Purpose and Psychology*. London: W. Hodge and Co. Ltd., 1937.

Honderich, T. *Punishment, Its Supposed Justifications*. New York: Harcourt, Brace and World, 1970.

Michael, J., and H. Wechsler, "A Rationale of the Law of Homicide," *Columbia Law Review*, 37(1937).

Michael, J., and H. Wechsler, *Criminal Law and Its Administration*. Brooklyn, NY: Foundation Press, 1940.

Model Penal Code. Philadelphia, PA: American Law Institute, 1962.

Morris, H. (ed.). *Freedom and Responsibility*. Stanford, CA: Stanford University Press, 1961. Chapter X.

Parkenham, F. *The Idea of Punishment*. London: Geoffrey Chapman, 1961.

Pincoffs, E. *The Rationale of Legal Punishment*. New York: Humanities Press, 1966.

Radzinowicz, L., and J. Turner (eds.). *The Modern Approach to Criminal Law*. London: Macmillan, 1948.

Stephen, J. A *History of the Criminal Law in England*. London: Macmillan, 1883.

Tarde, G. *Penal Philosophy*. Boston: Little, Brown and Co., 1912.

Williams, G. *Criminal Law: The General Part*. London: Stevens and Sons Ltd., 1953.

CHAPTER 1: THE CONCEPT OF PUNISHMENT

Benn, S., and R. Peters. *Social Principles and the Democratic State*. London: George Allen and Unwin Ltd., 1959, pp. 182–83.

Bentham, J. *The Rationale of Punishment*, in J. Bowring (ed.), *The Works of Jeremy Bentham*. Edinburgh: W. Tait, 1843, Chapter I.

Bobbio, N. "Law and Force," *The Monist*, 49(1965).

Durkheim, E. *The Division of Labor in Society*, trans. G. Simpson. New York: Free Press, 1965. Chapter II.

Flew, A. "The Justification of Punishment," *Philosophy*, 29(1954).

Gahringer, R. "Punishment and Responsibility," *Journal of Philosophy*, 66(1969).

Hart, H. L. "Prolegomenon to the Principles of Punishment," *Proceedings of the Aristotelian Society*, 60 (1959–60). Reprinted in Hart, *Punishment and Responsibility*.

Hart, H. M. "The Aims of the Criminal Law," *Law and Contemporary Problems*, 23(1958).

Honderich, T. *Punishment: The Supposed Justifications*. New York: Harcourt, Brace and World, 1970. Chapter III.

Kasachkoff, T. "Analysing 'Punishment,'" *Canadian Journal of Philosophy*, 2(1972).

Kaufman, A. "Anthony Quinton on Punishment," *Analysis*, 20(1959).

Lasswell, H., and R. Donnelly. "The Continuing Debate Over Responsibility: An Introduction to Isolating the Condemnation Sanction," *Yale Law Journal*, 68(1959).

McCloskey, H. "The Complexity of the Concepts of Punishment," *Philosophy*, 37(1962).

McPherson, T. "Punishment: Definition and Justification," *Analysis*, 28(1967).

Strömberg, T. "Some Reflections on the Concept of Punishment," *Theoria*, 23(1957).

CHAPTER 2: THE JUSTIFICATION OF PUNISHMENT

Aquinas, T. "Of the Debt of Punishment," in *Summa Theologica*. New York: Benziger Brothers, 1947. Question 87, Articles 1–8.

Aristotle. *Nicomachean Ethics*, trans. W. Ross, in *The Works of Aristotle*. Oxford: Clarendon Press, 1938. 1104b, 15–19.

Beccaria, C. *On Crimes and Punishment*, trans. H. Paolucci. Indianapolis, IN: Bobbs-Merrill, 1963.

Benn, S. "An Approach to the Problems of Punishment," *Philosophy*, 33(1958).

Bentham, J. *An Introduction to the Principles of Morals and Legislation*. Oxford: Basil Blackwell, 1948.

Bentham, J. *Theory of Legislation*. London: Routledge and Kegan Paul Ltd., 1950.

Bentham, J. *The Rationale of Punishment*, in J. Bowring (ed.), *The Works of Jeremy Bentham*. Edinburgh: W. Tait, 1843.

Bentham, J. *Of Laws in General*, in H. L. Hart (ed.), *Collected Works of Jeremy Bentham*. London: Athlone Press, 1970. Chapter XI.

Bosanquet, B. *The Philosophical Theory of the State*, 4th ed. London: Macmillan, 1966.

Bradley, F. *Ethical Studies*, 2nd ed. London: Oxford University Press, 1927. Essay I.

Bradley, F. "Some Remarks on Punishment," *International Journal of Ethics*, 4(1894).

Brandt, R. *Ethical Theory*. Englewood Cliffs: Prentice-Hall, 1959. Chapter 19.

Brentano, F. *The Origin of Our Knowledge of Right and Wrong*, English edition, ed. R. Chisholm. London: Routledge and Kegan Paul Ltd., 1969, pp. 118–122.

Carritt, E. *Ethical and Political Thinking*. Oxford: Clarendon Press, 1947. Chapter V.

Carritt, E. *The Theory of Morals*. London: Oxford University Press, 1952. Chapter XII.

Cohen, M. *Reason and Law*. Glencoc: Free Press, 1950. Chapter II.

Darrow, C. *Crime: Its Cause and Treatment*. New York: Crowell, 1922.

Dewey, J. *Human Nature and Conduct*. New York: Modern Library, 1930, pp. 17–19.

Feinberg, J. "On Justifying Legal Punishment," in C. Friedrich (ed.), *Responsibility*. New York: Liberal Arts Press, 1960.

Finnis, J. "Punishment and Pedagogy," *Oxford Review*, 1967.

Gahringer, R. "Punishment and Responsibility," *Journal of Philosophy*, 66(1969).

Gallie, W. "The Lords' Debate on Hanging, July 1956: Interpretation and Comment," *Philosophy*, 32(1957).

Gendin, S. "A Plausible Theory of Retribution," *Journal of Value Inquiry*, 6(1972).

Glover, J. *Responsibility*. New York: Humanities Press, 1970. Chapter 8.

Goldinger, M. "Punishment, Justice and the Separation of Issues," *The Monist*, 49(1965).

Goldinger, M. "Rule-utilitarianism and Criminal Reform," *Southern Journal of Philosophy*, 5(1967).

Grotius, H. *On the Rights of War and Peace*, trans. W. Whewell. London: John W. Parker, 1853. Chapter XX.

Hart, H. L. "Prolegomenon to the Principles of Punishment," *Proceedings of the Aristotelian Society*, 60(1959–60). Reprinted in Hart, *Punishment and Responsibility*.

Hegel, G. *Philosophy of Right*, trans. T. Knox. London: Oxford University Press, 1969. Section 100.

Hobbes, T. A *Dialogue Between a Philosopher and a Student of the Common Laws of England*, ed. and intro. J. Cropsey. Chicago: University of Chicago Press, 1971.

Kant, I. *Critique of Practical Reason*, trans. L. Beck. New York: Liberal Arts Press, 1956. Part I, Book I, Chapter 2.

Kant, I. *The Philosophy of Law*, trans. W. Hastie. Edinburgh: T. T. Clark, 1887. Part II.

Kaufman, A. "The Reform Theory of Punishment," *Ethics*, 71(1960).

Leibniz, G. *Theodicy*, ed. A. Farrer. New Haven: Yale University Press, 1962. Part I, Sections 73–75.

Lewis, C. "Humanitarian Theory of Punishment," *Res Judicatae*, 6(1953).

MacLaglan, W. "Punishment and Retribution," *Philosophy*, 14(1939).

Maimonides. *The Guide for the Perplexed*. London: Routledge and Kegan Paul, 1904.

Mill, J. *An Examination of Sir William Hamilton's Philosophy*. New York: H. Holt, 1884. Chapter XXVI.

Morris, H. "Punishment for Thoughts," *The Monist*, 49(1965).

Mundle, C. "Punishment and Desert," *Philosophical Quarterly*. 4(1954).

Paley, W. *The Principles of Moral and Political Philosophy*, 13th ed. London: R. Faulder, 1801. Chapters I, X.

Plamenatz, J. "Responsibility, Blame and Punishment," in *Philosophy, Politics and Society*, 3rd series, ed. P. Laslett and W. G. Runciman. Oxford: Basil Blackwell, 1967.

Price, R. *A Review of the Principal Questions in Morals*, ed. D. Raphael. London: Oxford University Press, 1948.

Raphael, D. *Moral Judgement*. London: George Allen and Unwin Ltd., 1955. Chapter V.

Rashdall, H. *Theory of Good and Evil*, 2nd ed. Oxford: Clarendon Press, 1924. Vol. I, Chapter 9.

Rawls, J. "Two Concepts of Rules," *Philosophical Review*, 64(1955).

Ross, W. "The Ethics of Punishment," *Philosophy*, 4(1925).

Sidgwick, H. *The Methods of Ethics*, 7th ed. Chicago: University of Chicago Press, 1962. Book III, Chapter V.

Smith, A. *The Theory of Moral Sentiments*. Philadelphia, PA: Finley, 1817. Part II, Section 3, Chapters 1, 2.

Strawson, P. "Freedom and Resentment," in *Studies in the Philosophy of Thought and Action*. London: Oxford University Press, 1968.

Strong, E. "Justification of Juridical Punishment," *Ethics*, 79(1969).

Thompson, D. "Retribution and the Distribution of Punishment," *Philosophical Quarterly*, 16(1966).

CHAPTER 3: THE DEATH PENALTY

Beccaria, C. *On Crimes and Punishment*, trans. H. Paolucci, Indianapolis, IN: Bobbs-Merrill, 1963.

Bedau, H. "A Social Philosopher Looks at the Death Penalty," *American Journal of Psychiatry*, 123(1967).

Bedau, H. "Deterrence and the Death Penalty: A Reconsideration," *Journal of Criminal Law, Criminology and Police Science*, 61(1971).

Bedau, H. "The Courts, the Constitution and Capital Punishment," *Utah Law Review*, 1968.

Bedau, H. (ed.). *The Death Penalty in America*. Garden City, NY: Doubleday, 1964.

Bentham, J. *The Rationale of Punishment*, in J. Bowring (ed.), *The Works of Jeremy Bentham*. Edinburgh: W. Tait, 1843. Chapters XI, XII.

Black, Charles L. Jr. 1981. *Capital Punishment: The Inevitability of Caprice and Mistake*. 2nd ed. (1st ed., 1974) New York: W.W. Norton.

Camus, A. "Reflections on the Guillotine," *Evergreen Review*, 1(1957), No. 3.

Capital Punishment. Staff Research Report, No. 46. Legislative Service Commission. Columbus: State of Ohio, 1961.

Capital Punishment. Department of Economic and Social Affairs. New York: United Nations, 1962.

Capital Punishment: Material Relating to Its Purpose and Value. Ottawa: Queen's Printer, 1965.

DiSalle, M., and L. Blochman. *The Power of Life or Death*. New York: Random House, 1965.

Ehrmann, H. *The Untried Case: The Sacco-Vanzetti Case and the Morelli Gang*, 2nd ed. New York: Vanguard Press, 1960.

Ehrmann, H. *The Case That Will Not Die: Commonwealth vs. Sacco and Vanzetti*. Boston: Little, Brown and Co., 1969.

Gahringer, R. "Punishment and Responsibility," *Journal of Philosophy*, 66(1969).

Gottlieb, G. *Capital Punishment*. Santa Barbara: Center for the Study of Democratic Institutions, 1967.

Hart, H. L. "Murder and the Principles of Punishment: England and the United States," *Northwestern Law Review*, 52(1958).

Johnson, J. (ed.). *Capital Punishment*. New York: H. W. Wilson Co., 1939.

Koestler, A., and C. Rolph. *Hanged by the Neck*. Harmondsworth, UK: Penguin Books, 1961.

Lawes, L. "Capital Punishment," in *Encyclopedia Americana*. New York: Americana Corp., 1966.

Lawrence, J. A *History of Capital* Punishment, 2d ed. New York: Citadel Press, 1960.

McClellan, G. (ed.). *Capital Punishment*. New York: H. W. Wilson Co., 1961.

Marx, K. "Capital Punishment," in L. Feuer (ed.), *Marx and Engels: Basic Writings on Politics and Philosophy*. Garden City, NY: Anchor Books, 1959.

Parliamentary Debate on Capital Punishment Within Prisons Bill. *Hansards Parliamentary Debates*, 3d series. London: Hansard, 1868.

Rousseau, J. *The Social Contract*, intro. C. Frankel, New York: Hafner, 1949. Book II, Chapter V.

Royal Commission on Capital Punishment 1949–1953 Report. London: Her Majesty's Printing Office, 1953.

Rush, B. "Considerations of the Injustice and Impolicy of Punishing Murder by Death," *American Museum*, 1792. Reprinted in D. Runes (ed.), *The Selected Writings of Benjamin Rush*.

Schneir, W. and M. Schneir. *Invitation to an inquest*. Garden City, Doubleday and Co., 1965.

Scott, G. *The History of Capital Punishment*. London: Torchstream Books, 1950.

Sellin, T. (ed.). *Capital Punishment*. New York: Harper and Row, 1967.

Sellin, T. (ed.) "Murder and the Death Penalty," in *The Annals of the American Academy of Political and Social Science*, 284(1952).

Sellin, T. *The Death Penalty*. Tentative Draft No. 9, Model Penal Code. Philadelphia: American Law Institute, 1959.

Van den Haag, E. "On Deterrence and the Death Penalty," *Ethics*, 78(1968).

Van den Haag, E. "On Deterrence and the Death Penalty," *Journal of Criminal Law, Criminology and Police Science*, 60(1969).

CHAPTER 4: GROUPS PUNISHED

Blumstein, Alfred. 1993a. "Making Rationality Relevant: The American Society of Criminology 1992 Presidential Address." *Criminology*, January 1993.

Bureau of Justice Statistics, *Sourcebook of Criminal Justice Statistics* (Washington, DC: U.S. Department of Justice, various years from 1978 to 1992), various tables.

Clark, Stover. 1992. "Pennsylvania Corrections in Context," *Overcrowded Times* 3(4): 4–5.

Clarke, Stephens H. 1992. "North Carolina Prisons Growing." *Overcrowded Times*. 3(4):1, 11–13.

Dailey, Debra L. 1993. "Prisons and Race in Minnesota." *Colorado Law Review* 64: 761–80.

Federal Bureau of Investigation, *Crime in America—1992* (Washington, DC: U.S. Government Printing Office, 1993), Table 43, p. 235.

Federal Bureau of Investigation. Various Years. *Uniform Crime Reports for the United States—[1993 and various years]*. Washington, DC: U.S. Government Printing Office.

Federal Bureau of Investigation, *Uniform Crime Reports for the United States—1992*. (Washington, DC: U.S. Government Printing Office, 1993).

National Institute on Drug Abuse. 1991. *National Household Survey on Drug Abuse: Population Estimates 1990*. Washington, DC: U.S. Government Printing Office.

CHAPTER 6: SOLITARY CONFINEMENT

ACLU, "Report: Too Many Teens in Solitary Confinement" (http://www.aclu.org/criminal-law-reform/report-too-many-teens-solitary-confinement) October 10, 2012.

Amnesty International, "USA urged to end inmates' 40 year-long solitary confinement" (http://www.amnesty.org/en/news-and-updates/report/usa-urged-end-inmates'-40-year-long-solitary-confinement-2011-06-06) June 6, 2011.

Gibbons, John J., and Nicholas de B. Katzenbach, commission co-chairs. "Confronting Confinement A Report of the Commission on Safety and Abuse in America's Prisons" (http://www.vera.org/download?file=2845/Confronting_Confinement.pdf) June 2006.

Human Rights Watch, "Growing Up Locked Down" (http://www.hrw.org/reports/2012/10/03/growing-locked-down) October 4, 2012.

Mears, Daniel P. "Evaluating the Effectiveness of Supermax Prisons" (http://www.urban.org/publications/411326.html) May 10, 2006.

National Religious Campaign Against Torture, "Torture in Your Backyard" (http://www.nrcat.org/index.php?option=com_content&task=view&id=591&Itemid=418)

Senate Judiciary Committee Subcommittee on the Constitution, Civil Rights and Human Rights "Reassessing Solitary Confinement: The Human Rights, Fiscal and Public Safety Consequences" (http://www.judiciary.senate.gov/hearings/hearing.cfm?id=6517e7d97c06eac4ce9f60b09625ebe8) June 19, 2012.

Testimony of Professor Craig Haney Senate Judiciary Subcommittee on the Constitution, Civil Rights, and Human Rights Hearing on Solitary Confinement (http://www.judiciary.senate.gov/pdf/12-6-19HaneyTestimony.pdf) June 19, 2012.

U.S. Supreme Court, Medley, Petitioner, 134 U.S. 160 (1890) No. 5, Original. Argued and submitted January 15, 1890, Decided March 3, 1890. 134 U.S. 160 (http://supreme.justia.com/cases/federal/us/134/160/case.html)

CHAPTER 7: ALTERNATIVES TO PUNISHMENT

Abrahamsen, D. *Crime and the Human Mind*. Montclair: Patterson Smith, 1969 (1944).

Alexander, F., and H. Staub. *The Criminal, the Judge and the Public*, rev. ed. Glencoe: Free Press, 1956.

Andenaes, J. "The General Preventive Effects of Punishment," *University of Pennsylvania Law Review*, 114(1966).

Andenaes, J. "General Prevention—Illusion or Reality?" *Journal of Criminal Law, Criminology and Police Science*, 43(1952).

Ball, J. "The Deterrence Concept in Criminology and Law," *Journal of Criminal Law, Criminology and Police Science*, 46(1955).

Barnes, H., and N. Teeters. *New Horizons on Criminology*, rev. ed. New York: Prentice-Hall, 1950.

Birnbaum, M. "The Right to Medical Treatment," *American Bar Association Journal*, 46(1960).

Bixby, F. "Treating the Prisoner: A Lesson from Europe," *Federal Probation*, 25(1961).

Bromberg, W. *Crime and the Mind*. Philadelphia: J. B. Lippincott Co., 1948.

Christie, *Research Into Methods of Crime Prevention*. Report to the European Council No. DPC-CDIR 10, 1964.

Conrad, J. *Crime and Its Correction*. Berkeley: University of California Press, 1965.

Conrad, J. *The Future of Corrections*, in *The Annals of the American Academy of Political and Social Science*, 381(1969).

Correction. Task Force Report. Washington: President's Commission on Law Enforcement and the Administration of Justice, 1967.

DeGrazia, E. "Crime Without Punishment: A Psychiatric Conundrum," *Columbia Law Review*, 52(1952)

Dershowitz, A. "The Psychiatrist's Power in Civil Commitment: A Knife That Cuts Both Ways." *Psychology Today*, 3(1969).

Ellingston, J. *Protecting Our Children From Criminal Careers*. New York: Prentice-Hall, Inc., 1948.

Elliot, M. *Conflicting Penal Theories in Statutory Criminal Law*. Chicago: University of Chicago Press, 1931.

Empey, L. *Alternatives to Incarceration*. Washington: Office of Juvenile Delinquency, 1967.

Feinberg, J. "What is So Special About Mental Illness?" in *Doing and Deserving: Essays in the Theory of Responsibility*. Princeton: Princeton University Press, 1970.

Ferenczi, S. "Psycho-Analysis and Criminology," in *Further Contributions to the Theory and Technique of Psycho-Analysis*, trans. J. Suttie and others. London: Hogarth Press Ltd., 1950.

Freud, S. "Psycho-Analysis and the Establishment of the Facts in Legal Proceedings," in J. Strachey (ed.), *The Standard Edition of the Complete Psychological Works of Sigmund Freud*. London: Hogarth Press, 1959, pp. 97–114. Volume 9.

Gibbons, D. *Changing the Lawbreaker: The Treatment of Delinquents and Criminals*. Englewood Cliffs, NJ: Prentice-Hall, 1965.

Glaser, D. *The Effectiveness of a Prison and Parole System*, abridged ed. Indianapolis, IN: Bobbs-Merrill, 1969.

Hakeem, M. "A Critique of the Psychiatric Approach to Crime and Correction," *Law and Contemporary Problems*, 23(1958).

Hall, J. *General Principles of Criminal Law*, 2nd ed. Indianapolis, IN: Bobbs-Merrill, 1960. Chapter 13.

Hess, A. *The Young Adult Offender: A Review of Current Practices and Programs in Prevention and Treatment*. New York: United Nations Department of Economic and Social Affairs, 1965.

Hood, *Research on the Effectiveness of Punishment*. Report to the European Council No. DPC/CDIR 9, 1964.

Karpman, B. "Criminality, Insanity and the Law," *Journal of Criminal Law, Criminology and Police Science*, 39(1949).

Kassenbaum, G., D. Ward, and D. Wilner. *Prison Treatment and Parole Survival: An Empirical Assessment*, pp. xi, 380. New York: John Wiley & Sons, 1971.

Kinberg, O. *Basic Problems of Criminology*. London: William Heinemann, Ltd. 1935.

Klare, H. (ed.). *Changing Concepts of Crime and Its Treatment*. London: Pergamon Press, 1966.

Landis, P. *Social Policies in the Making*. New York: D. C. Heath and Co., 1952.

Lipton, D., R. Martinson, and J. Wilks. *The Treatment Evaluation Survey*, to appear.

Manual of Correctional Standards. Washington: American Correctional Association, 1966.

Maudsley, H. *Responsibility in Mental Disease*. New York: Appleton, 1896.

Menniger, K. *The Crime of Punishment*. New York: Viking Press, 1968.

Menniger, K. "The Psychiatrist in Relation to Crime," *Reports of the American Bar Association*, 51(1926).

Middendorf, W. *The Effectiveness of Punishment*. South Hackensack: Fred B. Rothman, 1968.

Morris, N. *The Habitual Criminal*. Cambridge: Harvard University Press, 1951.

Owen, R. *Essays on the Formation of the Human Character*. Manchester: Heywood, 1837.

Packer, H. *The Limits of the Criminal Sanction*. Stanford: Stanford University Press, 1968.

Powers, E., and H. Witmer. *An Experiment in the Prevention of Delinquency: The Cambridge-Somerville Youth Study*. New York: Columbia University Press, 1951.

Ross, A. "The Campaign Against Punishment," *Scandinavian Studies in Law*, 14(1970).

Russell, B. *Roads to Freedom*, 3rd ed. London: Allen and Unwin Ltd., 1966, pp. 124–28.

Saleebey, G., H. Bradley, G. Smith, and W. Salstrom. *The Non-Prison: A New Approach to Treating Youthful Offenders.* St. Paul: Bruce Publishing Co., 1970.

Scarborough, D., and A. Novick (eds.). *Institutional Rehabilitation of Delinquent Youth.* Albany: National Conference of Superintendents of Training Schools and Reformatories, 1962.

Schwartz, L. (ed.). *Crime and the American Penal System,* in *The Annals of the American Academy of Political and Social Science,* 339(1962).

Shoham, S. *Crime and Social Deviation.* Henry Regnery Co., Chicago, 1966.

Slavson, S. *Reclaiming the Delinquent: New Tools for Group Treatment.* New York Free Press, 1965.

Street, D., R. Vinter, and C. Perrow. *Organization for Treatment: A Comparative Study of Institutions for Delinquents.* New York: Free Press, 1966.

Studt, E., S. Messinger and T. Wilson. *C-Unit: Search for Community in Prison.* New York: Russell Sage Foundation, 1968.

Sturop, G. *Treating the Untreatable.* Baltimore: Johns Hopkins University Press, 1968.

Toby, J. "Is Punishment Necessary?" *Journal of Criminal Law, Criminology and Police Science,* 55(1964).

White, W. *Crimes and Criminals.* New York: Farrar and Rinehart, Inc., 1933. Chapter XI.

Wilkins, L. *Evaluation of Penal Measures.* New York: Random House, 1969.

Wilkins, L. "Criminology: An Operational Research Approach," in A. Welford (ed.), *Society: Problems and Methods of Study.* London: Routledge and Paul, 1962.

Wiseman, F. "Psychiatry and Law: Use and Abuse of Psychiatry in a Murder Case," *American Journal of Psychiatry,* 118(1961).

Zilboorg, G. *The Psychology of the Criminal Act and Punishment.* New York: Harcourt Brace, 1954, p. 80.

Zimring, F. *Perspectives on Deterrence.* Washington, DC: U.S. Government Printing Office, 1971.

Made in the USA
Middletown, DE
28 December 2021

57197178R00276